GLOBAL AND TRANSNATIONAL BUSINESS

Strategy and Management

George Stonehouse | Jim Hamill | David Campbell | Tony Purdie

WILEY

GLOBAL AND TRANSNATIONAL BUSINESS

Strategy and Management

George Stonehouse, *University of Northumbria*
Jim Hamill, *University of Strathclyde*
David Campbell, *University of Northumbria*
Tony Purdie, *University of Northumbria*

JOHN WILEY & SONS, LTD
Chichester • New York • Weinheim • Brisbane • Toronto • Singapore

Copyright © 2000 by John Wiley & Sons, Ltd,
Baffins Lane, Chichester,
West Sussex PO19 1UD, England

National   01243 779777
International   (+44) 1243 779777
e-mail (for orders and customer service enquiries): cs-book@wiley.co.uk
Visit our Home Page on http://www.wiley.co.uk
or http://www.wiley.com

Other Wiley Editorial Offices

John Wiley & Sons, Inc., 605 Third Avenue,
New York, NY 10158-0012, USA

VCH Verlagsgesellschaft mbH, Pappelallee 3,
D-69469 Weinheim, Germany

Jacaranda Wiley Ltd, 33 Park Road, Milton,
Queensland 4064, Australia

John Wiley & Sons (Canada) Ltd, 22 Worcester Road,
Rexdale, Ontario M9W 1L1, Canada

John Wiley & Sons (Asia) Pte Ltd, 2 Clementi Loop #02-01,
Jin Xing Distripark, Singapore 129809

Library of Congress Cataloging-in-Publication Data

Global and transnational business : strategy and management / by George Stonehouse ...
[et al.].
    p. cm.
  Includes bibliographical references and index.
  ISBN 0-471-98819-7 (alk. paper)
    1. International business enterprises–Management. 2. Strategic planning. 3.
  Marketing–Management. 4. Competition, International. I. Stonehouse, George.

  HD62.4 .G528 2000
  658.4'012–dc21   99-059516

British Library Cataloguing in Publication Data

A catalogue record for this book is available from the British Library

ISBN 0-471-98819-7

Typeset in 10/14 pt Garamond by C.K.M. Typesetting, Salisbury, Wiltshire.
Printed and bound in Great Britain by Bookcraft, Midsomer Norton.
This book is printed on acid-free paper responsibly manufactured from sustainable forestry,
in which at least two trees are planted for each one used for paper production.

CONTENTS

PREFACE

Globalization is one of the most used and abused terms in the English language. It is used to describe phenomena like cultural convergence, global products and production, and the increasing inter-relatedness between the world's economies. Globalization means all of these things and more. This range of meanings illustrates that globalization is, indeed, a complex and sometimes contradictory force which not only affects huge transnational corporations but also impinges upon the activities of small, locally-based businesses and consumers alike. At the same time, as globalization is one of the major challenges facing modern business, other trends, like the information and communications revolution and growing consumer sophistication and fickleness, have given rise to an environment which is characterized by increasingly rapid and unpredictable change. This book sets out to challenge some of the assumptions underlying globalization and to consider approaches to strategy which, recent research suggests, are most appropriate under circumstances of hypercompetition and turbulence.

The book brings together some of the most recent developments in the fields of strategic management and international business. The first section of the book, which considers the development of global and transnational strategy, draws upon competence-based strategy, organizational learning, knowledge management, the virtual corporation, and Ecommerce. The second section, dealing with the management of global business, explores developments in global marketing, international finance, strategic human resource management, global logistics, mergers and alliances, and transnational network approaches to organizational structure. The reader is able to test her or his understanding of the concepts developed in the book through discussion questions and case study work. The book provides a comprehensive and up-to-date introduction to global and transnational business which will prove valuable to postgraduate and final-year undergraduate students, and practising managers alike.

Acknowledgements

The authors would like to thank their colleagues for their invaluable contributions to the completion of the book and their families and friends for their limitless patience and support. They would also like to thank the reviewers, in particular Annik Hogg of Kingston University, for their feedback and support.

AN INTRODUCTION TO GLOBAL BUSINESS

1

PART

The internationalization of business was one of the most prominent features of the second half of the twentieth century – and the pace increased as the decades passed. In the aftermath of the 1939–45 war, most of the world's developed countries were in some economic distress and the appetite for international business was not strong. The focus for some years after the war was on survival rather than cross-border growth as the redevelopment of the major economies progressed.

Events after this, however, created a climate of change which stimulated cross-border business growth. In the political arena, the United Nations was established in 1945, the General Agreement on Tariffs and Trade was initiated in 1948 and in Europe, the European Economic Community was set up in 1957. In other spheres, transport and communications technology advanced significantly in comparison to its pre-war state. The first UK motorways in the 1950s and 1960s were matched by similar developments throughout Europe and North America, making possible much more rapid transport of goods both within and between countries. The burgeoning air flight and telecommunications industries brought about similar effects.

The proliferation of television as the media of choice precipitated a significant growth in viewers' awareness of how people in other nations lived their lives as well as providing a platform for mass advertising. This made possible (alongside other influences) the growth of global brands and some internationally-accepted ideas (such as the value of free trade between countries). The popularity of cinema and televised sport provided other opportunities for organizations to develop their products across national boundaries that were hitherto closed.

And so by the end of the century, the international climate was fertile for business growth across borders. With the exception of a handful of countries that clung on to protectionist measures, the world was 'open for business'. Many companies took full advantage of this to the point where the world's largest global companies were larger than many countries in terms of GDP vs turnover.

As well as the new environment providing new opportunities for business, it also presented the managers of (especially) large companies with a much more complex range of threats than before. They could no longer rely on the support of traditional customers as competitor products flooded across borders to threaten the positions of established products. Accordingly, the importance of being able to manage international issues became a major issue in large businesses.

As more and more companies took their first steps into international business and the ability of political structures to influence business became apparent, many companies realized that they needed some kind of strategy for carrying out their activities in international markets. Some companies opted for a formal planning process whilst others preferred a less rigid and more flexible approach. What the two types had in common, however, was a realization that to carry out business on a global scale involved managing very many variables in turbulent environments. The strategy was important because the amount of money that could be won or lost was huge.

In this first part of the book (Chapter 1), we examine the core themes in strategy in general and in international strategy in particular. There has been a great deal of scholarship in this area of business studies and we begin by introducing some of the big debates and key themes.

STRATEGIC AND MANAGEMENT ISSUES IN GLOBAL AND TRANSNATIONAL BUSINESS

CHAPTER

LEARNING OBJECTIVES

After studying this chapter, students should be able to:

- define the key terms used in international business studies;
- describe the changes in international business behaviour in the second half of the twentieth century;
- explain the nature and causes of industry and market globalization;
- describe some of the key issues in global and transnational business management;
- define and distinguish between the 'big controversies' in strategic management such as those between the prescriptive and emergent approaches, and the competitive positioning and resource-based approaches;
- explain the management processes involved in successful global and transnational business management.

Global and transnational business – an introduction

Some important definitions

The complex strategic issues involved in global and international business comprise the central themes of this book. This chapter identifies the features which distinguish 'global' from 'international' business, examines the most important current developments in the field of strategic management and sets out the analytical frameworks which will form the core of the subsequent chapters.

The terms *international*, *multinational* and *global* business are often used interchangeably but to do so can result in some confusion. It is important to make a clear distinction between the terms. A spectrum of international business activity can be identified depending on the nature and extent of a business's involvement in international markets and the degree of co-ordination and integration of geographically dispersed operations. The importance of making this distinction lies in the fact that the strategic and management issues facing an organization will vary considerably depending on the breadth of its international presence.

International and multinational business

The term *international* simply implies that a business is operating in more than one country. A business which is *multinational*, on the other hand, operates in several countries but Bartlett and Ghoshal (1989) suggest that the term implies some decentralization of management decision-making to overseas subsidiaries, and little co-ordination of activities across national boundaries. This is in contrast to what we define as a *transnational* business.

Global and transnational business

The terms *global* and *transnational* must be used more carefully as they have much more specific meanings. Levitt (1983) made the case that a global market was one in which consumers had the same needs and preferences worldwide. Yet the term *global* refers to more than just markets and is used to indicate the potentially global scope of all of an organization's business operations and its ability to compete on a global scale (see Yip 1992). Bartlett and Ghoshal (1989) use the word *transnational* to describe the configuration, co-ordination and control of a global business activities across national boundaries in the pursuit of global competitiveness. Both markets and the ways in which international businesses configure and co-ordinate their activities are becoming *global in scope* and *transnational in nature*. It is the process of developing global and transnational strategies, and the management and co-ordination of worldwide operations which provide the main focus to this text. Table 1.1 shows how international business has developed over recent decades. Note how configuration of international activities has increased over time.

Table 1.1 The evolution of international and global strategy (1950–1990s)

Period	International strategy of the period
1950s/1960s	Multinational expansion through the establishment of miniature replica subsidiaries abroad. Predominance of multidomestic strategies, with largely autonomous foreign subsidiaries supplying local/regional markets. Limited global co-ordination or integration of geographically dispersed operations
1970s	Multinationals in retreat: divestments, rationalizations and host country plant closures
1980s	Shift towards co-ordinated and integrated global strategies by established MNEs (multinational enterprises); focus on global competitiveness and use of global scope as a competitive weapon in global industries involving plant specialization and national interdependency
1990s	Transition to global and transnational strategies. Businesses focus on developing core competences with outsourcing of other non-core activities. This results in the development of global networks and strategic alliances which are both horizontal and vertical. Increasing emphasis on knowledge as an asset and early forms of learning organization begin to develop
2000s	The era of the 'virtual' corporation and the 'intelligent' organization

Structure of the book

The emphasis of the book, on global and transnational strategy, rather than international or multinational strategy and management, reflects the major changes that have taken place in the environment of international business since the early 1980s. These changes accelerated in the 1990s and look set to continue (see Chapter 2). The overall theme is the link between the trend towards globalization of competition, markets and products, and the consequent imperative to adopt global or transnational strategies and approaches to management.

Competition in many industries and markets has become increasingly global rather than international in scope (Porter 1990; Yip 1992). As a consequence, many established international businesses have replaced their traditional country-centred multidomestic strategies with ones that involve closer co-ordination and integration of geographically dispersed operations. In other words, organizations and strategies are no longer best described as multinational, but as global and transnational.

The extent of globalization, however, varies both within and between industries and markets. Indeed, there are still many industries and markets which are largely national and others where local conditions dictate local adjustments to strategy and management. These factors raise major implications for management within businesses. It is therefore necessary to adopt a co-ordinated approach to global production, technology, marketing, financial management, human resource management and so on, combined with differentiated structures and strategies where and when local conditions dictate. A global or transnational strategy, therefore, does not imply total standardization of products.

Part Two of the book (Chapters 2–5) is concerned mainly with developing understanding of global business and globalization of the business environment. The implications of globalization for business strategies are examined in Part Three (Chapters 6–7); with Part Four (Chapters 8–14) examining global and transnational business management. The remainder of this chapter develops the concept of globalization further and explains the approach adopted to the processes of strategic management.

The globalization debate

Levitt and standardization

The terms *globalization* and *global business* have attracted considerable attention in both academic and non-academic circles since the publication of Levitt's influential article on *The Globalization of Markets* in 1983 (Levitt 1983). According to Levitt, technological change, social, political and economic developments have, in recent decades, driven the world towards a 'global village' or 'converging commonality' – a homogenized, unified global market in terms of consumer tastes and product preferences. The main beneficiaries of this convergence will be global organizations producing globally standardized products in order to achieve world economies of scale. Such global businesses are able (because of the scale economies) to undercut the prices of more nationally-orientated competitors.

The publication of Levitt's article triggered a debate on the extent to which there has been cultural convergence between countries and the extent to which businesses should, or should not, standardize marketing on a global scale. Douglas and Wind (1987) questioned the globalization hypothesis and the need for standardized global strategies and products. They argued that there are many barriers to standardization of products and strategies so that greater returns may be achieved by adapting products, production and marketing strategies to the needs of specific markets. Although they accepted that *some* markets are global, there are many others where it is not the case.

In seeking to develop this theme, we suggest that a standardized global marketing strategy:

- ignores regional or local consumer needs assuming them to be the same everywhere (so missing some potential sales opportunities arising from regional variation);
- is product rather than customer driven;
- ignores localized production advantages.

There is growing evidence that *many markets are becoming increasingly international and, in turn, global.* At the same time as markets become more global, however, consumers are becoming more sophisticated, demanding products and services which are differentiated rather than standardized. Thus, although the market may be essentially global, the sophistication of consumers' needs and wants will dictate that strategy must be flexible and responsive, rather than rigidly standardized. Flexibility of strategy and management is at the heart of *total global strategy* (Yip 1992) and *transnational strategy* (Bartlett and Ghoshal 1989).

Globalization of industries and markets

Development of the key terms

This globalization debate has been broadened from Levitt's narrow focus on markets and global product standardization to a much wider discussion of global industry, global strategy, global management and global competitiveness. Just as important as the trend towards global markets, has been the trend towards the globalization of businesses' value-adding activities. Industries, as well as markets, are becoming global. Today, businesses in many industries are paying increasing attention to the advantages of concentrating certain activities in specific locations all over the world on the basis of localized resource, cost, skill or quality advantages. This has increased the need for businesses to co-ordinate their dispersed operations across the world.

A major stimulus to this growing emphasis on co-ordination has come from the 'Oriental challenge' to western business. Jatusripitak *et al.* (1985) attributed the success of Japanese companies in world markets to the adoption of global strategies involving the co-ordination and integration of worldwide production and distribution. A large number of articles in the academic press then advised western business people on how best to manage their companies for global competitiveness in a rapidly changing global business environment. According to Bartlett and Ghoshal (1989), some of this advice was thoughtful and sound, although they argued that there was a need to maintain local responsiveness combined with a global approach. Globalization, however, soon became a term in search of a definition and many simplistic solutions and over-generalizations began to emerge.

The confusion surrounding the term *globalization* can be illustrated by referring to the two extreme uses of the term. At one end of the spectrum, the term 'global' has been used to describe only those businesses adopting completely standardized strategies in all world markets. At the opposite end, 'global' has been used to describe any company beginning to expand outside of its domestic market. In the former case the term is used too narrowly and in the latter it is confused with simply 'going international'.

It should be obvious that definitions of the term *globalization*, which are either overly prescriptive or vague, are not particularly useful. Few markets and industries are fully global although many display global characteristics (Yip 1992). A global strategy of complete world standardization is therefore unlikely to be successful and, as a result, very few (if any) organizations adopt such strategies. Even corporations like McDonald's and Coca-Cola make minor adjustments to their strategies as national circumstances demand. Using the term globalization to describe the strategy of any company expanding abroad is too wide in scope since it would encompass all businesses with any interests overseas, and clearly not all such organizations are global.

Definitions

In order to establish the focus of this book and to avoid the confusions described, it is necessary to define the terms global and transnational more clearly. We define the *globalization of markets* as the extent to which a market is characterized by broadly similar customer needs, global customers and global market segments. *Industry globalization* is the extent to which the value-adding activities of the players within an industry are configured and co-ordinated globally. A *transnational strategy* is one which combines a global configuration and co-ordination of business activities with local responsiveness. Yip (1992) uses the term 'total global strategy' more broadly than many other writers, arguing that 'a [global] strategy can be more or less global in its different elements'. To avoid confusion with more limited definitions of global strategy this book uses the term *transnational strategy*.

A *transnational strategy* consists of:

- a global core competence giving access to global markets;
- extensive participation in major world markets;
- global configuration of value-adding activities which exploits both national similarities and differences;
- global co-ordination and integration of activities;
- local responsiveness where required;
- differentiated structure and organization.

The definitions of globalization and transnational strategy above provide the focus of this book. A brief case study will help to illustrate the issues involved in global and transnational strategy and management (see chapter case I).

CASE EXAMPLE: INCREASING GLOBAL CO-ORDINATION IN PHILIPS ELECTRONICS

In 1991, Philips of the Netherlands – one of the world's largest electronic multi-nationals – celebrated its one-hundredth anniversary. The celebrations coincided with the announcement of a major change in Philips' corporate mission and strategy for the 1990s aimed at improving global competitiveness.

Although operating on a global scale with a very large number of geographically dispersed activities, Philips was not a global company. Historically, the company had adopted a multidomestic or country-centred strategy with national subsidiaries being responsible mainly for the domestic markets in which they operated; and with a lack of global co-ordination and integration of activity in different countries. By the late 1980s, it had become obvious to senior executives that this multidomestic strategy was becoming increasingly inappropriate given the rapid changes taking place in the world electronics industry.

The most important of these were:

- the globalization of the market and the emergence of strong global competitors, especially from the Far East;

- rapid technology change leading to a stream of new product developments and the closer convergence between consumer and professional electronics;
- changes in production processes (e.g. CAD/CAM) which were becoming much less labour intensive;
- new patterns of industry competition and co-operation through strategic alliances; and fluctuating exchange rates.

In response to these changes, electronics companies required global sales to achieve economies of scale and learning curve effects. They also needed to spread R&D costs and to justify new product developments.

The major change in Philips' corporate strategy and mission was the adoption of a global orientation or strategic vision with the objective of becoming a leading global electronics company with strengths in the major 'triad markets' of the USA, Europe and the Far East. The adoption of a global philosophy and a reorientation of strategy towards global markets was to be achieved through the implementation of several changes in the worldwide strategy and management of the company. The major measures included:

- the adoption of globalization and an orientation to global markets;
- restructuring of product development and production for global market distribution through the establishment of International Production Centres (IPCs) as manufacturing centres for products aimed at world markets;
- centralization of product policy and planning aimed at achieving a coherent, integrated global marketing strategy covering product planning, design, development etc. National marketing, sales and service programmes should complement the overall global product strategy;
- organizational restructuring to conform to the global orientation;
- production restructuring, especially a shift from local production for local markets to highly efficient factories for large volume production for world markets through IPCs;
- improving the management of resources through decentralizing the organization through the establishment of Business Units and Project Teams; an effective human resource management development programme; greater attention paid to the management of external relationships; and improving the management of operating systems.

These changes were aimed at achieving a balance act between global integration and national responsiveness, i.e. a balancing between centralization to achieve global integration and decentralization to achieve national responsiveness.

Global and transnational strategies and management – the issues

The Philips' case illustrates many of the complex strategic and management issues involved in global business, including:

- the importance of analysing change in a turbulent international business environment. Industry globalization had made Philips' traditional country-centred strategy inappropriate;
- global strategies involving co-ordination and integration of geographically dispersed operations were becoming essential to maintain competitiveness in global electronics;
- the adoption of global strategies requires an underlying global philosophy or strategic vision;
- the shift from country-centred to global strategies required major changes in the internal management of Philips – especially in production, logistics, R&D, human resource management and development, etc.;
- the shift to global strategies implied significant changes in organization and control.

In this complex area, we need to draw a distinction between the conception of strategy and that of management. Strategy concerns understanding the environment and formulating policies to position the organization favourably with regard to the variables in the environment (which in the case of international business are usually very complex and turbulent environments). Management is concerned with how the company configures and oversees its internal value-adding and support activities to achieve and maintain its strategic position.

The key issues surrounding global and transnational strategy and management are summarized in Table 1.2.

A framework for global and transnational strategic management

The controversies in strategic management

Strategic management is a comparatively young discipline and, in consequence, there is considerable debate over which approach managers should adopt in devising their strategies. The alternative approaches are

Table 1.2 Global and transnational business strategy and management: the issues

(a) Global and transnational *strategy*	Issues involved
Global/transnational strategy (how the organization positions itself with regard to the global business environment and how it formulates its strategies)	Global core competence and capability Global generic/hybrid strategy Competence and strategy relationships Global, transnational, regional and multidomestic strategies. Collaborative network strategies – the virtual corporation. Learning organizations – knowledge-based competition
Global/transnational marketing servicing (how the global organization sets about responding to and servicing its markets – its groups of customers in various parts of the world)	Market servicing strategies – the alternatives: Exporting; contractual agreements; joint venture strategies, foreign direct investment (FDI); crossborder mergers, acquisitions and strategic alliances
Subsidiary strategies (how the organization deals with its subsidiaries in other parts of the world)	Types of subsidiaries – subsidiary and global strategies. Evolution of subsidiary strategies. Subsidiary strategies and management

(b) Global and transnational *management*	
Human resource management (how the global organization manages its people)	Staffing and expatriate policies Global managers for global corporations Global management development Labour-relations management
Production and logistics management (how the organization manages its main value adding activities such as manufacturing and distribution)	Global production Global logistics Plant location Global procurement (purchasing)
Technology management (how the organization invests in and employs all technologies)	Technology accumulation, development, diffusion and deployment Technology and competitiveness
Marketing management (how the organization understands and communicates with its customers)	Role of marketing in global strategy Global marketing Global marketing strategies Segmentation and positioning for global markets Global marketing mix
Financial management (how the organization raises funds for global activity and how it manages it financial resources in a complex environment)	Financing international development Strategies for managing exchange rate risk Transfer pricing Financial strategies for global competitiveness
Organizational structure and global control (how the organization is structured and controlled to achieve its global objectives)	Organizational structures – types and evolution of Organizational culture Decision making and control Global strategy, structure and competitiveness

considered here before the frameworks used in this book are developed. McKiernan (1997) identifies four well-established approaches to strategic management. The approaches can be broadly identified as:

1. the prescriptive approach (also called the deliberate or planned approach);
2. the emergent (or learning) approach;
3. the competitive positioning approach;
4. the resource, competence and capability approach.

Each of these approaches to strategic management has its distinct characteristics and emphasis. Equally, however, the approaches are interlinked and share certain concepts. No single approach presents a prescription for a complete methodology of strategic management. As a consequence, we draw upon certain of the frameworks developed by each school of thought, in order to develop a methodology for devising transnational strategies. Global strategic management is by its nature an eclectic academic discipline.

The prescriptive or deliberate approach to strategy

This approach focuses on long-term planning aimed at achieving a 'fit' between an organization's strategy and its environment (Ansoff 1965; Learned *et al.* 1965; Argenti 1974, 1980; Andrews 1987). Internal competences are matched to opportunities and threats in the environment. Strategic management is presented as a highly systematized and deterministic process, from the setting of objectives through external and internal analysis, to the formulation and implementation of a grand organizational strategy aimed at achieving a 'fit' between the organization and its environment. Each stage of the process is highly structured and prescribed.

The major advantage of such systematized planning is that it structures complex information, defines and focuses business objectives, establishes controls and sets targets against which performance can be measured.

There are, however, dangers inherent in an approach which is overly prescriptive. The business environment (particularly complex international environments) can be very chaotic and complicated. The information upon which planning is based can, accordingly, be uncertain and often inaccurate. To adopt rigidly-defined plans based upon incomplete information may result in flawed decision making. Accordingly, strategies must be adapted to take advantage of unanticipated opportunities and to deal with unanticipated threats.

The emergent or learning approach to strategy

The complexity and dynamism of modern business organizations and their environments has led many writers to suggest that strategy will emerge and evolve incrementally over time (Lindblom 1959; Mintzberg and Waters 1985; Mintzberg *et al.* 1995). It has been suggested that organizations simply 'muddle through' in the face of complexity. The research of Quinn (1978), however, suggests that rather than 'muddling through' many organizations continually adapt their strategies to changing circumstances. He termed this approach *logical incrementalism*. In other words, strategy evolves rationally in response to changes in the environment.

Mintzberg (1987) argues that strategy is a combination of deliberate plans and emergent adjustments over time. There is likely to be a substantial difference between planned (or intended) strategy and the strategy that is actually realized by an organization. Some aspects of intended strategy will not be realized, while other elements of strategy, emergent strategy, will evolve as the strategy is carried out. Logical incrementalism is therefore a fusion of planning and incremental adaptation of plans.

The competitive positioning approach to strategy

Strategic management thinking in the 1980s was dominated by the work of Michael E. Porter of Harvard Business School, whose *five forces, generic strategy* and *value chain frameworks* (Porter 1980, 1985) added considerably to the tools available to the business strategist. In essence, Porter's approach to strategic management begins with analysis of the competitive environment using the five forces framework. This serves two major purposes. It indicates the potential profitability of the industry and it assists in identifying the appropriate generic strategy for acquiring competitive advantage. External analysis is followed by value chain analysis, which examines the value-adding activities of the organization and the linkages between them. The final stage is selection of a generic strategy, supported by the appropriate configuration of value-adding activities. This, Porter argued, will position the business in its competitive environment in such a way that it achieves competitive advantage. McKiernan

(1997) suggested that this approach can be termed *outside-in* as the initial focus is on the competitive environment rather than the resources of the organization.

Porter's approach has been criticized on the grounds that:

- It is prescriptive and static;
- Differences in industry profitability do not necessarily determine the profitability of the organizations within them (Rumelt 1991);
- It highlights (and presupposes) competition rather than collaboration;
- It emphasizes the environment rather than the competences of the corporation.

Despite these criticisms, Porter's work provides tools which are invaluable to managers seeking to make sense of complex environments and activities.

The resource, competence and capability approach to strategy

Just as the 1980s were dominated by the competitive positioning school of thought, the 1990s saw the rise of resource-based theories of strategic management. These emphasized the importance not of the organization's position in relation to its industry, but rather the way in which it manages its resource inputs in developing *core competences* and *distinctive capabilities* (Prahalad and Hamel 1990; Hamel and Prahalad 1994; Heene and Sanchez 1997; Kay 1993; Stalk *et al.* 1992). Research in the late 1980s and early 1990s (Rumelt 1991; Baden-Fuller and Stopford 1992) suggests that choice of industry is not a major factor in determining business profitability. The core competence of the organization is of greater importance. This indicates an 'inside-out' approach to strategic management based upon the premise that competitive advantage depends upon the behaviour of the organization rather than its competitive environment.

Competence-based theories are not new but they came to prominence in the 1990s. Prahalad and Hamel (1990) argued that an organization must identify and build upon its core competence.

Core competencies are the collective learning of the organization, especially how to co-ordinate diverse production skills and integrate multiple streams of technologies.

The organization must then exploit these competences in a wide variety of markets. The emphasis on organizational learning as a source of competitive advantage has resulted in renewed interest in knowledge as an organizational competence (Quinn 1992; Grant 1997; Sanchez and Heene 1997; Demarest 1997). The resource-based approach also emphasizes the potential advantages of collaboration between organizations whose competences are mutually complementary (Sanchez and Heene 1997).

To give an example of collaboration we can consider the UK retailer Marks and Spencer, whose core competences have traditionally lain in retailing and related activities and not in manufacturing. For this reason the manufacturing of the products sold in Marks and Spencer stores is outsourced to chosen manufacturers. Marks and Spencer collaborates with such manufacturers in the design and manufacture of the clothing, furniture and food products sold in its stores. There are advantages to both sides in such relationships. For Marks and Spencer there are advantages in terms of quality and cost control, input to the design process and freedom to concentrate on marketing and retailing activities. For the collaborating manufacturers there are advantages of the St Michael brand name, access to a large number of retail outlets, long-term supply agreements etc. Both sides benefit from collaboration by being able to concentrate on their respective areas of core competence. Furthermore, collaborative relationships are much more difficult for competitors to emulate. In this way, the ability of both Marks and Spencer and its suppliers to compete with other retailers and manufacturers is enhanced by their collaborative relationships.

Developments in information and communications technology have transformed collaborative relationships so that co-operating organizations can be characterized as what have become known as 'virtual' corporations (Davidow and Malone 1992; Alexander 1997). It is therefore no longer sufficient to analyse the strategies of individual organizations. The dynamics of linked organizations and their strategies must be examined.

Despite the insight that the competence-base approach provides, two criticisms can be levelled at it.

1. Lack of well-developed analytical frameworks – McKiernan (1997) points out that it is ironic that it is Michael Porter who has 'developed one of the most useful tools for internal resource analysis in the value chain'.
2. Neglect of the importance of the competitive environment – research by McGahan and Porter (1997) revived the view that industry is an important determinant of profitability as well as the business itself . There was not, until this book, a suitable framework for analysing the business environment from a resource-based perspective.

An increasing body of evidence (Prahalad and Hamel 1990; Narver and Slater 1990; Greenley and Oktemgil 1996) suggests that business must be market driven and sensitive to customer needs. The organization must therefore analyse those markets in which its competences can be exploited. It is evident that the competence-based approach is far from being a complete methodology of strategic management in these respects.

In this light, Mintzberg *et al.* (1995) made the point that the competence-based approach ought not to be viewed as an alternative to that of Porter. Rather, the two approaches may be viewed as 'complementary, representing two different forms of analysis both of which must be brought to bear for improving the quality of strategic thinking and analysis'.

The approach to global strategy in this book

The frameworks for global strategic management adopted by this book are, of necessity, eclectic. Each of the schools of thought in the field of strategic management has a contribution to make to the strategic management of global business enterprises.

The assumptions adopted can be summarized as:

1. strategy will inevitably be both planned and emergent;
2. competitive advantage can result from both internal competence development and from changing conditions in the business environment;
3. it is important to distinguish between industries and markets;
4. competitive advantage can result from both competitive and collaborative behaviour;
5. the complexity and unpredictability of change in both the business environment and in businesses themselves mean that businesses must be intelligent or 'learning' organizations.

The implications of these assumptions shape the approach to global strategy adopted in this book.

Assumption 1: Strategy is both planned and emergent

We base our discussion of strategy upon the working premise that both prescriptive and emergent understandings of strategy are valid in part and that it is possible to construct a model which includes elements of both.

Some *planning* of strategy is necessary so as to:

- set objectives and targets against which performance can be measured;
- organize activities in a meaningful way based upon prespecified objectives;
- guide actions and ensure consistency of behaviour.

Equally a strategy will always be *adapted* (and hence continually emerged) when:

- there are major or minor unanticipated changes in the global business environment;
- goals and targets are not being met (and hence they must be continually redefined);
- there are changes in the resources or competences of the organization.

The pace and unpredictability of change mean that strategy must be flexible. It is essential that strategic management is not viewed as a one-off planning activity but as a continuous series of loops constituting organizational learning and subsequent adaptation of strategy. Such learning must be focused upon the core competences of the organization and the changes taking place in its environment. This book attempts to reflect the need for both planning and adaptation of strategy.

Assumption 2:   Competitive advantage results from both internal competence development and from changing conditions in the business environment

The implication of this assumption is that both external analysis of the business environment and internal analysis of the business competences, resources, activities etc. are essential. The sequencing of external and internal analysis is not viewed as critical and, in reality, both types of analysis are likely to be undertaken simultaneously. It is critical, however, that both analyses are undertaken on a continuous basis through external scanning of the environment and through constant monitoring of business performance, activities and competences. Equally, it is vital that the results of internal and external analysis are linked together as they will define the critical strategic issues facing the business at any point in time.

Assumption 3: It is important to distinguish between industries and markets

Industries and markets are separate but linked concepts. Whereas industries are defined in terms of competences, technologies and products, markets are defined in terms of customers and customer needs. It is necessary to understand both concepts and the relationships between them as they will affect strategy. The nature of the industry will affect both competence development and organization of value-adding activities. Similarly, the market and customer needs will determine the ultimate success of any strategy.

Assumption 4: Competitive advantage results from organizational learning, and both competitive and collaborative behaviour

There is ample evidence that competitive advantage results from the way that individual businesses leverage, develop and deploy their resources and competences. Equally there is evidence that competitive advantage can be enhanced by the development of collaborative business networks which are often difficult for competitors to emulate. The potential for such collaboration has been increased by developments in information and communications technology which have resulted in the potential for the formation of a virtual corporation.

Assumption 5: The complexity and unpredictability of change in both the business environment and in businesses themselves mean that businesses must be intelligent (or learning) organizations

Chaos and complexity require that businesses are flexible and responsive. Such flexibility and responsiveness are critically linked to the ability of organizations to learn. Organizational learning both increases responsiveness and improves competitive performance.

A summary of the frameworks

The frameworks employed in this book have been developed by a number of different researchers and are drawn from each of the schools of strategic management. The frameworks employed are summarized in Figure 1.1.

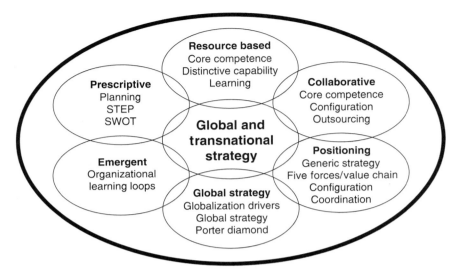

FIGURE 1.1   Global/transnational strategy and management – a conceptual summary

The global and transnational strategic management process

The management process matrix

The process of global strategic management is best represented as a series of learning loops which constantly iterate. The function of these 'learning loops' is to augment organizational learning so as to continuously develop and improve the transnational strategy of the organization. There is a strategic process which is both formal and informal, planned and emergent. The process is both 'inside-out' and 'outside-in' as strategy is inevitably shaped by both the environment and by the resources, competences and capabilities of the organization. The global strategic management process therefore forms a matrix (Figure 1.2) which is indicative of the complex series of relationships between the various elements of the framework employed in this book.

The major elements in the process matrix

Each chapter of this book examines one or more elements of the process matrix. The order in which the elements occur is not necessarily indicative of the order of analysis. For example, analysis of the global business, its resources, competences and capabilities is covered before analysis of the

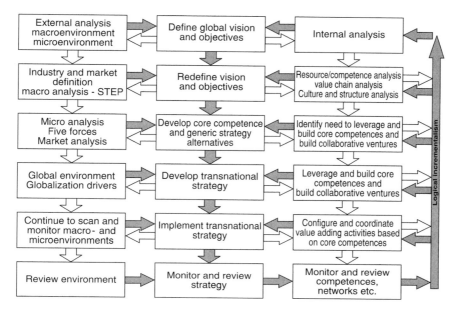

FIGURE 1.2   The process matrix used in transnational strategy

global business environment even although, in reality, the two key stages (internal and external analyses) are usually carried out concurrently. The elements are briefly outlined below and then explored in detail in the remainder of the book.

Globalization and the need for a global mission and objectives
Globalization means that managers must adopt a global strategy under-pinned by a global vision and global objectives.

   The overall strategic vision or mission of the company must be based upon the resources and competences of the organization and the extent of industry and market globalization. Globalization, to a large extent, is a business philosophy or way of thinking which emphasizes the similarities between national markets rather than the differences. The philosophy also highlights the potential for globalization of organizational activities whether through geographical concentration or dispersion. A trans-national strategy will be based upon a global vision but will engender appropriate local variations.

Analysis of global resources, competences and value-adding activities
Analysis of the business (internal analysis) is concerned with identification of its current and potential strengths and weaknesses in terms of its resources, competences and global activities. Globalization necessitates changes in the way that the value-adding activities of the business are organized, changes in its working practices and therefore changes in its structure and in its culture. Such analysis is aimed at identifying the nature and extent of the changes which are required to support a strategy which is both global and transnational. It will help to determine the global configuration and co-ordination of value-adding activities.

Analysis of the global business environment
Environmental analysis is concerned with understanding the macro- and microenvironments in which the business operates (external analysis). Its aim is to establish the key influences on the present and future well-being of the organization and therefore on the choice of strategy. These influences include environmental threats and opportunities. It is to be emphasized that strategy is determined by *both* the competences of the organization and its environment.

In global business, there are three particularly important aspects of environmental analysis. First, analysis of the global business environment enables identification of global opportunities and threats. Second, it increases understanding of the competitive environment in the form of the industry and associated markets so that critical success factors can be identified. Third, it establishes the nature and extent of sectoral globalization. The outcome of this analysis is essential in determining the precise nature of the global or transnational strategy of the organization.

Developing global and transnational competences and strategies
This element is concerned with the generation of global strategic options. Such options will be dependent upon the development and leveraging of those core competences and distinctive capabilities which support global and transnational strategies.

Various typologies of international business strategy have been developed (Porter 1986; Bartlett and Ghoshal 1989; Yip 1992) which address the issues of global configuration and co-ordination, local responsiveness and differentiated organizational structure. These are blended with recent developments in mainstream strategic management thinking relating to core competences, collaboration and organizational learning. This chapter should be viewed as central to the rest of the book since the type of strategy adopted will have major implications for global and transnational management, organization and control examined in subsequent chapters. The type of global strategy adopted will also have major implications for strategy at the level of overseas subsidiaries, with Chapter 7 examining the link between subsidiary and corporate strategy in global business.

Global and transnational management is concerned with the implementation of the chosen strategy in the context of a global organization. Issues relating to organizational structure and culture, marketing, finance, logistics, resource allocation, management of technology, location of value-adding activities and human resource management within global businesses are explored.

Conclusion

The rapid growth of international business over the last few decades and the increasing globalization of many industries has led to a proliferation of publications on the subject. The purpose of this book is to provide a review of the work of leading authors in the field and to present this within the context of an integrative framework which establishes clear linkages between global strategy, global management and global competitiveness.

This book is intended as a core text for courses in international and global business at advanced undergraduate, postgraduate and executive levels. It can be differentiated from the competition in at least three main ways. First, many of the currently available texts are intended as basic introductions to international business. This book, in contrast, is both comprehensive and up to date in its coverage of both strategic management and the major issues of global business. Second, this book has a much clearer focus on global and transnational business (strategy and management) than its competitors. Third, the book can be differentiated from the competition in the high level of integration of global and transnational strategy, management and competitiveness throughout the text.

REVIEW AND DISCUSSION QUESTIONS

1. Distinguish between globalization and internationalization.
2. Identify and discuss the major stages in the development of international and global strategy.

3. Do you agree with the view that a global strategy implies standardization of products, services, advertising and brand names?
4. Why are the activities involved in strategic management best represented as a matrix?
5. What are the major similarities and differences between the positioning and resource-based schools of strategic management? What are the major limitations of each approach?
6. Discuss the view that strategies cannot be planned because of the complexity and turbulence of the global business environment.
7. Why must strategies be both global and transnational?

References and further reading

Alexander, M. (1997) Getting to grips with the virtual organization, *Long Range Planning*, **30**(4).

Andrews, K. (1987) *The Concept of Corporate Strategy*, Irwin, Homewood.

Ansoff, H.I. (1965) *Corporate Strategy: An Analytical Approach to Business Policy for Growth and Expansion*, McGraw-Hill, New York.

Ansoff, H.I. (1991) Critique of Henry Mintzberg's the 'Design School' reconsidering the basic premises of strategic management, *Strategic Management Journal*, September, 449–461.

Argenti, J. (1974) *Systematic Corporate Planning*, Nelson, Sunbury-on-Thames.

Argenti, J. (1980) *Practical Corporate Planning*, Unwin, London.

Baden-Fuller, C. and Stopford, J. (1992) *Rejuvenating the Mature Business*, Routledge, London.

Bartlett, C.A. and Ghoshal, S. (1989) *Managing Across Borders: The Transnational Solution*, Harvard Business School Press, Boston.

Campbell, D., Stonehouse, G. and Houston, B. (1999) *Business Strategy: An Introduction*, Butterworth-Heinemann, Oxford.

Contractor, F. and Lorange, P. (1988) Why should firms co-operate?, in: *Co-operative Strategies in International Business*, Lexington Books, Lexington.

Cravens, D.W., Greenley, G., Piercy, N.F. and Slater S. (1997) Integrating contemporary strategic management perspectives, *Long Range Planning*, **30**(4), August, 493–506.

Davidow, W.H. and Malone, M.S. (1992) *Structuring and Revitalising the Corporation for the 21st Century – The Virtual Corporation*, Harper Business, London.

Demarest, M. (1997) Understanding knowledge management, *Long Range Planning*, **30**, 374–384.

Douglas, S.P. and Wind Y. (1987) The myth of globalization, *Columbia Journal of World Business*, Winter, 19–29.

Doz, Y. (1986) *Strategic Management in Multinational Companies*, Pergamon Press, New York.

Gamble, P.R. (1992) The virtual corporation: an IT challenge, *Logistics Information Management*, **5**(4), 34–37.

Grant, R.M. (1997) The knowledge-based view of the firm: implications for management practice, *Long Range Planning*, **30**, 374–384.

Greenley, G.E. and Oktemgil, K. (1996) A development of the domain of marketing planning, *Journal of Marketing Management*, **12**.

Hamel, G. and Prahalad, C.K. (1985) Do you really have a global strategy? *Harvard Business Review*, July/August, 139–148.

Hamel, G. and Prahalad, C.K. (1994) *Competing for the Future*, Harvard Business School Press, Boston.

Hamel, G., Doz, Y. and Prahalad, C.K. (1989) Collaborate with your competitors – and win, *Harvard Business Review*, January/February, 133–139.

Heene, A. and Sanchez, R. (1997) *Competence-Based Strategic Management*, John Wiley, New York.

Hood, N. and Young, S. (1982) *Multinationals in Retreat: The Scottish Experience*, Edinburgh University Press, Edinburgh.

Jatusripitak, S., Fahey, L. and Kotler, P. (1985) Strategic global marketing: lessons from the Japanese, *Columbia Journal of World Business*, **20**(1), Spring.

Johanson, J. and Mattson, L.G. (1992) Network positions and strategic action, in: Axelsson, B. and Easton, G. (Eds), *Industrial Networks: A New View of Reality*, Routledge, London.

Johnson, G. and Scholes, K. (1997) *Exploring Corporate Strategy: Text and Cases*, Prentice Hall, Hemel Hempstead.

Kashani, K. (1990) Why does global marketing work – or not work?, *European Management Journal*, **8**(2), June.

Kay, J. (1993) *Foundations of Corporate Success*, Oxford University Press, Oxford.

Learned, E.P., Christensen, C.R., Andrews, K.R. and Guth, W.D. (1965) *Business Policy: Text and Cases,* Irwin, Homewood.

Levitt, T. (1983) The globalization of markets, *Harvard Business Review*, May/June, 92–102.

Lindblom, C.E. (1959) The science of muddling through, *Public Administration Review*, **19**, 79–88.

McGahan, A.M. and Porter, M.E. (1997) How much does industry matter, really?, *Strategic Management Journal*, 18 (Summer Special Issue), 15–30.

McKiernan, P. (1997) Strategy past; strategy futures, *Long Range Planning*, **30**(5), October.

Mintzberg, H. (1987) The strategy concept I: five Ps for strategy, *California Management Review*, Fall, 11–24.

Mintzberg, H. (1990) The design school: reconsidering the basic premises of strategic management, *Strategic Management Journal*, **XI**, March, 171–195.

Mintzberg, H. and Waters, J.A. (1985) Of strategies deliberate and emergent, *Strategic Management Journal*, **6**, 257–272.

Mintzberg, H., Quinn, J.B. and Ghoshal, S. (1995) *The Strategy Process: Concepts, Contexts and Cases* (European Edition), Prentice Hall, Englewood Cliffs.

Narver, J. and Slater, J.C. (1990) The effect of market orientation on business profitability, *Journal of Marketing*, **54**, October, 20–35.

Ohmae, K. (1989) Managing in a borderless world, *Harvard Business Review*, May/June, 152–161.

Porter, M.E. (1980) *Competitive Strategy: Techniques for Analysing Industries and Competitors*, The Free Press, New York.

Porter, M.E. (1985) *Competitive Advantage*, The Free Press, New York.

Porter, M.E. (1986) *Competition in Global Industries*, Harvard Business School Press, Boston.

Porter, M.E. (1990) *The Competitive Advantage of Nations*, The Free Press, New York.

Prahalad, C.K. and Doz, Y.L. (1987) *The Multinational Mission: Balancing Local Demands and Global Vision*, The Free Press, New York.

Prahalad, C.K. and Hamel, G. (1990) The core competence of the corporation, *Harvard Business Review*, May/June, 79–91.

Quinn, J.B. (1992) *Intelligent Enterprise: A Knowledge and Service Based Paradigm for Industry*, The Free Press, New York.

Quinn, J.B. (1978) Strategies for change: logical incrementalism, *Sloan Management Review*, Fall, 1–21.

Quinn, J.B., Dooley, T. and Paquette, P. (1990) Technology in services: rethinking strategic focus, *Sloan Management Review*, Winter.

Reve, T. (1990) The firm as a nexus of internal and external contracts, in: Aoki, M., Gustafsson, M. and Williamson, O.E. (Eds), *The Firm as a Nexus of Treaties*, Sage, London.

Rumelt, R. (1991) How much does industry matter? *Strategic Management Journal*, **12**(3), 167–186.

Sanchez, R. and Heene, A. (1997) *Strategic Learning and Knowledge Management*, John Wiley, New York.

Stalk, G., Evans, P. and Shulmann, L.E. (1992) Competing on capabilities: the new rules of corporate strategy, *Harvard Business Review*, March/April, 57–69.

Yip, G.S. (1992) *Total Global Strategy – Managing for Worldwide Competitive Advantage*, Prentice Hall, Englewood Cliffs.

GLOBAL BUSINESS ANALYSIS

2

PART

Part 2 of this book (Chapters 2–5) looks at environmental analysis. In many textbooks – and this is no exception – environmental analysis is considered in three categories or 'layers' of environmental influence.

The environment of any organization can be conceptualized as comprising concentric strata of influence.

Internal analysis is concerned with providing management with a detailed understanding of the business, how effective its current strategies are and how effectively it has deployed its resources in support of its strategies. Research in the 'core competence' school of strategic thought has suggested that internal analysis has increased importance because it is predominantly the actions of the business itself which determine its ability to outperform its competitors. Internal analysis aims to provide the managers of a business with an understanding of its potential for competitive advantage and, equally, those areas where it must take remedial action to ensure its survival. We examine these themes in Chapter 3.

The external business environment comprises two strata of influence. One level contains a number of influences that individual businesses – even very large ones – find difficult to control. The posture adopted in the face of such influences is to learn to 'cope' with them. Thus, macroenvironmental factors (political, economic, sociological and technological factors) can affect all of an industry and can determnine the performance parameters of competitors within it. We examine this level of influence with regard to international businesses in Chapter 5.

The other level of influence concerns the industry and market and is referred to as the microenvironment. This is the sphere in which the organization interacts often – usually on a day-to-day basis. Any changes in the microenvironment can affect an organization very quickly and sometimes, very dramatically. In the case of most organizations, the microenvironment comprises influences from the competitive environment. We introduce these themes in Chapter 4.

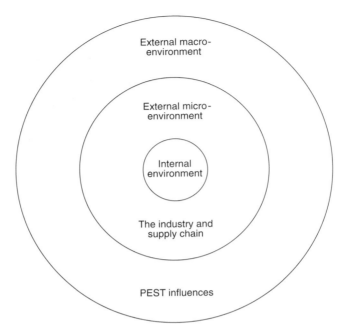

A schematic of the business environment

GLOBALIZATION AND GLOBAL VISION

2

CHAPTER

LEARNING OBJECTIVES

After studying this chapter, students should be able to:

- explain what globalization means with regard to industries and markets;
- describe the broad forces that have stimulated increased globalization;
- describe the effects that increased environmental turbulence has had on globalization;
- explain the major trends that have occurred over recent years in the globalization of industries and markets;
- define and distinguish between global mission, objectives and strategy.

Introduction

In chapter 1 we examined the concept of globalization and we learned how the globalized business differs from the merely 'international' business. In this chapter, we observe that some markets are globalized (such as that for fragrances) whilst others seem to be located only in one region or one country (such as that for regional foods like black pudding). Similarly, some industries compete on a global scale whilst others comprise smaller businesses competing on a regional basis. In this chapter we ask why these disparities exist and what causes some industries and markets to be globalized whilst others are not.

The concept of globalization

Industries and markets

'Globalization' is a frequently used term which is almost as frequently misused. This misuse probably arises from attempts to oversimplify what is, in reality, a complex concept. It is important to distinguish between globalization of markets and globalization of industries, as each of these forms of globalization has different implications for different aspects of business strategy and activity. It is also important to understand the linkages between global industries and markets as the nature of a global and transnational strategy will be influenced by industry and market characteristics.

At its simplest, we can understand the concepts of industry and market by considering them as the two sides of any economic system of exchange. Industries *supply* and markets *demand*. Such a simple definition, however, should not lead us to think that understanding industries and markets in an international setting is as straightforward.

Globalization of markets

Markets are defined by customers and their needs. The extent to which a market is global will depend upon the extent to which customer needs for a product or service are similar throughout the world. It may well be true that customer needs are becoming increasingly homogeneous with respect to certain products and services. American jeans have become ubiquitous as have many other items of fashion clothing. Yet there are many products and services for which markets remain nationally or regionally differentiated. In most nations of the world there is a customer need for bread, so it might be supposed that a global market for bread exists. In one sense there is, as the market for bread is worldwide. On the other hand the customer needs for bread differ significantly between countries. For example, the French prefer the baguette, the Indians the chapati or the nan bread, the Greeks pitta bread and so on throughout the world. The market is not global in the sense that customer needs are different in each country. There is evidence that the market is becoming more global in that in many countries, it is possible to obtain types of bread associated with other countries. Supermarkets in the UK typically supply all the types of bread listed above, in addition to traditional British white and wholemeal sliced breads. Despite this trend, the market is far from global and, even as it becomes more global, there is unlikely to be the standardization of products that Levitt predicted. In fact, customers are likely to demand a variety of products previously associated with a variety of countries.

This demand for variety is a consequence of the fact that globalization has made customer needs more informed and sophisticated. They demand more varied and complex products and services, rather than the standardized offerings which many predicted would become the norm. It was also predicted that global customers would be more price conscious. This may be the case but they are often more conscious of quality, technical features and design than price. In serving seemingly global markets, the business must be alert to the similarities in customer needs but also to the differences and to the increasing complexity of their requirements.

Globalization of industries

The globalization of industries is linked, but different in nature, to the globalization of markets. Whereas market globalization is centred on customer needs, industry globalization centres on the ability of businesses to configure and co-ordinate their productive or value-adding activities globally and across national boundaries. A business can choose to disperse all its activities around the world or to disperse some activities and concentrate others in locations which possess specific advantages. For example, Benetton outsources much of its manufacturing to a group of producers concentrated in a particular region of Italy because their is a high density of skilled workers in the area. At the same time as manufacturing activities are concentrated, Benetton retail outlets are dispersed throughout the world so as to reach customers in different parts of the world. Globalized industries are characterized by worldwide competition, opportunities for economies of scale and scope, rapid technological change, common technical standards and favourable trading conditions.

A global industry is capable of serving fragmented markets by producing products or services which are adapted to meet local requirements. In most cases, however, global industries serve markets which are themselves increasingly global.

Causes of market and industry globalization

An overview

The causes of globalization are, like their effects, complex. Although globalization is itself regarded as a relatively recent phenomenon, its roots can be traced back to many of the forces causing the internationalization of business activity. There are many excellent accounts of this process (see, for example, Dicken 1992) and only a summary is presented here. International business can be traced back to many of the earliest civilizations and the Egyptians, Phoenicians, Greeks and Romans were all heavily involved in trade across national boundaries. Yet the roots of globalization really lie in the eighteenth, nineteenth and twentieth centuries. It is major technological, economic, social and political forces, some recent and others more distant, which have caused businesses to become internationalized and then globalized. All of these forces are closely linked to each other and are largely interdependent (Figure 2.1).

Technological forces

Industrial development
The technological origins of globalization lie in the industrial revolution, beginning in the late eighteenth century and continuing into the nineteenth and twentieth centuries. *Industrialization* marked the beginning of the factory system and mass production of goods. It marked the beginning

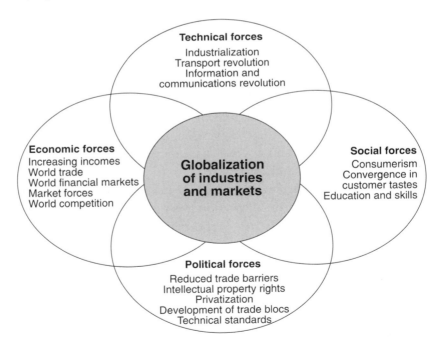

FIGURE 2.1 Forces leading to globalization

of 'a new pattern of geographical specialization' (Dicken 1992). The continued development of mass production techniques underlies the globalization of industries and the concentration of activities in certain locations but this has also been dependent upon other global forces. Mass production also contributed to the development of mass markets and, ultimately, to global markets. As mass production forced prices down, the global attractiveness of certain products increased.

Improved transportation

Development in transportation is the second technological force without which globalization could not have taken place. The development of railway networks throughout the world, and the impact of steam and diesel power on shipping provided the means for moving materials and finished goods around the world. This opened national markets to international products on a previously unknown scale, at the same time as reinforcing the benefits of concentrated manufacturing. Air travel has played a major role in the globalization of businesses both by allowing managers to travel quickly anywhere in the world and by allowing consumers to travel widely, giving them experience of products and services which were previously denied to them.

Improved information management

The most recent technological development, which arguably completes the jigsaw of globalization, is that of what has been called the information 'revolution'. Developments in information and communications technology have had major impacts directly on the advance of globalization itself and on its underlying forces. Global communications, like the telephone, the fax, the internet and electronic mail, have made it possible for businesses to co-ordinate their activities throughout the world. Global communications, like satellite television, have also played a major role in creating global customer needs, increasing awareness of products and brands across the globe.

As well as contributing directly to globalization of industries and markets, all three groups of technological developments have played a major role in bringing about the economic, political and social changes which have also contributed to globalization.

Social forces

Rising levels of income, coupled to the boom in consumer credit, have contributed to worldwide consumerism. Demand for consumer goods and services has increased beyond recognition in post-war years. This has been most evident in the case of motor vehicles, consumer electronics products like televisions, hi-fis, video recorders, telephones and home computers, and white goods like washing machines and refrigerators.

Such products are closely associated with increasing affluence and also with converging consumer tastes and wants. Technological developments have played a major role in converging consumer tastes. Travel, satellite television and global advertising have all assisted in developing global markets. Improvements in education and training have also contributed to technological progress and to rising levels of productivity throughout the world which have helped to give rise to the globalization of production.

Political and legal forces

Increasing world trade and globalization have also resulted from reducing barriers to international trade. Under the provisions of the World Trade Organization (WTO and its predecessor, GATT, the General Agreement on Tariffs and Trade) barriers to trade have fallen substantially in post-war years, although progress has been uneven. Trading blocs (sometimes called *customs unions*), like the European Union and the North American Free Trade Area, have also played a major role in fostering the inter-country trade which is the forerunner of global business.

The increasing legal recognition of intellectual property rights in most countries of the world has played a major part in protecting global products and brands. There have been similar moves to secure acceptance of similar technical standards throughout the world which are particularly important to the development of global consumer electronics products.

Many governments have taken steps to reduce their levels of intervention in economic matters. Privatization has become commonplace alongside reductions in taxation and government spending. In Eastern Europe the collapse of communism has opened up markets which were previously closed to international trade. This increasing prevalence of market forces over government regulation has helped to reduce the political barriers to globalization.

Economic forces

Competition in many industries and markets has become increasingly global as the role of governments diminishes and free market forces are allowed to play a more significant role. In addition, the increasing volume of world trade has gone hand in hand with rising income levels in the major First World economies. Both are interdependent and are also closely associated with technological and political developments. Increasing levels of income have created the demand for global products and services. Finally, the finance for world trade has been made available through the development of world financial markets between which transactions charges have been made insignificant by technological developments.

The extent of globalization

From the previous discussion it might seem that the world has already become a global economy and that its industries and markets are already fully globalized. This is far from the truth. Different countries have been affected to differing extents by global trends. World trade remains dominated by the 'Triad' of Western Europe, North America and the Pacific Rim countries of Asia. These three areas account for 80 per cent of the world's output and only 20 per cent of its population and are at the heart of global business. Their dominance is based upon their technological and economic superiority. Other parts of the world like Eastern Europe, Africa and South America are both economically and technologically disadvantaged. As a consequence the spread of global business is far from geographically complete. Similarly there are many markets and industries which remain largely localized and even within global industries there are businesses which operate successfully either only locally or regionally.

For Yip (1992), the debate is not about whether industries and markets are global but rather the *extent* of globalization in an industry and the impact that this has upon business strategy. Yip's *globalization driver framework* is developed in Chapter 4 as a tool for analysing the extent of industry and market globalization. The remainder of this chapter, however, is concerned with the forces at work in the global macroenvironment which stimulate globalization rather than the techniques which are used to analyse them. We describe the context in which global managers must make their decisions before the subsequent chapters introduce the techniques available to support the making of such decisions.

Despite many important exceptions, the overall trend is still towards the increased globalization of business. The benefits of globalization are, however, accompanied by some difficulties.

Globalization and environmental turbulence

The example of the South Korean economy

Alongside the forces driving many industries and markets towards globalization, the business environment is becoming increasingly turbulent, complex and interdependent. The impact of overseas debt and the falling value of the 'won' in 1997/8 on Korean business is an illustration of these unpredictable forces. In the 1990s the Korean economy was growing at a rate averaging almost 9 per cent and Korean corporations like Samsung were investing heavily overseas. Then the country, along with many other South East Asian economies, was hit by a mounting financial crisis as currency values plummeted. Despite the positive impact that this might have had on Korean exports, its impact on foreign debt and investment plans was devastating. No-one could have predicted such a rapid economic collapse nor that it could affect so many countries.

There are many changes taking place in the global environment with long- and short-term implications. The success of GATT has had a significant impact on increasing the volume of world trade since World War II, although progress slowed in the 1990s as the USA and EU wrangled over further reductions in cross-border tariffs. The development of the single European market has significantly affected trade within Europe and between Europe and other regions. At the global level, the opening of Eastern Europe, the Gulf War and its aftermath, and the growing importance of 'green' issues have all affected global business activity.

Currents and cross-currents

Porter (1986a), in discussing these globalization trends, made a distinction between *currents* and *cross-currents* of change.

Currents are the broad forces which have led to the widespread globalization of business since World War II including:

- the growing similarity of countries in many important areas of demand;
- increased fluidity in global capital markets;
- falling tariff barriers;

- technological restructuring and improvement;
- the integrating role of technology;
- the emergence of new global competitors.

Cross-currents are those factors which have made the patterns of international competition different and more complex since the 1960s and 1970s. These include:

- slowing rates of economic growth in some countries which push businesses to internationalize;
- eroding types of competitive advantage (e.g. labour costs which upset the traditional competitive balance between countries);
- new types of government inducements to attract inward investment;
- the proliferation of coalitions between companies and countries;
- the growing ability to tailor products to local demand conditions.

The major cross-currents of global business in the last decade or so are examined later in this chapter. Prior to this, it is necessary to present an analytical framework for examining global trends.

Changes in the *macro* or *far environment* are major causes of the globalization of industries and markets. Chapter 5 introduces analysis of the macro-environment in terms of changes and trends in *social* and *cultural*, *demographic*, *political*, *legal*, *technological*, *economic* and *financial* factors, and their effects on international industries and markets – and the businesses which compete within them. These classifications are employed in subsequent sections of this chapter to assist in understanding the nature of changes in the global macroenvironment.

Major trends in the macroenvironment

The most commonly-mentioned trends

In their book *Megatrends 2000*, Naisbitt and Aburdene (1990) identified what, in their view, would be the major social, economic, political and technological changes that would shape the 1990s. Other authors such as Dicken (1992) and the various reports published by international organizations such as the World Bank and UNCTC focused more specifically on globalization trends. Among the major trends identified by Dicken (1992) were:

- the increasing globalization of economic activity;
- turbulence and volatility resulting in rapid and fundamental changes in economic life;
- the increasing complexity and interconnectedness of the world economy;
- de-industrialization in North America and Europe and the global shift of many traditional industries to developing countries;
- the crippling financial debts of many developing nations inhibiting economic growth;
- trade tensions between both industrialized and newly industrialized countries, and amongst industrialized countries themselves, e.g. between the USA, Europe and Japan;
- closely related to the above, the division of the world into regional trading blocs as in the single European market, and the North American Free Trade;
- the difficulties encountered in GATT negotiations in reducing trade friction;
- dramatic political changes in Eastern Europe and the beginnings of a transformation from centrally-planned to market economies;
- continuing political volatility as evidenced in the Gulf War, Africa and in the former Yugoslavia;
- the growing importance of 'green' issues.

Changes in international businesses

These broad trends in the global business environment have been accompanied by equally important developments in world investment flows, international trade and the strategies of global companies. Among the most important trends in this respect include:

- a more even distribution in FDI (foreign direct investment) reflecting the rapid increase in outward direct investment flows from Europe and Japan; and declining US power;
- a wave of crossborder mergers and acquisitions replacing the establishment of greenfield subsidiaries as the dominant form of FDI;
- the changing sectoral composition of FDI with a rapid increase in the service sector at the expense of traditional manufacturing;
- the growing importance of collaboration in global business strategy through various forms of strategic alliance;

- the emergence of international businesses from newly industrialized countries.

All of these changes in businesses and in the macroenvironment are likely to have a serious impact upon the nature and structure of global industries and markets. If international businesses are to cope and thrive in the face of these changes then they must adopt a more global outlook.

Global mission, objectives and strategy

Globalization implies that managers must develop perspectives which are both global and transnational. They must evolve a global philosophy and culture within their business which underpins a transnational approach to organization and strategy.

Strategy, purpose and objectives

It is not only an organization's competences, strategy and operations which distinguish it from its competitors. Sanchez *et al.* (1996) argued that 'firms are distinguished by their distinctive sets of goals, as well as by their individual approaches to achieving those goals'. As objectives set out the purpose of the organization, its priorities and standards of performance, it is essential that they are also reviewed as part of the analysis process. Objectives shape global strategy as they set out both the broad and specific intentions of the organization.

Objectives define:

- the purpose and raison d'être of the organization;
- long- and short-term aims and goals of the organization;
- the decision-making framework of the organization;
- anticipated outcomes of its plans and actions.

The objectives of any organization will be determined by:

- the nature of its business activities;
- the resources at its disposal;
- its culture;
- its stakeholders and their influence;
- the environment in which it operates.

A major purpose of the analysis of objectives is to ensure that they continue to be relevant in such a rapidly changing environment. Objectives should lead rather than lag behind organizational change. The need to develop a global vision as the strategic intent guiding a global strategy is an excellent example of this.

Global vision

The highest and broadest level of business objective is the *vision* of the organization. This is a statement of broad aspiration. It deals with where an organization hopes to be in the future. The vision is concerned with the *strategic intent* of the organization (Hamel and Prahalad 1989, 1994). It is an attempt by managers to identify the gap between where the organization currently is and where it expects to be in the future. Hamel and Prahalad argued that the vision of the organization must relate to its core competences and to its future environment.

A *global vision* is an essential prerequisite to global and transnational strategy. This implies that the whole world is treated as a potential market, competition is viewed as global, that activities are configured to exploit global advantages, that activities are globally co-ordinated and, perhaps most importantly, that the organization has a global philosophy, ethos and outlook.

Examples of global vision statements (Pitts and Lei 1996) are:

- CNN – 'to be the best and most reliable news source on any topic, anywhere, anytime';
- Coca-Cola – to ensure that 'a Coke is in arm's reach' of any potential customer anywhere in the world;
- McDonald's – 'to be the leading provider of quality food to anyone, anywhere'.

Vision, philosophy and transnational strategy

Hamill (1992) suggested that a global strategy is, to a large extent 'a business philosophy or way of thinking'. It is therefore important to understand how far a business is globally orientated. Perlmutter (1969) argued that the value system of the company, its history and development, its methods and practices, its vision and corporate culture will shape managerial outlook towards global strategy.

One useful framework for categorizing organizational philosophy is known as the EPRG matrix. Company philosophy can fall into one of four categories. An *ethnocentric* philosophy is one where there is a predisposition towards the home country based upon a belief that the home industry is superior. A *polycentric* philosophy is orientated towards the host country (or foreign market) but which emphasizes adaptation to local conditions in other locations. A *regiocentric* philosophy is an approach which emphasizes an orientation towards a regional grouping of countries such as Europe, North America or the Far East. A *geocentric* philosophy implies a global approach to business.

Each philosophy has implications for the likely strategy of the business adopting it. Ethnocentricity implies that foreign markets are seen as inferior to the home market and the strategy adopted will be the same as that in the home market with the same product offering. Polycentricity results in a multidomestic strategy adapting fully to the requirements of each national market. Regiocentricity implies regional co-ordination of strategy but not global. Geocentricity suggests that strategy is developed on a global basis and is not determined by home or host country factors. Managers must assess the underlying philosophy of the business and determine the extent to which it is to be geared to support and encourage *a transnational approach to business*.

REVIEW AND DISCUSSION QUESTIONS

1. Outline the major trends in the macroenvironment which have brought about the increasing globalization of (a) markets and (b) industries.
2. Why is the global environment becoming more turbulent?
3. What is the relationship between strategic intent and global vision?

References and further reading

Abell, D.F. (1980) *Defining the Business: the Starting Point of Strategic Planning*, Prentice Hall, Englewood Cliffs.

Boettcher, R. and Welge, M.K. (1994) Strategic information diagnosis in the global organization, *Management International Review*, 1st Quarter.

Chakravarthy, B. (1997) A new strategy framework for coping with turbulence, *Sloan Management Review*, Winter, 69–82.

Chakravarthy, B.S. and Perlmutter, H.V. (1985) Strategic planning for a global business, *Columbia Journal of World Business*, Summer, pp. 3–10.

Dicken, P. (1992) *Global Shift – The Internationalization of Economic Activity*, Paul Chapman, London.

Elenkov, D.E. (1997) Strategic uncertainty and environmental scanning: the case for institutional influences on scanning behaviour, *Strategic Management Journal*, **18**(4), 287–302.

Fahey, L. and Narayanan V.K. (1994) Global environmental analysis, in: S. Segal-Horn (Ed.), *The Challenge of International Business*, Kogan Page, London.

Ginter, P. and Duncan, J. (1990) Macroenvironmental analysis, *Long Range Planning*, December.

Hamel, G. and Prahalad, C.K. (1989) Strategic intent, *Harvard Business Review*, **67**(3), pp. 63–76.

Hamel, G. and Prahalad, C.K. (1994) *Competing for the Future*, Harvard Business School Press, Boston.

Hamill, J. (1992) *Global Marketing*, in: Baker, M.J. (ed.) *Perspective on Marketing Management*, **2**, Prentice Hall, Englewood Cliffs, NJ.

Heene, A. and Sanchez, R. (1997) *Competence-Based Strategic Management*, John Wiley, New York.

Helms, M.M. and Wright, P. (1992) External considerations: their influence on future strategic planning, *Management Decision*, **30**(8), 4–11.

Henzler, H. and Rall, W. (1986) Facing up to the globalization challenge, *McKinsey Quarterly*, Winter.

Kay, J. (1993) *Foundations of Corporate Success*, Oxford University Press, Oxford.

Kay, J. (1995) Learning to define the core business, *Financial Times*, 1st December.

Klugt, C.J. Van der (1986) Japan's global challenge in electronics – The Philips' response, *European Management Journal*, **4**(1), 4–9.

Lindsay, W.K. and Rue, L.W. (1980) Impact of organization environment on the long range planning process, *Academy of Management Journal*, 23.

Mascarenhas, B. (1982) Coping with uncertainty in international business, *Journal of International Business Studies*.

Mintzberg, H. (1973) Strategy-making in three modes, *California Management Review*, **16**.

Mintzberg, H. (1991) *The Strategy Process – Concepts, Contexts, Cases*, Prentice Hall, Englewood Cliffs.

Naisbitt, J. and Aburdene, P. (1990) *Megatrends 2000*, Morrow, New York.

Negandhi, A.R. (1987) *International Management*, Allyn and Bacon, Boston.

Perlmutter, H.V. (1969) The tortuous evolution of the multinational corporation, *Columbia Journal of World Business*, January–February.

Phatak, A.V. (1963) *International Dimensions of Management*, Kent, Boston.

Pitts, R.A. and Lei, D. (1996) *Strategic Management – Building and Sustaining Competitive Advantage*, West Publishing, St Pauls.

Porter, M.E. (1990) *The Competitive Advantage of Nations*, Macmillan, London.

Porter, M.E. (1980) *Competitive Strategy: Techniques for Analysing Industries and Competitors*, The Free Press, New York.

Porter, M.E. (1985) *Competitive Advantage*, The Free Press, New York.

Porter, M.E. (1986a) *Competition in Global Business*, Harvard University Press, Boston.

Porter, M.E. (1986b) Changing patterns of international competition, *California Management Review*, **28**(2), Winter, 9–40.

Prahalad, C.K. and Doz, Y.L. (1986) *The Multinational Mission: Balancing Local Demands and Global Vision*, The Free Press, New York.

Prahalad, C.K. and Hamel, G. (1993) Strategy as stretch and leverage, *Harvard Business Review*, March/April.

Prahalad, C.K. and Hamel, G. (1995) *Competing for the Future*, Harvard Business School Press, Boston.

Prahalad, C.K. and Hamel, G. (1989) Strategic intent, *Harvard Business Review*, pp. 63–76.

Prahalad, C.K. and Hamel, G. (1990) The core competence of the corporation, *Harvard Business Review*, 79–91.

Sanchez, R. (1995) Strategic flexibility in product competition, *Strategic Management Journal*, **16**, Summer, 135–159.

Sanchez, R. (1995) Strategic flexibility, firm organization, and managerial work in dynamic markets: A strategic options perspective, *Advances in Strategic Management*, **9**, 251–291.

Sanchez, R., Heene, A. and Thomas, H. (1996) Towards the theory and practice of competence-based competition, in: Sanchez, R., Heene, A. and Thomas, H. (eds), *Dynamics of Competence-Based Competition: Theory and Practice in the New Strategic Management*, Elsevier, Oxford.

Segal-Horn, S. (1992) Global markets, regional trading blocs and international consumers, *Journal of Global Marketing*, **5**(3).

Smith, D. (1997) Wrinklies timebomb waiting to explode, *Sunday Times*, 23rd February.

Stalk, G., Evans, P. and Shulmann, L.E. (1992) Competing on capabilities: the new rules of corporate strategy, *Harvard Business Review*, March/April.

Strebel, P. (1992) *Breakpoints*, Harvard Business School Press, Boston.

Turner, I. (1996) Working with chaos, *Financial Times*, 4th October.

Yip, G.S., Loewe, P.M. and Yoshino, M.Y. (1988) How to take your company to the global market, *Columbia Journal of World Business*, Winter, 37–48.

Yip, G.S. (1992) *Total Global Strategy*, Prentice Hall, Englewood Cliffs.

ANALYSIS OF THE GLOBAL BUSINESS

3

CHAPTER

LEARNING OBJECTIVES

After studying this chapter, students should be able to:

- explain the components of an internal analysis;
- define and distinguish between an organization's competences, resources and capabilities;
- describe the value chain framework and understand its components;
- explain how value chains differ in global organizations;
- define and distinguish between configuration and co-ordination as the terms apply to global value adding activities;
- describe the importance of organizational culture and structure as they affect the strategy of global businesses;
- explain how to analyse an organization's products, portfolio and performance.

Introduction

Strategic analysis of any business enterprise involves two stages. Internal analysis is the systematic evaluation of the key internal features of an organization and we address this in this chapter. The second stage, external analysis is covered in Chapters 4 and 5.

Internal analysis enables managers to gain a picture of their organization. Such information is essential when deciding upon strategic options or on adjusting global strategy to provide an optimum performance. Superior performance (this is, returning higher profitability that the industry average) depends upon management's ability to employ their resource inputs into core competences more effectively than competitors. This, in turn, depends upon how well-configured the organization's value-adding activities are and how it configures and co-ordinates its value-adding activities in the various parts of the world.

Product analysis is important in internal analysis because the product is the final expression of value added and the output of the whole organizational process. The extent to which products are balanced in a portfolio or are adjusted to suit regional preferences can be a vital factor in the success or failure of a global strategy.

Analysis of the global organization

Internal analysis

When considering the internal analysis of any organization, four broad areas need to be considered. These are the analysis of:

- the organization's resources capabilities and competences;
- the way in which the organization configures and co-ordinates its key value-adding activities;
- the structure of the organization and the characteristics of its culture;
- the performance of the organization as measured by the strength of its products. This, in turn, is largely determined by the three aforementioned factors (see Figure 3.1).

These categories of enquiry form the basis of the structure of this chapter.

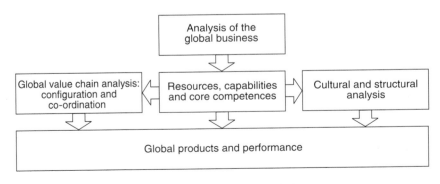

FIGURE 3.1   Internal analysis

Competences, resources and capabilities

Understanding global competences

Many researchers in strategy including Prahalad and Hamel (1990), Heene and Sanchez (1997) and Kay (1993) have made the case that internal factors (resources, capabilities and competences) are more important in acquiring and sustaining competitive advantage than the organization's position in relation to its competitive environment. In other words, the major sources of global competitive advantage are business, rather than industry, specific. It is therefore important to understand what constitutes core competence or distinctive capability as they form the basis of successful strategy. These concepts are also explored further in Chapter 6 which deals with the 'sources' of global and transnational strategy.

This understanding of strategy (sometimes called the 'resource-based' approach) can be traced back to the work of Penrose (1959). It is only recently, however, that researchers have begun to develop the conceptual frameworks which allow this approach to make a valuable contribution to global strategic analysis.

Definitions of resources, capabilities and competences

Although core competences are widely acknowledged as important sources of competitive advantage, there is no precise and universally-agreed definition of the term. As a result, according to Kay (1995) 'Core competence is one of the most used and abused phrases in business strategy'. Accordingly, the terms *resource*, *capability*, *core competence* and *distinctive capability* are often used imprecisely in the literature. It is therefore necessary to define each of the concepts, explaining their major characteristics and the relationships between them.

Prahalad and Hamel (1990) defined core competence as 'the collective learning in the organization, especially how to co-ordinate diverse production skills and integrated multiple streams of technologies'. This definition does little, however, to reduce the ambiguity. Instead definitions based upon those proposed by Kay (1993, 1995), Heene and Sanchez (1997), Gorman and Thomas (1997) and Petts (1997) are developed and illustrated in Figure 3.2.

There are significant difficulties in identifying and analysing core competences. This is because they tend to be complex bundles of resources and

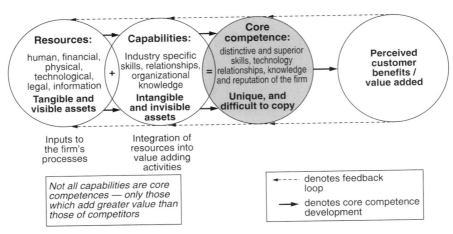

FIGURE 3.2   The relationships between resources, capabilities and core competences

capabilities which are invisible and intangible, and are, therefore, difficult to describe precisely and are equally difficult to evaluate.

Despite these limitations, however, we suggest that analysis of core competences is possible by examining the factors that go to create them – resources and general competences.

Resources

Resources are assets which are employed in the activities and processes of the organization. Such assets can be either tangible or intangible. They can be obtained externally from suppliers in resource markets or can be internally generated. Internally-generated resources are *organization-specific* while externally obtained resources are *organization-addressable* (Heene and Sanchez 1997). Resources can be highly specific or non-specific. Specific resources can only be used for highly specialized purposes and are very important to the organization in adding value to goods and services. Assets which are less specific are less important in adding value, but are usually more flexible.

Resources fall within several categories: human, financial, physical, technological or informational. An audit of resources would be likely to include an evaluation of resources in terms of availability, quantity and quality, extent of employment, sources, control systems and performance. The audit would also be likely to employ benchmarking techniques including internal and external comparisons:

- against objectives and strategies – are the resources adequate to achieve organizational objectives?
- against benchmarks like competitors – is the organization in question stronger or weaker?
- against performance indicators over time – has the organization matched, exceeded or fallen short of the key indicators?

Table 3.1 illustrates some of the resource audits that may be carried out within a global organization.

General competences/capabilities

These are assets like *industry-specific skills*, *relationships* and *organizational knowledge* which are largely *intangible* and *invisible assets*. Competences and capabilities will often be internally generated but may be obtained by collaboration with other organizations. In other words, competences may be shared or created across organizational boundaries. They are often shared between the organization and one or more of its suppliers, distributors or customers.

Certain competences are likely to be common to competing businesses within a global industry or strategic group. These competences relate to the

Table 3.1   Content of a resources audit

Human	Physical	Financial	Technological	Informational
Numbers of staff	*Buildings and equipment*:	Global sources and availability of finance	Technology – 'know how'	Customer information
Deployment				
Age distribution			Patents	Supplier information
Education	Locations	Global accounts	R&D facilities	Competitor
Skills	Age	Global assets	IT and	information
Training	Repair	and liabilities	communication	Internal process
(including	Flexibility	Control systems	systems (internal	information
linguistic skills)	Configuration	International	and external)	Agreements with
Motivation	Expansion	accounting	Production	suppliers,
Attitudes and	potential	systems	systems	customers,
cultural awareness	Capacity	Taxation		distributors
Flexibility	Utilization	systems		Note: the
Productivity				information resource
Job specifications	*Materials*:			is generated both
Recruitment	Sources			within the business as
Industrial relations	Quality			a result of its activities
Remuneration	Costs			and outside the
	Availability			business

critical success factors in the industry or market. Most competitors in the brewing industry, for example, will possess certain competences or capabilities which are essential to the production and selling of beer. Such competences are not distinctive, however, and do not account for distinctive or superior performance. They simply mean that the business in question has sufficient competence to produce and distribute beer.

Core competences/distinctive capabilities

Core competences or distinctive capabilities are combinations of resources and capabilities which are unique to a specific organization and which are responsible for generating its competitive advantage. Core competences only create competitive advantage when they are applied in markets, thus creating benefits which are perceived by customers as adding value over and above those of competitors. Core competences often have the potential to produce competitive advantage in more than one market.

Kay (1993) identified four potential sources of distinctive capability: reputation, architecture (that is, internal and external relationships), innovation and strategic assets.

Core competences or distinctive capabilities may well be based upon unique external relationships with other organizations or with customers. Benetton's competitive advantage, for example, rests in large part upon its reputation, its knowledge of the fashion clothing industry and markets, and its unique network of relationships with manufacturers and retailers.

Core competences must be perceived *by customers* as providing benefits if they are to create competitive advantage. Thus reputation is vitally important to businesses like Porsche, Nike and Tommy Hilfiger, in achieving global competitive advantage, because customers place a high value on the reputations of such companies when purchasing their products.

Core competence development depends upon the distinctive way that the organization combines, co-ordinates and deploys its resources and capabilities (Heene and Sanchez 1997) as well as upon the resources and capabilities themselves. Core competences can be evaluated against a set of criteria:

- *complexity* – how elaborate is the bundle of resources and capabilities which comprise the core competence?
- *identifiability* – how difficult is it to identify?
- *imitability* – how difficult is it to imitate?

- *durability* – how long does it endure?
- *substitutability* – how easily can it be replaced by an alternative competence?
- *superiority* – is it clearly superior to the competences of other organizations?
- *adaptability* – how easily can the competence be leveraged or adapted?
- *customer orientation* – how is the competence perceived by customers and how far is it linked to their needs?

(Adapted from Petts 1997).

By evaluating core competences against these criteria, managers can gain a valuable insight into their ability or likelihood to bring about any sustained advantage. The strengths and weaknesses of existing competences can be assessed and any opportunities or needs for competence building and leveraging can be identified. These opportunities and needs may refer to resource markets, the industry, competing industries or product markets. Resources, capabilities and competences are both critical to, and interdependent with, the value adding activities of the business. Value adding activities are therefore analysed in the following section of this chapter.

Global value chain analysis

Organizations as systems

Heene and Sanchez (1997) described an organization as 'an open system of asset stocks and flows including tangible assets like production equipment and intangible assets like capabilities and cognitions'. This system converts inputs (resources) into outputs (goods and services). A major objective of the system is to add value to the inputs so that the value of the outputs exceeds the value of the resources used in their creation. Competitive advantage depends upon the ability of the organization to organize its resources and value adding activities in a way which is superior to its competitors thus enabling more value to be added and more quickly. Value chain analysis is a technique developed by Porter (1985) for understanding an organization's value-adding activities and the relationships between them. Value can be added in two ways:

- by producing products at a lower cost than competitors;
- by producing products of greater perceived value than those of competitors.

Analysis of value-adding activities allows managers to identify where value is currently added and where there is potential to add further value in the future by reconfiguration of activities. Porter extended value chain analysis to the value system so that, as well as internal activities, the technique also includes analysis of the relationships between the organization, its suppliers, distribution channels and customers.

The value chain

The value chain is the chain of activities which results in the final value of a business's product. Value added, or margin, is indicated by sales revenue (units sold multiplied by price) minus total costs (variable costs like materials, wages etc., plus fixed costs of capital equipment, rents etc.). In other words 'the margin is the difference between the total value and collective cost of performing the value activities' (Porter 1985).

In Porter's framework, value is added as a result of value-adding activities and the linkages between them. Porter divided the internal parts of the organization into primary and support activities as indicated in Figure 3.3. *Primary activities* (inbound logistics, operations, outbound logistics, marketing, and sales and service) are those which directly contribute to the production of the good or services and its provision to the customer. *Support activities* (firm's infrastructure, human resource management, technology development and procurement) are those which aid the primary activities but do not themselves add value.

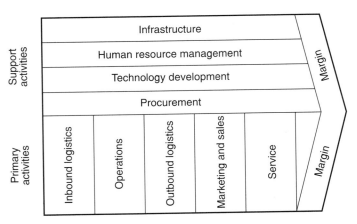

FIGURE 3.3   The value chain (adapted from Porter 1985)

Certain activities or combinations of activities are likely to relate closely to the organization's core competences. Logically, these can be termed *core activities*. They are those activities which:

- add the greatest value;
- add more value than the same activities in competitors' value chains;
- relate to and reinforce core competences.

Other value chain activities relate to capabilities, but do not add greater value than competitors and therefore do not relate to core competence (because they do not contribute towards competitive advantage).

Value chain analysis involves analysis of all the company's activities, and its internal and external linkages, in order to determine how the company's activities are currently organized and how they can be better organized so that competitive advantage can be achieved. The activities in the company's value chain must be organized in such a way as to support its corporate strategy.

A value chain analysis will therefore include:

- a breakdown and analysis of all the activities of the organization;
- an examination of the match between configuration and current strategy (e.g. cost- or differentiation-based strategy);
- identification of internal and external *linkages* between activities which result in additional added value;
- identification of *blockages* which reduce the organization's competitive advantage.

The primary and support activities can be broken down into several elements for analysis.

Primary activities

Inbound logistics
These are activities concerned with the receipt and storage of materials (inputs), stock control, and distribution of inputs to those areas of the business concerned with operations.

Operations
Operations transforms inputs into final products or services. It may be concerned with manufacturing processes, assembly, testing etc.

Outbound logistics
This function is responsible for storage and distribution of finished goods to customers. It includes warehousing, order processing, transport and distribution.

Marketing and sales
This includes activities which are concerned with analysis of markets and customers, persuading customers to buy the product, and making the product accessible to customers via appropriate channels.

Service
This consists of activities concerned with installation of the product and after-sales service.

Support activities

Procurement
This is concerned with purchasing the resource inputs used in the organization's activities (other than those which directly add value, which are part of inbound logistics). Certain purchasing functions may be centralized so as to obtain economies and control quality of inputs. Other purchasing activities may be decentralized. Purchasing has a clear impact on value added both in terms of controlling costs and in terms of controlling quality of inputs and therefore of final products.

Technology development
All activities within the business employ technology both in the production and distribution of physical products and also in terms of producing information and services. Technology development is concerned with product, process and resource development, and improvement. It includes the research and development function if the organization has one.

Human resource management
Human resource management is concerned with obtaining, training and motivating appropriate employees. It therefore involves recruitment, selection, training, rewards and motivation. Again, human resources are employed throughout the organization's value chain. The quality and 'appropriateness' of the human resources is closely associated with its ability to add value.

Firm infrastructure

Firm infrastructure includes management systems, planning, finance, accounting, information systems, and quality management. The infrastructure is vital to the success of the business and its global corporate strategy.

Using the value chain framework

All the primary and support activities described contribute to the final value of the product to the consumer so the organization must analyse each activity, and the linkages between the activities to see if any improvements can be made which will increase the final value of the product or decrease the costs of making it.

Just as important as the internal activities are the external linkages – with suppliers of inputs and services, and linkages with distribution channels and customers. The value of the product may depend upon linkages with retailers, for example. Similarly, linkages with suppliers may be critical to competitive success if the business operates a Just-In-Time (JIT) operational philosophy.

Every different type of organization will have a very different value chain. Adidas, for example is not generally involved in the retailing of its product but is heavily involved in the design and marketing activities. Nissan is involved in design and manufacturing and also has involvement in the distribution of its products. Other businesses' value chains may be centred on manufacturing with no design, little marketing and no retailing. The businesses that manufacture the products sold under the Nike or St Michael (Marks and Spencer) brand names would fall into this category.

The analysis helps us to add to our picture of the organization's strengths and weaknesses. It may be possible to compare one value chain with that of organizations in similar sectors so as to make comparisons of performance.

The value chain of an individual organization, however, provides an incomplete picture of its ability to add value as many value-adding activities are shared between organizations often in the form of a collaborative network. As organizations identify and concentrate on their core competences and core activities, they increasingly outsource activities to other businesses for which such activities are core. For example Marks and Spencer, the UK retailer, would regard its core competence as being based upon its skills in design and retailing which have established its reputation for quality. Marks and Spencer has no expertise or core competence in manufacturing and therefore it obtains its products from a network of suppliers, for which manufacturing is a core competence and activity. The ability to add value is enhanced for all members of the network as they benefit from each other's core competences. Marks and Spencer benefits from the core competences of its suppliers in manufacturing quality products, while the suppliers benefit from Marks and Spencer's retailing skills and reputation.

It is therefore necessary to analyse the *value system* of the business so as to establish the effectiveness of its external linkages.

The value system

The value system (Figure 3.4) is the chain of activities from supply of resources through to final consumption of a product.

The total value system, in addition to the organization's own value chain, can consist of *upstream* linkages with suppliers and *downstream* linkages with distributors and customers. A single organization can form any part or the whole of the value system for a product or service. The value system is a similar concept to that of the *supply chain* and illustrates the interactions between an organization, its suppliers, distribution channels and customers. It also illustrates the fact that such relationships may also be common to its competitors. Managing these external relationships can be equally as important to competitive advantage as the management of internal activities and linkages.

Co-ordinating activities and linkages

Competitive advantage arises from an organization's core competences and core activities. Businesses make themselves distinctive by the way in which they configure and co-ordinate their competences and value-adding

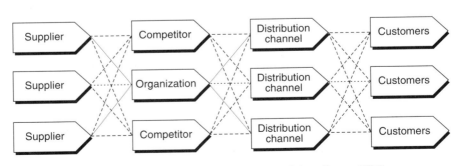

FIGURE 3.4   The value system. (Adapted from Porter 1985)

activities. Competitive advantage is also enhanced by the distinctive network of relationships that a business has with its suppliers, distribution channels and customers. Inter-company relationships must be co-ordinated and integrated with those competences and activities which are core to the business itself. There may well be synergies between the core competences of an organization and those of linked organizations. Certainly, the linking of core competences increases the range of competences which can be deployed competitively and at the same time, they can create a more complex source of competitive advantage which is more difficult for competitors to emulate.

At the same time, effective management of complex linked activities can further extend advantage. To summarize, managing internal and external linkages between competences and activities is just as important as the management of the individual primary and support activities which make up the value chain. An important aspect of strategic analysis is therefore the examination of internal and external relationships between competences and activities.

The 'global' value chain

A more complex value chain

Globalization offers new opportunities and new challenges for the configuration and co-ordination of value-adding activities (Porter 1986, 1990). The configuration of an organization's activities relates to where and in how many nations each activity in the value chain is performed. Global businesses can configure their activities to take advantage of both global and localized advantages. Co-ordination is concerned with the management of dispersed international activities and the linkages between them. Co-ordination of globally dispersed activities is, of course, a complex matter but it is because of this complexity that it offers considerable potential for achieving competitive advantage. Managers must therefore examine the current configuration of value-adding activities and the extent and methods of co-ordination as part of their strategic analysis. This analysis makes it possible to determine possibilities for reconfiguration or improved co-ordination.

In understanding the complexity of global value chain management, two concepts are important – configuration of activities and co-ordination between them.

Configuration

In terms of each value-adding activity a global business has two broad choices of configuration: *concentration* of the activity in a limited number of locations to take advantage of benefits offered by those locations (such benefits may relate to availability of materials or labour, to cost advantages, demand conditions, markets, government incentives etc.) or *dispersion* of the activity to a large number of locations (when transport costs are high, when national markets differ significantly etc.).

Changes in the business environment, for example technological change, may well lead to changes over time in the configuration which give greatest competitive advantage. Businesses must therefore constantly monitor their current configuration in conjunction with the environment in order to identify opportunities to re-configure their global activities to take advantage of changing conditions.

Co-ordination

Competitive edge can also be increased by more effectively co-ordinating diverse activities which are located in a number of different nations. Co-ordination is essentially about overseeing the complexity of the organization's configuration such that all value-adding parts of the business act in concert with each other to facilitate an effective overall synergy. The more complex the configuration becomes (and some global businesses can have very complex configurations) then the greater the difficulties will be in retaining control over each value-adding part.

Those businesses which overcome the potential difficulties of co-ordination are those that sustain the greatest competitive advantage. New technology and organizational structures offer new possibilities for co-ordinating diverse activities. The increasing ability to co-ordinate activities more effectively also expands the range of alternative configurations accessible to global business.

Analysis of configuration and methods of co-ordination assists in the process of understanding current competences and identifying the potential for strengthening and adding to them. Core competences are closely related to value-adding activities. Configuring the value chain globally offers further opportunities to develop competences which are both distinctive and difficult to emulate. Figure 3.5 illustrates the issues which must be

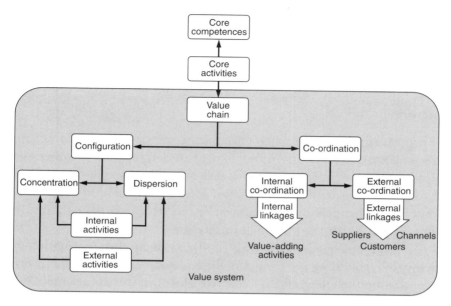

FIGURE 3.5   Managing the value system

considered in relation to analysing the management of a business's value system.

Global organizational culture and structure

The importance of culture and structure

A global business must have a culture and structure which allow it to carry out its global activities. Culture and structure are investigated in more detail in Chapter 13 but they are examined briefly here as part of the process of internal business analysis.

In attempting to answer the question why an organization has a particular culture and structure, we find a complicated range of explanations (see, for example, Campbell *et al.* 1999).

The culture and structure of an organization are the result of a number of factors including:

- its history;
- its size;
- the nature of its product and production processes;

- the nature of its business environment, markets and industry;
- its country of origin and areas of operation;
- the nature of its strategy;
- the philosophy of key members of the organization.

Structure

Major problems can arise when either structure or culture is not adapted in response to changes in strategy, size, the environment, processes or philosophy. As organizations grow they must restructure to continue to co-ordinate and control their activities. More clearly defined roles, responsibilities and channels of communication are required than the informal arrangements which exist in small businesses.

Some large businesses with very rigid and hierarchical structures have difficulty in responding to changes in the environment. As the environment becomes more turbulent and as activities globalize it becomes increasingly difficult to reconcile the need for flexibility with that for control and co-ordination. Similarly, different strategies require different structures. As the pace of environmental change increases, there is the potential for misalignment between an organization's structure and its strategy. Analysis of structure on an ongoing basis is therefore necessary to ensure it is the most appropriate given its ephemeral environmental conditions.

Aspects of structure which require analysis include:

- grouping of activities and functions;
- roles and responsibilities;
- communication channels;
- lines of authority;
- rules and regulations.

The structure of the business must allow it to accomplish its objectives as effectively and as efficiently as possible. The larger and more diverse the activities of an organization, the more complex its structure will usually need to be.

Culture

What is culture?
One of the best definitions of culture was offered by Stacey (1996).

The culture of any group of people is that set of beliefs, customs, practices and ways of thinking that they have come to share with each other through being and working together. It is a set of assumptions people simply accept without question as they interact with each other. At the visible level the culture of a group of people takes the form of ritual behaviour, symbols, myths, stories, sounds and artefacts.

Hence, the culture of any organization consists of the shared values, attitudes, assumptions and beliefs of the managers and employees of the organization which shape their behaviour and actions. The culture of an organization shapes its style and 'feel'. It will govern attitudes to work and dictate how people think things ought to be done. Culture will be an important determinant of how effectively the organization operates and has important implications for employee motivation

Culture and success
Although this is not a textbook designed to explore culture in any depth, we do make the following observations about the linkages between culture and successful strategy.

Firstly, successful organizations tend to have cultures which emphasize excellence, quality and customer service. Culture affects interactions between people within the business and between the business its customers, its suppliers and its other stakeholders.

Secondly, culture should not be seen as static – it must change as environmental conditions change. As is often the case with structure, a frequent problem for businesses is that culture does not change quickly enough to account for environmental changes. Culture is thought to change relatively over time through the process of socialization. The pace of culture change cannot always be controlled by managers. These difficulties in achieving change arise because people's long-held attitudes and beliefs do not alter unless they can be persuaded that the alterations are both justified and necessary. It is therefore important to appraise organizational culture as part of the analysis process. Yet the process of appraisal is problematic because there are difficulties inherent in 'measuring' culture. Culture cannot be readily described nor quantified.

Finally, culture is closely linked to the vision and mission of the organization. Vision and mission can help to shape organization culture and vice versa. To develop a global and transnational outlook is clearly dependent upon both vision and culture (see Chapter 2).

Products, performance and portfolio analysis

The concept of portfolio

A global business exploits its resources, capabilities and competences in the production of goods and services which meet the needs of its customers. A key concept with regard to successful product or subsidiary strategy is that of portfolio.

Many, although not all, global companies consist of a portfolio of businesses offering multiple products and services. Portfolio analysis is used in evaluating the balance of an organization's range of products. Successful product management relies upon maintaining a portfolio of products that increase the organization's ability to withstand and exploit opportunities and threats in the environment. In this regard, the key advantage of a broad portfolio is that risk can be spread across more than one market. Offsetting this is the fact that a narrower portfolio can mean that the organization becomes more specialized in its knowledge of fewer products and markets – its expertise is less 'diluted'.

Several matrices have been developed to allow analysis of an organization's products and markets. Probably the best known of these is the Boston Consulting Group (BCG) growth-share matrix. The matrix is most often used by organizations in multi-product and multi-market situations. It considers products in terms of their market share and the growth rate of the market in which they are sold.

The BCG matrix

The Boston Consulting Group matrix offers a way of examining and making sense of a company's portfolio of product and market interests. It is a relatively sophisticated approach, based on the idea that market share in mature markets is highly correlated with profitability, and that it is relatively less expensive and less risky to attempt to win share in the growth stage of the market, when there will be many new customers making a first purchase. This is the approach taken by the BCG matrix. It is used to analyse the product range with a view to aiding decisions on how the products should be treated in an internal strategic analysis. Figure 3.6 shows the essential features of the Boston matrix.

The market share measure
The horizontal axis is based on a very particular measure of market share – share relative to the largest competitor. A product with a share of 20 per

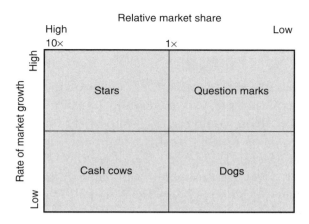

FIGURE 3.6   The Boston Consulting Group matrix

cent of the market, where the next biggest competitor had a share of 10 per cent would have a relative share of 2, whereas a product with a market share of 20 per cent and the biggest competitor also had 20 per cent, would have a relative share of 1. The cut-off point between high and low share is 1, so high market share products in this analysis are market leaders. This arrangement of scale is sometimes described as being *logarithmic* in nature.

The market growth measure

The vertical axis is the rate of market growth, with the most relevant definition of the market being served. A popular point used to divide high and low growth in the market is 10 per cent year-on-year growth, but the authors have found it useful in practical situations to use growth that is faster than the rate of growth in the economy as a whole, which, after inflation in most Western countries, is usually between 1 and 2.5 per cent per annum.

Using the BCG matrix

Cash cows

A product with a high market share in a low growth market is normally both profitable and a generator of cash. Profits from this product can be used to support other products that are in their development phase. Standard strategy would be to manage conservatively, but to defend strongly against competitors. Such a product is called a *cash cow* because profits from the product can be 'milked' on an ongoing basis. This should not be used as a justification for neglect.

Dogs

A product that has a low market share in a low growth market is termed a *dog* in that it is typically not very profitable. To cultivate the product to increase its market share would incur cost and risk, not least because the market it is in has a low rate of growth. Accordingly, once a dog has been identified as part of a portfolio, it is often discontinued or disposed of.

More creatively, opportunities might be found to differentiate the dog and obtain a strong position for it in a niche market. A small share product can be used to price aggressively against a very large competitor as it is expensive for the large competitor to follow suit.

The matrix does not have an intermediate market share category, but there are large numbers of products that have large market share, but are not market leaders. They may be the biggest profit earners for the companies that own them. They usually compete against the market leader at a disadvantage that is slight, but real. Management need to make very efficient use of marketing expenditure for such products and to try to differentiate from the leader. They should not normally compete head on, especially on price, but to attempt to make gains if the market changes in a way that the leader is slow to exploit.

Stars

Stars have a high share of a rapidly growing market, and therefore rapidly growing sales. They may be the sales manager's dream, but they could be the accountant's nightmare, since they are likely to absorb large amounts of cash, even if they are highly profitable. It is often necessary to spend heavily on advertising and product improvements, so that when the market slows, these products become cash cows. If market share is lost, the product will eventually become a 'dog' when the market stops growing.

Question marks

Question marks are aptly named as they create a dilemma. They already have a foothold in a growing market, but if market share cannot be improved, they will become dogs. Resources need to be devoted to winning market share, which requires bravery for a product that may not yet have large sales, or the product may be sold to an organization in a better position to exploit the market.

Limitations of the BCG matrix

Accurate measurement and careful definition of the market are essential to avoid mis-diagnosis when using the matrix. Critics, perhaps unfairly, point out that there are many relevant aspects relating to products that are not taken into account, but it was never claimed by the Boston Consulting Group that the process was a panacea, and covered all aspects of strategy. Above all, the matrix helps to identify *which* products to push or drop, and *when*. It helps in the recognition of windows of opportunity, and can provide strong evidence against simple rules of thumb for allocating resources to products.

The matrix has also been criticized for the imprecise nature of its four categories and because of the difficulties inherent in predicting future market growth. There are alternatives to the BCG matrix which indicate competitive position and market development (Hofer and Schendel 1979) but these share similar limitations. Despite these limitations, evaluating the performance and potential performance of products is a necessary part of the process of analysis.

Global activity may add an extra dimension to the process of portfolio analysis. The market for a global product may be at different stages of development in different countries. Similarly the market share which a product commands may differ from country to country. Global portfolio analysis must take these factors into account.

Global products and services

Yip (1992) argued that 'The benefits of global products (or services) can be achieved by standardizing the core product or large parts of it, while customizing the peripheral or other parts of the product'. Analysis of an organization's products must identify those features of a product which appeal to customers on a worldwide basis and those features which must be adapted to meet local preferences. A global product will have core features which will appeal to all customers. For example, most of Sony's consumer electronics products are generally standardized but some parts are adapted to meet national electrical standards (Yip 1992). Similarly McDonald's offerings are largely standardized, but there are minor variations, from country to country in terms of the products offered and in their presentation.

There are several benefits to be obtained from offering global products: reduced costs, enhanced quality, increased consumer preference, competitive leverage (Yip 1992). The analysis of global products must be closely related to analysis of the global competitive environment (see Chapter 4).

Performance analysis

Strategic analysis of the global organization must also include appraisal of past and present performance. Current performance can be evaluated against:

- stated objectives and targets;
- past performance;
- competitors' performances;
- external and internal benchmarks.

In addition, the performance of different divisions within the same organization can be compared.

Measures of performance can include the following areas:

- finance – accounting information including profits, return on investment, sales etc.;
- products – price, quality, value for money, functionality, design etc.;
- customer interfaces – delivery times, after sales service etc.;
- marketing – market share etc.;
- production – productivity, quality standards etc.

Establishing objectives, targets and performance standards can be extremely effective in improving organizational performance but it is important that standards are prioritized and related to critical success factors. They should also relate to areas of core competence which generate competitive advantage.

Benchmarking

A benchmark is the value of some parameter which is used as a reference point in comparisons, e.g. the top speed of a car or the number of pages per minute from the leading laser printer. The benchmark may also be the performance of a business, e.g. ROCE, profit/employee or customer satisfaction. Benchmarking is used to compare the effectiveness of the various *processes* within a business with those in other organizations and using this information, to help improve the original processes. Benchmarking can be:

- internal – using other businesses owned by the parent company;
- external – using divisions of multinationals or companies in different sectors;
- best practice – identifying the *leader* in whatever sector they operate.

Note that unlike conventional comparative analysis, the benchmark for any given process may be selected from businesses of different size and in different sectors – often the best solutions are to be found in businesses which are not competitors. To summarize, benchmarking is:

- a continuous process of evaluating and developing products, services and practices by comparison with the *best* that can be recognized globally;
- an integral part of Total Quality Management;
- essential for continuous improvement of products and performance.

Successful benchmarking must be based upon:

- commitment from the managers of the organization;
- acceptance of the need for improvement;
- willingness to take on other peoples' ideas;
- a supportive vision, mission and clear objectives;
- subsequent development of competences;
- a supportive culture.

Performance measures, although imprecise and potentially misleading, provide important indications of past and current performance. They help in identifying strengths and weaknesses which form the basis of future developments in global strategy.

Outside in or inside out?

In understanding internal analysis, we need to understand the two 'sources' of strategy and how they relate to this part of the strategic process.

'Outside in' strategy

The positioning school implies an approach to strategic analysis which is 'outside in'. That is to say the strategic process begins with analysis of the environment in order to establish which industries are potentially the most profitable. Global strategy is then determined by adopting a strategy which best matches industry conditions. In other words the business looks for a 'strategic fit' between its resources and strategies so as to exploit opportunities and reduce threats in the global environment.

'Inside out' strategy

The resource-based school emphasizes the importance of organization-specific resources, capabilities and competences in acquiring competitive edge. The approach is therefore 'inside out'. Analysis begins inside the organization to identify core competences and how new competences can be built or existing competences can be leveraged in new markets.

The two approaches and internal analysis

Despite the different starting points there is more common ground than is apparent at first glance. The positioning school accepts the importance of organization-specific factors in gaining competitive advantage as part of a generic strategy. In fact, value chain analysis (Porter 1985) is a fundamental part of its methodology, just as the way that a business's value-adding activities are configured and co-ordinated will determine its strategy and therefore its competitiveness.

Similarly, the resource-based approach, although focused on the organization, accepts the necessity to analyse the environment so as to identify the potential for competence building and leveraging opportunities. The reality is that no business can ignore its environment and that competitive advantage depends upon the competences of the organization and the way that it deploys them. In practice, the rapidly changing environment indicates that both external analysis and analysis of competences and activities must be continuous and therefore simultaneous. The purpose of strategic analysis remains, as it has always been, to determine the organization's strengths and weaknesses, to identify opportunities and threats in the environment prior to developing a strategy, based upon core competences, which produces and sustains competitive advantage.

REVIEW AND DISCUSSION QUESTIONS

1. Distinguish and explain the relationships between resources, capabilities and core competences.

2. Evaluate the role of core competences in delivering sustainable competitive advantage.
3. Choose a transnational business that you know of. Identify its core competences. Assess the competences against the criteria specified in the chapter.
4. Using the same business as in the previous question, identify and evaluate the key activities and relationships in its value chain and value system.
5. Using the same company again, explore the relationships between its core competences and key value-adding activities.
6. Obtain the annual company report of an international business and gather any other relevant materials that you can, covering a recent period of as many years as you can. Using the appropriate measures, evaluate its performance.

References and further reading

Bogner, W.C., Thomas, H. and McGee, J. (1996) A longitudinal study of the competitive positions and entry paths of European firms in the US pharmaceutical industry, *Strategic Management Journal*, **17**, 85–107.
Campbell, A. (1997) Mission statements, *Long Range Planning*, **30**(4), 931–932.
Campbell, D., Stonehouse, G. and Houston, B. (1999) *Business Strategy – An Introduction*, Butterworth-Heinemann, Oxford. See especially p. 44 on culture and p. 171 on structure.
Collis, D.J. and Montgomery, C.A. (1995) Competing on resources: strategy in the 1990s, *Harvard Business Review*, July/August, 199–128.
Cravens, D.W., Greenley, G., Piercy, N.F. and Slater S. (1997) Integrating contemporary strategic management perspectives, *Long Range Planning*, **30**(4), 493–506.
Day, G.S. (1994) The capabilities of market-driven organizations, *Journal of Marketing*, **38**, 37–52.
Gorman, P. and Thomas, H. (1997) The theory and practice of competence-based competition, *Long Range Planning*, **30**(4), 615–620.
Hamel, G. and Prahalad, C.K. (1994) *Competing for the Future*, Harvard Business School Press, Boston.
Hamill, J. (1992) Global marketing, in: Baker, M.J. (ed.), *Perspectives on Marketing Management*, vol. 2, Prentice Hall, Englewood Cliffs.
Heene, A. and Sanchez, R. (eds) (1997) *Competence-Based Strategic Management*, John Wiley, New York.
Hofer, C. and Schendel, D. (1979) *Strategy Formulation: Analytical Concepts*, West Publishing Company, St Paul.
Kay, J. (1993) *Foundations of Corporate Success*, Oxford University Press, Oxford.
Kay, J. (1995) Learning to define the core business, *Financial Times*, 1st December.
Penrose, E. (1959) *The Theory of the Growth of the Firm*, Oxford University Press, Oxford.
Perlmutter, H.V. (1969) The tortuous evolution of the multinational corporation, *Columbia Journal of World Business*, January/February.
Petts, N. (1997) Building growth on core competences – a practical approach, *Long Range Planning*, **30**(4), 551–561.
Pitts, R.A. and Lei, D. (1996) *Strategic Management – Building and Sustaining Competitive Advantage*, West Publishing Company, St Paul.
Porter, M.E. (1985) *Competitive Advantage*, The Free Press, New York.
Porter, M.E. (1986) *Competition in Global Industries*, Harvard Business School Press, Boston.
Porter, M.E. (1990) *The Competitive Advantage of Nations*, Macmillan, London.
Prahalad, C.K. and Hamel, G. (1990) The core competence of the corporation, *Harvard Business Review*, May/June, 79–91.

Sanchez, R., Heene, A. and Thomas, H. (1996) Towards the theory and practice of competence-based competition, in: Sanchez, R., Heene, A. and Thomas, H. (eds), *Dynamics of Competence-Based Competition: Theory and Practice in the New Strategic Management*, Elsevier, Oxford.

Stacey, R. (1996) *Strategic Management and Organizational Dynamics*, 2nd ed, Pitman, London.

Stalk, G., Evans. P. and Shulmann, L.E. (1992) Competing on capabilities: the new rules of corporate strategy, *Harvard Business Review*, March/April, 57–69.

Yip, G.S. (1992) *Global Strategy – Managing for Worldwide Competitive Advantage*, Prentice Hall, Englewood Cliffs, NJ.

ANALYSIS OF THE COMPETITIVE ENVIRONMENT

4

CHAPTER

LEARNING OBJECTIVES

After studying this chapter, students should be able to:

- define and distinguish between the micro- and macroenvironments;
- define and distinguish between industries and markets;
- explain and apply Porter's five forces framework for analysing industries and markets;
- explain and apply Yip's framework for international business drivers;
- explain the importance of strategic groupings in competitive strategy.

Introduction

The strategy of any organization will be shaped in part by its own capabilities and competences, and, in part, by its competitive environment. The micro or competitive environment consists of the industry and markets in which the organization carries out its business. Industries are concerned with the production of goods and services while markets are concerned with the demand side of the economic 'equation'.

In this chapter, we introduce Yip's (1992) globalization driver framework to explain the factors in the environment that stimulate the increased globalization of industries and markets. This is important when seeking to understand why some competitive situations are globalized whilst others are more regional or localized in nature.

Two key frameworks for understanding competition in industries are then explained. Firstly, Michael Porter's five forces framework can be used to understand the competitive forces at work in industries. The five forces framework suggests that competitive advantage depends upon how strongly an organization is positioned with regard to the five competitive forces. Secondly, the resource-based school of thought is introduced. This suggests that competitive advantage rests more upon how well the organization captures and develops resources into competences which can then be exploited in markets. The features of markets as they influence competitive behaviour is discussed.

Finally, the importance of strategic groupings is discussed. Competition in any industry will be at its most intense between the competitors in such a group and we discuss what factors come together to form such a grouping.

The nature of the business environment

The importance of environmental analysis

Analysis of the external business environment is a major factor in determining the strategy adopted by a business. For businesses that are international, this stage in strategic analysis is even more important.

Factors in the environment, the industry and the market will drive the enterprise towards one type of international strategy – either one that is fully global or one which makes concessions to localized customer needs. Environmental analysis is therefore a key element of the strategic process yet it is probably the stage of the process about which there is greatest ambiguity. This ambiguity arises from the problem of gaining external information which is reliable and based upon which, the business can make decisions about its strategic future.

One way of conceptualizing the external environment is as a network of macro- and microenvironments, all of which are related to each other. Every international enterprise operates within one or more industries and one or more markets which are found in more than one country. National and global industries and markets all interact with each other and are interdependent to varying degrees. Similarly, industries and markets exist in the context of global and national macro business environments which also interact with each other. These global and national macro business environments are important in shaping individual industry and market characteristics at both national and global levels. Changes in the macro-environment at both global and national levels cause changes in customer needs, products and production techniques, competition, and industry and market structures. Managers must therefore be aware of both the global and national contexts in which their business operates, and the complex network of relationships between each of these environments.

The macroenvironment

The macroenvironment (sometimes called the *far* or *remote* environment) consists of the forces at work in the general business environment which will shape the industries and markets in which an organization competes. Analysis of the macroenvironment is concerned with changes and trends in *social and cultural, demographic, political, legal, technological, economic* and *financial factors*. The effects of such changes upon international industries and markets is assessed and also upon the businesses that compete within them.

The macroenvironment can be further subdivided into both global and local (or national) elements:

- the global macroenvironment – this is concerned with global trends;
- the national macroenvironment – this is concerned with trends and changes at the level of the individual country.

The forces at work in these two subdivisions fall into the same categories, and are often linked. Their magnitude and direction may well differ at the global and national levels.

The microenvironment

The microenvironment (sometimes called the *near* environment) is the competitive environment facing a business and it consists of the industries and markets in which the organization conducts its business. The micro-environment can also be subdivided into:

- the global microenvironment – concerned with global industry and market trends;
- the national or regional microenvironment – concerned with national industry and market trends.

The microenvironment will be largely shaped by the forces at work in the global and national macroenvironments. The near environment is the part of the environment over which the business is likely to be able to exercise some direct influence and control through its corporate strategies.

There are several techniques available for analysing the microenvironment. Porter's 'five forces' model (Porter 1980, 1985) is the most widely used in strategic management texts, but Yip's globalization drivers (Yip 1992) is a useful model in the context of studying global businesses. This chapter will consider both of these models, but we begin with exploring the key concepts of industries and markets – the two major components of the microenvironment.

Industries and markets

Identifying industries and markets

Some strategic management texts wrongly use the terms industry and market interchangeably. Kay (1995) pointed out that to confuse the two concepts can result in flawed analysis of the competitive environment and, hence, in flawed strategy. Matters are sometimes complicated because many businesses operate in one or more industries and in one or more markets. Each will have its own distinctive structure and characteristics which will have particular implications for the formulation of corporate strategy. Kay (1993) also pointed out that a distinctive capability, or core competence, 'becomes a competitive advantage only when it is applied in a market or markets'. Industries are centred on the supply of a product while markets are concerned with demand. It is essential, therefore, to understand and analyse both industry and market when undertaking microenvironmental analysis.

The industry

An industry consists of a group of businesses producing similar outputs (goods or services). Although there is no precise way of defining an industry, all of the businesses in a particular industry might be expected to share the following related features:

- skills and competences;
- technology;
- processes and value-adding activities;
- materials (especially input stocks);
- supplier channels;
- distribution channels;
- products.

Analysis of these features of an industry will inform the process of strategy formulation.

The players in a given industry may produce products for more than one market. For example, businesses in the 'white goods' industry produce both washing machines and refrigerators. The materials, technology, skills, and processes employed in the manufacture of both products are very similar. The materials used are obtained from similar suppliers and the products are sold to consumers through the same distributors. There is therefore clearly a 'white goods' industry. Yet both products (washing machines and refrigerators) satisfy very different customer needs, are used for entirely different purposes and are therefore sold in separate markets. One make of washing machines competes with another, while one make of refrigerators competes with another.

The market

We generally think of a market as comprising the demand side of an economic system (the industry is the supply side). Unlike an industry, a market is defined in terms of shared:

- products or services;
- customers;
- customer requirements;
- distribution channels;
- competitors.

Thus, a market centres on products or services which meet a specific set of consumer requirements. Given that their needs are met, the skills involved in the production of the product or service are generally of little consequence to consumers. It is important to note that businesses operate within two distinct groups of markets, those where they sell their products and services and those where they acquire their resource inputs. In addition, markets for substitute products and services will have an important bearing upon the attractiveness of a particular market. Whereas understanding the industry is concerned with skills, technology and so on, understanding the market is centred upon awareness of customers and their needs.

The importance of the distinction between industry and market

Businesses gain competitive advantage by developing core competences within an industry which are then deployed in markets to satisfy customer demands. An industry may well produce more than one product and may serve more than one market or group of customers. For example, the players in the chemical industry can produce a variety of products like pharmaceuticals, fertilizers, paints etc. These are then sold in completely separate markets. Similarly, a market may be served by more than one industry. For example, the transport needs of commuters are met by the automobile industry, the railways and bus companies. While there is a world automobile industry there are still several distinct markets for automobiles. Despite the fact that consumer needs have converged in recent years, their preferences in the North American market remain significantly different from those of their European counterparts.

The distinction between industry and market is important to make as the success of a business will depend upon its competitive position in both areas of operation – as a supplier of outputs and as a buyer of inputs.

Understanding of the nature of the industry and markets in which a business conducts, or may potentially conduct, its business allows its managers to determine the most effective ways to exploit its resources, competences and technology in the context of existing and potential markets. The ability of a business to achieve competitive advantage depends upon the development of company-specific competences and capabilities, and the identification of those markets to which they may give access. Such awareness is provided by internal and external analysis of the business and its environment. Internal analysis helps to identify the core competences of the business whilst external analysis, particularly of the microenvironment, assists in identifying those industries and markets where the competences apply.

Globalization of industries and markets

Industries and markets differ vastly in the extent to which they are globalized. The consumer electronics industry and its markets are largely globalized. On the other hand, both the market for personal banking and the associated industry providing banking services are still largely localized (in that they operate in limited geographical regions). Yet as deregulation of financial services develops throughout the world, both banking industry and market are becoming increasingly globalized.

The dynamic nature of the business environment means that the trend towards globalization is gaining momentum both in terms of the number of industries and markets which are becoming global and the extent to which they are globalized. There are a number of notable examples, however, where industries are largely globalized but markets remain locally differentiated in terms of customer needs, product specifications, legal requirements, branding, advertising and other factors. In the paint industry, for example, the processes of making paint and the products of the paint industry are almost completely standardized but the packaging, advertising and brand names are often adapted for both linguistic and cultural reasons.

Yip's globalization drivers

The four categories of drivers

Yip (1992) provided the most widely-used framework for assessing the extent of, and potential for, industry and market globalization. Yip's research suggested that there are four categories of drivers (market, cost, government and competitive) which must be analysed in order to determine the degree of globalization within an industry. The strength of each of these drivers will vary from industry to industry and from market to market. It is important not to regard any industry or market as being either entirely global or local. In the case of a specific industry, certain drivers may be strongly indicative of globalization and the others more suggestive of localization. In such a situation it is appropriate for a transnational strategy that incorporates both global and local features matched to the industry drivers.

There is a strong relationship between the factors at work in the macroenvironment and the globalization drivers. This relationship is illustrated in Figure 4.1. Changes in the macroenvironment will affect both the general extent of globalization and the degree of globalization in specific industries. For example, cultural convergence and developments in transport and communications technology have been important factors increasing the strength of market, cost and competitive drivers pushing towards globalization in a number of industries. Yip's framework therefore establishes the linkages between the macro- and microenvironments and the extent to

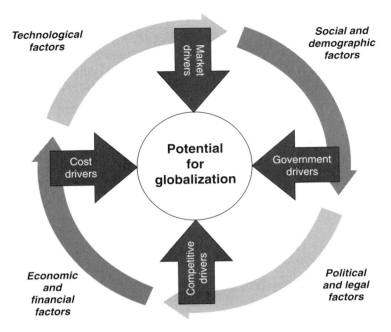

FIGURE 4.1   The macroenvironment and globalization drivers (adapted from Yip 1992)

which changes in the macroenvironment cause globalization of the micro-environment.

Each of the drivers must be analysed in detail in order to assess the extent of the pressures on an industry and market for globalization or localization. Table 4.1 shows aspects of the drivers which are indicative of globalization or localization potential. By such detailed analysis it is possible to match transnational strategy to each of the drivers. Equally, the transnational strategy of a business will seek to modify the drivers so that they match its core competences and distinctive capabilities.

Market globalization drivers

The extent to which customers, customer needs, distribution channels and marketing strategy are global will together determine the extent of market globalization or localization. The role of 'lead' countries in promoting the globalization of industries and markets is also an important determinant.

Customer needs
Similarities and differences in customer needs for a product or service will depend upon similarities and differences in culture, economic development,

Table 4.1 The globalization drivers

Driver		Pressure for globalization	Pressure for localization
Market	Customers	Global customers	Local customers
	Channels	Global channels	Local channels
	Marketing	Transferable marketing	Differentiated marketing
	Countries	Lead countries	No obvious lead countries
Cost	Economies of scale	High fixed costs	Low fixed costs
	Experience curve	Steep learning curve	Shallow learning curve
	Sourcing	Centralized purchasing	Decentralized purchasing
	Logistics	Low transport costs, perishable products, no need to locate near customers	High transport costs, perishable products, need to locate near customers
	Country costs	Differences in costs	Similarities in costs
	Product development costs	High	Low
	Technological change	Rapid	Slow
Government	Trade policies	Low trade barriers	High trade barriers
	Technical standards	Compatible	Incompatible
	Marketing regulations	Common	Different
	Government ownership	Government-owned competitors present	Government-owned competitors absent
	Host government concerns	Policies which favour global businesses	Policies which hinder global businesses
Competitive	Volume of exports and imports	High exports and imports	Low exports and imports
	Competitors	Competitors from different continents	Local competitors
		Competitors globalize	
	Interdependence of countries	Countries largely interdependent	Countries largely independent

climate, physical environment and whether countries are at the same stage in the product's life cycle. Cultural and economic convergence are causing customer needs to converge in many markets (Levitt 1983).

Customers and channels

Some customers – often global organizations themselves – purchase goods and services on a global basis. They seek those suppliers that can offer the best worldwide product, service and price package. These businesses often demand inputs that are globally standardized. The leading motor vehicle manufacturers, for example, source components globally. The world's largest motor manufacturer, General Motors, spends about UK£44bn

(US$70bn) per annum on components. These are sourced globally from a smaller and smaller number of larger and larger suppliers so as to ensure both lower costs and consistent quality. The increasing number of global businesses, of course, has increased the number of global customers as such businesses increasingly co-ordinate their activities globally including purchasing decisions.

Although global distributors that buy on a global basis are less common, they exist on a regional basis in large numbers. Major supermarket chains in Europe co-ordinate their purchasing largely within the European Union but they demand uniform product standards.

Marketing

In an increasing number of markets, like fashion clothing, global brand names and marketing mixes have been established. In others, product names and advertising are varied locally. For example, the Ford Mondeo, as it is known in Europe, is badged as the Ford Contour and the Mercury Mystique in the USA. Similarly, the advertising campaign for the Renault Clio in the UK featuring 'Nicole and Papa' was not used in France. In those markets where standardized marketing is possible, it clearly indicates the existence of a global market.

Lead countries

Certain countries take the lead in product innovation in certain industries and it is essential that global competitors compete in such lead countries. It is Japan which leads in consumer electronics, the USA in computer software, and Italy in ceramic tiles (Porter 1990). Such countries tend to set global standards for the products and services in which they are leaders creating global markets.

To summarize, globalization is stimulated by common customer needs, global customers, the presence of lead countries and transferable marketing messages.

Cost globalization drivers

Those industries where fixed costs are high will tend to be global so that such costs can be diluted by higher sales volumes. Higher sales volumes reduce unit fixed costs as the organization benefits from greater scale economies.

Economies of scale and scope

When a national market is not large enough for the players in an industry to achieve economies of scale then they will be driven to enter global markets. Similarly, the desire to obtain economies of scope (advantages gained by providing two or more distinct goods or services together rather than providing them separately) has pushed industries towards globalization.

Scope economies often arise because products share the same distribution outlets or because consumers require a group of goods to be packaged together. For example, many travel agents provide currency exchange *and* insurance services alongside their normal travel services. This is thought to attract customers requiring the full range of travel-related services rather than because they possess a particular competitive advantage in the provision of such goods. Indeed global economies of scope drive an industry towards globalization. Yip (1992) gave the example of household products like detergent and toothpaste whose manufacture gives little scope for economies of scale. In spite of this, the industries that produce these things are dominated by global companies like Unilever, Procter and Gamble, and Colgate-Palmolive. This suggests that global economies of scope derived from marketing, consumer needs and research are the drivers towards globalization rather than economies of scale.

Experience curve

If there are substantial learning and experience effects in an industry then global operation is likely to produce substantial competitive advantages.

Sourcing

There may be cost and quality advantages to be obtained by centralizing the acquisition of supplies and services on a global basis. Global customers like Ford and other large motor manufacturers source components so as to reduce costs and 'Such cost advantages are often multiplied by the fact that big component specialists supply more than one carmaker giving them greater economies of scale' (Simonian 1996). Global sourcing will drive an industry towards globalization.

Logistics

If transport costs are low and products are non-urgent and non-perishable then there are advantages to be gained from global concentration of production.

Country costs, productivity and skills
Countries differ considerably in terms of production costs, productivity levels, infrastructure and availability of skilled labour. There are sometimes global cost advantages to be obtained by concentrating activities in countries where productivity is high and costs are relatively low.

Product life cycles and product development costs
The speed with which new products are required is increasing and, at the same time, the development costs of new products are high. In order to cover these costs it is necessary to sell such products in global markets because national markets are not sufficiently large to provide the necessary returns (again, especially if the business has relatively high fixed costs).

Government globalization drivers

Government policies, legislation and regulation can also drive an industry towards globalization.

Trade policies
The increasing liberalization of world trade (with falling barriers to trade) has greatly increased the potential for globalization even though in some countries, there are still substantial government-imposed trade barriers.

Technical standards
If technical standards for a product are common between countries, then this will drive an industry towards globalization while incompatible standards will tend to fragment the market. In the 1970s, technical standards for telecommunications tended to be different from country to country although the digitization of the 1990s increased compatibility. The resultant compatibility was one of the most important stimulants behind global communications media such as the internet.

Marketing regulations
Marketing regulations like those governing advertising tend to vary from country to country which can sometimes inhibit the use of global advertising. Yet even in this case there is a tendency towards global standards. As a consequence, major companies like Nike and Coca-Cola have been able to design advertising campaigns which meet advertising standards across the world such that the advert's ability to offend in some cultures is minimized.

Government-owned competitors

Yip argued that the existence of government-owned competitors in an industry can spur an industry towards globalization. Government subsidies and protection of home markets encourage such businesses to seek foreign customers and this can increase global competition.

Government-owned customers

Government-owned customers tend to reduce globalization potential as they often tend to favour domestic suppliers for local political reasons.

Host government concerns

Global businesses will seek those countries where national conditions are the most favourable. Governments can advance globalization business by policies which encourage global businesses to locate value-adding activities within their national boundaries.

Competitive globalization drivers

Indicators of global competition are the existence of global competitors from several countries; high levels of exports and imports; and inter-dependence between countries.

Exports and imports

The level of exports and imports will indicate the extent of globalization of an industry. The higher their levels the greater the potential for the industries and markets to become globalized.

Competitors

The greater the number of competitors from different countries and continents the greater will be the level of global competition.

A business which faces global competitors making use of global strategies will, almost inevitably, be forced to compete globally itself. If competitors are largely domestic then a business will not be forced to adopt a global strategy and can continue to operate within its national boundaries.

Interdependence of countries

If there is a high level of interdependence in an industry between countries, then this will also stimulate global competition. In most industrial sectors, both markets and industries are becoming increasingly interdependent.

A summary of the drivers

Analysis of the extent of globalization in industries and markets will require examination of the strength of Yip's four drivers: market; cost; government; and competitive drivers. There are several advantages to be gained by using Yip's framework:

- it allows identification of those drivers which are global and those which are local so that attributes of transnational strategy can be tailored to match the drivers;
- it can be used to analyse both industry and market;
- it can be mapped onto Porter's five forces;
- changes in the drivers can be indicated by macroenvironmental analysis;
- it assists in the identification of critical success factors in a global industry and market.

Industry analysis

Industry analysis aims at establishing the intensity and nature of competition in an industry, and the competitive position of the individual business with it. Industry dynamics are, in turn, affected by changes in the macroenvironment. For example, ageing populations in many developed countries have significantly affected the need to develop drugs suitable for treating the ailments of older people. There is a danger that industry analysis will be treated as a one-off activity but, on the contrary, it is usually important that it is given a dynamic perspective and repeated on a regular basis. The framework developed by Michael E. Porter (1980) is the most widely used in industry analysis and it is explained in this section.

Porter's five forces framework (Figure 4.2)

According to Michael Porter (1979)

> Every industry has an underlying structure, or set of fundamental economic and technical characteristics that gives rise to ... competitive forces. The strategist

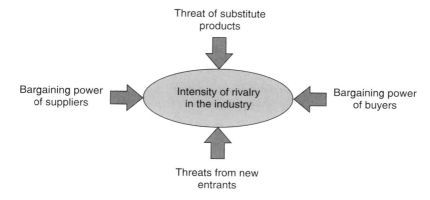

FIGURE 4.2   Porter's five forces framework (adapted from Porter 1979)

wanting ... to influence that environment in the company's favour, must learn what makes the environment tick. The state of competition in an industry depends on five basic forces, the collective strength of which determines the ultimate profit potential of the industry.

The competitive forces in question are:

- threat of new entrants to the industry (that is, the height of barriers to entry);
- threat of substitute products;
- bargaining power of customers;
- bargaining power of suppliers;
- rivalry among current competitors in the industry.

Porter (1980) argued that it is the strength of these forces in an industry which determines its potential for profitability and which strongly influences its structure.

This view was challenged by Baden-Fuller and Stopford (1992) who observed that 'There is little difference in the profitability of one industry versus another'. Their argument is based upon the research of Rumelt (1991) which suggested that company-specific factors like preferred strategy were of much greater importance in determining the profitability of a business rather than its competitive environment.

There are two reasons why Rumelt's argument should not deter managers from undertaking industry and market analysis. Firstly, whether or not industry structure determines profitability, managers must understand the environment in which they operate to assist in the choice of strategy.

Secondly, McGahan and Porter (1997) carried out a broader and more rigorous study than that of Rumelt and concluded that industry structure influences profitability alongside company-specific factors.

The strength of each of the five forces will differ within an industry over time and between different industries. Equally it is true that each of the forces will be of different strengths. In fact, it is likely that just one or two of the forces will be of critical importance within a particular industry at a given point in time. The analysis of an industry will, therefore, seek to identify the nature and relative strength of each of the forces over time. Analysis must begin with an explanation of the nature of each of the forces and will culminate in an assessment of:

- the relative strength of each force;
- any changes likely to occur in the future;

The analysis of each of the five forces is now considered in detail.

Force 1: the threat of new entrants

The more easily new competitors can enter an industry, the greater will be the level of competition. The threat from new entrants will depend on the 'height' of the barriers to entry to an industry. Barriers to entry consist of:

- the economies of scale which existing businesses in the industry already enjoy which give them a cost advantage over new entrants;
- product differentiation and brand loyalty which make it difficult for new players to attract customers from existing competitors;
- the start-up capital required to enter the industry;
- switching costs incurred by customers which deter them from buying from new entrants;
- difficulty in accessing supply or distribution channels which may make it difficult for new entrants to gain key inputs or to provide their products to the customer;
- government policy which may restrict entry;
- the resistance offered by existing players like price cuts and advertising campaigns which may deter customers from switching to new entrants.

The greater the height of the entry barriers for a particular industry, the fewer competitors will be in the industry and hence, the higher the potential profits available to the businesses within it. As a consequence, one objective of corporate strategy will be to create and increase barriers to entry.

Force 2: the threat of substitute products

A substitute is the product of (usually) another industry which meets very similar customer needs to those of the product of the industry in question. The threat from substitutes will depend upon the number available and how readily they can be substituted for the product in question (i.e. what the switching costs are). For example, butter, margarine and low fat spreads are all produced in different ways but satisfy the same customer needs. They are very close substitutes for each other so resulting in a high level of competition between them. When there are few close substitutes for a product the level of competition will be reduced (such as for patented medicines).

The degree of competition from substitutes will depend on:

- how effectively they meet the specific customer need;
- their relative price and performance;
- the cost of switching to the product for buyers;
- the willingness of buyers to substitute.

A business can reduce the competition from substitutes by taking action to differentiate its product, to enhance its performance and to increase switching costs for consumers.

Force 3: the bargaining power of buyers (customers)

The customers purchasing a product can include manufacturers, service businesses, retailers, wholesalers and distributors as well as retail consumers. Such customers have, to varying degrees, the power to bargain with the players in an industry over price, product features, availability etc.

The extent of buyer or customer power will depend upon factors such as:

- the number of large and powerful customers that there are for a product;
- the ease with which customers can switch to substitute products;
- the ability of the customer to threaten to take over any of the businesses supplying the particular product by backward integration;
- the skills of the customer in negotiating price with the suppliers in the industry;

- the ability of customers to act collectively when dealing with the industry;
- the availability of information to customers.

In short, customers are powerful if individually they are large purchasers of the industry's product, switching costs are low, or if they pose a credible threat of backward integration etc. The businesses in an industry will obviously try to reduce the power of their customers by differentiating their products and taking other action to increase actual or perceived switching costs.

Force 4: the bargaining power of suppliers

The suppliers to an industry include providers of raw materials, components, labour, energy, plant and equipment, finance, etc.

Their power will depend upon:

- the size and power of individual suppliers compared to the size and power of the businesses in the industry (which, in this case, are the buyers);
- the importance of suppliers' products to the businesses in the industry;
- the costs for the players in the industry of switching to alternative suppliers;
- the importance of the buyers in the industry as customers of the suppliers;
- the threat of forward integration by the suppliers.

Supplier power will be greatest when they are few in number and large in size, their products or services are important to the industry, when switching costs are high, when the industry is unimportant as a customer and when there is a threat of forward integration by suppliers. There are several ways in which supplier power can be reduced, such as by locating alternative sources of supply.

Force 5: the rivalry among existing competitors in the industry

Rivalry among the players in an industry can take several forms. The most common are price competition, product development, product differentiation, promotion and advertising.

The intensity of rivalry can be related to a number of factors:

- the number of competitors in the industry;
- the similarity of the size of the competitors;
- the overall rate of industry growth;
- the extent of differentiation and brand loyalty among consumers;
- the costs to competitors of exiting the industry (exit costs).

Rivalry will be greatest when there are a large number of roughly evenly-sized businesses, when industry growth is limited, when brand loyalty is low and when exit costs are high.

Such competition may have both positive and negative effects upon the industry. If competition results in enhanced innovation, it may cause the industry to expand. It is just as possible, however, that competition may result in reduced levels of profit.

Use of the five forces framework

The five forces framework can be used as either a tool for understanding industry structure and dynamics or as a means of identifying and understanding the key forces at work in the industry (or both).

Some criticisms can be made of the five forces framework as an analytical tool. There seems to be an assumption that the threat of substitutes, the power of buyers and the power of suppliers will be equally important to *all* of the competitors in an industry. In reality, some of the players in an industry may be able to manage the effects of the forces more effectively than others.

Managers must seek to establish the strength of the five forces in relation to their business as well as for the industry as a whole. This analysis will help in determining how the business's strategy can modify competitive forces in its favour without providing similar benefits to the competitors in the industry. Finally, the framework has been criticized as being static when, in reality, environmental analysis must be undertaken on an ongoing basis.

Globalization drivers and the five forces

Synthesizing the two frameworks

The strength of the globalization drivers can affect the strength of the competitive forces at work within an industry. The potential relationships are illustrated in Table 4.2.

Table 4.2   Globalization drivers and Porter's five forces

Competitive force	Globalization driver impact
Threat of entry	Common customer needs increase threat of entry Global economies of scale reduce threat of entry Global marketing reduces threat of entry High product development costs reduce threat of entry Global competition increases threat of entry to national markets from global competitors
Threat of substitutes	Threat of substitutes is increased by presence of lead nations Threat of substitutes is increased by research and development of global businesses that use innovation as means of competition
Power of buyers and suppliers	Existence of global customers can weaken supplier power Existence of global suppliers can counteract the power of global customers
Competitive rivalry	Common customer needs make it difficult for businesses to differentiate themselves which increases competition Global customers increase competition as businesses compete to supply them Economies of scope increase competitive rivalry Global sourcing increases competitive rivalry Compatible technical standards and favourable trade policies increase competitive rivalry Increased number of businesses operating across national boundaries increases competition

Although the effect of the drivers will differ from industry to industry, it is evident that globalization will increase competition in almost all cases. At the same time, however, there is also potential for the growth of global businesses that can compete with smaller businesses that are locally and nationally based. The smaller businesses usually suffer in such a competitive situation – often to the point of going out of existence.

Market analysis

Market identification

Besides developing an appreciation of the forces at work within their industry, strategic decision-makers must also develop an understanding of the markets in which they sell their products. Unless they can sell the organization's products at a profit the business cannot succeed.

Kay (1993) pointed out that it is only when core competences or distinctive capabilities are applied in the context of one or more markets that they become sources of competitive advantage. Markets are based upon customer needs so that success in the marketplace is largely dependent upon a business being customer driven. In addition to meeting existing customer needs, this implies that a business must also seek to create new ones. Sony for example created a customer need for the personal hi-fi when it launched the Walkman concept. An organization can attempt to shape the needs of its customers through new product development and advertising. Similarly, market research attempts to identify and test out ideas for new products. It is evident that the major aim of market analysis is an increased understanding of customers and their needs. Equally, markets are defined in terms of competitors and distribution channels so that analysis also endeavours to increase understanding of these facets of the market.

Customers and their needs

Customer analysis attempts to develop knowledge of customer groupings (segmentation analysis), customer motivations and the unmet needs of customers (Aaker 1992). We consider each of these below.

Market segmentation analysis

This analysis seeks to identify the largest and most profitable customers and to group them according to shared characteristics. Such shared characteristics will cause specific customer groups to have different needs and to act and behave differently to other customer groups. Fundamentally, segmentation means subdividing a market into customer sub-groupings, each with their own distinctive attributes and needs. Customer groups are commonly segmented according to factors like age, sex, occupation, socio-economic grouping, race, lifestyle, buying habits, geography (i.e. where they live) etc. Where the customers are other businesses, they can be grouped by the nature of their business, organization type and by their size. Each segment is then analysed for its size and potential profitability, for customer needs and for potential demand, based on ability and willingness to buy. Segmentation analysis assists in the formulation of strategy by identifying particular segments and consumer characteristics which can be targeted. Computer games, for example, are largely targeted upon young males between the ages of 11 and 25. This is not to say that other groups and individuals do not play computer games but the segment identified is easily the largest and most profitable.

Customer motivations

Once market segments have been identified they must be analysed to reveal the factors which influence customers to buy or not buy products. It is particularly important to understand factors affecting customer motivations. These include:

- sensitivity to price;
- sensitivity to quality;
- the extent of brand loyalty.

Differences in customer motivations between market segments can be illustrated by reference to the market for air travel. The market can be segmented into business and leisure travel. Customers in each group have very different characteristics and needs. Business travellers are not particularly price conscious but are sensitive to standards of service, to scheduling and to the availability of connections. Leisure travellers are generally much more price rather than service conscious and are less sensitive to scheduling and connections. Market research has an important role in building understanding of customer needs so that they can be targeted by appropriate product or service features.

Unmet needs

Aaker (1992) defined an unmet need as 'a customer need that is not now being met by the existing product offerings'. There are many relevant examples in markets for pharmaceutical products. There are many illnesses for which there is no current cure and often, when a cure exists, treatment has undesirable side effects. Cancer, for example, is often incurable and even where a cure is possible, it sometimes involves a number of unpleasant side effects. Clearly a cure which was successful in a greater number of cases, and which eliminated harmful side effects, would both meet patient needs and, as a result, be potentially very profitable. The identification of unmet customer needs, as a basis for future product development, is a vital function of market research.

In addition to analysis of market segmentation, customer motivations and unmet customer needs, Porter's five forces framework 'can also be applied to a market or submarket within an industry' (Aaker 1992).

Although the framework is designed primarily for industry analysis, it can also be useful in the analysis of competition within an organization's markets.

Strategic group and competitor analysis

What are strategic groups?

Although businesses compete within industries and markets, they face the strongest competition from businesses possessing similar core competences, pursuing similar strategies, and satisfying similar customer demands. Strategic group analysis (Porter 1980) attempts to compare an organization with the group of businesses which are its closest competitors.

A strategic group consists of organizations which:

- possess similar core competences;
- pursue similar strategies;
- serve a similar customer group and similar market segments;
- employ similar technology;
- utilize similar distribution channels;
- produce similar products or services of comparable quality.

The importance of each of these attributes in circumscribing the strategic group will differ from industry to industry. It is necessary to decide which attributes are the most significant, for the industry under analysis in defining its strategic groupings. In the motor industry, for example, businesses like Porsche, Ferrari, Aston Martin and Lotus fall into the same strategic group for which technology, quality and customer group are probably the most definitive characteristics. In the brewing industry, businesses like Heineken, Carlsberg and Kronenberg fall into the same group which is best characterized by their similarity of product range and distribution channels.

Whilst the similarities between the businesses are used to define the group, it is the purpose of strategic group analysis to facilitate analysis of direct competitors and to highlight differences as well as similarities. In other words, the businesses which constitute a particular strategic group can then be compared in terms of a range of indicators which include:

- shared or similar objectives;
- core competences;

- strategies;
- markets and segments served;
- market share;
- profitability;
- cost structure;
- price structure;
- access to finance;
- product quality;
- customer loyalty;
- approach to marketing;
- organization of value-adding activities;
- suppliers and distribution channels;
- organizational culture;
- research, development and innovation.

Information on competitors can be obtained from several sources including:

- company accounts and annual reports;
- market research reports;
- suppliers;
- the government and other regulators;
- the press.

Strategic group and competitor analysis make it possible for the managers of an organization to better understand their own position, and that of their competitors, in the context of both industry and market. Such knowledge is essential because it:

- identifies and focuses on an organization's closest competitors;
- assists in assessing competitive potential; highlights opportunities for development;
- provides external performance benchmarks;
- helps to identify critical success factors.

A resource-based approach to environmental analysis

Limitations of traditional frameworks

This chapter has concentrated on explaining the traditional strategic management frameworks employed in analysis of the competitive environment. The resource-based approach to strategic management, which emphasizes the importance of core competence in achieving competitive advantage, employs a different approach to analysis of the competitive environment.

We suggest that there are several limitations to existing frameworks:

- they do not integrate external and internal analysis (Heene and Sanchez 1997);
- they emphasize the competitive and not the collaborative behaviour of businesses;
- they emphasize product and service markets rather than those where organizations obtain resources;
- they do not adequately recognize the fact that businesses themselves may alter their own competitive environments by their competence leveraging and building activities;
- they do not adequately recognize that organizations currently outside of an organization's industry and market may pose a significant competitive threat if they possess similar core competences and distinctive capabilities;
- similarly, they do not recognize that the leveraging of existing competences and the building of new ones may enable businesses to compete outside their current competitive arenas.

Understanding the framework

A resource-based framework for analysis of the business and its competitive environment is shown in Figure 4.3. Analysis is divided into five interlinked areas:

1. the organization itself;
2. the industry;
3. product markets;
4. resource markets;
5. competing industries.

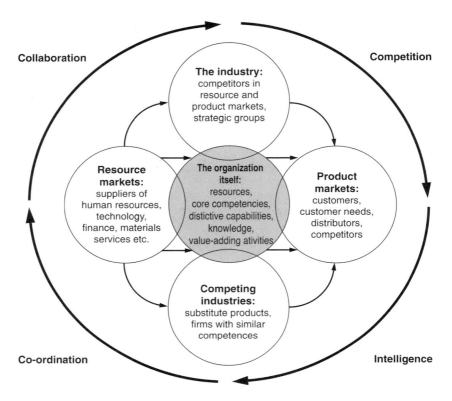

Collaboration

Competition

The industry:
competitors in
resource and
product markets,
strategic groups

Resource markets:
suppliers of
human resources,
technology,
finance, materials
services etc.

The organization itself:
resources,
core competencies,
distictive capabilities,
knowledge,
value-adding ativities

Product markets:
customers,
customer needs,
distributors,
competitors

Competing industries:
substitute products,
firms with similar
competences

Co-ordination

Intelligence

FIGURE 4.3   The competence-based competitive environment

The organization itself

The internal features of the organization itself as it relates to the resource-based view are discussed in Chapter 3. To introduce these themes again here would be an unnecessary duplication.

The industry

The industry consists of a group of businesses producing similar products, employing similar capabilities and technology.

Analysis of the industry therefore examines over time:

- the skills and competences of the companies in the industry;
- the organization of their value-adding activities;
- the technology that they employ;
- the number of competitors in the industry;
- ease of entry to and exit from the industry;
- strategic groupings.

Product markets

Product markets are those in which businesses sell their products. A business may operate in one or more product markets. Each of these markets will have its own characteristics and each market will typically be analysed in terms of:

- the number of businesses in the market and their relative market shares;
- the number of customers and their relative purchasing power;
- segments and their profitability;
- customer motivations;
- unmet customer needs;
- access to distribution channels;
- potential for collaboration with customers.

Resource markets

Resource markets are those where organizations obtain finance, human resources, materials, equipment, services etc. It is evident that businesses will normally operate in several such markets, each with its own characteristics, depending upon the company-addressable resources that they require.

Resource markets need to be analysed in terms of:

- the resource requirements of businesses;
- the number of actual and potential resource suppliers;
- size of suppliers;
- supplier capabilities and competences;
- potential for collaboration with resource suppliers;
- access by competitors to suppliers.

Competing industries

Competing industries are those which produce substitute products or services. These must be analysed for:

- substitutability of the product – how close the substitute is to satisfying the same consumer demands as the original product or service;
- key competences of the businesses in the industry;
- the number and size of the businesses in the industry.

Critical success factors (CSFs) and core competences

What are CSFs?

Analysis of the industry, market and competitive position provides the means for managers to identify critical success factors (CSFs). CSFs are those factors which are fundamental to the success of all businesses in a particular industry and associated markets. CSFs will dictate the skills which a business must possess to ensure survival in the context of its competitive environment. Competitive advantage, however, depends on the possession of company-specific attributes which are superior to and distinctive from those of competitors. These are known as core competences and distinctive capabilities.

CSFs will differ from industry to industry and from market to market. For example, in the financial services industry, a reputation for reliability, attractive interest rates and an extensive sales force are essential while in the motor vehicle industry research and development of new models, efficient and cheap supply of components, extensive dealer networks and heavy advertising are essential.

Critical success factors are shaped by the competitive environment in which the organizations operate but are also influenced by the way in which individual businesses develop their core competences. They are heavily influenced by customer demands and by the actions of competitors. It is therefore essential to understand the competitive environment and its effect on CSFs.

REVIEW AND DISCUSSION QUESTIONS

1. Define and distinguish between the following: industry; product market; resource market; strategic group.
2. Discuss the extent to which the personal computer market is globalized using Yip's framework.
3. Discuss the extent to which the profitability of a business is due to industry-dependent or business-specific factors.
4. Why is analysis of the competitive environment so important?
5. Explain the major forces which may cause the competitive environment to change.
6. Discuss the major similarities and differences between the traditional and resource-based approaches to analysis of the competitive environment?
7. Define and distinguish between critical success factors and core competences.

References and further reading

Aaker, D.A. (1992) *Strategic Market Management*, John Wiley, New York.

Abell, D.F. (1980) *Defining the Business: the Starting Point of Strategic Planning*, Prentice Hall, Englewood Cliffs.

Arthur, W.B. (1996) Increasing returns and the new world of business, *Harvard Business Review*, **74**, July/August.

Baden-Fuller, C. and Stopford, J. (1992) *Rejuvenating the Mature Business*, Routledge, London.

Boettcher, R. and Welge, M.K. (1994) Strategic information diagnosis in the global organization, *Management International Review*, 1st Quarter.

Chakravarthy, B. (1997) A new strategy framework for coping with turbulence, *Sloan Management Review*, Winter, 69–82.

Chakravarthy, B.S. and Perlmutter, H.V. (1985) Strategic planning for a global business, *Columbia Journal of World Business*, Summer.

D'Aveni, R.A. (1994) *Hypercompetition: Managing the Dynamics of Strategic Manoeuvring*, Free Press, New York.

Fahey, L. and Narayanan, V.K. (1994) Global environmental analysis, in: S. Segal-Horn (ed.), *The Challenge of International Business*, Kogan Page, London.

Ginter, P. and Duncan, J. (1990) Macroenvironmental analysis, *Long Range Planning*, December.

Hamel, G. and Prahalad, C.K. (1989) Strategic intent, *Harvard Business Review*, **67**(3).

Hamel, G. and Prahalad, C.K. (1994) *Competing for the Future*, Harvard Business School Press, Boston.

Heene, A. and Sanchez, R. (1997) *Competence-Based Strategic Management*, John Wiley, New York.

Helms, M.M. and Wright, P. (1992) External considerations: their influence on future strategic planning, *Management Decision*, **30**(8).

Henzler, H. and Rall, W. (1986) Facing up to the globalization challenge, *McKinsey Quarterly*, Winter.

Kay, J. (1993) *Foundations of Corporate Success*, Oxford University Press, Oxford.

Kay, J. (1995) Learning to define the core business, *Financial Times*, 1st December.

Klugt, C.J. Van der (1986) Japan's global challenge in electronics – the Philips' response, *European Management Journal*, **4**(1).

Levitt, T. (1983) The globalization of markets, *Harvard Business Review*, May/June, 92–102.

Lindsay, W.K. and Rue, L.W. (1980) Impact of organization environment on the long range planning process, *Academy of Management Journal*, **23**.

Mascarenhas, B. (1982) Coping with uncertainty in international business, *Journal of International Business Studies*.

McGahan, A.M. and Porter, M.E. (1997) How much does industry matter, really?, *Strategic Management Journal*, **18** (Summer Special Issue), 15–30.

McGahan, A.M. and Porter, M.E. (1997) The persistence of profitability: Comparing the market-structure and Chicago views, manuscript, Harvard Business School, Boston.

Porter, M.E. (1979) How competitive forces shape strategy, *Harvard Business Review*, March/April.

Porter, M.E. (1980) *Competitive Strategy: Techniques for Analysing Industries and Competitors*, The Free Press, New York.

Porter, M.E. (1985) *Competitive Advantage*, The Free Press, New York.

Porter, M.E. (1990) *The Competitive Advantage of Nations*, Macmillan, London.

Prahalad, C.K. and Hamel, G. (1990) The core competence of the corporation, *Harvard Business Review*, May/June, 79–91.

Rumelt, R. (1987) Theory, strategy and entrepreneurship, in: Teece, D.J. (ed.), *The Competitive Challenge*, Ballinger Publishing Company, Cambridge, MA.

Rumelt, R.P. (1991) How much does industry matter?, *Strategic Management Journal*, **12**(3).

Sanchez, R. (1995) Strategic flexibility in product competition, *Strategic Management Journal*, **16** (Summer).

Sanchez, R. (1995) Strategic flexibility, firm organization, and managerial work in dynamic markets: A strategic options perspective, *Advances in Strategic Management*, **9**, 251–291.

Simonian, H. (1996) Star parts for bit players, *Financial Times*, 28th October.

Strebel, P. (1992) *Breakpoints*, Harvard Business School Press, Boston.

Turner, I. (1996) Working with chaos, *Financial Times*, 4th October.

Yip, G.S. (1992) *Total Global Strategy*, Prentice Hall, Englewood Cliffs.

Yip, G.S., Loewe, P.M. and Yoshino, M.Y. (1988) How to take your company to the global market, *Columbia Journal of World Business*, Winter.

ANALYSIS OF THE GLOBAL MACRO-ENVIRONMENT

5

CHAPTER

LEARNING OBJECTIVES

After studying this chapter, students should be able to:

- describe the nature of the macroenvironment;
- define and distinguish between continuities and discontinuities in the business environment;
- explain each of the factors to be analysed in a STEP analysis;
- describe why macroenvironmental analysis is more complex for international businesses;
- explain how national circumstances can affect global strategy;
- describe the stages in carrying out a STEP analysis.

Introduction

Strategic planning is made more difficult by the rate of change, complexity and associated uncertainty in the environment. Heene and Sanchez (1997) stated that 'In dynamic environments, building and leveraging competences requires flexibility in acquiring and deploying new resources effectively in changing circumstances'. It is evident therefore that successful strategy and associated competence development must be informed by a detailed understanding of the business environment.

In Chapter 4, we examined the importance of industry analysis. In this chapter, we look outside of the industry to learn about those forces at work that are outside of an organization's control and with which, the business must usually learn to 'cope'. A thorough macroenvironmental analysis is an ambitious task for a non-internationalized business, but for a global company, the task is made all the more complex because of the number of industries, markets and countries in which it may operate.

Change in the business environment

The nature of environmental change

The global business environment may be described as possessing three important characteristics:

- it is *dynamic* – this describes the rate of change. Environmental factors tend to change with increasing dynamism as time passes;
- it is *complex* – the forces at work in the environment are numerous, difficult to understand individually and the relationships between them are increasingly intricate;
- it is *turbulent* – the changes taking place are variable in direction, uneven in magnitude and do not always conform to a recognizable or predictable pattern.

Change in the network of business environments can be regarded as either continuous or discontinuous.

- Continuous change is a series of minor developments in technology, the world economy, political alignments and societies which is constantly taking place.
- Discontinuous change describes major developments in the global business environment which arise almost at random and which may cause major alterations in the way that business is conducted. They tend to be 'one-off' occurrences but they can precipitate significant change in business strategies.

The effects of discontinuities on governments and businesses can bring about changes in the balance of power in society, such is their potential influence. The oil crisis of 1974 brought about a large increase in the price of crude oil in Western economies. The effect of this was recession, very high inflation and numerous business failures. Similarly, the demise of communism in Eastern Europe (an example of a political change) opened up these countries, their markets and their industries to the rest of the world. In Europe, the creation of the Single European Market in 1992 eliminated many of the barriers to trade between member countries.

Discontinuities can also result from 'industry breakpoints' (Strebel 1992; Turner 1996) which can be 'caused by a revolutionary product or by fundamental changes in process or distribution channels'. Strebel identified the major indicators of breakpoints as falling demand for standardized products, availability of new sources of supplies or technologies, the breaking down of traditional customer segment groups and convergence of separate industries.

Organizations must respond to continuous and discontinuous changes in their environment if they are to compete and survive. It may be tempting to assume that it is impossible to make sense of the chaos which sometimes comprises the modern business environment but such a negative approach is unlikely to result in commercial success. It may be impossible to predict some discontinuities, but awareness and understanding of the environmental forces at work increase the likelihood of prompt and appropriate organizational responses.

Change and prescriptive strategy

For the planning or prescriptive school of strategists, environmental analysis is supposed to allow the prediction of future events so that strategic plans can be formulated accordingly. The fact that the complexity and turbulence of the environment make accurate prediction problematic may suggest that environmental analysis is of little value. However even the incrementalists (Lindblom 1959) and the logical incrementalists (Mintzberg and Waters 1985) acknowledged the need for business to anticipate and respond to changes in the environment. Chakravarthy (1997) and D'Aveni (1994) argued that businesses should actively seek to modify their environment, constantly challenging and changing the rules of the game. Analysis of the environment is therefore vital, whether it is to act as the basis of a long-term plan, to inform incremental modifications to strategy or to increase understanding of those 'rules' that the business may wish to change.

The complex and chaotic nature of the global business environment rules out (in most cases) a rigidly planned approach to strategic management. Complexity theory, however, advocates that organizations foster cultures which are flexible and experimental, and which place an emphasis on learning (Turner 1996) . Both individual and organizational learning imply the acquisition of information and knowledge. In consequence, monitoring and analysis of the business environment can be regarded as fundamental to organizational learning within the global enterprise.

The complexity of the global environment means that the process of analysis must attempt to structure, simplify and summarize events so as to facilitate their evaluation prior to management decision making. The dynamics of the environment and the pace of change mean that external analysis must be a continuous process. The frameworks employed in environmental analysis provide the means to order and relate seemingly random and isolated events in a format which is understandable to the managers of international enterprises. Managers must, however, continue to recognize the imperfections of the analytical frameworks that they employ and the often incomplete and inaccurate nature of the information upon which they base their decisions. Environmental analysis can never remove risk from business activities but it provides a means of understanding the nature and extent of the risks involved. The next section of this chapter explores the major forces at work in the macroenvironment (in contrast to the micro-environment which was considered in Chapter 4).

The macroenvironment

STEP analysis

The macro (or 'far') environment is the part of the environment over which the business can rarely exert any direct influence but to which it must respond. Conventionally, it is analysed by categorizing environmental influences at the macro level into broad groupings. In this context the most commonly used framework is STEP (sociological, technological, economic and political factors). This chapter uses an alternative categorization of forces which is more appropriate for global analysis. The forces at work in the macroenvironment are grouped under the headings of social and cultural, demographic, political, legal, technological, economic and financial. Each of these forces must be considered at both global and national levels. Global trends in these forces will significantly affect national trends but there will frequently be differences in magnitude and direction at the global and national levels. For example, the information revolution has transformed global business activities but its effects on individual countries has been uneven.

Table 5.1 shows the major groupings of forces at work in the macroenvironment and the variables associated with them. It is essential that information on these forces and associated variables is gathered continuously both globally and within each country of operation. The information must then be assessed for relevance to industry and markets.

Global and national macroenvironments

The process of analysis of the global macroenvironment is concerned with global movements in culture and society, demography, politics, international law, economics and technology. It is such movements which can create the conditions for breakpoints (Strebel 1992) which may, in turn, drastically alter competitive conditions either in favour of, or against, countries, industries and organizations.

International enterprises operate within several national environments. Each country in which a business operate presents a different set of environmental influences at the macro, industry and market levels. It is therefore necessary to monitor the macroenvironmental situation in each country of operation, as national trends will differ from those taking place in the global environment in terms of pace, size and direction. Again the national macroenvironment must be analysed in terms of the social, cultural, demographic, political, legal, technological, economic and financial forces at work.

The relationship between global and national macroenvironments

The global macroenvironment will influence the development of individual national conditions but each nation will have its own unique set of macroenvironmental conditions related to its history and development. Trends in the global macroenvironment will play a major part in shaping the global industry and market for particular products. Similarly, the national macroenvironment will substantially shape national industry and market conditions.

A major purpose of macroenvironmental analysis is to identify both similarities and differences that exist between countries. Levitt (1983) emphasized the advantage which can be gained by concentrating on national similarities. There are two dangers, however, in overemphasizing similarities between countries as a source of competitive advantage. Firstly, while there are benefits to be gained by concentrating on similarities in

Table 5.1 Macroenvironmental forces

Social and cultural	Legal (vary between countries)
Values, attitudes and beliefs	Contract law
Lifestyle and tastes	Employment law
Ethics	Trade union law
Working practices and attitudes	Monopoly and restrictive practices legislation
Levels of education and training	Consumer protection legislation
Language	Tax law
Ecological and environmental concern	Company law
Religion and moral dispositions	Corruption law
Health and related issues	International law
Openness (to international products and new technology)	
Individualism vs collectivism (in national culture)	

Demographic	Technological
Size and growth of population (birth and death rates)	Research and development
Composition of population (age, sex, ethnic mix)	Information technology and communications systems
Geographic distribution and population movements (internal migration, emigration and immigration).	Transport systems and infrastructures
	Production technologies
	Design technologies and new products
	Levels of technology, adoption rates and availability of technology

Political	Economic and financial
Constitutional issues in the country	Economic systems – market, centrally planned, mixed
National parties and groupings	Size of economies (usually measured by GDP)
Stability (or lack of)	Structures and structural changes
International groupings and trading blocs	Cyclical changes – recessions, booms etc.
Government economic intervention	Growth rates and levels of economic development
Levels of taxation	Levels and distribution of income
Availability of government subsidies	Price/inflation levels
Levels of trade protectionism	Cost levels (labour, energy, transport, materials)
	Employment levels
	Currency and exchange values
	Interest rates; levels of investment and capital markets
	International groupings
	Banking systems

global customer requirements, there are also advantages to be gained by remaining responsive to differences in customer needs (Prahalad and Doz 1986). Such thinking is at the heart of transnational strategy. Secondly, exploitation of national differences in relation to core business activities can be important as a source of competitive advantage. Porter (1990) stressed the role of national circumstances in fostering competitive advantage. Differences in wage and price levels, availability of skilled labour and the availability of government assistance can all be important sources of competitive advantage. The ability to exploit both national similarities and differences is central to international competitive advantage. Analysis of international business environments makes it possible to identify where potential sources of competitive advantage can be found both in terms of actual and potential markets, and the location of value-adding activities.

The role of national circumstances in international business

Porter (1990) argued that global competitive advantage 'results from an effective combination of national circumstances and company strategy'. It is therefore useful to examine those factors which are likely to make a country attractive as a market and as a base for value-adding activities. In other words, national circumstances may be important in determining the success of a business which chooses to locate certain of its activities in a country. It is therefore important to consider what factors constitute the major determinants of national competitive advantage.

Determinants of national competitive advantage

Porter (1990) identified four sets of circumstances (represented in Porter's Diamond – see Figure 5.1) which are crucial in determining national competitive advantage.

(a) Factor conditions
Factor conditions refer to the quality and availability of the key inputs to a business's processes. Typically, this includes an analysis of the quality and quantity of the nation's human, physical, knowledge, capital technological and capital resources, and the national infrastructure. The stock of factors is important in determining national competitiveness but more important still is the rate at which the factors are created, upgraded and made more

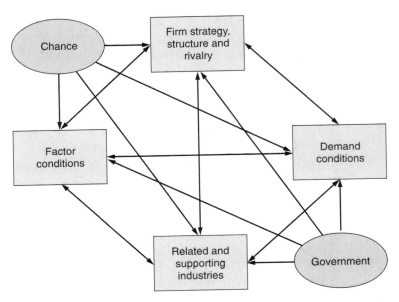

FIGURE 5.1   Determinants of national competitive advantage – Porter's diamond (adapted from Porter 1990)

specialized in particular industries. As well as the role of businesses in factor creation and improvement, the government can also have an important role to play via its policies on education, training and industry.

(b)   Demand conditions

The quantity and quality of home demand for an industry's product will also help to determine national advantage in that industry. If domestic buyers are sophisticated and demanding, and if domestic demand is internationalized, this will stimulate competitive advantage as domestic businesses will be forced to innovate faster and will be more accustomed to catering for international preferences.

(c)   Related and supporting industries

Supporting industries are those such as suppliers or downstream buyers, whilst related is a more generic term to describe those industries that interlink with the industry in question such that there is some degree of reciprocal advantage. If these industries are stronger in some countries than others, then such regions will tend to have more competitive industry. For example, many Japanese car companies benefit from the fact that

Japanese component manufacturers (a supporting industry) are extremely competitive in international markets.

(d)   The business's strategy, structure and rivalry

The context in which businesses are established, organized and managed as well as the nature of domestic rivalry will also help to determine national competitive advantage in specific industries. Factors like attitudes to risk-taking and commitment to goals are important. Similarly vigorous domestic rivalry, both price and non-price, produces companies which are likely to be able to compete in international markets. Technological rivalry is also important as it will help to create technological superiority.

As well as these four factors there are two others factors which can play an important role in national competitive advantage. These are *chance* and *government*.

(e)   The role of chance

Chance can also affect national competitive advantage. Events like major technological discontinuities, wars, political decisions by foreign governments, significant shifts in world financial markets or exchange rates can all create or destroy national advantages. The problem with chance events is their inherent unpredictability.

(f)   The role of government

Porter argued that government can affect national competitiveness by influencing the other four factors. Factor conditions are affected by government subsidies, policies towards education, capital markets, the setting of product standards etc. Governments provide the framework within which businesses compete and formulate their structures and strategies hence playing a significant role in determining national advantage.

Porter's diamond

Porter's diamond is a way of conceptualizing the six circumstantial influences that are relevant in determining national competitiveness. These determinants, individually and collectively, create the context in which a country's businesses are born and compete. The factors and the relationships between them are illustrated in Figure 5.1. Nations are most likely to succeed in industries or segments where the combination of factors is most favourable. Similarly, from the perspective of the individual business, those countries with the most favourable combination of circumstances are likely to be chosen as markets and as locations for value-adding activities by global businesses.

The analytical process

Stages in the process

At each stage of analysis of the macro- and microenvironments a number of activities are carried out. Ginter and Duncan (1990) argued that environmental analysis 'consists of four interrelated activities – scanning, monitoring, forecasting and assessing'. The process of analysis, which must be applied to all the global and national environments in which the organization conducts business, may alternatively be conceived as comprising three stages.

- *Information gathering* – identification of sources of information and obtaining relevant information from those sources.
- *Information processing* – organization of information into a manageable and meaningful format which identifies indicators of change, trends and patterns.
- *Knowledge generation* – the assessment of information to identify and prioritize those external events which are critical to the success of the organization, the creation of models and scenarios which are used to evaluate different possibilities so as to augment organizational learning and inform strategic decision making.

We will now consider each of these stages in turn.

Information gathering

Data and information about the environment can be obtained from a variety of sources (Table 5.2) which must be constantly scanned and monitored for changes which may affect markets, competition and industry structures. Two major problems exist with regard to information gathering.

Table 5.2 Data sources in international strategic analysis

Type of data source	Examples
World organizations (reports and statistics)	OECD, World Bank, International Monetary Fund, United Nations
Computerized sources	Internet, commercial databases both on-line and CD-ROM (e.g. Datastream, Mintel, Extel, FAME)
Government sources	National government reports and statistics
General and academic publications	Quality newspapers and magazines (e.g. *The Economist* and associated publications, the *Financial Times* etc.). International academic journals
Business publications	Market research reports (Neilsen's etc.) *The Economist*, banks, trade journals, *Financial Times*, national and international market research agencies, commercial bank reports
Directories	International Directory of Marketing Research Agencies, Market Research Society, London. International Directory of Marketing Research Houses and Services, American Marketing Association, Chicago

The number and variety of sources

There are so many diverse sources of data and information that it is extremely difficult to monitor them all so that it may be necessary to be selective. This carries the danger of missing some vital information.

The accuracy, relevance and reliability of sources

It is very difficult to gauge the accuracy, relevance and reliability of sources, particularly as much of the information may be speculative in nature.

In both cases experience and judgement are essential to the selection process.

Information processing

Once the information has been gathered it must be processed into a usable format. There are many methods of processing the data once gathered. These will often require the use of information technology (IT) to manipulate, summarize, tabulate, model and graph data. Database and spreadsheet software is helpful but in recent years developments in decision support systems, expert systems and intelligent databases have transformed the ability of managers to generate the quality of information required to support decision making.

Knowledge generation

The more rapid the pace of change, the greater is the need for accelerated learning by both the individual and the organization. In such a dynamic environment, it is those organizations which learn rapidly and generate organizational knowledge which survive and outperform their rivals. The boundaries between information processing and knowledge generation have become increasingly blurred as a result of the major developments which have taken place in information technology. IT greatly assists knowledge generation by allowing the development of sophisticated models and the ability to simulate a range of situations.

Turbulence in the environment makes the process of knowledge generation uncertain but scenario analysis, game theory and computer simulations make it possible to explore a range of possibilities in terms of both change in the environment and appropriate organizational responses. As Boettcher and Welge (1994) put it, 'the diagnosis of strategic information by globally dispersed organizations has been identified as a largely neglected but extremely relevant field of inquiry'.

Summary – analysis of the global macroenvironment

The links between the micro- and macroenvironments

Analysis of the macroenvironment is a fundamental prerequisite to the formulation of global strategy. The macroenvironment plays a vital role in shaping industry and market structures. Consequently, the process of analysis must begin with definition of the industry and markets in which the business operates so that analysis of the macroenvironment is focused and the dynamic relationships between the macro- and microenvironments are highlighted.

As has been shown, changes in social, demographic, political, legal, technological, economic and financial factors can create new industries and markets and can drastically alter existing ones. Additionally, it is important to understand the interaction between global and national business environments at the micro and macro levels. Global trends may affect each country, industry and market differently, thus changing the balance of competitive forces between different nations and creating a complex set of opportunities and threats for global business organizations.

The process of analysis seeks to gather information and to process it in such a way as to enhance organizational learning and knowledge, thus adding to the organization's stock of strategic assets. Although such knowledge is inevitably imperfect because of the complexity and turbulence of the environment, it is invaluable in the process of managing risk. Sanchez (1995a) and Heene and Sanchez (1997) argued that 'in dynamic environments, creating "higher order" capabilities like organizational learning that improve the strategic flexibility of an organization becomes critical to building, leveraging, and maintaining competences'. Such competence development and flexibility are essential to successful global strategy in a complex and rapidly changing environment.

In Chapter 4 we discussed the links between the micro- and macro-environments with particular emphasis on the globalization drivers. We can also develop a framework which shows how changes in the macroenvironment affect the five forces in Porter's model of the competitive environment. This enables us to predict how trends in the macroenvironment will change industry profitability.

An example of such a link is the trend towards reduction of tariff and non-tariff trading barriers between trading nations. This reduces the barriers to entry into formerly protected national or regional industries and hence the threat of new entrants into such industries is increased. The increased threat, in turn, is likely to apply a downward pressure on the prices charged by the industry and thus lower the profitability of the industry as a whole.

Review of the key stages

Despite the emphasis in the literature on competences and capabilities as internal sources of competitive advantage, environmental analysis is still of vital importance to strategy formulation. Organizations must assess both their current and potential capabilities, and the competitive, and sometimes collaborative, global context in which they must conduct their business.

In terms of specific stages, we suggest that a thorough environmental analysis for an international business will involve the following:

- definition of industry and market and identification of their chief characteristics;

- analysis of the macroenvironment at both global and national levels;
- an understanding of the role of nations in competitive advantage;
- analysis of the globalization drivers affecting the industry and market;
- analysis of industry and market structures (product and resource);
- identification and analysis of strategic groupings;
- identification of critical success factors.

The main output of the analysis is the identification of the opportunities and threats facing the business and the factors which are critical to success in the business environment. It is important to remember that such analysis must be undertaken on a continuous basis because of the dynamic and turbulent nature of the business environment. Similarly, such analysis must be recognized as inherently imprecise. Nevertheless, knowledge of the environment in which it operates is essential to the learning process of an intelligent organization.

External analysis also forms the basis of the assessment of how well the capabilities of a business are matched to its environment. It may demonstrate that there are opportunities, or requirements, for an organization to develop new competences, or leverage existing ones, if it is to succeed in the future.

REVIEW AND DISCUSSION QUESTIONS

1. Explain the importance of the macroenvironment in shaping competition and global strategies.
2. Discuss the major trends that are forcing the globalization of industries and markets. Illustrate your answer with examples.
3. Explain the difference between an industry and a market.
4. Discuss the effects of changes in the macroenvironment in an industry you know about (such as in the fast-food industry).

References and further reading

Abell, D.F. (1980) *Defining the Business: the Starting Point of Strategic Planning*, Prentice Hall, Englewood Cliffs.

Boettcher, R. and Welge, M.K. (1994) Strategic information diagnosis in the global organization, *Management International Review*, 1st Quarter.

Chakravarthy, B. (1997) A new strategy framework for coping with turbulence, *Sloan Management Review*, Winter, 69–82.

Chakravarthy, B.S. and Perlmutter, H.V. (1985) Strategic planning for a global business, *Columbia Journal of World Business*, Summer.

D'Aveni, R.A. (1994) Hypercompetition: *Managing the Dynamics of Strategic Manoeuvring*, The Free Press, New York.

Elenkov, D.E. (1997) Strategic uncertainty and environmental scanning: the case for institutional influences on scanning behaviour, *Strategic Management Journal*, **18**(4), 287–302.

Fahey, L. and Narayanan V.K. (1994) Global environmental analysis, in: S. Segal-Horn (Ed.), *The Challenge of International Business*, Kogan Page, London.

Ginter, P. and Duncan, J. (1990) Macroenvironmental analysis, *Long Range Planning*, December.

Hamel, G. and Prahalad, C.K. (1989) Strategic intent, *Harvard Business Review*, **67**(3).

Hamel, G. and Prahalad, C.K. (1994) *Competing for the Future*, Harvard Business School Press, Boston.

Heene, A. and Sanchez, R. (1997) *Competence-Based Strategic Management*, John Wiley, New York.

Helms, M.M. and Wright, P. (1992) External considerations: their influence on future strategic planning, *Management Decision*, **30**(8), 4–11.

Henzler, H. and Rall, W. (1986) Facing up to the globalization challenge, *McKinsey Quarterly*, Winter.

Kay, J. (1993) *Foundations of Corporate Success*, Oxford University Press, Oxford.

Kay, J. (1995) Learning to define the core business, *Financial Times*, 1st December.

Klugt, C.J., Van der (1986) Japan's global challenge in electronics – the Philips' response, *European Management Journal*, **4**(1), 4–9.

Levitt, T. (1983) The globalization of markets, *Harvard Business Review*, May/June, 92–102.

Lindblom, C.E. (1959) The science of muddling through, *Public Administration Review*, **19**, 79–88.

Lindsay, W.K. and Rue, L.W. (1980) Impact of organization environment on the long range planning process, *Academy of Management Journal*, **23**.

Mascarenhas, B. (1982) Coping with uncertainty in international business, *Journal of International Business Studies*.

Mintzberg, H. (1973) Strategy-making in three modes, *California Management Review*, **16**.

Mintzberg, H. (1991) *The Strategy Process – Concepts, Contexts, Cases*, Prentice Hall, Englewood Cliffs.

Mintzberg, H. and Waters, J.A. (1985) Of strategies deliberate and emergent, *Strategic Management Journal*, **6**, 257–272.

Negandhi, A.R. (1987) *International Management*, Allyn and Bacon, Boston.

Phatak, A.V. (1963) *International Dimensions of Management*, Kent, Boston.

Porter, M.E. (1980) *Competitive Strategy: Techniques for Analysing Industries and Competitors*. The Free Press, New York.

Porter, M.E. (1985) *Competitive Advantage*, The Free Press, New York.

Porter, M.E. (1986a) *Competition in Global Business*, Harvard University Press, Boston.

Porter, M.E. (1986b) Changing patterns of international competition, *California Management Review*, **28**(2), Winter, 9–40.

Porter, M.E. (1990) *The Competitive Advantage of Nations*, Macmillan, London.

Prahalad C.K. and Doz Y.L. (1986) *The Multinational Mission: Balancing Local Demands and Global Vision*, The Free Press, New York.

Prahalad, C.K. and Hamel, G. (1989) Strategic intent, *Harvard Business Review*, 63–76.

Prahalad, C.K. and Hamel, G. (1990) The core competence of the corporation, *Harvard Business Review*, 79–91.

Prahalad, C.K. and Hamel, G. (1993) Strategy as stretch and leverage, *Harvard Business Review*, March/April.

Prahalad, C.K. and Hamel, G. (1995) *Competing for the Future*, Harvard Business School Press, Boston.

Sanchez, R. (1995a) Strategic flexibility in product competition, *Strategic Management Journal*, **16** (Summer), 135–159.

Sanchez, R. (1995b) Strategic flexibility, firm organization, and managerial work in dynamic markets: A strategic options perspective, *Advances in Strategic Management*, **9**, 251–291.

Segal-Horn, S. (1992) Global markets, regional trading blocs and international consumers, *Journal of Global Marketing*, **5**(3).

Smith, D. (1997) Wrinklies timebomb waiting to explode, *Sunday Times*, 23rd February.

Stalk, G., Evans P. and Shulmann, L.E. (1992) Competing on capabilities: the new rules of corporate strategy, *Harvard Business Review*, March/April.

Strebel, P. (1992) *Breakpoints*, Harvard Business School Press, Boston.

Turner, I. (1996) Working with chaos, *Financial Times*, 4th October.

Yip, G.S., Loewe, P.M. and Yoshino, M.Y. (1988) How to take your company to the global market, *Columbia Journal of World Business,* Winter, 37–48.

Yip, G.S. (1992) *Total Global Strategy*, Prentice Hall, Englewood Cliffs.

GLOBAL AND TRANSNATIONAL BUSINESS STRATEGIES

3
PART

Part 3 is the core of this book. Having considered the core themes of global and transnational business (Part 1) and the international business environement (Part 2), we turn to the central themes of international strategy itself.

In Chapter 6 we explore the core competence vs competitive positioning debate as it relates to international strategy. The issues raised in the controversy are brought into sharp focus by the turbulent nature of international environments. The concept of the 'global' strategy is discussed in both contexts and we attempt to synthesize a common approach stressing the importance of both core competences and competitive positioning in global and transnational strategy. As thought in the academic literature is still evolving in this important area of strategic thought, we attempt to inform on the debate rather than reflect a particular prescriptive model.

Chapter 7 discusses the strategies that businesses can adopt with a view to entering and consolidating their positions in foreign markets. In order to service foreign markets, organizations need to take into account a number of variables including changes in the global macro- and microenvironments and the core competences of the business itself. An exhaustive list of market entry options is discussed and the pros and cons of each approach is detailed. Collaborative arrangements for market servicing have increased in 'popularity' over recent years and we reflect this by drawing a distinction between the presupposition that business behaviour is always intended to subjugate competition and the belief that collaborative ventures can serve the reciprocal strategic aims of participants in such arrangements.

GLOBAL AND TRANSNATIONAL STRATEGY

6

CHAPTER

LEARNING OBJECTIVES

After studying this chapter, students should be able to:

- define the terms competitive advantage and sustainability and explain how the two concepts are linked;
- describe how transnational strategy can be formulated;
- explain how the competitive positioning and core competence schools contribute to our understanding of global strategy;
- describe and critically evaluate the core competence approach to understanding global strategy;
- describe and critically evaluate Porter's generic strategy framework for understanding superiority in global strategy;
- understand how the two ways of thinking can be seen as mutually enriching rather than mutually exclusive;
- explain the essential elements of transnational strategy;
- describe the concept of 'total' global strategy.

Introduction

In many ways this chapter is the core of the book. It links with subsequent chapters on international and global business management and also links back to Chapters 2–5 which examined the most important influences on global strategy, namely core competences, industry/market characteristics (especially the extent of globalization) and the global vision and philosophy of the business.

This chapter focuses on the competitive strategies of global businesses and is pivotal to the rest of the book, drawing together analysis of the global business and its environment with global management. Global and transnational strategies are developed on the basis of analysis of global competences, activities and the global environment. The choice of strategy is by no means simple. Industries and markets cannot be classified as either entirely global or multidomestic. Yip's research (1992) showed that an industry or market may simultaneously possess both global and local characteristics, based upon the relative strength of each element of each of the globalization drivers. It is likely that most industries and markets will be both global and local in some respects. On this basis, a global and transnational strategy must be 'a flexible combination of many elements' (Yip, 1992). That is to say, the strategy of a global business must be tailored to match each element of each globalization driver, being in part global and in part adapted to local requirements, as conditions dictate. The use of the term 'global strategy' could be seen as slightly misleading when describing a complex strategy which combines global and local components. For this reason, we use the term 'transnational strategy' to describe a worldwide strategy based upon core competences integrating both global and local elements.

Transnational strategies and global competitiveness

Sustainability and competitive advantage

One of the key objectives of any business strategy is to achieve competitive advantage that is sustainable. This implies two things. Firstly, it implies that a strategy will lead to superior performance in an industry and secondly, that the superior performance can be sustained over time (i.e. not just for a limited period of time).

Competitive advantage
The strategy literature makes a number of observations with regard to competitive advantage. It tends to be explained in terms of a number of interlinked concepts.

- *Superior performance* – there is no precise measure but this is often measured in terms of above average profits or return on investment, higher unit revenue, lower unit costs, higher market share etc.

- *Strategy* – the plan or course of action by which the business hopes to achieve competitive advantage.
- *Core competences/distinctive capabilities* – the distinctive knowledge, skills and organization of activities which make the corporation different and superior to its competitors.
- *Configuration/architecture* – the way in which the value-adding activities of the organization are configured on an international or global basis. They may be geographically concentrated or dispersed.
- *Co-ordination/integration* – how the value-adding activities are co-ordinated on a transnational or global basis.
- *Responsiveness* – the ability of the organization to respond to local needs. At another level this may also imply responsiveness to a rapidly changing environment.

Sustainability

This is best considered as the time period over which superior performance is maintained. The extent to which competitive advantage is sustainable will usually depend upon a number of organizational features:

- Its ability to build and leverage core competences, build an architecture, and develop strategies which are superior to those of competitors and which are difficult to emulate;
- Its ability to co-ordinate and integrate its worldwide activities more effectively than its competitors;
- Its ability to continuously improve strategies, competences, architecture and co-ordination.

Sustainability will also depend upon the ability of competitors (or lack of ability) to imitate or surpass the business which has achieved a superior level of performance. Finally, it will depend upon changes in the business environment, like technological change, which may be beyond the control of the leading competitor and which may enhance or reduce its competitive advantage.

Transnational, global and international business strategies

A successful international strategy must create and then sustain competitive advantage across national boundaries whether on a regional or worldwide basis. Global, regional and multidomestic strategies were once perceived as the only international strategic alternatives. A key concept to emerge in the late 1990s, however, was that of *transnational* strategy. This is a concept that combines the efficiency gains of a global strategy (with its scale economies) with the advantages of local responsiveness.

The next section considers the various theories which seek to explain how competitive advantage is created and sustained. Figure 6.1 is illustrative of the process of formulating a transnational strategy. It incorporates the various approaches to global strategic management. The approach is both 'inside-out' and 'outside-in' (see Chapter 3), in that the importance of simultaneous, continuous and iterative internal and external analysis of the business and its environment are recognized as inseparable from the process of developing core competences, generic and transnational strategy.

Strategies – the choice

Various authors have developed typologies of global strategy which provide the focus of this section. Broadly speaking, the various typologies can be divided into three main categories.

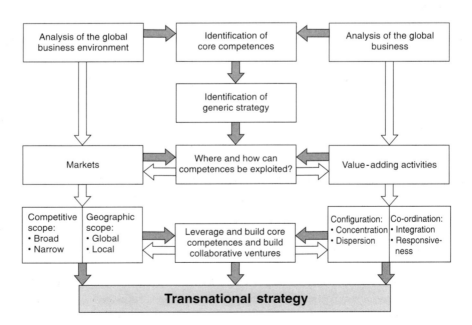

FIGURE 6.1   Global and transnational strategy formulation

1. Those which centre on the organization's generic strategies and its competitive positioning as the sources of competitive advantage.
2. Those which focus on resources, capabilities and competences as sources of sustained superior performance.
3. Those which emphasize the co-ordination and integration of geographically dispersed operations in the pursuit of global competitiveness.

This chapter integrates all three approaches into a framework for evaluating the transnational strategies of global organizations. There are three well-established frameworks which explain the ways in which sustainable competitive advantage can be achieved. These approaches are summarized below.

Competitive positioning

This approach is based largely on the work of Porter (1980, 1985) on industry analysis, value chain analysis and generic strategy (see Chapters 3 and 4). Industries are assessed for their potential profitability, value-adding activities are assessed for their effectiveness and efficiency, and a generic strategy is developed which creates a strategic fit between the opportunities and threats in the environment and the strengths and weaknesses of the business itself. According to the competitive positioning school of thought, it is the ability of the business to select the appropriate generic strategy for its industry, and to configure its value-adding activities in support of it, which will generate competitive advantage.

Resource or competence-based strategy

This approach is based on the work of theorists including Penrose (1959), Prahalad and Hamel (1990), Stalk *et al.* (1992), Kay (1993) and Heene and Sanchez (1997). In this model of strategy, businesses are viewed as open systems interacting with their environments to acquire resources and deliver outputs (products). According to this school of thought, superior performance is based upon the ability of the business to develop core competences which are not possessed by its competitors, and which create perceived benefits for consumers. Existing core competences can be leveraged, and new competences can be built, in order to generate competitive advantage in both new and current markets. Additionally, competitive advantage can result from collaboration with suppliers, customers and even competitors.

Global strategy

Writers on global strategy, who include Porter (1986a, 1990), Prahalad and Doz (1987) Bartlett and Ghoshal (1987, 1988, 1989) and Yip (1992) argued that in international business there are significant advantages to be gained from the global scope, configuration and co-ordination of a firm's international activities. Yip argues that global strategy must be tailored to match each of the globalization drivers in an industry.

Although they are often seen as alternative approaches, the competitive positioning and resource-based approaches are viewed as being complementary to each other in this book. By drawing upon all three approaches it is possible to develop a comprehensive overview of all the strategic alternatives available to a global business.

In the remainder of this chapter, we discuss each of these schools of thought in more detail.

Competence-based strategy

The emphasis on the organization itself

We introduced the ideas behind competences when we discussed internal analysis in Chapter 3. In this chapter, we consider the competence-based idea of strategy as it relates to competitive success.

The resource-based approach to strategy focuses on the business itself, rather than the industry, as the primary source of competitive advantage (in contrast to the competitive positioning school). Within any global industry or market, those businesses that perform exceptionally do so because they possess qualities which make them both distinctive from, and superior to, their competitors. These qualities are known as *core competences* (Prahalad and Hamel 1990) or *distinctive capabilities* (Kay 1993). This section explains what constitutes a core competence or distinctive capability and how such competences can be deployed as the essence of a successful transnational strategy.

In Chapter 3, we learned that to distinguish between competences and core competences was an important starting point in understanding this approach. Whilst competences are abilities possessed by all competitors in an industry, core competences are possessed only by those who achieve superior performance.

Prahalad and Hamel (1990) argued that a core competence might:

- provide potential access to a wide variety of markets;
- make a significant contribution to the perceived consumer benefits of the end product;
- be difficult for competitors to emulate.

The components of core competences

Core competences have three essential components: resources, capabilities and perceived consumer benefits. This make-up of a core competence is illustrated in Figure 3.2 (p. 48).

Resources
The first two of these, resources and general competences, were introduced in Chapter 3. Resources, the inputs into an organization's processes, include human, financial, physical, technological, legal and informational resources. They can be both tangible and intangible but are much easier to identify and evaluate than capabilities and competences which may be invisible. The quality, cost and availability of resources to a business will affect its ability to compete but the same or similar resources can often be acquired by competitors. Accordingly, resources alone are unlikely to create a core competence or sustainable competitive advantage. Nevertheless resources contribute to core competences.

Human resources in particular are important in forming core competences. In addition, human resources can significantly affect an organization's ability to co-ordinate its activities and to learn from its experiences. Thus, according to Prahalad and Hamel (1990), 'the value of human capital in the development and use of capabilities and core competencies cannot be overstated'.

In a dynamic environment, businesses must be flexible and 'a firm's strategic flexibility can be increased by acquiring resources that are flexible (i.e. can be switched among a range of different uses quickly and at low cost) (Heene and Sanchez 1997). Resources are valuable in creating core competences when they are superior to those of competitors, when they are not accessible to competitors, when they cannot be substituted and when they cannot be copied. Resources are both generated within the business and are obtained from external suppliers. The importance of a resource to the development of a core competence 'depends on the way a firm combines, co-ordinates, and deploys that resource with other firm-specific and firm-addressable resources' (Heene and Sanchez 1997).

General competences and capabilities

Competences or capabilities are assets which are essential to the operation of the competitors within an industry. Capabilities are specific skills, relationships, organizational knowledge and reputation. Capabilities are much less tangible and visible than resources. A capability may or may not be 'core'. This will depend upon the extent to which it is a capability which is possessed by competitors. In other words, all core competences stem from an organization's capabilities but not all capabilities are core competences. A core competence will be a capability which is unique to the individual business and which adds value to its products. A capability must therefore meet certain criteria before it is regarded as a core competence (see below).

Core competences and distinctive capabilities

'Owning' core competences

Core competences, or distinctive capabilities, are a combination of resources and capabilities which are unique to a specific business and which generate its competitive advantage.

Resources and capabilities form core competences when they create sustainable competitive advantage for a business. This will arise when a combination of resources and capabilities:

- *adds to perceived customer value of the product* – the product is perceived as possessing advantages over those of competitors;
- *is superior* – it adds greater value than capabilities possessed by competitors;
- *is complex, difficult to imitate and durable* – this will prevent competitors from identifying the characteristics of the capability and copying it;
- *is unique* – it is not available to competitors;
- *is non-substitutable* – it cannot be substituted by other resources and capabilities;
- *is adaptable* – it can be leveraged to give competitive advantage in other markets.

A business will create a core competence when it combines its resources and capabilities in such a way that the competence produced meets the criteria above.

Core competences and collaboration

Core competences are also often based upon unique external and/or collaborative relationships. Marks and Spencer's competitive advantage is, in part, due to its unique relationships with its manufacturers and suppliers, which contribute to its core competence as a retailer. This is largely based upon its reputation for high quality and reliability.

Collaboration can add to competitive advantage by:

- combining the core competences of two different organizations to add greater value and to increase complexity so reducing the danger of imitation;
- allowing the partners to specialize on a smaller number of competences;
- denying access to resources for competitors;
- increasing strategic flexibility.

Cravens *et al.* (1997) demonstrated the benefits of collaboration in producing competitive advantage through the example of the sportswear company Tommy Hilfiger.

> A network organization linked with independent global suppliers and marketers, Hilfiger designs its own products and licenses its name to other organizations for products such as fragrances and jeanswear. Innovative versions of traditional casual wear clothing, high quality products and efficient production enables Hilfiger to appeal to the price segment between Polo and The Gap. Sales and net product growth have been impressive. Remarkably, the company has less than 500 employees, generating about $1 million in sales per employee compared with only $55 000 per employee for a leading competitor. (Cravens *et al.* 1997)

Prahalad and Hamel (1990) cited numerous examples of core competence producing competitive advantage. Philips' development of optical media, notably the laser disk, has spawned a whole new range of products. Honda's engine technology has led to advantage in car, motor cycle, lawn mower and generator businesses. Canon's mastery of optics, imaging and microprocessor controls has allowed it to compete in diverse markets including copiers, laser printers, cameras and image scanners.

Prahalad and Hamel (1990) went on to argue that global leadership in a market is likely to be based upon no more than five or six competences.

These competences will allow an organization's management to produce new and unanticipated products and to be responsive to changing opportunities because of production skills and the harnessing of technology. Given the turbulence of the global business environment, such adaptability is essential if competitive advantage is to be built and sustained.

Competence building and leveraging

Key to the success of organizations possessing core competences is the extent to which they can build new ones to account for changes in their environments and the extent to which they can be leveraged to establish an advantage in another market. When international markets are concerned, this ability can be one of the most crucial of all.

- *Competence building* is the development of new competences which are required to compete either in an existing market which is changing or in a new market.
- *Competence leveraging* is the application of existing competences in a new market.

Entry to a new market will often require both competence leveraging and competence building. Similarly collaboration between organizations may well provide access to new markets by combining the core competences of different businesses.

Global organizations must develop core competences which provide the organization with the ability to access a range of global markets. Many of the leading fashion design houses like Ralph Lauren and Calvin Klein have exploited their core competence in fashion to enter the global market for fragrances.

The process of gaining competitive advantage through global competences involves the organization in:

- identification of its resources, capabilities and competences;
- identification of the need for competence leveraging and building within existing markets to preserve or enhance competitive position;
- identifying industries and markets where core competences may give competitive advantage;
- identifying the need for competence leveraging and competence building to enter new markets.

Implicit in the processes of competence building and leveraging is analysis of the environment (macroenvironment, industry, market, competitors and strategic group) to identify the need or opportunity for competence development (leveraging or building). In particular this concerns organizations seeking to leverage competences and actually seeking the opportunities that the strategic analysis throws up.

Globalization of business activities provides several opportunities which relate to a business's core competences:

- core competences can be exploited globally in a large number of countries and markets;
- new sources of resources can be identified and exploited making use of localized advantages to potentially strengthen core competences;
- value-adding activities can be reconfigured to enhance core competences.

Summary of competence-based strategy

In overview, competence-based (or resource-based) strategic management emphasizes the importance of an 'inside-out' approach to the development of transnational strategy. A transnational strategy must be based upon core competences which provide access to global markets. Adopting a transnational approach also provides opportunities for competence strengthening, building and leveraging. A number of factors can contribute to a global core competence. Each one needs to be distinctive and unique in order to achieve competitive advantage.

- Products and relationships to distributors and customers.
- Resources and relationships to suppliers.
- Company-specific information, knowledge and organizational learning.
- Collaboration with businesses with complementary core competences.
- Configuration or architecture of global internal and external activities.
- Methods of co-ordinating global activities.
- Culture of the organization.
- Technology and the way that it is employed.

Alternative approaches to resource-based strategy

Stalk *et al.* (1992) advanced similar ideas on what they called 'capabilities-based competition'. They suggested four basic principles upon which such competition should be based. By focusing upon these four factors, they argued that these would, in turn, enhance the organization's ability to achieve a superior performance.

- Corporate strategy consists of a focus on business processes rather than products and markets (superior processes will, in turn, result in superior products).
- Competitive success depends on transforming a company's key processes into strategic capabilities that consistently provide superior value to the customer.
- Companies create these capabilities by making strategic investments in a support infrastructure that links together and transcends traditional strategic business units and functions.
- Because capabilities necessarily cross functions, the champion of a capabilities-based strategy is the CEO (chief executive officer).

A capability, in the context of Stalk *et al.*'s (1992) meaning of the term, is a set of business processes whose strategic importance has been understood. In other words, organizations must identify which of their processes are of strategic importance and must focus upon them.

Distinctive capabilities

Kay (1993) developed the concept of capability and that of the value chain a stage further. He argued that the achievement of competitive advantage relies on distinctive capability. This idea of distinctive capability is similar to that of core competence. In both cases, the organization acquires competitive advantage by possession of attributes which make it superior to its competitors. These attributes may be features of products or services or may result from the way that activities are organized.

According to Kay (1993), distinctive capability depends upon:

- architecture – the networks of relationships both within and outside a business which are critical to determining its success;
- reputation – this is based upon product quality and characteristics, but equally as important is how effectively the information is conveyed to consumers;
- innovation – the ability to successfully develop and market new products;

- strategic assets – these are advantages based upon dominance or market position and include natural monopoly, cost advantages and market restrictions like licensing.

Although resource-based strategy can be viewed as an alternative to the generic strategy or competitive positioning approach, there are advantages in viewing strategy from both perspectives in seeking to identify sources of competitive advantage.

Competitive positioning – Porter's generic strategies

The generic strategy framework (Figure 6.2)

The competitive positioning school of thought is the second major way in which competitive advantage is explained. Porter (1985) argued that competitive advantage depends upon selection of the most appropriate *generic strategy* for achieving business objectives in the context of the competitive environment. This generic strategy can be one of, or a combination of, three types – cost leadership, differentiation and focus.

Although we introduce these strategies here, the global and international variants are explored later in this chapter. Although Porter's work has been criticized (Cronshaw *et al.* 1990; Heene and Sanchez 1997; Kay 1993), it is still a very widely used model of competitive behaviour.

Cost leadership strategy

A cost leadership strategy implies that a business endeavours to be the lowest cost producer within an industry. The main advantages of such a

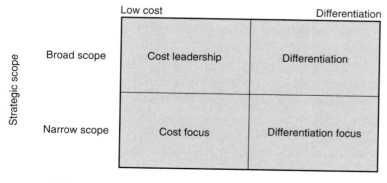

FIGURE 6.2   The generic strategy framework (adapted from Porter 1985)

strategy to a business are twofold. Firstly, there is the potential to earn profits above the industry standard while charging a price comparable to the average for the industry. Secondly, the strategy places the business in a position where it is able to compete effectively on the basis of price, both with existing competitors, and with potential new entrants to the industry. Value chain analysis (see Chapter 3) is central to identification of where cost savings can be made at various stages in the value chain and its internal and external linkages.

To establish a position as cost leader depends upon the organization of value chain activities so as to:

- advertise and promote the product to achieve large volume sales;
- achieve economies of scale in the production process;
- invest in and utilize the latest production technology thus lowering production costs;
- achieve the highest levels of productivity thus reducing labour costs;
- copy designs rather than producing originals;
- acquire cheaper raw materials (as measured on a unit cost basis);
- reduce distribution costs;
- obtain locational cost advantages;
- secure government assistance;
- exploit organizational knowledge and experience.

A cost leadership strategy will normally entail charging a price equal to or slightly lower than competitors so as to increase sales, although the real aim is to charge a price roughly equivalent to the industry norm, selling a similar volume to competitors but earning higher than normal profits because unit costs are lower. Such a strategy can be most effective in a situation where price elasticity of demand for the product is high. In this situation a slightly lower price than competitors will result in a more than proportionate gain in sales.

It is often used as the strategy for entering a new market. For example, some of the major Japanese car and motor cycle manufacturers initially entered overseas markets on the basis of low cost and low price strategies (see hybrid strategies below), often coupled to focus on a particular market segment (see focus strategies below). Similarly, international markets provide the opportunity for the large volume sales which are essential to the success of a cost leadership strategy.

Differentiation strategy

A differentiation strategy seeks to distinguish a company and its products from its competitors by establishing characteristics for the company and its products which are perceived as both unique and desirable by customers. The aim is to reduce the price elasticity of demand for the company's product so that higher prices can be charged without significant reductions in demand (because consumers perceive the product as superior to those of competitors).

Differentiation can be achieved in a variety of ways including creating distinctiveness in brand name, technical superiority, quality, packaging, distribution, image, or after sales service.

A business can create differentiation by organizing activities so as to:

- provide superior service relative to price;
- innovate continually providing the technical superiority to stay ahead;
- make customers perceive and believe that the product is superior by branding and advertising of products and services.

The differences between a company's product and those of its competitors may be real (e.g. in design) or perceived (they may be created by advertising and brand image). Levi jeans, for example, may be of high quality, but the ability of Levi's to charge a premium price may well be more to do with the perception of consumers that they are also a fashionable brand name. Consumer perceptions are the decisive influence in such a situation.

Focus strategy

In some situations, businesses choose to target only certain segments of the market in which they operate. This is termed a focus strategy. This can imply focus on a specific geographical segment or concentration on a particular group of buyers within the market. To compete with other companies within the chosen market segment, businesses may employ a cost focus strategy which is essentially cost leadership confined to one market segment. Alternatively they may utilize a differentiation focus strategy whereby they seek to differentiate themselves and their product from other products within the chosen market segment.

A good example of differentiation focus is that of Porsche, the German sports car manufacturer. It focuses on the performance car segment of the automobile market and does not produce cars for other segments of the market. Its cars are sold on the basis of brand name based upon consumer perceptions that its products are technically superior to those of competitors, are better designed, have superior performance and are more reliable than those of their competitors.

Focus strategy is based upon identification of a market segment with distinct characteristics and selecting a strategy which matches those characteristics. There are two possibilities for strategy based upon segmentation:

- focus – on a single segment;
- multi-focus – focus on a number of segments. A variation of the same generic strategy will be used in each segment of the market to match its characteristics.

A focus strategy is most suitable for a business which is not large enough to target the whole market so that targeting only one segment is the most viable possibility. It is also appropriate in markets where distinct segments can be clearly identified. This makes it possible to minimize costs and/or to achieve differentiation.

Hybrid strategies

Porter argued that to acquire sustainable competitive advantage, a business must select one of the generic strategies. To attempt to be cost leader and to differentiate simultaneously will (he argued) result in the organization being 'stuck in the middle'. This, according to Porter, is unlikely to result in competitive advantage which is sustainable.

Both the underlying assumptions of the generic strategies and the idea of being 'stuck in the middle' have been criticized. In the case of cost leadership, low cost itself does not establish competitive advantage, as it does nothing to promote sales of a product. Low price may, however, encourage sales. Thus the combination of low cost and low price may jointly produce competitive advantage. In the case of differentiation, Porter emphasized that it allows the company to charge a premium price. Differentiation, however, also presents the alternative of charging a price comparable to that of competitors so as to increase sales volume and augment market share. Equally, there is evidence to support the view that many companies pursue a strategy which combines very low costs with differentiation to produce competitive edge. The Japanese automobile manufacturer Nissan is a good example of a business broadly adopting such a strategy.

A strategy which combines elements of low cost, price and differentiation is known as a *hybrid* strategy (Johnson and Scholes 1999). The extent of each of these elements in the strategy will depend upon the nature of the market in which the business is operating. In markets where consumers show a preference for quality then the emphasis will be less on price and costs whilst in markets where demand is price sensitive the emphasis will be on keeping both price and costs as low as possible. A hybrid strategy can be successful but only where it is a conscious decision. Being stuck in the middle because of lack of awareness is usually a recipe for failure. Mintzberg (1991) made the point that 'price can be viewed as simply another way of differentiating a product'. A business which uses price as a major element of its strategy must also concentrate on keeping costs low.

The generic and hybrid strategy frameworks provide an alternative explanation of the sources of competitive advantage to those provided by competence theory. It must be accepted that there is a difference of emphasis between the two approaches but there are also linkages. The success of the generic strategy adopted by a business is dependent upon its ability to configure its value-adding activities in a way which appropriately supports the strategy. Similarly, there are strong relationships between resources, capabilities, core competences and configuration and co-ordination of value-adding activities. In this way, the two approaches provide different but complementary perspectives on the various sources of competitive advantage.

Core competence and generic strategy – a synthesis

Drawing the threads together

Different strategies require different configurations of value chain activities and are associated with different areas of core competence. For example, a differentiation strategy is likely to place a strong emphasis on design and marketing activities. Core competences in these areas are likely to be distinctive from those of competitors. In this way the value chain provides the bridge between generic strategy and core competence. Porsche pursues a focus differentiation strategy. Its core competences in design, technology development and marketing underpin its brand name, which is the basis of its differentiation. Its value-adding activities emphasize design, technology development and marketing so as to enhance its reputation. Thus Porsche's core competences are rooted in its value-adding activities. The relationship between generic strategies, core competences and value-adding activities is illustrated in Table 6.1.

Grant (1991) presented a similar line of argument stating that 'capabilities are developed in functional areas'. Table 6.2 illustrates the capabilities associated with functional areas of several businesses.

Table 6.1   Generic strategies and core competences

Generic strategy	Associated value chain activities	Associated areas of core competence
Differentiation	Design	Innovation to deliver improved product quality, new products, and new product features
	Marketing	Strong brand identity created through reputation, advertising and promotion and design features
	Distribution	Product available to target consumer groups Distributors add value to the product
	Service	Superior service adds to product differentiation
Cost leadership/price-based	Production	Lowering of production costs through use of latest technology
	Marketing	Market on basis of price to achieve economies of scale Knowledge of customer's price preferences
	Purchasing	Purchase in volume and use cheaper materials Collaborative relationships with suppliers

Table 6.2   Capability development in functional areas

Functional area	Capabilities	Examples
MIS	Data processing skills	American Airlines
Marketing	Promoting brand name	Nike
R&D	Innovation	Honda
Manufacturing	Rapid change in product lines	Benetton
	Miniaturization of components and products	Sony

Clearly differentiation strategies will rely on core competences centred around design, marketing and distribution while cost- or price-based strategies will be more dependent upon production, purchasing and marketing. Having reviewed the strategy alternatives generally available to all businesses it is now necessary to explore those specific to transnational businesses.

Global and transnational strategy

Domestic and global strategies have much in common. They are both based upon core competences, generic strategies and the way in which value-adding activities are organized.

Equally, however, global strategy differs from domestic strategy in the following respects:

- the scale and scope of activities are greater;
- there are far more alternatives for the configuration of value-adding activities;
- there are greater difficulties in co-ordinating global activities but also greater scope for competitive advantage if activities are effectively co-ordinated;
- the strategy must take account of cultural and linguistic similarities and differences;
- national economic and factor conditions differ and can be harnessed to give competitive advantage.

Porter's work (1986b, 1990) focused on global generic strategies and the possibilities for global configuration and co-ordination of activities. Prahalad and Doz (1987) examined the importance of integration and responsiveness in global strategy. Yip (1992) and Bartlett and Ghoshal (1987, 1989) presented the models for global strategy and transnational organization from which the model of transnational strategy in this book is drawn.

Porter's model of global strategy – the value system

Porter (1986a) proposed a model of international global strategy based upon the generic strategy framework. He argued that the generic cost leadership or differentiation strategies can be operated on a global scale as either *global cost leadership* or *global differentiation* – targeting either an entire global market or a particular global segment. In other words the scope of the strategy can be either broad or narrow but on a global scale. The success of such global strategies will depend upon the market being global. When global market conditions do not exist a *country-centred strategy* can be implemented based on responsiveness to local needs.

Of much greater significance is Porter's work (1986b, 1990) which advanced two unique options, based upon the value chain concept and which are available to enhance corporate strategy in global markets. These choices are:

- *configuration* – where and in how many nations each activity in the value chain is performed;
- *co-ordination* – how dispersed international activities are co-ordinated.

The decisions of the business relating to these two choices are the key to international competitive advantage.

Configuration

The way in which a business configures its upstream, downstream and internal value-adding activities presents several alternatives. A business may choose to concentrate its manufacturing activities in one nation and to export and market in a range of countries. Alternatively, a global business may decide to disperse its value-adding activities to several nations. In both cases, the advantages of alternative locations for each activity will influence the architecture of value chain activities which is finally selected. It is important to note that changes in technology may well lead to changes over time in the configuration which gives greatest competitive advantage. Organizations must constantly strive for the optimal configuration of their international operations showing flexibility in dynamic conditions.

There are two broad directions of configuration of value-adding activities – concentration or dispersal.

Concentrating activities

In some industries there are advantages to be obtained from concentrating activities in a small number of nations and exporting to foreign markets. This is true when locational factors are important and regional advantages may be gained.

Dispersing activities

Competitive advantage may arise from dispersing activities in several nations. Dispersed activities involve foreign direct investment. It is best to disperse activities when:

- transportation, communication, or storage costs are high;
- factors like exchange rates and political risk are important;
- national markets differ because of culture;
- governments exert influence via tariffs, subsidies and nationalistic purchasing (governments tend to favour location of whole value chain in their country).

Dispersed global strategies involving FDI are typical in industries such as services, health care, telecommunications etc.

Co-ordination

In addition to adopting the optimum configuration, competitive edge can be gained by efficient and effective co-ordination of diverse activities which are located in a number of different nations. According to Porter (1990), 'Co-ordination involves sharing information, allocating responsibility, and aligning efforts'. It is differing linguistic, cultural, political, legal, technological and economic factors, coupled to geography and distance, which pose the problems which beset multinational co-ordination. It is the global businesses which overcome these problems most effectively that will gain the greatest competitive advantage from a global strategy.

Figure 6.3 shows the various alternatives which exist for global organizations from a country based strategy with widely dispersed activities, requiring minimal co-ordination, to what Porter called purest global strategy. In this purest global strategy, activities are concentrated and extensive co-ordination is in evidence. The configuration chosen, and the extent of global co-ordination of activities, will depend upon the nature of the industry and markets in which the business operates.

Integration and responsiveness

Prahalad and Doz (1987) reached conclusions which are in some respects similar to those of Porter (1986a,b, 1990). Prahalad and Doz identified three major characteristics of global management:

	Geographically dispersed	Geographically concentrated
High co-ordination of activities	High foreign investment in dispersed activities with a high degree of co-ordination among subsidiaries	Purest global strategy (with extensive co-ordination and concentration)
Low co-ordination of activities	Country centred strategy for company with several national subsidiaries each operating in only one country	Strategy based upon exporting of product/ service with decentralized marketing in each host country

Configuration of activities

FIGURE 6.3   Configuration and co-ordination for international strategy (adapted from Porter 1986a)

1. Global integration of activities

This is the centralized management of geographically dispersed activities which is necessary to reduce costs and optimize investment. In striving to reduce costs, corporations may use low wage labour in South East Asia shipping products to well-developed markets in Europe and America. Thus there is a need to manage across national boundaries.

2. Global strategic co-ordination

This is the strategic management of resources across national boundaries. It includes co-ordination of research and development, pricing, and technology transfer to subsidiaries. Prahalad and Doz argued that 'The goal of strategic co-ordination is to recognise, build and defend long-term competitive advantages'.

3. Local responsiveness

This requires that decisions are taken locally by subsidiaries where local market conditions dictate the need for local responsiveness. Such markets are not global in nature.

To summarize, Prahalad and Doz (1987) suggested that corporate success at an international level is dependent upon the ability of the business to co-ordinate and integrate global activities whilst, at the same time, retaining responsiveness to the demands of local markets and changing circumstances when necessary.

Pressures for and against increased global co-ordination

Stimulating forces

Pressures for global strategic co-ordination include:

- importance of multinational customers – dependence on customers on a worldwide basis makes it necessary to co-ordinate activities globally;
- presence of multinational competitors – global competition demands global co-ordination;
- investment intensity – where investment costs are high (e.g. research and development costs) the need to recoup investment costs increases the need for global co-ordination;
- technology intensity – where technology encourages businesses to manufacture in only a few locations to control quality and product development;
- pressure for cost reduction – often stimulates global integration of activities to intensify scale economies;
- universal consumer needs – lead to standard global products requiring integration;
- access to raw materials and cheap energy – often means that manufacturing has to be concentrated in a single area remote from other activities thus necessitating integration and co-ordination.

Restraining forces

Whilst the above forces work in favour of increased global co-ordination of value-adding activities, some factors act to partly offset these. These are factors that stimulate local responsiveness and include:

- differences in customer needs – when these differ between countries local responsiveness is required;
- differences in distribution channels – when such differences exist between countries, local responsiveness is required in relation to differences in pricing, promotion and product positioning;
- availability of local substitutes – if local substitutes with different specifications exist then there is a need to adapt products in order to compete;
- market structure – where local competitors are important and there is a high concentration then businesses must respond locally;
- host government demands – when such governments promote self sufficiency a business may be forced to be more locally responsive.

FIGURE 6.4   The integration–responsiveness matrix (adapted from Prahalad and Doz 1987)

Prahalad and Doz (1987) represented the relationships between these factors on an integration–responsiveness matrix (see Figure 6.4).

The conclusions reached by Prahalad and Doz's research are remarkably similar to those of Porter. Both emphasize the need for global co-ordination and integration of activities when a global strategy is adopted, and the need for local responsiveness when conditions dictate.

Regional strategies

Under certain circumstances a business may elect to adopt an international regional strategy as opposed to a multidomestic, global or transnational strategy. A regional strategy focuses on one or more geographical regions of the world rather than on an entire world market. Prahalad and Doz (1987) argued that, although businesses must be multimarket competitors, they may benefit from choosing to operate in certain 'critical markets'. These are markets which, at the minimum:

- are reliable 'profit sanctuaries' of the key competitors in that market;
- provide volume and include state-of-the-art customers;
- have competitive intensity which allows suppliers to achieve reasonable margins.

International businesses may therefore choose to adopt a regional strategy for a variety of reasons. These reasons include:

- the existence of critical markets (as described above) which make regional operation viable;
- the removal of barriers which have inhibited cross border trade within a region. Customs unions such as the European Union, the North Atlantic Free Trade Area etc. have assisted in this;
- the size and importance of certain regional markets (which tend to be those where trade barriers have been reduced);
- the limited importance of cultural differences within a particular regional market in comparison to more important differences which exist between certain regions;
- limited business resources and objectives which confine the operations of the business to a regional scale.

Within a region, the organization faces several strategic alternatives. The regional strategy may be little more than a multidomestic strategy. This will be the case when there are one or more of the following distinctions between the national markets within the region: political, cultural, linguistic or legal. Such distinctions will inhibit the possibilities for standardization and increased economies of scale. On the other hand, the less such distinctions exist within a region, the greater the opportunities for standardization, co-ordination and integration of strategies, products and operations.

Total global strategy

Development of total global strategy

For Levitt (1983), globalization implied that the focus of a global strategy ought to be standardization of products and marketing. In reality, globalization is far more complex than this and requires the development of more complex strategies to reflect this. Yip (1992) argued that an industry may be more or less global in several respects, according to the strength of each of its globalization drivers. Chapter 4 shows how the extent of globalization of an industry can be assessed by analysis of the extent to which its market, cost, competitive and government drivers are global. Global strategy must then be tailored to match each of the drivers. Yip's concept of Total Global Strategy is, therefore, not rooted in the idea of global standardization but rather in the idea that global strategy must be flexible.

Yip (1992) stated that a total global strategy has three separate components or stages:

1. *developing the core strategy* – this is the basis of the organization's global competitive advantage;
2. *internationalising the core strategy* – the international expansion of activities and the adaptation of the core strategy;
3. *globalizing the international strategy* – integrating the strategy across countries.

Yip's three stages are considered below.

Stage 1
The *core business strategy* is viewed as consisting of several elements:

- types of products or services that the business offers;
- types of customers that the business serves;
- geographic markets served;
- major sources of competitive advantage;
- functional strategy for each of the most important value-adding activities;
- competitive posture, including the selection of competitors to target;
- investment strategy.

Stage 2
Internationalizing the core business involves:

- selecting the geographic markets in which to compete;
- adapting products.

Stage 3
Globalizing the core business requires:

- identification of the areas of strategy to be globalized (based on the globalization drivers);
- integration of activities.

Global strategy levers
The business must then identify its 'global strategy levers' which determine the way in which the global strategy is used. They are:

- global market participation (which markets and countries in which to participate);
- global products (standardized products);
- global location of activities;
- global marketing;
- global competitive moves.

The extent to which each of these aspects of strategy is global will depend upon the relative strength of the globalization drivers. A global strategy can give benefits in terms of reduced costs, improved quality, enhanced customer preference and competitive leverage.

Transnational organizations

There is a further dimension to global management, that of transnational strategy (Figure 6.5). These are strategies which although global in nature, incorporating a global configuration and a high degree of co-ordination, allow the business to retain local responsiveness. Bartlett and Ghoshal (1987, 1988, 1989) found that managers often oversimplified the choices

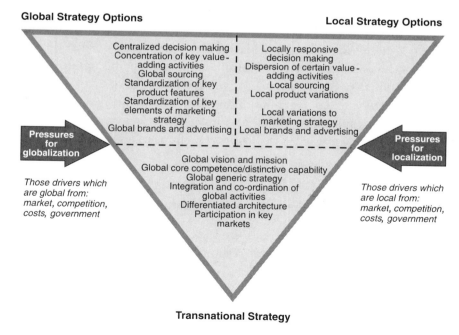

FIGURE 6.5   Transnational strategy

available to them. They found erroneous management attitudes such as a belief that it had to be:

- global strategy vs local responsiveness;
- centralized vs decentralized key resources;
- strong central control vs subsidiary autonomy.

They went on to argue that the transnational business strategy ought to incorporate the following features:

- strong geographical management to allow responsiveness to local markets based on sensitivity to local needs;
- strong business management based on global product responsibilities so as to achieve global efficiency and integration through product standardization, manufacturing rationalization and low-cost global sourcing;
- strong worldwide functional management to develop and transfer its core competencies via organizational learning.

Bartlett and Ghoshal (1989) argued that strong geographical management, business management and worldwide functional management incorporating a differentiated organization with extensive co-ordination would enable the business to develop multiple strategic capabilities to adapt to local and global needs. Such an organization can be said to have *transnational capability* – an essential ingredient of a transnational strategy which is at the same time global and locally responsive. In fact, there is much in common between Yip's approach and that advocated by Bartlett and Ghoshal.

Global and localized elements of transnational strategy

A transnational strategy combines the benefits of global scope, configuration and co-ordination with local responsiveness. Certain components of the strategy will be essentially global whilst others will be more or less global according to the pressures for globalization or localization. These pressures are assessed through the normal procedures of macroenvironmental analysis and an analysis of how the globalization drivers affect the business.

Globalized components of transnational strategy

The following elements of a transnational strategy are always likely to be global:

- *global vision* – this determines the outlook of the business which will always be to take a global perspective on business activities;
- *global core competences* – these are core competences which can be built, enhanced and leveraged to enter global markets;
- *global generic strategy* – the generic strategy, based upon core competences, will be applied globally;
- *global co-ordination* – global value-adding activities will be co-ordinated on a worldwide basis;
- *differentiated architecture* – activities will be structured so as to maximize global advantages but this is likely to mean that some activities are concentrated while others are dispersed. Structures will be adapted to accommodate this;
- *participation in key markets* – the transnational organization will always view the whole world as a potential market but may choose only to target key markets.

Activities that can be global or localized components in transnational strategy

Certain components of transnational strategy can be globalized or localized according to changes in the macroenvironment and to the globalization drivers:

- *decision making* – conditions may dictate that decisions are made centrally or are devolved when local responsiveness is required;
- *value-adding activities* – may be dispersed or concentrated or some combination of the two according to locational advantages;
- *products* – may be standardized or adapted when conditions dictate;
- *marketing strategy* – may be global or local according to consumer and product characteristics;
- *branding* – may be global or local according to consumer and product characteristics;
- *sourcing* – resources may be globally or locally sourced according to locational advantages.

REVIEW AND DISCUSSION QUESTIONS

1. Explain what is meant by sustainable competitive advantage.

2. Explain the factors which determine the choice of a global or locally responsive strategy.
3. What will determine the competitive scope of the strategy of a global business?
4. Explain and critically evaluate Porter's generic strategy framework? What does the concept of the hybrid strategy add to the debate?
5. What are the major differences between domestic and international strategies?
6. Provide an example of a global business in each of these categories (at least in part of its activities):
   - adopts a differentiation strategy;
   - adopts a cost leadership strategy;
   - adopts a cost focus strategy;
   - adopts a differentiation focus strategy;
   - adopts a hybrid strategy.
7. Explain the significance of each of the following to a multinational business:
   - core competence/distinctive capability;
   - configuration/architecture;
   - co-ordination/integration;
   - responsiveness.
8. Discuss the nature of the relationships between:
   - generic strategy and core competence;
   - core competence and configuration/architecture;
   - configuration/architecture and co-ordination/integration.
9. Explain the similarities and differences between regional, global and transnational strategies.

References and further reading

Arthur, W.B. (1996) Increasing returns and the new world of business, *Harvard Business Review*, **74**, July/August.

Barney, J.B. (1991) Firm resources and sustained competitive advantage, *Journal of Management*, **17**(1), 99–120.

Bartlett C. and Ghoshal, S. (1987) Managing across borders: new organizational responses, *Sloan Management Review*, Fall, 45–53.

Bartlett C. and Ghoshal, S. (1988) Organizing for a worldwide effectiveness. The transnational solution, *California Management Review*, **30**, 54–74.

Bartlett C. and Ghoshal, S. (1989) *Managing Across Borders: The Transnational Solution*, Harvard Business School Press, Boston.

Chakravarthy, B. (1997) A new strategy framework for coping with turbulence, *Sloan Management Review*, Winter, 69–82.

Chakravarthy, B.S. and Perlmutter, H.V. (1985) Strategic planning for a global business, *Columbia Journal of World Business*, Summer, 3–10.

Collis, D.J. and Montgomery, C.A. (1995) Competing on resources: strategy in the 1990s, *Harvard Business Review*, July/August, 199–128.

Cravens, D.W., Greenley, G., Piercy, N.F. and Slater S. (1997) Integrating contemporary strategic management perspectives, *Long Range Planning*, **30**(4), August, 493–506.

Cronshaw, M., Davis, E. and Kay, J. (1990) On being stuck in the middle or Good food costs less at Sainsburys, working paper, *Centre for Business Strategy*, London School of Business, London.

D'Aveni, R.A. (1994) *Hypercompetition: Managing the Dynamics of Strategic Manoeuvring*, Free Press, New York.

Day, G.S. (1994) The capabilities of market-driven organizations, *Journal of Marketing*, **38**, October, 37–52.

Doz, Y. (1986) *Strategic Management in Multinational Companies*, Pergamon Press, New York.

Fayerweather, J. (1981) Four winning strategies for the international corporation, *Journal of Business Strategy*, **1**(2).

Gorman, P. and Thomas, H. (1997) The theory and practice of competence-based competition, *Long Range Planning*, **30**(4), August, 615–620.

Grant, R.M. (1991) The resource based theory of competitive advantage: Implications for strategy formulation, *California Management Review*, **33**, Spring, 114–135.

Hamel, G. and Prahalad, C.K. (1985) Do you really have a global strategy? *Harvard Business Review*, July/August.

Hamel, G. and Prahalad, C.K. (1994) *Competing for the Future*, Harvard Business School Press, Boston.

Heene, A. and Sanchez, R. (1997) *Competence-Based Strategic Management*, John Wiley, New York.

Helms, M.M. and Wright, P. (1992) External considerations: their influence on future strategic planning, *Management Decision*, **30**(8), 4–11.

Henzler, H. and Rall, W. (1986) Facing up to the globalization challenge, *McKinsey Quarterly*, Winter.

Hitt, M.A. and Ireland, R.D. (1985) Corporate distinctive competence, strategy, industry and performance, *Strategic Management Journal*, **6**(3), 273–293.

Johnson, G. and Scholes, K. (1997) *Exploring Corporate Strategy*, Prentice Hall, Englewood Cliffs.

Johnson, G. and Scholes, K. (1999) *Exploring Corporate Strategy*, 2nd edn, Prentice Hall, Englewood Cliffs.

Katz, D. (1993) Triumph of the swoosh, *Sports Illustrated*, 16th August.

Kay, J. (1993) *Foundations of Corporate Success*, Oxford University Press, Oxford.

Klugt, C.J., Van der (1986) Japan's global challenge in electronics – the Philips response, *European Management Journal*, **4**(1), 4–9.

Kogut, B. (1985a) Designing global strategies: comparative and competitive value-added claims, *Sloan Management Review*, Summer, 15–27.

Kogut, B. (1985b) Designing global strategies: profiting from operational flexibility, *Sloan Management Review*, Fall, 28–38.

Leontiades, J.C. (1985) *Multinational Corporate Strategy: Planning for the World Markets*, Lexington Books, Lexington.

Levitt, T. (1983) The globalization of markets, *Harvard Business Review*, May/June, 92–102.

Miller, D. (1992) The generic strategy trap, *Journal of Business Strategy*, **13**(1), 37–42.

Mintzberg, H. (1991) *The Strategy Process – Concepts, Contexts, Cases*, Prentice Hall, Englewood Cliffs.

Penrose, E. (1959) *The Theory of the Growth of the Firm*, Oxford University Press, Oxford.

Perlmutter, H.V. (1969) The tortuous evolution of the multinational corporation, *Columbia Journal of World Business,* January/February.

Petts, N. (1997) Building growth on core competences – a practical approach, *Long Range Planning*, **30**(4), August, 551–561.

Porter, M.E. (1980) *Competitive Strategy: Techniques for Analysing Industries and Competitors*, The Free Press, New York.

Porter, M.E. (1985) *Competitive Advantage*, The Free Press, New York.

Porter, M.E. (1986a) *Competition in Global Business*, Harvard University Press, Boston.

Porter, M.E. (1986b) Changing patterns of international competition, *California Management Review*, **28**(2), Winter, 9–40.

Porter, M.E. (1990) *The Competitive Advantage of Nations*, The Free Press, New York.

Prahalad C.K. and Doz Y.L. (1987) *The Multinational Mission: Balancing Local Demands and Global Vision*, The Free Press, New York.

Prahalad C.K. and Hamel, G. (1989) Strategic intent, *Harvard Business Review*, 63–76.

Prahalad C.K. and Hamel, G. (1990) The core competence of the corporation, *Harvard Business Review*, 79–91.

Stalk, G., Evans, P. and Shulmann, L.E. (1992) Competing on capabilities: the new rules of corporate strategy, *Harvard Business Review*, March/April, 57–69.

Yip, G.S. (1992) *Total Global Strategy – Managing for Worldwide Competitive Advantage*, Prentice Hall, Englewood Cliffs.

GLOBAL AND TRANSNATIONAL MARKET SERVICING STRATEGIES

7

CHAPTER

LEARNING OBJECTIVES

After studying this chapter, students should be able to:

- explain what is meant by market servicing and market entry;
- describe the market entry options in international business;
- describe the factors that are relevant when selecting a mode of entry;
- explain how market servicing strategies are relevant to a global business;
- understand the nature of collaborative arrangements as they relate to market entry.

Introduction

An important element of the global strategy of a transnational organization is its market servicing strategy. This is the method of entry and operation chosen by a business for a particular overseas market. A business can select from a wide range of alternative strategies for servicing foreign markets. Possible strategies include exporting, licensing, joint ventures, wholly owned subsidiaries etc. Each alternative may be suitable under particular circumstances but each is subject to limitations. The choice of strategy from the alternatives available can be described as a 'frontier issue' in international business. This is because the method of market servicing is one of the most important factors influencing company performance in foreign markets.

Given its importance, it is not surprising to learn that the issue of foreign market servicing strategies has been extensively covered in the international marketing literature (see Root 1987; Young *et al.* 1989). Literature on the subject of foreign market servicing strategies concentrates on methods for selecting the most efficient alternative for a particular market. Choice of servicing strategy will depend upon the characteristics of the market and upon the global strategy of the organization.

Alternative foreign market servicing strategies

What is market servicing?

Foreign market servicing strategies can be regarded as one of a series of linked decisions which any company must make in the process of internationalization and globalization. In an 'ideal' international marketing plan (as shown in Table 7.1 and in the simplified schematic in Figure 7.1) businesses would first of all decide the strategic reasons for internationalization. Environmental scanning would then take place to identify external threats and opportunities; and internal strengths and weaknesses. Following this, international marketing opportunities would then be identified, taking into account product suitability for foreign markets and country market choice. Once the firm has decided 'which product in which foreign market', it would then need to examine the best way of entering and developing that market. This final stage, that of deciding upon the mode of market entry, is the essence of market servicing analysis.

Table 7.1   An 'ideal' international marketing plan

Stage	Focus
1	Deciding to go abroad: reasons for internationalization
2	Scanning the international marketing environment (opportunities/threats; strengths/weaknesses)
3	Product suitability and choice of products for foreign markets
4	Country market choice
5	Choosing the foreign market entry and development strategy
6	Designing the international marketing mix
7	Financing international operations

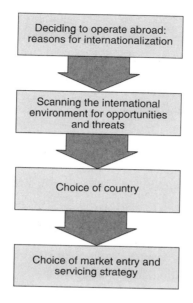

FIGURE 7.1   Stages in the market servicing and entry decision

Market servicing options

An organization seeking to develop activities in international markets has a number of options open to it. We consider each one in turn (see Young *et al.* 1989).

1. Direct exporting (Table 7.2)

Exporting normally begins as domestic sales of a product begin to slow down due to home market saturation. Exporting usually begins by simply shipping a product upon receipt of payment but as sales expand, an export office may be set up in the domestic office, then sales offices may be set up overseas. At its simplest the product is manufactured in the home country

Table 7.2   Pros and cons of exporting

Advantages of exporting	Disadvantages/potential problems
Least expensive	Remote from customers
Least complicated	Lack of market knowledge
Profits do not have to be shared	Difficult to control remotely
Risk is limited to the value of the shipment	Distribution arrangements can be complex

and then marketed abroad. The costs of exporting may be reduced by 'piggyback' distribution, i.e. by using an already established distribution network in the overseas country, e.g. a chain of stores. Direct exporting may be carried out using a local agency. This has the benefit of exploiting local knowledge and links, but will mean that a commission has to be paid which will reduce profitability.

2. Contractual agreement type 1: licensing (Table 7.3)

Licensing involves a producer renting out certain intellectual property rights to a licensee. Payment is made to the licensor on the basis of an agreed licensing contract, possibly on the basis of *pro rata* with profits earned on the use of the intellectual property or against sales. For the licensor, this can be a low cost but effective way of setting up an operation overseas while retaining control over the product. It protects the technology and know how of the licensor and can also help to circumvent protectionist measures imposed by host governments. There may, however, be problems including the danger that the licensee may become a competitor when the licence expires. Licensing is used in industries where branding is important (such as food FMCGs like soft drinks), in scientific industries such as pharmaceuticals and in brewing.

3. Contractual agreement type 2: patents (Table 7.4)

Patenting is a method of safeguarding an innovation against illegal copying by competitors. It involves patenting the exporting company's product in

Table 7.3   Pros and cons of licensing

Advantages for licensor	Disadvantages/potential problems
Little capital outlay Some control of operations Risks are shared and limited Licensee has local knowledge	Limited contact with customers No direct control of operations Profits must be shared with licensee

Table 7.4   Pros and cons of patenting

Advantages of patenting	Disadvantages/potential problems
Prevents copying Protects product standards Protects profits	Different laws in different countries Laws not enforced in some countries Protects technology

the domestic home and in the foreign countries in which it hopes to do business. Patent rights are protected by the Patent Co-operation Treaty, the European Patent Convention, and the European Community Patent Convention. These can help to protect the products of an exporter from competition but there are many less developed countries where the patent laws do not apply. It is used in industries where competitors are technically able to copy but must be prevented from doing so (such as in pharmaceuticals).

4. Contractual agreement type 3: franchising (Table 7.5)

Franchising is similar in concept to licensing. In licensing, the licensor (the licence holder) allows the licensee to use a piece of intellectual property such as a brand name, a formulation, recipe or similar. In franchising, the franchiser allows a franchisee, possibly in a foreign country, to use an entire business idea, including a brand, an 'image' (if appropriate) and a set of procedures and systems that have proven themselves to have worked previously by the franchiser.

In most franchise situations, the franchisee is encouraged to maintain the same business format as the franchiser. It becomes a rather more complicated situation if the franchisee deems it to be necessary to make some modifications to the franchise idea in order to accommodate national or regional differences in lifestyles, tastes, socio-cultural factors and legal requirements. Franchising tends to work best in retailing industries and is widely used in multiple chains such as fast food, hotels, specialist chains and car hire.

5. Contractual agreement type 4: contract manufacturing

This involves a business entering a foreign market by contracting local organizations in the foreign country to produce all or some portion of a product. This reduces the amount of direct investment required but still allows the business to retain control of its product and technology.

Table 7.5 Pros and cons of franchising

Advantages for the franchiser	Disadvantages/potential problems
Little capital outlay	Limited contact with customers
Some control of operations	No direct control of operations
Risks are shared and limited	Profits must be shared with franchisee
Franchisee has local knowledge	

6. Contractual agreement type 5: management contract

Under this arrangement a business provides the management functions for another. Many major airlines including PanAm, BA etc. supply maintenance and technical services to smaller airlines in this way. The same is true of civil engineering and construction management consultancies which manage construction projects abroad such as dams and bridges.

7. Contractual agreement type 6: turnkey operations

This arrangement involves a foreign business constructing an entire production facility such as a chemical plant in a host country. Upon completion, the facility is duly handed over to the recipient, which then operates it. The majority of recipients of turnkey operations are governments of developing countries. Because of the high costs involved, payments are made in instalments with the last payment being made upon satisfactory completion.

8. Local assembly (Table 7.6)

The components are imported to the host country and are assembled into the finished product which is then marketed and distributed in the host country (i.e. the foreign country) but perhaps also in other markets in that region.

9. Local manufacture (Table 7.7)

The product is manufactured, either partly or wholly in the host country and sold in the host country but perhaps in other markets. It is the next stage in terms of commitment after local assembly.

Table 7.6   Pros and cons of local assembly

Advantages	Disadvantages/potential problems
Possibility of lower labour costs	May be difficult to obtain skilled labour
Reduced transport costs	Difficult to control quality standards
Creates local jobs	More expensive to set up than some other
May avoid import restrictions in host country	options due to transport costs

Table 7.7   Pros and cons of local manufacture

Advantages	Disadvantages/potential problems
Possibility of lower labour costs	Difficult to obtain skilled labour
Reduces transport costs	Difficult to control quality standards
Creates local jobs	
May avoid import restrictions in host country	

10. Coproduction

A domestic and a foreign business may enter into an arrangement to produce a certain product using both domestic and foreign components. The advantages of this are economies of scale, use of specialist technologies, local materials and experience. The development of the Eurofighter in the 1990s was an example of coproduction, with different parts of the aircraft being built by various companies throughout Europe.

11. Establishing foreign subsidiaries (Table 7.8)

This is the case when a parent company has total control of its overseas operations, decision making and profits. Wholly owned subsidiaries may, however, give rise to opposition from the foreign government and there may also be labour relations problems.

12. Joint ventures and strategic alliances (Table 7.9)

The joining of two or more separate businesses for a mutually-beneficial project is a relatively common arrangement in domestic business. When it is used in international business, cultural and political differences can partly offset the opportunities it presents.

Table 7.8 Pros and cons of foreign subsidiaries

Advantages	Disadvantages/potential problems
Retain central control	Possible opposition from host government
Provides sensitivity to local conditions	Possible labour relations problems
Creates local jobs	May be conflict between HQ and local managers
May avoid import restrictions in host country	

Table 7.9 Pros and cons of international joint ventures and international strategic alliances

Advantages	Disadvantages/potential problems
Synergy	Conflicts of interest
Shared knowledge, expertise and skills	Some partners gain more than others
Shared technology	Difficult to sustain in long run
Shared costs and benefits	Competitive instincts prevail
Mutual profits	Decision making is slower
Knowledge of local markets	
Existing business contacts can be used	
Reduces political risks	
Less costly than a merger	

Table 7.10   Pros and cons of foreign mergers and acquisitions

Advantages of mergers and acquisitions	Disadvantages/potential problems
Synergy between the two parties Shared knowledge, expertise and skills Shared technology	Costs are higher than most other modes of entry May create resentment in host country May take over a business with a poor local reputation
Full operational control can be gained in an acquisition (less so in a merger) Control of quality Knowledge of local markets	May take over a business whose image does not match May take over a business with problems Financial exposure is much higher than for exporting, licensing, etc. as an investment is made abroad which may be lost.
Existing business contacts can be used Reduces political risks as partner company will already be established Locally known trading name	

Two or more companies from different countries contribute resources to carry out certain activities without forming a new company. Each partner contributes a specialized resource or skill. We consider this arrangement in some detail in Chapter 14.

13. Mergers and acquisitions (Table 7.10)
In a merger, two companies join to form a new business entity. In an acquisition, one company purchases a controlling interest in another. Both are used in international business (the two parties in the arrangement are from different countries). Again, we consider this matter in detail in Chapter 14.

14. Global business
Many large companies configure their business in such a way as to spread their activities around the world so as to maximize the locational advantages to be obtained from each of their activities. The sportswear producer Nike is an example of a global business in this regard. The company bases its design and development in the USA. Manufacturing is concentrated primarily in the Far East to meet high quality standards while maintaining low unit costs (especially for labour). Marketing and distribution is spread around the world to allow maximum flexibility and responsiveness to local markets.

Table 7.11   Costs and benefits of the alternative modes of entry (4 is highest, 1 is lowest)

Criteria	Exporting	Contractual agreements (e.g. licensing)	Joint ventures and alliances	Wholly owned subsidiary
Cost of capital	2	1	3	4
Potential revenue	3	1	2	4
Political risk	2	1	3	4
Revenue stability	?	4	?	?
Corporate control	2	1	3	4

A summary of the modes of entry

Companies should consider the costs and benefits of the above strategies in relation to the foreign market to select the most appropriate. Table 7.11 is an example of how this might be done. The range of alternative foreign market servicing strategies available is summarized in Appendix 7.1 at the end of this chapter. Various attempts have been made to classify these alternatives. Brooke (1986), for example, distinguished between exporting, knowledge agreements and foreign investment as shown in Figure 7.2.

Root (1987) adopted a similar classification which distinguished between:

(a) export entry modes including indirect exporting, direct exporting through agents and distributors, and direct branch/branch subsidiary exports;
(b) contractual entry modes including licensing, franchising, technical agreements, service contracts, management contracts, construction/turnkey contracts, contract manufacturing, coproduction agreements; and
(c) investment entry modes including new plants, acquisitions and joint ventures.

Luostarinen's (1979) classification (see Figure 7.3) distinguished foreign market servicing strategies according to three main dimensions, namely:

- the location of production whether domestic or overseas, e.g. domestic production in exporting; overseas production in licensing, FDI etc.;
- whether foreign direct investment occurs or not, i.e. direct investment vs non-direct investment operations;
- the type of activity undertaken whether manufacturing, marketing or the transfer of 'know-how'.

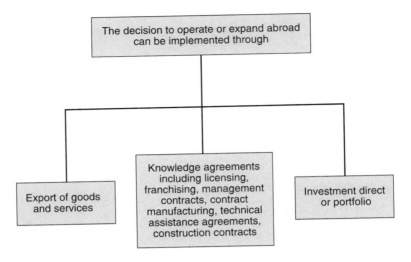

FIGURE 7.2   International business options (according to Brooke 1986)

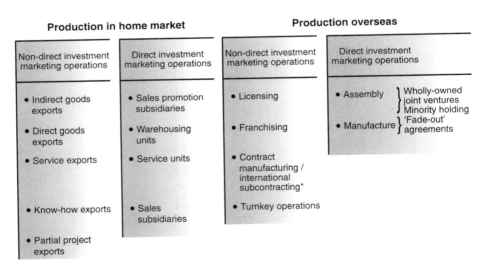

FIGURE 7.3   Luostarinen's (1979) forms of international market entry and development excludes industrial co-operation agreements and the range of forms of contractual joint ventures because of their variety. *Assuming that international subcontracting takes place between independent companies in home and overseas markets

Selection of mode of entry

Choosing the most appropriate mode of entry

A range of factors will influence the choice between these alternative modes of entry. Particularly important will be the costs, risks and control considerations of each option. The various modes can be considered to exist on a continuum ranging from low cost, low risk, low control (such as indirect exporting) to high cost, high risk, high control modes such as FDI. Other factors influencing strategic choice regarding market entry and development modes include the following.

The nature of the product provided

Certain entry and development modes are more appropriate for certain products or services than others. Thus, exporting would not be an appropriate supply mode for products where transportation costs are high as a proportion of value added. Similarly, subcontracting arrangements are more appropriate in labour intensive products such as in the textile industry and certain parts of the electronics industry. For technology intensive products, the business may wish to retain control over access to know-how, thus favouring a higher-control option such as a foreign wholly-owned subsidiary.

Management commitment

For small-to-medium sized companies the range of alternative supply modes may be limited because of limits on managerial time and resources.

Host country legislation

Depending upon the political leanings of host governments, some countries make impositions such as: import controls; restrictions on profit and royalty payments; controls on technology transfer through licensing; incentives and disincentives for foreign investors.

Marketing objectives

Supply mode choice will vary depending on the organization's objectives in the foreign market. Where market share is important, more direct forms of entry may be desirable. Alternatively, a company which wishes to skim a number of foreign markets may prefer less direct modes such as franchising etc.

Culture

More direct forms of involvement may be encouraged where there are cultural similarities between the foreign and domestic markets since this reduces the risk of cultural clashes.

Criteria for choosing mode of entry

Various models have been developed to assist companies in choosing between alternative foreign market entry and development strategies. These can be classified into three different approaches.

The economic approach

This emphasizes the rate of return or profitability of different entry and development modes. After considering the return profile of each option, the one offering the highest return is chosen regardless of any other considerations.

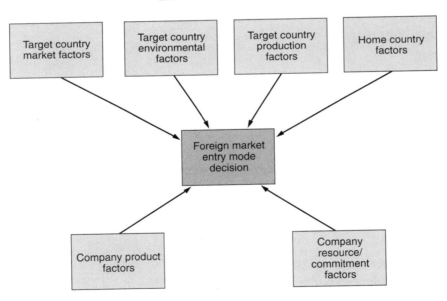

FIGURE 7.4   Factors in the entry mode decision (adapted from Root 1987)

The stage of development approach

This approach relates the entry and development mode decision to the internationalization process. Different entry/development modes are 'best-suited' at different stages of internationalization (exporting, for example, is typically the first foray that a business makes into international business).

The business strategy approach

This approach relates the entry and development mode to the strategic motivations to be achieved and to the internal environmental and external environmental factors influencing the decision (see Figure 7.4).

Global market servicing strategies

Literature summary

While there is an extensive literature on foreign market entry mode choice, there has been little attempt to incorporate such decisions into the wider context of global strategy. The existing literature tends to view market servicing decisions as specific to each new market entered. They largely ignore the interdependencies which may exist between operations across borders. This is a major weakness in the literature from the perspective of this book with its emphasis on the co-ordination and integration of geographically dispersed operations. Thus, it may reasonably be expected that the overall global strategy of a business may be an important determinant of the choice of foreign market servicing mode. Decisions regarding the mode of entry must be consistent with and support the overall strategic development of the business in global industries.

The importance of global strategic considerations in the choice of market servicing modes has been recognized in the literature since the 1980s. Hout *et al.* (1982), Porter (1986a), Yip (1992) and Young *et al.* (1989) extended the traditional approach to market entry choice (as discussed in the previous section) to include aspects of global strategy. In addition to the environmental and transaction-specific variables extensively covered in the previously-cited literature, entry-mode decisions are influenced by three global strategic variables: global concentration, global synergies and global strategic motivations.

Three key variables

Global concentration

Many global industries have become highly concentrated with a high level of competitive or oligopolistic interdependence. In other words, the actions taken by one company in one national market will have repercussions in other national markets. This leads to the hypothesis that when the global industry is highly concentrated, companies will favour high control entry modes.

Global synergies

This refers to the synergies which can arise from the shared utilization of core competencies among strategic business units (such as Honda's transfer of advanced engine technology from motorcycles to automobiles). The achievement of such synergy requires a degree of hierarchical control. This, in turn, leads to the hypothesis that businesses will demand higher levels of control over foreign operations as the extent of potential global synergies between the subsidiary and other sister business units increases.

Global strategic motivations

Companies entering or developing a particular foreign market may have strategic motivations which are wider than simply choosing the most efficient entry mode. These global strategic motivations are set at corporate level for the purpose of overall corporate efficiency maximization rather than efficiency of individual national markets. Foreign business units, for example, may be established as a strategic outpost for future global expansion, as global sourcing, or to attack a competitor. To successfully achieve these global strategic motivations requires tight co-ordination across global business units. This leads to the hypothesis that businesses exercising global strategic motivations will favour high control entry modes.

Collaborative arrangements

Collaboration rather than competition

Collaborative networks or strategic alliances are arrangements between businesses to co-operate with the express purpose of gaining competitive advantage. The conventional model of business behaviour is that of competition but collaborative relationships have become increasingly important as a means of acquiring competitive advantage for the businesses that are members of the collaborative network. The basis of collaborative behaviour can be related to conventional theories explaining sources of competitive advantage.

Porter (1986a, 1990) stressed the importance of *configuration* of business activities and their *co-ordination* as a means of achieving competitive advantage.

Kay (1993) identified *distinctive capability* as the source of competitive edge. Distinctive capabilities rest upon architecture, reputation, innovation and strategic assets (see Chapter 6).

Prahalad and Hamel (1990) argued that an international business must identify and build upon its core competences. Core competences are 'the collective learning in the organization, especially how to co-ordinate diverse production skills and integrate multiple streams of technologies'. Three criteria can be applied in identifying a core competence:

- it provides potential access to a wide variety of markets;
- it should make a significant contribution to the perceived consumer benefits of the end product;
- it should be difficult for competitors to emulate.

Core competence should lead to core products which in turn should lead to competitive advantage.

A study by Prahalad and Doz (1987) of a number of multinationals, spanning a decade, reached similar conclusions to those of Porter (1986a, 1990). They found that corporate success at an international level was dependent upon the ability of the multinational to *co-ordinate* and *integrate* global activities while, at the same time, retaining *responsiveness* to the demands of local markets and changing circumstances.

Achieving competitive advantage will therefore require:

- identification of the core competences of the organization;
- identification and focus upon activities which are critical to the core competence of the organization and outsourcing those which are not;
- achieving the internal and external linkages in the value/supply chain which are necessary for effective co-ordination of activities and which permit responsiveness.

Literature has for many years stressed the competitive elements of the behaviour of organizations in achieving competitive advantage. More recently research has pointed to collaboration between companies as a potential source of competitive edge.

The nature and rationale of collaboration

Partners for collaboration
Collaboration may take place between an organization and any of the following:

- suppliers;
- customers;
- financiers;
- competitors;
- governments and other public organizations.

Taken to one extreme collaboration may lead to mergers and acquisitions (see our discussion of this in Chapter 14). More often it can take place between businesses that retain their separate identities but which collaborate in a network on a short- or long-term basis.

Reasons for collaboration
Contractor and Lorange (1988) identified several rationales for collaboration:

- risk reduction (e.g. of investment exposure);
- the sharing of different but like core competencies;
- economies of scale and/or rationalization;
- complementary technologies and patents;
- blocking competition;
- overcoming government mandated investment or trade barriers;
- initial international expansion;
- vertical quasi integration – access to materials, technology, labour, capital, distribution channels, buyers, regulatory permits.

In addition, we suggest that collaboration can enable each party to bring unique core competences to the alliance. By combining their core competences, partners can enjoy synergy. In this regard, collaboration can provide similar benefits to a business to outsourcing – taking advantage of another business's core competences to add value more effectively that could be accomplished in-house.

Reve (1990) identified two explanations of what holds alliances together.

1. The economic approach which states that alliances exist between businesses because the parties involved see the possibility of increased profits. Such relationships depend upon safeguards to protect the interests of the participants and the relationship is therefore 'impersonal and unstable'
2. The behavioural approach which says that there is value attached to the relationship between the parties involved, social ties are built, there is trust and integrity and personal contacts are important. Such alliances are usually longer lasting and more stable

Potential problems
There are, however, problems associated with collaboration.

- the initial rationale for collaboration may shift over time, e.g. technology changes, or one partner has a reduced need for the other;
- language problems;
- cultural differences (differences in values and norms);
- incompatibilities between management styles and systems;
- co-ordination and integration problems;
- an increase in competitive pressures (that changes the competitive environment for one or both parties);
- changes in the market.

Horizontal and vertical collaboration

Horizontal relationships
Horizontal collaboration is an arrangement involving two or more companies at the same stage in the supply chain. It usually takes place between competitors (although rarely on anything other than a limited scale). They can serve to strengthen the participating companies against outside competition, possibly an aggressive (and larger) competitor.

The nature of collaboration necessitates sharing between the partners. This can be shared technology, skills, costs (say of an overseas investment) or risks. It can also increase scale economy benefits to both parties, thus giving vertical advantage over suppliers.

Vertical relationships
These can be upstream in the supply chain (towards suppliers) or downstream (towards distributors and customers). Collaboration in either

direction can enable a business to gain cost or price advantage against its competitors. If the upstream or downstream partner is in another country, the arrangement can be used to circumvent local import or export restrictions.

Benefits
Both horizontal and vertical relationships offer benefits:

- each partner in the alliance can concentrate upon its core competences and thus add greater value at lower cost;
- create barriers to entry (the two act in concert and thus are effectively one when attacked by a would-be new entrant);
- produce logistical economies of scale;
- superior information on activities at all stages of the supply chain;
- ties in suppliers and customers to the focal business;
- the creation of synergy between partners and a lowering of unit costs.

Alliances

An alliance is one type of collaborative arrangement (see Chapter 14 for a detailed discussion of this topic). With regard to considering alliances as a market servicing strategy, the participants must consider a number of issues.

- Deciding which activities and assets are core and should therefore be carried out by the business itself (configuration).
- Deciding which activities are of medium specificity and should be obtained via alliances and outsourcing (configuration).
- Deciding which activities are of low specificity and should be obtained through the market (configuration).
- Integration of core and alliance activities (co-ordination).
- Management and operation of the alliances (co-ordination).

Summary – advantages of collaborative arrangements as modes of entry

Collaborative networks have the potential to deliver sustainable competitive advantage by:

- enhancing core competence and distinctive capability;

- making possible and improving organizational architecture;
- creating new organizational assets;
- creating synergy;
- reducing unit costs;
- increasing efficiency;
- increasing flexibility.

The survival and prosperity of a collaborative relationship depends upon:

- its ability to co-ordinate intra-organizational activities;
- its ability to integrate business strategies;
- external contracts and motivations to foster the alliance;
- its ability to adapt to a changing environment and changing network relationships.

Appendix 7.1:   Some additional notes on foreign market servicing strategies (Adapted from Young *et al.* 1989)

Firms can choose from a wide range of alternative strategies when entering and developing foreign markets. These include: (a) export entry and development modes; (b) contractual entry and development modes; and (c) modes of entry and development involving direct investment abroad.

Exporting

This involves the transfer of goods and/or services across national boundaries from a domestic production base. Exporting may be either indirect (which involves little effort on the part of the firm itself) or direct (which involves a greater internal commitment). The main forms of indirect and direct exporting include

Indirect exporting
  Export houses
  Confirming houses
  Trading companies
  Piggybacking

Direct exporting
  Agents
  Distributors
  Company export salespeople
  Overseas sales subsidiaries

Contractual agreements

This covers a wide range of alternatives including the following.

Licensing
Contracts in which licensor provides licensees abroad with access to one or a set of technologies or know-how in return for financial compensation. Typically, the licensee has rights to produce and market a product within an agreed area in return for royalties.

Franchising
Contracts in which franchiser provides franchisee with a 'package' including not only trade marks and know-how, but also local exclusivity and management and financial assistance and joint advertising. Management fees are payable. Most important in services.

Management contracts
An arrangement under which operational control of an enterprise, which would otherwise be exercised by a board of directors or managers elected and appointed by its owners, is vested by contract in a separate enterprise which performs the necessary management functions in return for a fee.

Turnkey agreements
A contractor has responsibility for establishing a complete production unit or infrastructure project in a host country – up to the stage of the commissioning of total plant facilities. Payment may be in a variety of forms including countertrading. 'Turnkey plus' contracts include product-in-hand and market-in-hand contracts.

Contract manufacturing or international subcontracting
A company (the principal) in one country places an order, with specifications as to conditions of sale and products required, with a firm in another country. Typically the contract would be limited to production, with marketing being handled by the principal.

Industrial co-operation agreements
Conventionally applied to arrangements between Western companies and government agencies or enterprises in the Eastern Bloc. Include licensing, technical assistance agreements, turnkey projects and contract manufacturing, as well as contractual joint ventures and tripartite ventures.

Contractual joint ventures

Formed for a particular project of limited duration or for a longer-term co-operative effort, with the contractual relationship commonly terminating once the project is complete. May relate to *co-production, co-research and development, co-development, co-marketing* plus *co-publishing, consortium ventures* by banks to finance large loans etc.

Foreign direct investment

The three main types of foreign market servicing strategy involving direct investment abroad are:

- the establishment of wholly owned, greenfield subsidiaries;
- crossborder acquisitions;
- equity joint ventures.

REVIEW AND DISCUSSION QUESTIONS

1. Why do organizations seek to develop markets abroad?
2. What are the market entry options open to a business seeking to service foreign markets?
3. Which market entry option carries the highest risk?
4. Summarize the criteria for selecting a market entry strategy.
5. Why might an organization seek to develop a collaborative arrangement as a mode of foreign market entry?
6. Distinguish between vertical and horizontal relationships.

References and further reading

Borys, B. and Jemison, D.B. (1988) Hybrid organizations as strategic alliances: theoretical issues in organizational combinations, *Graduate School of Business*, March, Stanford University.

Bowerson, D.J. (1990) The strategic benefits of logistics alliances, *Harvard Business Review*, **90**(4), 36–47.

Brooke, M.Z. (1986) *International Management: A Review of Strategies and Operations*, Hutchinson, London.

Buckley, P.J. and Casson, M. (1976) *The Future of the Multinational Enterprise*, Macmillan, London.

Buckley, P.J. and Casson, M. (1981) The optimal timing of a foreign direct investment, *Economic Journal*, **92**, (361), 75–87, reprinted in Buckley, P.J. and Casson, M. (1985) *The Economic Theory of the Multinational Enterprise*, Macmillan, London.

Buckley, P.J. and Casson, M. (1988) A theory of co-operation in international business, in: Contractor, F.J. and Lorange P. (eds), *Competitive Strategies in International Business*, Lexington Books, Lexington.

Buckley, P.J., Pass, C.L. and Prescott, K. (1990) Foreign market servicing by multinationals – an integrated treatment, *International Marketing Review*, **7**(4), 25–40.

Buckley, P.J., Pass, C.L. and Prescott, K. (1992) Foreign market servicing strategies of UK retail financial service firms in continental europe, in: Young, S. and Hamill, J. (eds), *Europe and the Multinationals: Issues and Responses for the 1990s*, Edward Elgar, Aldershot.

Contractor, F. and Lorange, P. (1988) Why should firms co-operate? in: *Co-operative Strategies in International Business*, Lexington Books, Lexington.

Contractor, F.J. and Lorange, P. (1988) Competition vs. co-operation: a benefit/cost framework for choosing between fully-owned investments and co-operative relationships, *Management International Review*, **28** (Special Issue), 88.

Cooke, T.E. (1986) *Mergers and Acquisitions*, Basil Blackwell, Oxford.

Cooke, T.E. (1988) *International Mergers and Acquisitions*, Basil Blackwell, Oxford.

Davidow, W.H. and Malone, M.S. (1992) *Structuring and Revitalising the Corporation for the 21st Century – The Virtual Corporation*, Harper Business, London.

Davidson, K.M. (1990) Mergers and acquisitions: anatomy of the fall, *Journal of Business Strategy*, **11**(5), 48–51.

Davidson, K.M. (1991) Mergers and acquisitions: innovation and corporate mergers, *Journal of Business Strategy*, **12**(1), 42–45.

De Noble, A.F., Gustafson, L.T. and Hergert, M. (1988) Planning for post-merger integration – eight lessons for merger success, *Long Range Planning*, **21**(110), 82–86.

Devlin, G. and Bleackley, M (1988) Strategic alliances – guidelines for success, *Long Range Planning*, **21**(5), 18–23.

Douglas, S.P. and Craig, C.S. (1989) Evolution of global marketing strategy: scale, scope and synergy, *Columbia Journal of World Business*, Fall, 47–59.

Doz, Y.L., Hamel, G. and Prahalad, C.K. (1986) Strategic partnerships: success or surrender? the challenge of competitive collaboration, Paper presented at Joint Academy of International Business/European International Business Association Conference, London, November.

Gall, E.A. (1991) Strategies for merger success, *Journal of Business Strategy*, **12**(2), 26–30.

Gamble, P.R. (1992) The virtual corporation: an IT challenge, *Logistics Information Management*, **5**(4), 34–37.

Ghoshal, S. and Bartlett, A. (1990) The multinational corporation as an interorganizational network, *Academy of Management Review*, **15**, 603–625.

Gilbert, X. and Stebel, P. (1989) From innovation to outpacing, *Business Quarterly*, **54**(1), 19–22.

Gogler, P. (1992) Building transnational alliances to create competitive advantage, *Long Range Planning*, **25**(1), 90–99.

Goldberg, W.H. (1983) *Mergers – Motives, Modes, Methods*, Gower, Aldershot.

Goodnow, J.D. and Hanz, J.E. (1972) Environmental determinants of overseas market entry strategies, *Journal of International Business Studies*, Spring, 33–50.

Hamel, G., Doz, Y. and Prahalad, C.K. (1989) Collaborate with your competitors and win, *Harvard Business Review*, January/February.

Hamill, J. (1988a) British acquisitions in the US, *National Westminster Bank Quarterly Review*, August.

Hamill, J. (1988b) US acquisitions and the internationalization of British industry, *Acquisitions Monthly*, November.

Hamill, J. (1991a) Strategic restructuring through international acquisitions and divestments, *Journal of General Management*, **17**(1), Autumn.

Hamill, J. (1991b) Changing patterns of international business: crossborder mergers, acquisitions and alliances, *Proceedings of the UK Region, Academy of International Business Conference*, London, April.

Hamill, J. (1992) Global marketing, in: Baker M.J. (ed.) *Perspectives on Marketing Management*, Vol. 2, John Wiley, New York.

Hamill, J. and Crosbie, J. (1989) Acquiring in the US food and drink industry, *Acquisitions Monthly*, May.

Hamill, J. and El-Hajjar, S. (1990) Defending competitiveness, *Acquisitions Monthly*, April, 36–39.

Harrigan, K.R. (1984) Joint ventures and global strategies, *Columbia Journal of World Business*, Summer.

Harrigan, K.R. (1985) *Strategies for Joint Ventures*, Lexington Books, Lexington.

Harrigan, K.R. (1988a) Joint ventures and competitive strategy, *Strategic Management Journal*, **9**.

Harrigan, K.R. (1988b) Restructuring industries through strategic alliances, *Strategic Management Journal*.

Helms, M.M. and Wright, P. (1992) External considerations: their influence on future strategic planning, *Management Decision*, **30**(8), 4–11.

Hout, T.E., Porter, M.E. and Rudden, E. (1982) How global companies win out, *Harvard Business Review*, Sept.–Oct., pp. 98–103.

Jain, S.C. (1987) Perspectives on international strategic alliances, *Advances in International Marketing*, JAI Press Inc., Greenwich, pp. 103–120.

Jarillo, J.C. and Stevenson, H.H. (1991) Co-operative strategies – the payoffs and pitfalls, *Long Range Planning*, **24**(1), 64–70.

Jemison, D.B. and Sitkin, S.M. (1986) Acquisitions: the process can be a problem, *Harvard Business Review*, March.

Johanson, J. and Mattson, L.G. (1992) Network positions and strategic action, in: Axelsson, B. and Easton, G. (Eds), *Industrial Networks: A New View of Reality*, Routledge, London.

Kay, J. (1993) *Foundations of Corporate Success*, Oxford University Press, Oxford.

Keenan, M. and White, L.J. (1982) *Mergers and Acquisitions*, Lexington Books, Lexington.

Kobayashi, N. (1988) Strategic alliances with Japanese firms, *Long Range Planning*, **21**(108), 29–34.

Kohn, R.L. (1990) Japanese–US alliances: resolving economic conflict, *Journal of Business Strategy*, **11**(4), 48–50.

Lorange, P. (1988) Co-operative strategies: planning and control considerations, *Centre for International Management Studies*, WP-512.

Lorange, P. and Roos, J. (1991) Why some strategic alliances succeed and others fail, *Journal of Business Strategy*, **12**(1), 25–31.

Lorange, P. and Roos, J. (1992) *Strategic Alliances: Formation, Implementation and Evolution*, Basil Blackwell, Oxford.

Love, J.H. and Scouller, J. (1990) Growth by acquisition: the lessons of experience, *Journal of General Management*, **15**(3), Spring.

Luostarinen, R. (1979) *The Internationalization of the Firm*, Acta Academic Oeconumicae Helsingiensis, Helsinki.

Luostarinen, R. (1980) *The Internationalisation of the Firm*, Acta Academic Oeconumicae, Helsinki.

Lyons, M.P. (1991) Joint ventures as strategic choice – a literature review, *Long Range Planning*, **24**(4), 130–144.

Malekzadeh, A.R. and Nahavindi, A. (1990) Making mergers work by managing cultures, *Journal of Business Strategy*, **11**(3), 55–58.

Morgan, N.A. (1988) Successful growth by acquisition, *Journal of General Management*, **14**(2), Winter.

Morris, D. and Hergert, M. (1987) Trends in international collaborative agreements, *Columbia Journal of World Business*, Summer.

Ohmae, K. (1989) The global logic of strategic alliances, *Harvard Business Review*, March/April.

Oman, C. (1984) *New Forms of International Investment in Developing Countries*, Paris, OECD.

Payne, A.F. (1987) Approaching acquisitions strategically, *Journal of General Management*, **13**(2), Winter.

Perlmutter, H.V. and Heenan, D.H. (1986) Cooperate to compete globally, *Harvard Business Review*, March/April.

Porter, M.E. (1995) *Competitive Advantage*, The Free Press, New York.

Porter, M.E. (ed.) (1986a) *Competition in Global Industries*, Harvard Business School Press, Boston.

Porter, M.E. (1986b) Changing patterns of international competition, *California Management Review*, **28**(2), Winter, 9–40.

Porter, M.E. (1986c) *Competition in Global Business*, Harvard University Press, Boston.

Porter, M.E. and Fuller, M.B. (1987) Coalitions and global strategy, in: Porter, M.E. (ed.), *Competition in Global Industries*, Harvard Business School Press, Boston.

Porter, M.E. (1990) *The Competitive Advantage of Nations*, The Free Press, New York.

Prahalad C.K. and Doz Y.L. (1987) *The Multinational Mission: Balancing Local Demands and Global Vision*, The Free Press, New York.

Prahalad C.K. and Hamel, G. (1989) Strategic intent, *Harvard Business Review*, 63–76.

Prahalad C.K. and Hamel, G. (1990) The core competence of the corporation, *Harvard Business Review*, 79–91.

Quinn, J., Dooley, T. and Paquette, P. (1990) Technology in services: rethinking strategic focus, *Sloan Management Review*, Winter.

Reich, R.B. and Mankin, E.D. (1986) Joint ventures with Japan give away our future, *Harvard Business Review*, March/April, 78.

Reve, T. (1990) The firm as a nexus of internal and external contracts, in: Aoki, M., Gustafsson, M. and Williamson, O.E. (eds), *The Firm as a Nexus of Treaties*, Sage, London.

Root, F.R. (1987) *Entry Strategies for International Markets*, Lexington Books, Lexington.

Shelton, L.M. (1988) Strategic business fits and corporate acquisitions: empirical evidence, *Strategic Management Journal*, **9**.

Stalk, G. (1988) Time – the next source of competitive advantage, *Harvard Business Review*, July/August.

Steiner, P.O. (1975) *Mergers, Motives, Effects, Control*, University of Michigan Press, Ann Arbor.

Teece, D.J. and Pisano, G. (1987) *Collaborative Arrangements and Technology Strategy*, School of Business Administration, University of California, Berkeley.

Toyne, B. and Walters, P.G.P. (1993) *Global Marketing Management: A Strategic Perspective*, Allyn and Bacon, Boston.

United Nations Centre on Transnational Corporations (1988) *Transnational Corporations in World Development: Trends and Prospects*, UNCTC, New York.

Wissema, J.G. and Euser, L. (1991) Successful innovation through inter-company networks, *Long Range Planning*, **24**(6), 33–39.

Yip, G. (1992) *Total Global Strategy*, Prentice Hall, Englewood Cliffs, NJ.

Young, S., Hamill, J., Wheeler, C. and Davies, J.R. (1989) *International Market Entry and Development: Strategies and Management*, Harvester Wheatsheaf, Hemel Hempstead.

GLOBAL BUSINESS MANAGEMENT

4

PART

The fourth and largest section of the book concerns the many aspects of managing global and transnational business strategy. The fact that strategic management (whether domestic or international) is holistic in nature, insofar as it encompasses the whole organization, means that any section on managing strategy must take into account each part of the organization's activity. Accordingly, this section explores each area of organizational activity that has an influence on the outcome of international strategy.

Each part of an organization can add to its overall competitive advantage if it acts in congruence with the overall strategy and adds value faster or more effectively than competitors. Similarly, however, any part of a business can prevent the organization as a whole performing in an optimal manner. For this reason, we conclude that every part of an organization's value-adding activity should come under review as part of successful international strategy.

Chapter 8 deals with the central value-adding decisions of the international business. For most companies, the operational, production and logistical departments will be the largest consumers of resource and the producers of the output for which the organization is known. Accordingly, the strategic importance of this part of the business is difficult to overestimate. Chapter 9 (on human resource strategy), Chapter 10 (on technology) and Chapter 12 (on global finance) discuss the three major resource inputs into the operational process. The core competence approach to strategic management stresses the importance of resources, their acquisition in resource markets and the way in which they are converted into outputs, and we reflect the importance of resource contribution to strategy in these chapters.

The global business's interface with its customers and other aspects of global marketing strategy are discussed in Chapter 11 whilst the issues surrounding structure and control are discussed in Chapter 13. Global integrations and alliances are considered in a separate chapter in this text (Chapter 14) due to the increased incidence of these methods of growth in international business and the increased prominence given to the subject in the academic literature.

Finally, Chapter 15 makes an attempt to review the broad themes in global and transnational business strategy and prognosticates what we believe will be the key subjects of academic discussion in the sphere of international business in future years. The key themes in this context are introduced and briefly discussed.

GLOBAL PRODUCTION AND LOGISTICS MANAGEMENT

8

CHAPTER

LEARNING OBJECTIVES

After studying this chapter, students should be able to:

- explain what is meant by production and logistics in the context of international business;
- review the most relevant literature as it relates to global operations strategy;
- describe Dicken's four production strategies;
- explain the factors that influence where transnational businesses locate their production facilities;
- describe the issues surrounding procurement decisions for international businesses;
- explain how logistics is managed by multi-site transnational businesses.

Introduction

The core of any global strategy is the use of the company's international scope as a key competitive weapon in global industries. This implies a degree of central co-ordination and integration of geographically dispersed operations, and involves complex decisions across a range of functional management areas. Nowhere is this more important than in the co-ordination and integration of global production and logistics management – the focus of this chapter.

Global production and sourcing is concerned with the what, where and how of worldwide production. In other words, it is concerned with global management decisions relating to the number, size and location of production facilities throughout the world; plant roles and specialization (by either products or markets); and inter-plant relationships. Especially important is the extent of co-ordination and integration of production facilities in different countries. Global logistics is concerned with the physical movement of final goods (and services) from producer to end-user; and the flow of intermediate products, parts and components between plants, i.e. both external and internal logistics.

Production strategy and competitive advantage

The critical success factors in operations

An efficient, co-ordinated and integrated global production and logistics system can be an important source of competitive advantage in global industries. Co-ordinated global production can provide advantages in terms of costs (production and transportation); production flexibility; and market responsiveness.

The major sources of value added in external logistics relate to:

1. place – the availability of a product in a location that is convenient to customers;
2. time – the availability of a product at a time that fulfils a customer's needs;
3. information – that answers questions and communicates useful product and applications knowledge to customers (Keegan 1995).

An efficient internal logistics network is essential to achieve the benefits of plant specialization and integration.

The overall global competitive strategy of the business will have a major impact on production and logistics management. The latter needs to be consistent with and integrated upon the former. The major influence on production and logistics management in transnationals adopting country-centred strategies will be the requirement of national responsiveness. Global strategies, on the other hand, imply greater co-ordination and integration of worldwide production and logistics. Global strategies were defined by Doz (1986) as the 'specialization of plants across countries into an integrated production and distribution network involving substantial cross border flows of components or products'. Similarly, Porter's (1986) definition of global strategy emphasized the configuration (location) and co-ordination (control) of value added activities throughout the world.

This chapter is largely concerned with configuration and co-ordination issues as they relate to global sourcing and distribution.

The issues raised in this chapter have become highly topical over recent years as a consequence of the globalization of markets and the emergence of global competition. Globalization has reduced the need for a market-by-market approach to sourcing and distribution and provided the international business with greater strategic flexibility in this area. The emergence of global competition has forced many companies to reassess their sourcing and distribution strategies aimed at greater cost effectiveness. As a consequence of these two trends, a number of international businesses have rationalized their sourcing and distribution systems by consolidating activity into fewer, larger plants serving multi-country markets.

Global production strategies

The 'big' decisions in production strategy

This section examines global production strategies taking into account the issues involved, the alternative strategies available and the important links between global strategy and production strategy.

In designing its global production strategy, an international business needs to make decisions in a number of important areas.

- The number and location of plants throughout the world, with plant location, in turn, being determined by a number of factors including costs, risks, return and government regulation.
- Plant roles and inter-plant relationships including decisions regarding plant specialization and integration. Important issues here are whether to establish largely self-contained manufacturing plants or assembly plants which rely on a high proportion of bought-in parts and components; whether these bought-in components are from related or unrelated concerns; the product line of the plant; and markets to be supplied. The three main strategic options in terms of plant roles are:
  - (a) to operate a number of plants each producing the same product for different markets;
  - (b) to operate a number of factories each producing non-competitive products for the same market;
  - (c) to have plants specializing on component manufacture with assembly being undertaken elsewhere.

- Transnational procurement policies where three types of purchasing policy are possible – central purchasing; autonomous subsidiary purchasing; and partial central purchasing.

Plant roles and inter-plant relationships

Reference has already been made in previous chapters to the different classifications of companies in international business where a distinction can be made between international, multinational and global companies (see Chapter 1). Keegan (1995) used this distinction to classify the alternative production/sourcing strategies available to global businesses. The three alternatives are described below.

'International' sourcing

This relies heavily on home country manufacturing, with foreign markets being mainly served through exports from a domestic production base. The main advantage of this strategy is that it reduces the requirement for international transfers of know-how and manufacturing capability.

'Multinational' sourcing

This establishes production operations in each foreign market. The three main advantages of this strategy are that it can overcome any barriers to market entry (e.g. import controls); it takes advantage of local factors of production and shortens supply lines; production is more responsive to country customer needs and wants. The main disadvantage is that multiple production facilities limit the possibilities of economies of scale

'Global' sourcing

In this strategy, production activities are located in such a way as to maximize quality and availability while minimizing costs. Global sourcing implies considerable co-ordination and integration of worldwide manufacturing and distribution.

Research in global production strategy

The issue of global production involving cross border co-ordination and integration of activity has attracted significant attention in the academic literature. We review the work of three of the most important thinkers in this area: Doz (1978), Starr (1984) and Dicken (1998).

Doz – opportunities from relaxations in trade restrictions

One of the earliest attempts to examine the process of manufacturing rationalization in international businesses was that by Doz (1978). Although published in the late 1970s, the study remains highly relevant, especially in the context of the development of trading blocs and customs unions (such as the European single market and NAFTA).

The main argument developed by Doz was that reduction of tariffs and other trade barriers and the emergence of free trade zones in Western Europe during the 1970s provided an opportunity for international businesses to specialize and integrate their European manufacturing plants. Instead of multiproduct–multistage plants autonomously serving national markets, it had become feasible and economic to develop plants that manufacture only one model or one product line, or are involved in only certain stages of the production process for worldwide markets. This represents a shift from local-for-local plants (local production for local markets) to an integrated network of large-scale production-specialized plants serving world markets. The process of manufacturing rationalization is particularly important for companies with less-differentiated (standardized) products; where production costs are high in relation to total costs; where major economies of scale can be derived from plant specialization; and for companies facing strong competition from strong competitor nations.

The above factors were then incorporated by Doz into a framework which helps to: (a) diagnose the need for rationalization; and (b) manage the rationalization process itself. This is shown in Table 8.1.

Manufacturing rationalization is most needed in mature industries with significant price competition and where there are unexploited economies of scale (with the European automobile industry being given as an example). Even when the benefits of rationalization are diagnosed clearly, there will be major problems in the implementation of rationalization strategies arising from the conflict between analytical (i.e. the diagnostic need for rationalization) and behavioural issues. The latter refer to social and political difficulties within the international business which hinder the start of rationalization.

The major pitfalls to rationalization implementation include a lack of perception of the new competitive forces; the search for local solutions by local managers; and subsidiary opposition to rationalization. To overcome these difficulties, a number of guidelines are suggested (deriving from examples of successful rationalizations) for managing the rationalization

Table 8.1 A framework for managing the rationalization process (source: Doz 1978)

Diagnosis	Product/market maturity; price competition; unexploited economies of scale
Start-up	Product type inventory; co-ordination group; staff experts; co-ordinators
Changes in the management process	Marketing co-ordination; export co-ordination and sourcing control; logistics; overall market share; production programming; technical co-ordination; funding for R&D and capital expenditure
Corporate management actions to support rationalization	Communication of purpose; planning integration; changes in measurement, evaluation and reward systems; changes in career paths and management development
Pitfalls	Lack of perception of new competition; autonomous subsidiary structure favours national responses rather than diagnosis of rationalization need; rationalization may be opposed by national subsidiary managers' diagnosis; too assertive co-ordinator; too little top management support of co-ordinators; co-ordinators subordinate to group of subsidiary managers; too many subsidiaries; joint ventures; wrong timing; inappropriate sequencing; poor choice of co-ordinators; lack of top management visible support; continuation of country based evaluation and compensation schemes; poor choice of country managers

process. These fall into three main groups covering start-up; implementation of changes in the management process; and actions by corporate management to support rationalization. To start-up the process an initial inventory of redundant product types and plants should be established. The process then shifts to gaining the co-operation of subsidiary managers to rationalization through co-ordination and strategic planning groups to facilitate social interaction. The process overall can be greatly assisted by clear communications from the corporate centre and a clear commitment to the need for rationalization. The process of manufacturing rationalization has accelerated considerably in recent years in response to the pressures of global competition.

Starr's network

Starr (1984) provided an exposition of the strategic considerations important to the development of a successful global production operation. This is defined to include global sourcing, fabrication, assembly, marketing and distribution. A global network model is developed to illustrate the alternative strategies available in this respect. The network shows the various connections (links) between suppliers, fabricators, assemblers and marketers (nodes). In most cases the network will involve complicated arrangements (and various combinations) between domestic and international nodes. According to the author, the choice of network will depend on a cost/benefit analysis of the alternatives. Important issues to consider include the costs of various suppliers; the effects of exchange rate movements; inflation rates in different countries which can affect purchasing as well as production and marketing decisions; the quality of supplies; proximity to markets etc.

Dicken and international value adding

The view of global production as a network of relationships was developed in more detail by Dicken (1998). Two sets of relationships are explored:

1. the internal network of relationships within the global business;
2. the network of external relationships with independent and quasi-independent businesses, both large and small, transnational and domestic.

The basic building block to understand both internal and external networks is the model of the production chain shown in Figure 8.1, where the term production is used in its widest sense to include the provision of services as well as physical production.

This model shows the whole range of activities (value-added activities in Porter's (1985) terminology) performed within the production system, i.e. a

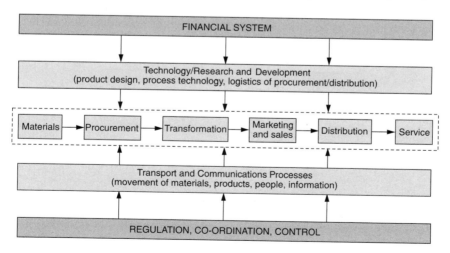

FIGURE 8.1 The basic production chain (source: Dicken 1998)

chain of linked functions (see Chapter 3 on the value chain). The way in which the chain of transactions is organized and co-ordinated determines the international business's internal and external network of relationships. At one extreme, the chain of transactions can be performed entirely within the business itself, i.e. internalization. At the other extreme, each function could be the responsibility of individual, independent businesses, i.e. externalization. A wide variety of relationships may exist between these two extremes.

In terms of the transnational business's internal production network, Dicken (1998) drew on Porter's (1986) configuration and co-ordination alternatives (see Chapter 3) to identify the alternatives available. Four main types of internal production strategy are identified as summarized in Figure 8.2.

(a) Globally concentrated production

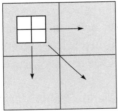

All production occurs at a single location. Products are exported to world markets

(b) Host-market production

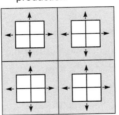

Each production unit produces a range of products and serves the national market in which it is located. No sales across national boundaries. Individual plant size limited by the size of the national market

(c) Product specialization for a global or regional market

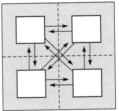

Each production unit produces only one product for sale throughout a regional market of several countries. Individual plant size very large because of scale economies offered by the large regional market

(d) Transnational vertical integration

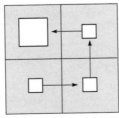

Each production unit performs a separate part of a production sequence. Units are linked across national boundaries in a 'chain like' sequence

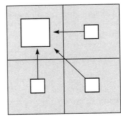

Each production unit performs a separate operation in a production process and ships its output to a final assembly plant in another country

FIGURE 8.2   Some major ways of organizing the geography of transnational production units (source: Dicken 1998)

Dicken's four production strategies

Globally concentrated production

The simplest case is where the business concentrates all production in one central location and supplies world markets through its marketing and sales network. This is consistent with Porter's (1986) purest global strategy of geographically concentrated and highly co-ordinated operations.

Host market production

According to Dicken (1998) this has become a common production strategy amongst global businesses. It is essentially local production for local markets consistent with Porter's (1986) multidomestic strategy of geographically dispersed and uncoordinated (autonomous) operations.

Product specialization for a global or regional market

A strategy of production as part of a rationalized product or process strategy, i.e. specialization of production in a few plants supplying multi-country markets. According to Dicken (1998), this strategy is becoming increasingly popular, especially in large regionally integrated markets such as the EU.

Transnational vertical integration of production

This is a strategy of specialization by process or by semi-finished products (rather than by final products as in the product specialist above) and is consistent with Porter's (1986) strategy of high FDI with extensive co-ordination amongst subsidiaries. A particularly important aspect of this strategy according to Dicken (1998) is the increasing use of offshore processing as part of a vertically integrated global production network. Two main types of activities are particularly suited to offshore sourcing:

- products at the mature stage of the product life cycle, in which technology has become standardized, long production runs are needed, and semi-skilled or unskilled labour costs are very important;
- there are certain parts of the production process of newer industries (e.g. electronics) which are labour intensive and amenable to the employment of semi-skilled and unskilled labour, even though the industry as a whole is capital and technology intensive.

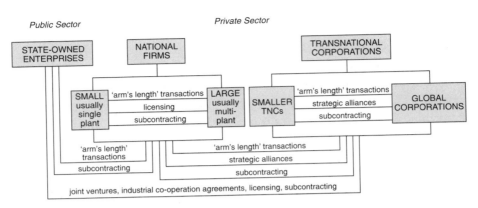

FIGURE 8.3   Major organization segments within a global economic system (source: Dicken 1998)

Selecting the most appropriate strategy

The choice between Dicken's alternatives involves a balance between the economies of scale to be achieved through plant specialization against the extra costs of moving products either between plants or from plants to markets. Other factors requiring consideration are the risks associated with plant specialization, whether local manufacturing is required for product adaptation and government policy regarding investment incentives or disincentives and import regulations. The internal production network is also highly dynamic and subject to rapid change due to both changes in the organization's external environment and internal pressures that may necessitate reorganization and rationalization.

In addition to the internal network discussed above, Dicken (1998) also stressed the importance of external networks. International businesses are often engaged in many external interconnections with other businesses. The linkages can be with domestic companies (large and small), public and private organizations as shown in Figure 8.3.

Plant location decision-making

Decision criteria

For transnational companies that have decided to manufacture abroad through foreign direct investment (FDI), a complex decision on plant location must be made. Scully and Fawcett (1993), in their study of 103 US companies with international operations, found that the level of formal planning for facility location was greater than that for overall planning, production systems and logistics decisions. They suggested that this may be 'the result of the many mathematical models and software programs which exist to assist in making this decision'.

There are a number of factors which have to be taken into consideration in making the location decision. Dunning (1980), as part of his 'eclectic' theory of international production, identified five major location-specific factors derived from FDI considerations:

1. markets – size, growth, type of products/services demanded, degree of competition;
2. resources – availability of raw materials and services, availability of a workforce with appropriate skills (or which is 'trainable');
3. production costs – labour and productivity, raw materials, transportation, energy, currency exchange;
4. political conditions – attitude of host government to FDI, e.g. restrictions on ownership, tax rates, incentives, trade barriers, government and economic stability (the degree of risk), employment legislation;
5. cultural and linguistic affinities – product attractiveness and other marketing issues, similar ways of doing business, no need to communicate in a different language, attractiveness of host country to parent company nationals.

The perceived relative importance of these factors will vary from one industry to another but will also depend on the type of production that the individual business intends to use in the host country. Dunning (1993) described six types of production with the main location-specific advantages for each. These are summarized in Table 8.2.

The most frequently-used criteria

The majority of FDI has been for the first three types of production. Dicken (1998) discussed these in terms of market-, supply- and cost-oriented production.

Market-oriented production

In the first case, businesses aim to supply an overseas market by locating production within that market, often to circumvent trade barriers such as tariffs and quotas. In simple terms, the major factors to be considered are market size and growth. A crude estimate of these can be made by examining the gross national product (GNP) per capita and how it is changing. In these terms, the USA and Western Europe are the most attractive markets.

Table 8.2 Factors affecting location decisions for each type of international production (source: adapted from Dunning 1993)

Type of international production	Location advantages sought
Natural resource seeking	Possession of natural resources and related transport and communications infrastructure; tax and other incentives
Market seeking	Material and labour costs; market size and characteristics; government policy (e.g. with respect to regulations and to import controls, investment incentives etc.)
Efficiency seeking (a) of product (b) of processes	(a) Economies of product specialization and concentration (b) Low labour costs; incentives to local production by host governments
Strategic asset seeking	Any countries from the first three that offer technology, markets and other assets in which the business is deficient
Trade and distribution (import and export merchanting)	Source of inputs and local markets; need to be near customers; after-sales servicing etc.
Support services	Availability of markets, particularly those of 'lead' clients

However the picture is more complex – the type of products demanded vary with GNP per capita, with poorer countries requiring more basic goods while richer countries spend more income on 'higher order' goods and services.

Supply-oriented production

Supply-oriented production is the dominant form of production for businesses dependent on natural resources for their output such as those in the extractive industries. However, Dicken (1998) argued that only some of the operations of such companies may be located at the source of supply; for example some oil companies transport crude oil relatively long distances to refineries located in countries considered to be more attractive for such investment.

Cost-oriented production

Cost-oriented production has accounted for many of the global shifts in production in the last 30 years, away from the developed to the less-developed countries whose labour costs were much lower. For manufacturing industries where labour inputs are a relatively high proportion of costs, there are major potential savings by locating production in low wage areas. Dicken (1998) compared the changes in patterns of production of the textiles and clothing industries. In both cases there was been a decline in production in the industrialized countries and a growth in production in the developing countries. The shift, however, was more marked for clothing manufacture where automation has been less successful in replacing manual labour. Although variations in labour costs are well documented it is also necessary to consider variations in productivity levels, workforce adaptability and workforce 'manageability' between different countries.

Dornier *et al.* (1998) questioned both market- and cost-orientation as viable long-term reasons for locating overseas. They found that the notional advantages of proximity to market are often offset by government restrictions on domestic content, technology transfer and domestic ownership which can severely limit the control that the parent has over its subsidiary. Furthermore, wage rates change as today's newly developing countries become tomorrow's industrialized nations and in addition, the recent collapse of the Far Eastern economies has created major uncertainties on future exchange rates and government policies towards FDI. Dornier *et al.* (1998) argued that the key to successful location overseas is a commitment to strategic planning. Once the FDI has been made, the development of the facility must be guided by strategic, rather than operational, thinking.

The location decision

The way in which the decision is made depends on many company-related factors such as experience in FDI; type of production; inter-plant relationships, type of product etc. Many production and operations management textbooks describe analytical methods of determining optimal locations for new investment. Most of these involve the calculation of tangible costs and returns followed by a factoring in of other intangible variables through some kind of weighting. Such approaches are probably more suited to cost-oriented production than market-oriented production. One approach is to use a hierarchical screening of options beginning with continent followed by country then actual site.

Choice of continent
For a business with a wide spread of international manufacturing plants, the choice of continent may be a significant one as the company may have to decide between competing proposals from subsidiaries in various parts of the world. In such a case, the company should be able to compare the

expected costs, returns and risks of the alternative proposals. In cases where the company has a narrow spread of international investment, some form of broad screening will be required based on the type of production required.

Choice of country

Unless the business is present in a large number of countries already, it will probably limit consideration to a few obvious candidates which either have an attractive market or offer low cost manufacturing. However in a major trading bloc such as the EU, a much more detailed country by country comparison may be made, particularly if different incentives are offered by host governments.

Choice of site

A much more detailed investigation is required examining factors such as labour availability, transport infrastructure, regional incentives, other related industries and general attractiveness of the area. The analytical methods mentioned earlier may be used to rank the shortlist. Large businesses investing in the EU are likely to have a shortlist of 2–3 sites in different countries with the final decision coming down to the most attractive financial package being offered by the host government.

Procurement and transnational business

Procurement policy

Procurement policies are closely linked to the plant roles and inter-plant relationships discussed earlier in the chapter. The policies are linked to the overall global strategy of the business and the issues affecting procurement can be discussed in terms of a number of variables:

- in-house manufacturing vs external purchasing/subcontracting;
- corporate vs third party suppliers;
- domestic vs other country purchasing;
- single vs multiple sourcing.

Birou and Fawcett (1993) in a survey of US companies identified a range of perceived benefits of international sourcing (Table 8.3).

Table 8.3 Benefits obtained from international sourcing. Rating is on a seven-point Likert scale with 7 = greatest benefit (source: Birou and Fawcett 1993)

Rank	Benefits from international sourcing	Rating
1	Access to lower priced goods	5.56
2	Enhanced competitive position	5.29
3	Access to higher quality goods	4.89
4	Access to worldwide technology	4.49
5	Better delivery performance	3.48
6	Better customer service	3.38
7	Increased number of suppliers	2.76
8	Helps meet countertrade obligations	2.60

Types of purchasing policy

Broadly speaking, three types of purchasing policy are possible: central purchasing; autonomous procurement and a mixture of these two extremes.

Central purchasing

In the most extreme case, a single part of the corporation is responsible for carrying out all purchasing, for all parts of the company, with the objective of gaining economies of scale and uniformity of quality. Purchasing is carried out on a global basis and is mainly of standard products such as electronic components. Subsidiaries are then required to buy from (usually through a quasi market or transfer pricing arrangement) the central purchasing organization. In less extreme cases, groups of plants located in a particular regions may set up their own regional purchasing organizations.

Autonomous purchasing

Individual plants are responsible for their own procurement. This may be forced on the business because of government policies on local sourcing or it may be part of a corporate country-centred policy. The plant will still have to ensure that vendors meet the company's agreed standards of quality, cost and delivery particularly in cases of transnational vertical integration.

In many cases a mixture of the two extremes is used with central purchasing for standard components and local procurement for more specialized components.

Global logistics

The 'flow' of materials

'Logistics' is defined (Slack *et al.* 1998) as activities concerned with the flow of material from supplier to production and from production to the customer. The meaning has extended, however, to include reverse flows of material (e.g. returned or faulty goods, packaging etc.) and flows of information. This wider definition reflects the greater emphasis on logistics as part of the overall global strategy of a business. This view of logistics as linking the operations of the business is summarized in Figure 8.4.

Logistics is thus the means through which the competitive advantage sought by globalized business will be realized. Conversely weaknesses in logistics may undermine that competitive advantage through the creation of 'blockages' in the organization's primary value-adding activities (Porter 1985 – see discussion on this in Chapter 3).

Logistics and strategy

The type of global production strategy adopted will have important implications for logistics management. Decisions will be made concerning both internal logistics (i.e. the flow of intermediary products, parts and components between subsidiaries) and external logistics (i.e. the flow of final goods from producer to end-user).

In transnationals adopting country-centred or multidomestic strategies, logistics management will be concerned mainly with distribution within countries since production is located in the markets being served. Companies adopting 'purest' global and export-based strategies, on the other hand, will be concerned more with international (across border) logistics given that dispersed foreign markets are supplied through centralized production facilities. The most complicated arrangement arises in

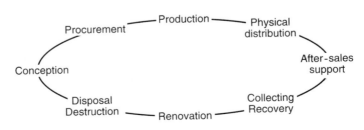

FIGURE 8.4   Operations and logistics flows (source: Dornier *et al.* 1998)

companies adopting strategies of high FDI with extensive co-ordination amongst subsidiaries. In addition to within-country and across-border product flows, this involves the global co-ordination and integration of worldwide production and distribution into a global logistics network.

Scully and Fawcett (1993) analysed the comparative costs of production and logistics in different regions of the world for a number of US companies. They noted that while management time tends to be concentrated on seeking production locations which offer cost advantage, there is relatively little time spent on the co-ordination of the organization's dispersed productive operations. They also found that some areas which offered very advantageous production costs also suffered from comparatively high logistics costs. The reasons for this are that areas which offer lower labour costs tend to have less well developed infrastructures and management practices.

Scully and Fawcett also showed that, for US-based companies, any move out of the USA resulted in higher logistics costs. This can be explained by considering that over 90 per cent of logistics costs come from documentation, stock and transport costs. Documentation costs, despite attempts to reduce these within trading blocs such as the EU and NAFTA, are invariably higher than when all operations take place in a single country. Stock costs rise because companies tend to carry more stock when distribution lines are lengthened in order to guard against delays and stock-outs. Finally longer distances raise transport costs.

A further study by Ghosh and Cooper (1997) of the impact of NAFTA on US companies showed that while logistics in Mexico were expected to improve as a result of NAFTA, customs inefficiencies, poor transport infrastructure and different management practices were still likely to be a significant barrier to increased trade between the US and Mexico.

Managing logistics

The complexity of managing logistics for organizations with global operations can be immense and the potential for problems correspondingly large. Companies have identified a number of techniques to manage and reduce logistics lead times.

Fawcett (1992) listed a number of examples including:

- developing partnership relationships with providers of transportation services;

- developing partnership relationships with domestic and foreign suppliers of sourced components;
- reliance on third party transportation companies;
- use of advanced information systems such as EDI to track and/or expedite shipments.

The emphasis on partnerships and alliances, a growing feature of global business, is discussed further in Chapter 14 and the use of information systems to co-ordinate activities is discussed in Chapter 10.

REVIEW AND DISCUSSION QUESTIONS

1. What are the critical success factors that enable production strategy to contribute to competitive advantage?
2. Explain how the three types of materials sourcing can help a business's strategy.
3. What features of a business's strategy would influence the choice between Dicken's four production strategies?
4. Explain the key decision criteria when deciding on plant location.
5. Define and distinguish between central and autonomous purchasing.
6. Define and distinguish between internal and external logistics.

References and further reading

Agodo, O. (1978) The determinants of US private manufacturing investments in Africa, *Journal of International Business Studies*, Winter, 95–107.

Birou, L.M. and Fawcett, S.E. (1993) International purchasing: benefits, requirements and challenges, *International Journal of Operations and Production Management*, **29**(2), 27–37.

Channon, D.F. and Jalland, M. (1978) *Multinational Strategic Planning*, AMACOM.

Dicken, P. (1998) *Global Shift – Transforming the World Economy*, Paul Chapman, London.

Dornier, P., Ernst, R., Fender, M. and Kouvelis, P. (1998) *Global Operations and Logistics*, John Wiley, New York.

Doz, Y.L. (1978) Managing manufacturing rationalization within multinational companies, *Columbia Journal of World Business*, **13**(3), Fall.

Doz, Y.L. (1986) *Strategic Management in Multinational Companies*, Pergamon Press, New York.

Dubin, M. (1975) Foreign acquisitions and the growth of the multinational firm, Doctoral Thesis, Harvard Business School, Boston.

Dunning, J.H. (1973) The determinants of international production, *Oxford Economic Papers*, **25**(3), 289–336.

Dunning, J.H. (1980) Towards an eclectic theory of international production: some empirical tests, *Journal of International Business Studies*, **11**, 9–31.

Dunning, J.H. (1986) *Japanese Participation in British Industry*. Croom Helm.

Dunning, J.H. (1993) *Multinational Enterprises and the Global Economy*, Addison-Wesley, Reading, MA.

Economist, The Hanson Trust: Low Tech, High Profit, April 20, 1985.

Fawcett, S. (1992) Strategic logistics in co-ordinated global manufacturing success, *International Journal of Production Research*, **30**(4), 1081–1099.

Ghosh, A. and Cooper, M. (1997) Manager's perceptions of NAFTA, *The International Journal of Logistics Management*, **8**(2), 33–45.

Goldar, J.D. and Jelinek, M. (1983) Plan for economies of scope, *Harvard Business Review*, November/December, 141–148.

Graham, E.M. (1978) Transatlantic investment by multinational firms: a rivalistic phenomenon, *Journal of Post Keynesian Economics*, **1**(1), 82–98.

Groo, E.S. (1972) Choosing foreign locations: one company's experience, *Columbia Journal of World Business*, September/October.

Guisinger, S.E. and Associates (1985) Investment incentives and performance requirements, *Patterns of International Trade, Production, and Investment*, Praeger.

Hamill, J. (1988) British acquisitions in the US, *National Westminster Bank Quarterly Review*, August.

Hood, N. and Young, S. (1981) *The R&D Activities of US Multinational Enterprises: A Review of the Literature*, Report to the Department of Industry, UK, June.

Hood, N. and Young, S. (1982) *Multinationals in Retreat: The Scottish Experience*, Edinburgh University Press, Edinburgh.

Hood, N. and Young, S. (1983) *Multinational Investment Strategies in the British Isles*, HMSO, London.

Keegan, W.J. (1995) *Global Marketing Management*, 5th edn, Englewood Cliffs, NJ: Prentice Hall.

Kitching, J. (1974) Winning and losing with European acquisitions, *Harvard Business Review*, March/April.

Knickerbocker, F.T. (1973) Oligopolistic reaction and the multinational enterprise, *Harvard Business School*, Division of Research.

Malecki, E.J. (1980) Corporate organization of R&D and the location of technological activities, *Regional Studies*, **14**, 219–234.

Mansfield, E. (1978) *Studies of the Relationship between International Technology Transfer and R&D Expenditure by US Firms*, report for the National Science Foundation.

Merritt, G. (1985) How Europe's governments are 'aiding' the multinationals, *Multinational Info*, February, 6–8.

Nigh, D. (1986) Political events and the foreign direct investment decision: an empirical examination, *Managerial and Decision Economics*, **7**(2).

OECD (Organization for Economic Cooperation and Development) (1986) *Impact of Multinational Enterprises on National Scientific and Technological Capacities: Analytical Report*, OECD.

OECD (Organization for Economic Co-operation and Development) (1981) *Relationships of Incentives and Disincentives to International Investment Decisions*, USA-BIAC Committee on International Investment and Multinational Enterprise, OECD.

Porter, M.E. (1985) *Competitive Advantage*, Free Press.

Porter, M.E. (1986) *Competition in Global Industries*, Harvard Business School Press, Boston.

Ricks, D.A. and Ajami, R.A. (1981) Motives of non-American firms investing in the United States, *Journal of International Business Studies*, Winter, 25–34.

Ronstadt, R. (1977) *Research and Development Abroad by US Multinationals*, Praeger.

Rugman, A.M., Lecraw, D.J. and Booth, L.D. (1985) *International Business, Firm and Environment*, New York, McGraw Hill.

Scully, J. and Fawcett, S. (1993) Comparative logistics and production costs for global manufacturing strategy, *International Journal of Operations and Production Management*, **13**(12), 62–78.

Slack, N., Chambers, S., Harland, C., Harrison, A. and Johnston, R. (1998) *Operations Management*, 2nd edn, Pitman, London.

Starr, M.K. (1984) Global production and operations strategy, *Columbia Journal of World Business*, **18**(4), Winter.

GLOBAL STRATEGIC HUMAN RESOURCE MANAGEMENT

9

CHAPTER

LEARNING OBJECTIVES

After studying this chapter, students should be able to:

- understand the need for, and basis of, a strategic approach to human resource management (HRM);
- understand the benefits of a global approach to HRM;
- summarize the advantages and disadvantages of alternative staffing policies (home, host or third country nationals);
- identify the main reasons for the high failure rate amongst expatriate employees and the possible solutions to the problem through an effective expatriate policy;
- summarize the main aims and issues covered in a global management development programme;
- compare the different approaches of transnational businesses towards the management of labour abroad;
- identify the link between the transnational's value system and global strategy, and its human resource strategy.

Introduction

Human resources are viewed as having a central role in determining the success of global and transnational strategy. Human resources are regarded as being of singular importance because:

- they play a unique part in organizational learning and competence building;
- their management poses particular questions in a global context;
- they are crucial in converting strategies into action.

Heijltjes *et al.* (1996) stated that 'Human resource management (HRM) carries the promise that, if people are regarded and managed as strategic resources, it can help the firm to obtain a competitive advantage and superior performance'.

The implementation of effective managerial and labour strategies within global businesses is complicated by variations in culture, value systems, language, business environment and industrial relations systems between countries. In terms of its managerial strategy global companies need to resolve four key issues including:

- human resource strategy – the means by which the human resource strategy is determined and the extent to which it is integrated with global and transnational strategy;
- staffing policies – the extent to which key managerial positions at foreign subsidiaries should be staffed by home, host or third country nationals;
- expatriate policies – the establishment of effective policies for ensuring the smooth exchange of managerial/executive personnel between the parent company and overseas subsidiaries;
- global management development – to ensure an adequate supply of globally experienced managers at all levels in the organization.

These four issues are discussed in this chapter.

Strategic human resource management

The importance of human resources

An important determinant of the success of global strategy is the management of an organization's human resources. Human resource management (HRM), according to Beer *et al.* (1984), 'involves all management decisions and actions that affect the nature of the relationship between the organization and its employees – its human resources'. People have a crucial role to play in devising and implementing strategy, in strategic decision making and in making strategy successful. HRM has been defined thus: 'a strategic and coherent approach to the management of an organization's most valued assets: the people working there who individually and collectively contribute to the achievement of its objectives for sustainable competitive advantage' (Armstrong 1992). Strategic HRM is therefore concerned with making the most effective use of people in determining and operationalizing strategy.

It is also concerned with ensuring that HR strategy is fully congruent with corporate strategy. When the business is globalized, the importance of arriving at an appropriate human resource strategy is very great. Global and transnational HR strategy is more complex but also offers more strategic alternatives. Human resources are central to achieving global competitive advantage so they must be managed strategically by ensuring that an organization has an HRM strategy which is fully integrated with its global and transnational strategy.

Walker (1992) made the following case for adopting a strategic approach to HR management:

- it defines opportunities and barriers for achievement of business objectives;
- it prompts new thinking about issues; orientates and educates participants and provides a wider perspective;
- it tests management commitment for actions; creates a process for allocating resources to specific programmes and activities;
- it develops a sense of urgency and commitment to action;
- it establishes selected long-term courses of action considered high priority over the next 2–3 years;
- it provides a strategic focus for managing the business and developing management talents.

Features of HR strategy

Anthony *et al.* (1993) listed six key features of an HR strategy:

1. *recognition of the impact of the external environment* – need to take advantage of opportunities and to minimize the effects of threats;
2. *recognition of the impact of competition and the dynamics of the labour market* – organizations compete for employees and must recognize the forces affecting local, regional and national labour markets. Labour market dynamics of wage rates, unemployment levels, working conditions, minimum wage

legislation, benefit level and competitor reputation all affect or are affected by strategic HR decisions

3. *long-range focus* – a time frame of three to five years is normal;
4. *choice and decision-making focus* – strategy implies choosing between alternatives and making major decisions about HR that commit the organization's resources toward a particular direction;
5. *consideration of all personnel* – the value of all employees from top level management to unskilled workers is seen as being important;
6. *integration with corporate strategy and functional strategies* – HR strategy must be fully integrated with both corporate strategy and the strategies of the other functional areas of the business.

As well as these general characteristics of a strategic approach to HR, it is important to consider the impact of core competence and generic strategy on the organization's HR strategy.

HR strategy, core competences and organizational learning

Globalization, turbulence and hypercompetition in markets demand increased organizational flexibility and accelerated organizational learning. In addition, a customer focus is also an essential element of sustained competitive advantage. These twin needs for responsiveness and customer orientation have profound implications for global strategic human resource management.

We learned in Chapter 6 that a global business can adopt a competence-based approach to strategic management. This, in turn, implies the adoption of an open systems perspective to human resources which looks across and beyond organizational boundaries. Furthermore, the development of core competences is often based upon organizational learning and knowledge building. Organizational learning and knowledge building are based upon individual knowledge and learning, which is stored and shared.

The importance of human beings in the development of both individual and organizational knowledge is as evident as it is paramount. Strategic human resource management, therefore, has a pivotal role to play in knowledge management and development, and in competence building. Hagan (1996) argued that a competence-based human resource strategy 'will demand major changes in the way we organize, the way we structure work, the importance we place on learning and innovation, and the way we approach the management of our employees'.

Table 9.1 Strategic HRM – implications of a core competence approach (adapted from Hagan 1996)

Job design	1. Greater technical knowledge will be required for individual jobs. Project teams and rotation of jobs will be used to foster the sharing of knowledge
	2. Jobs will increasingly combine thinking and doing
Staffing issues	3. Most challenging positions will be filled by internal transfers. Externally hired employees will be mainly at entry level
	4. Businesses will enter relationships with educational institutions to obtain suitably qualified employees
	5. Personality and attitudinal tests will be used to assess the potential of individuals
Training and development	6. Investment in training and development programmes will increase to facilitate personal and organizational development
	7. Training and development personnel will be increasingly decentralized to operating departments
	8. Training and development will move away from traditional skills building to development
	9. Performance review will be used to assess the contribution of employees rather than to determine pay. This will be based on feedback from peers and customers rather than supervisors and subordinates
Rewards systems	10. A greater proportion of pay will be based upon group or organizational outcomes
	11. Traditional hierarchical pay plans will be replaced by broader banding of jobs. Job evaluation will shift from a quantitative to a qualitative focus
	12. Compensation systems will become flexible

Hagan proposed 12 hypotheses believed to govern a competence-based approach to strategic HRM (see Table 9.1)

HR strategy and generic strategy

Research by Heijltjes *et al.* (1996) suggested that the HR strategy of the organization ought to, and in most cases does, support its generic strategy. Their findings identified that the HR strategies of businesses pursuing cost leadership, differentiation and combination (hybrid) strategies, in most cases, had readily identifiable characteristics. These characteristics are shown in Table 9.2.

Heijltjes *et al.* (1996) identified a possible conflict for companies pursuing a combination (hybrid) strategy of cost leadership, differentiation and

Table 9.2 Generic and HR strategies – key linkages (adapted from information in Heijltjes *et al.* 1996)

	Cost leadership	Differentiation
Selection and training		High emphasis on recruiting and training quality trained personnel
Level of supervision	Intense supervision of labour	
Level of cost control	Tight cost control	
Level of reporting	Frequent and detailed control reports	
Emphasis on training	Low emphasis on training and development	
Emphasis on improved productivity	High emphasis on improving productivity	
Reward systems	Incentives based on quantitative targets	Reward systems are not based on quantitative targets only
Organizational structure	Highly structured organizations	

focus. In these cases (which they related to competitors in the food and drink industry) Heijltjes *et al.* argued that differentiation is primarily achieved through marketing and, therefore, that HR policy at management level and in marketing will be that of a differentiator. In the area of production, HR policy would be likely to be similar to that adopted by a company whose strategy was cost leadership. Their research found evidence that 'In the majority of cases, the HRM strategy supports the generic strategy chosen'. There is thus strong support for the view that the generic strategy element of a global and transnational strategy must be complemented by its HR strategy.

Integration of HRM with corporate strategy and functional strategies

The importance of congruence

A common assumption made in American models of HRM is that the corporate strategy of an organization drives its functional strategies. In other words, an organization determines its overall strategy and then sets functional strategies in order to implement it. However, the functional strategies can also impact on corporate strategy in that senior management must consider existing functional strategies when setting corporate strategy. For example, current HR strategy and capabilities will be important considerations when developing the corporate strategy of a transnational business. Brewster (1994) suggested that 'the development of strategy is in fact a complex, iterative and incremental process, so that it is difficult to define a point at which the corporate strategy can be finalized sufficiently to allow the HRM strategy to be created'.

Accordingly, human resource must be acutely aware of overall corporate strategy and how HR strategy aligns with it. Furthermore, they must be aware of functional strategies and endeavour to integrate HR strategy with them. In aiming to integrate HR strategies with business strategies, the HR strategy can be modelled on the business strategy and can use it as a starting point. Table 9.3 illustrates some of the possible relationships.

Problems of integrating HRM with global and transnational strategies
A number of problems are commonly encountered when attempting to integrate HR strategy with transnational strategy.

1. An organization will have a number of business strategies, especially if it operates in a variety of product-markets, therefore different approaches to HR might be needed for each. This is particularly true of global and transnational businesses.
2. If business strategy changes, it might be difficult to change HR strategy because it involves the internal structure and culture of the organization. Softer features of organizations like culture are notoriously difficult to change to a desired state.
3. HRM is often qualitative, meaning that it is not easy to prove the relationship between HRM and the performance of the organization.

Table 9.3 HR implications of business strategy

Business strategy questions	HR implications
What industry and markets are we in?	What people do we need?
Are organizational culture, structure and value systems appropriate or inappropriate?	How do we change them?
Strategic direction	Who will we need in the future?
New businesses and new markets	What systems and procedures might be developed?
Strengths, weaknesses, opportunities, threats	To what extent are they related to existing use of HR?
	Demand and supply in the labour market?
Critical success factors	To what extent do these depend on employees rather than other factors?

Table 9.4 Examples of organizational strategies and associated human resource strategies (source: Anthony *et al*. 1993)

Corporate strategy (strategic direction)	Example company	HR strategies
Retrenchment (cost reduction)	General Motors	Layoffs, wage reduction, productivity increases, job redesign, re-negotiated labour agreements
Growth	Intel	Aggressive recruiting and hiring, rapidly rising wages, job creation, expanding training and development
Renewal	Chrysler	Managed turnover, selective layoff, organizational development, transfer/replacement, productivity increases, employee involvement
Niche focus	Kentucky Fried Chicken	Specialized job creation, elimination of other jobs, specialized training and development
Acquisition	General Electric	Selective layoffs, transfers/placement, job combinations, orientation and training, managing cultural transitions

4. HRM is often long-term and large-scale but can easily be subverted. For example, a change in culture can be undermined by quick-fix management decisions or by management which pays only lip-service to change.

Criticisms of the concept of strategic HRM

The concept of HRM and the strategic approach originated in the USA, but there has been criticism of the view that American models of HRM can be applied universally, particularly in European literature on the subject. Some of the main criticisms of the American concept are that it:

- lacks clarity and precision;
- is too prescriptive and normative;
- lacks supporting empirical evidence;
- is difficult to distinguish from traditional personnel management;
- is too derivative in its approach to HRM strategy, which is seen as being driven by corporate strategy, rather than contributing to it;

- is overly prescriptive with regard to industrial relations history and practice in Europe (and perhaps in other continents as well).

European and American approaches to HRM

Two common elements of American models of HRM are the ideas of:

- organizational independence and autonomy;
- the integration of HRM and business strategy.

A survey of HRM policy and practice in Europe (Brewster and Hegewisch 1994) found important differences between the USA and Europe in respect of these two elements.

1. Organizational autonomy is more restricted in Europe because of:

- *culture and legislation* – US culture is more individualistic and achievement oriented. HRM in Europe is influenced and determined to a greater degree by state regulations;
- *patterns of ownership* in the private sector vary between Europe and the USA. For example, in Germany a network of a small number of large banks owns most of the major companies. Public ownership is more extensive in Europe;
- *trade unions and workforce communication* – Europe is more heavily unionized and union influence is still strong (in most European countries, more than 70% of employers recognize trade unions for the purpose of collective bargaining);
- *the controlled labour market* – In Europe, higher levels of state support in the external labour market enable European organizations to develop both internal and external labour market strategies with a lower degree of risk (although employers are also faced with restrictions in recruitment methods, for example.

2. HRM and business strategy
Brewster and Hegewisch (1994) argued that there is little evidence of the integration of HRM and business strategy in the USA, but there appears to be a higher degree of integration of HRM at the top levels of organizations in Europe.

A transnational model of HRM

Brewster (1994) proposed 'a model of HRM which places HR strategies firmly within, though not entirely absorbed by, the business strategy'. The model (Figure 9.1) shows that the business strategy, HR strategy and HR practice are all affected by, and interact with, an external environment of national culture, legislation, patterns of ownership, employee representation, education etc.

Global staffing policies

An important element of an organization's global and transnational HR strategy is its staffing policy. Three main alternatives are available to the global business in terms of staffing managerial positions abroad. The first three alternatives are the employment of home country nationals (ethnocentric), host country nationals (polycentric), or a combination of home, host and third country nationals (geocentric or global). Although only the third approach is consistent with a global and transnational approach, each of the alternatives has its own advantages and disadvantages (see the discussion of the EPRG framework in Chapter 2).

Home country managers
The employment of expatriate or home country managers provides the advantages of:

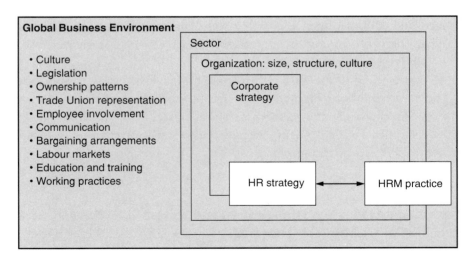

FIGURE 9.1   A transnational model of HRM (adapted from Brewster 1994)

- providing cultural consistency as such managers share the dominant culture of the parent company;
- assisting the parent company in transferring its best business practices and customs to subsidiaries;
- enhancing parent control and co-ordination of overseas operations;
- providing the parent company with a pool of mangers with international experience;
- increasing the international orientation of the parent organization.

The employment of expatriate managers can also have some disadvantages:

- problems of adaptation to the local culture;
- language problems;
- costs – employment of expatriates is usually more costly, and significantly so, than the employment of local nationals because of higher salaries and other transfer costs;
- political sensitivity – failure to employ local managers may cause political problems;
- personal and family problems for such managers (see later) which can result in a high staff turnover rate;
- a disincentive effect on the motivation and morale of indigenous managers who see promoted posts being retained for parent country nationals.

In a number of countries, the employment of expatriates may not be possible because of government regulations. A study by the Business International Corporation (1982) identified five situations where an international business would seek to use expatriate managers:

- when its foreign subsidiary is either entering the start-up phase, changing major corporate strategies or implementing new technologies;
- when no adequate local talent is available;
- during periods where control is critical and few deviations from corporate policies can be tolerated;
- when the foreign unit is short-lived;
- in order to staff specific managerial positions – especially the general manager, head of finance, R&D manager – for purposes of control and co-ordination.

Host country managers

The advantages of using local managers are basically the reverse of the disadvantages of employing expatriate managers. Such local managers:

- are more familiar with the language, customs, business practices and other conditions of the host country;
- may reduce the 'foreignness' of the subsidiary in the eyes of local officials;
- are usually cheaper than employing expatriates;
- reduce the need for establishing expatriate policies designed to reduce the problems involved in foreign assignments (see later), as well as meeting host government regulations;
- may improve local management motivation and morale by providing promotion opportunities within the subsidiary.

The disadvantages of employing local nationals include the lack of familiarity with the business practices and product technology of the parent company. These disadvantages can lead to potential control and communications problems; a parochial rather than a multinational perspective; and a shortage of internationally experienced managers.

Home, host and third country managers

The third alternative available to transnational corporations is a geocentric or global policy of filling overseas management positions with the 'best person for the job', regardless of their nationality. This can combine the advantages of both the previous approaches. It may also result in some of the disadvantages. The use of third country nationals, however, runs the risk of combining the disadvantages associated with both the ethnocentric and polycentric policies. Thus, third country nationals will be unfamiliar with both the local environment and with the business practices of the parent company. In addition, the employment of third country nationals can be very expensive in terms of training, language orientation and compensation complications. For these reasons a formalized geocentric staffing strategy is rare in practice.

In the absence of geocentric policy, global businesses have often adopted other strategies to reduce the disadvantages of ethnocentric and polycentric staffing policies. Thus, host country nationals may be employed, but only after extensive training at the parent company designed to incorporate such individuals into the parent company's business philosophy. An alternative strategy is to employ local nationals, but to reduce subsidiary decision-making autonomy.

Staffing policies and strategy

The staffing policies adopted by global business organizations will be influenced by several factors including the characteristics of both parent and subsidiary; characteristics of the host country; and the relative costs of the alternatives. Thus, the availability of local management talent in the host country and government restrictions on the employment of expatriates will obviously be important in the choice of home, host or third country nationals. Similarly, differences in salary levels, expatriate transfer costs and failure costs will also be important. The employment of home country nationals is generally greater in new subsidiaries (especially in the start-up phase); greenfield entrants as opposed to acquisitions; poor performers; and large subsidiaries.

Despite the importance of such factors, the dominant influences on global organization staffing policies are likely to be related to the strategic predispositions and value systems of the parent company and its global corporate strategy. In this respect, there is a clear link between staffing policies and the broader strategy of the organization as discussed in earlier chapters. This is explored in more detail in the final section of this chapter. Ondrack (1985) examined the relationship between the staffing policies of the business and its value system using Chakravarthy and Perlmutter's (1985) EPRG profile.

It was suggested that exchange and transfers of personnel within an international business occur for three main reasons:

1. *transfers for staffing* – whereby HQ executives are temporarily transferred abroad to fill key management positions at the overseas subsidiary;
2. *transfers for management development* – which involves a two-way flow of personnel from parent company to foreign subsidiary for management training and development;
3. *transfers for organizational development* – which involves the creation of a pool of internationally-experienced and trained executives through frequent foreign assignments, and the development of an informal network of interpersonal communications within the organization.

Ondrack (1985) suggested that both the number of international transfers and their direction (parent to subsidiary and vice versa) will vary with the underlying philosophy of the organization. In ethnocentric businesses, transfers of staff will be one-way only; from parent to subsidiary for staffing purposes. Career opportunities for host and third country nationals in ethnocentric companies will be confined to their own countries. In polycentric organizations on the other hand, host and third country nationals will spend time at the parent company as part of their management development. The international exchange and transfer of personnel will be most frequent in regiocentric and geocentric businesses. This will involve a three-way flow between parent, regional HQs and local subsidiary for staffing, management development and organizational development purposes. This can be viewed as the most 'global' of the approaches and likely to support a corporate strategy which is both global and transnational.

Expatriate management

Expatriate failures

Regardless of the staffing policy adopted, there will usually still be significant international transfers of staff within most international business organizations. Somewhere between 25 and 40 per cent of foreign assignments fail in US transnationals and this ensures that the effective transfer of such personnel is one of the most important human resource problems facing the HR function. Both the monetary and non-monetary costs of failure are high and they can cause a lot of personal problems for the individuals concerned. In contrast, the failure rate of expatriates in European transnationals is extremely low, at less than 3 per cent (Hamill, 1989).

Several reasons have been suggested for the high failure rate amongst expatriate employees, including the failure to adapt to a foreign working environment, inadequate compensation and a feeling of loss of status resulting from working at the periphery. Several studies have shown, however, that family-related problems are perhaps the most important cause of failure amongst expatriates (Tung 1981, 1984; Harvey 1985). Such family problems include those relating to the adaptation of both spouse and children to a new cultural and social environment.

The problems associated with foreign assignments highlight the importance to the global business of introducing effective expatriate policies aimed at ensuring the smooth international transfer of staff. A successful expatriate policy should cover a number of key variables including the recruitment and selection of employees for overseas assignments, the compensation package and repatriation. The training and development of managers for overseas assignments is also essential.

Recruitment and selection

Many of the problems associated with expatriate employees may be reduced by the careful recruitment and selection of employees for overseas assignments. Although the same skills which make an executive successful in the home country are also essential for foreign assignments, additional qualities will usually be required, including the ability to adapt to different cultures and work environments, flexibility, empathy, family stability and foreign language ability. Recruitment and selection procedures should be sufficiently rigorous to identify individuals possessing such qualities.

The selection process should focus on two main areas, namely, adaptability screening and a careful assessment of the individual's (and family's) potential for acculturating in a new environmental setting. Holmes and Piker (1980) found that effective recruitment and selection procedures can considerably reduce the incidence of failure amongst expatriate employees from 40 to 25 per cent.

Reward systems

One of the major difficulties relating to cross-national transfers of staff is arriving at the appropriate package to be paid to expatriate employees. The important issues are:

- payment of home or host country salary levels;
- payment of a foreign-service premium to cover relocation and disruption;
- allowances for variations in inflation, tax and exchange rates between countries.

There are significant variations between businesses as to how these problems are addressed and these variations are likely to continue in the foreseeable future.

Repatriation

An effective expatriate policy should also establish firm criteria for the repatriation of the executive, given that most foreign assignments are temporary. Reference has already been made to the cultural and social problems encountered by expatriates working abroad. However, reverse culture shock is also a significant problem on repatriation. Businesses must take steps to address these problems within their HR policy and procedures. Harvey (1982, 1985) provides a useful review of the problems and some of the potential solutions.

Global management development

Global organizations require a management team which is both multinational and global in its outlook. The establishment of such a team requires a management development programme, based on a global and transnational perspective of business, which covers the recruitment, training and remuneration of international executives. The aim of such a programme, in addition to covering basic management skills and techniques, is to increase the global awareness of managers. Home country managers, whose training and experience will have been confined to the parent country, will often need to improve their understanding of the complexities involved in operating globally, especially those relating to variations in cultural and environmental conditions in different countries. Subsidiary (host country) managers will usually need to be aware that they are part of a global network, with local decisions having implications elsewhere in the organization.

Labour management

This chapter has been concerned mainly with human resource management in the transnational in relation to its managers. Relationships with other employees in different cultural environments are also crucial to the success of such businesses. This is especially the case in globally-integrated organizations, where industrial relations problems at one subsidiary may have wider effects on the global network. The effective management of labour and industrial relations within transnational corporations is also much more difficult than in purely domestic companies due to variations in culture, attitudes towards work, working practices, industrial relations systems and the legal environment governing labour and management relations.

Such variations create two major difficulties for the business.

1. The extent to which labour and industrial relations decision-making should be centralized at the level of the parent company.
2. The extent to which the business should transfer its country of origin HR and industrial relations practices abroad.

In addition, the trade union movement has been active in recent years in internationalizing its activities in response to the perceived 'challenge' of the transnational. Although international trade unionism was once a source of concern for many transnational organizations, its importance has reduced in recent years with the weakening of trade union powers by many governments.

Labour and industrial relations decision-making

Transnational organizations face conflicting pressures when determining the extent of centralization or decentralization of parent company control over industrial relations. Variations in the cultural, legal and institutional framework of industrial relations between host countries provide a strong incentive for the decentralization of industrial relations decision-making within the business. Similarly, many human resource management and industrial relations matters like wage determination, recruitment and training are often best dealt with at a local level for legal and cultural reasons.

Despite such influences, it is unlikely that labour and industrial relations decision-making will be completely decentralized. Some standardization and centralized control may be necessary to prevent concessions granted by one subsidiary being used as a bargaining tactic by trade unions at another subsidiary. The progress made by trade unions in the area of information exchanges and consultations between unions in different countries may reinforce this trend. Similarly, some centralization of industrial relations decisions may be necessary in cases of foreign acquisitions if the acquired company has a history of industrial relations problems. Finally, the source of the transnational's competitive advantage may lie in its more advanced human resources and industrial relations practices. Again, some centralized control may be necessary to ensure the effective transfer of such practices abroad.

Empirical evidence in this area (Young *et al*. 1985; Hamill 1984; Bomers and Peterson 1977; Van Den Bulcke and Halsberghe 1984) shows that industrial relations are indeed one of the most decentralized functional areas within transnational companies. The extent of parent company control, however, varies significantly with the particular industrial relations issue in question and between different businesses. Industrial relations decisions with important cost or financial implications for the parent company are more centralized than other issues. Included here would be the determination of subsidiary employment levels, wage determination, pensions and employee fringe benefits. Many organizations (for example in the electronics sector) also have worldwide philosophies opposed to the involvement of third parties (both trade unions and employers' associations) in the firm's internal industrial relations. The extent of centralized control also depends on the definition of industrial relations, with employers adopting a narrow definition including union recognition, collective bargaining etc. Trade unions, on the other hand, argue that investment and divestment decisions are legitimate areas for bargaining because of their implications for employment levels at the foreign subsidiary. Such decisions will be centralized in most transnationals.

The locus of decision-making with respect to labour and industrial relations decisions also varies significantly between different businesses. For example, Hamill's (1984) survey of foreign businesses operating in the UK concluded that 33 per cent of the companies surveyed were highly decentralized in industrial relations decision-making. At the other extreme, however, 20 per cent of businesses were found to be extremely centralized, with the parent company exerting close control over labour relations at the UK subsidiary. The other 47 per cent of companies lay somewhere between these two extremes, with some industrial relations decisions being centralized and others decentralized.

Transfer of industrial relations practices

Closely related to the issue of industrial relations decision-making within an international business is the industrial relations practices adopted by such companies abroad. Again, transnationals may adopt an ethnocentric approach of transferring home country personnel and industrial relations practices to their overseas subsidiaries, or a polycentric approach of adopting local (host country) industrial relations practices. As in the decision-making area, transnationals face conflicting pressures in choosing between the alternatives, with differences in the cultural, legal and institutional framework of industrial relations between countries, exerting strong pressures for the adoption of a polycentric approach. The need for standardization; the problems of acquisitions; and the more effective labour utilization practices of many businesses, on the other hand, would suggest the adoption of an ethnocentric approach. Similarly, many host country industrial relations practices (such as in the UK) may be detrimental to labour productivity or contribute to a high level of industrial disputes (e.g. multi-unionism; demarcation disputes; informal bargaining etc.). Again, the transnational may attempt to overcome these problems by transferring its own home country practices.

Significant variations exist in the extent to which different businesses have transferred home country industrial relations practices abroad (Hamill 1983). Many US companies (especially in the electronics sector) have well-defined global industrial relations policies covering such issues as union recognition, employer association membership, communications procedures, employee fringe benefits etc. Such policies have been extensively transferred overseas. For example, most US electronics companies have global policies opposed to the involvement of third parties (both trade unions and employers' associations in the subsidiary's internal industrial relations). Japanese companies have also transferred their distinctive industrial relations approach to their overseas subsidiaries. European companies and certain US businesses, on the other hand, have generally adopted the existing industrial relations customs and practices of the host country. Such differences are related to the different international strategies of the business. The relationship between human resource management and international strategy is discussed in the concluding section of this chapter.

Porter's global strategy and human resource strategy

Congruence between HR and corporate strategy

Several references have already been made in this chapter to the link between the global and transnational strategy of a company and its HR strategy. Porter's global strategy model can be employed to indicate various aspects of a transnational's HR strategy (Figure 9.2).

According to Porter, there are two key dimensions to a global as opposed to a domestic strategy, namely, configuration and co-ordination.

High co-ordination strategies Low local responsiveness	*Dispersed activities/high degree of co-ordination*	*Purest global strategy (with extensive co-ordination and concentration)*

HR Strategy requiring high degree of co-ordination:
- May necessitate the employment of home country nationals at subsidiary level
- Significant cross-national exchange of personnel
- Effective expatriate policies needed to ensure smooth exchange of staff
- A pool of internationally experienced executives
- Extensive international management development programme
- Labour problems at one location must not affect operations elsewhere
- Standardization of employee benefits between subsidiaries is necessary
- Significant transfer of parent country industrial relations practices to subsidiaries.

Low co-ordination strategies High local responsiveness	*Country centred strategy, dispersed activities/little co-ordination*	*Strategy based upon exporting of product with decentralized marketing in each host country*

HR strategy requiring local responsiveness:
- Predominance of host country nationals in key management positions at subsidiary level
- Limited cross-national transfers of personnel
- Little need for well-defined expatriate or international management development policies
- Industrial relations decision-making will be decentralized at subsidiary level
- Subsidiary industrial relations practices will be based on host country customs and practices.

Geographically dispersed activities   Geographically concentrated activities

Configuration of activities

FIGURE 9.2   HR strategy and degree of co-ordination of global activities (source: based on Porter 1986)

The former refers to the location of activities; the latter to the extent of co-ordination between locations. The combination of configuration and co-ordination options gives rise to Porter's four categories of international strategy (see Figure 9.2).

The human resource management problems will vary with the type of international strategy adopted. Thus, in country-centred businesses, the need for national responsiveness is more important than global co-ordination and direction. This implies a predominance of host country nationals in key management positions at subsidiary level and only limited cross-national transfers of personnel. Thus, country-centred businesses may have little need for well-defined expatriate or international management development policies. The need for national responsiveness also implies that industrial relations decision-making will be decentralized at subsidiary level and that subsidiary industrial relations practices will be based on host country customs and practices. A similar approach may be expected in businesses adopting an export-based strategy of concentration and minimum co-ordination.

The opposite approach to human resource management may be expected in geographically dispersed but highly co-ordinated transnationals (high foreign investment/extensive co-ordination). Here the need for global co-ordination and direction outweighs the need for national responsiveness. This may necessitate the employment of home country nationals at subsidiary level and a significant cross-national exchange of personnel. Effective expatriate policies will, therefore, be needed to ensure the smooth exchange of staff. The achievement of global co-ordination and direction also requires a pool of internationally experienced executives, which requires an extensive international management development programme. In the labour area, highly co-ordinated businesses must ensure that labour problems at one location do not affect operations elsewhere. Similarly, some standardization of employee benefits between subsidiaries will also be necessary. This implies an active parent company involvement in subsidiary industrial relations issues and a significant transfer of parent country industrial relations practices.

REVIEW AND DISCUSSION QUESTIONS

1. Explain the relationship between a business's transnational and human resource strategies.
2. Describe the basis of a 'strategic' approach to global human resource management.
3. Explain the relationships between a business's: (a) core competences and human resource strategy; and (b) generic strategy and human resource strategy.
4. Explain the importance of a transnational's expatriate and management development policies and practices.

5. Explain the relationship between an organization's global strategy (using Porter's model) and its expatriate and management development policies and practices.

References and further reading

Anthony, W.P., Perrewe, P. and Kacmar, K.M. (1993) *Strategic Human Resource Management*, Dryden Press, Harcourt Brace Jovanovich, New York.

Armstrong, M. (1992) *Human Resource Management: Strategy and Action*, Kogan Page, London.

Beer, M., Spector, B., Lawrence, P.R., Quinn, M.D. and Walton, R.E. (1984) *Managing Human Assets*, The Free Press, New York.

Bomers, G.B.J. and Peterson, R.B. (1977) Multinational corporations and industrial relations: the case of West Germany and the Netherlands, *British Journal of Industrial Relations*, **XV**(1).

Borrowman, W. (1969) The problem of expatriate personnel and their selection in international business, *Management International Review*.

Brewster, C. (1994) European HRM: reflection of, or challenge to, the American concept? In: Kirkbride, P.S. (ed.), *Human Resource Management in Europe*, Routledge, London.

Brewster, C. and Hegewisch, A. (eds) (1994) *Policy and Practice in European Human Resource Management: The Price Waterhouse Cranfield Survey*, Routledge, London.

Business International Corporation (1982) *Worldwide Executive Compensation and Human Resource Planning in Multinational Corporations*, BIC.

Chakravarthy, B.S. and Perlmutter, H.V. (1985) Strategic planning for a global business, *Columbia Journal of World Business*, Summer, 3–10.

Desatnick, R.L. and Bennett, M.L. (1977) *Human Resource Management in the Multinational Company*, Gower, Aldershot.

Doeringer, P.B. and Piore, M.J. (1971) *Internal Labour Markets and Manpower Analysis*, Heath, Lexington.

Edstrom, A. and Galbraith, J. (1977) Transfer of managers as a co-ordination and control strategy in multi-national firms, *Administrative Science Quarterly*, **22**(2).

Edwards, P., Ferner, A. and Sisson, K. (1996) The conditions for international human resource management: two case studies, *International Journal of Human Resource Management*, **7**(1), February, 20–40.

Fombrun, C.J., Tichy, N.M. and Devanna, M.A. (1985) *Strategic Human Resource Management*, John Wiley, New York.

Gunnigle, P. and Moore, S. (1996) Linking business strategy and human resource management: issues and implications, *Personnel Review*, **23**(1).

Hagan, C.M. (1996) The core competence organization: implications for human resource practices, *Human Resource Management Review*, **6**(2), 147–164.

Hamill, J. (1983) The labour relations practices of foreign-owned and indigenous firms, *Employee Relations*, **5**(1).

Hamill, J. (1984) Labour relations decision-making within multinational corporations, *Industrial Relations Journal*, Summer.

Hamill, J. (1989) Expatriate policies in British multinationals, *Journal of General Management*, **14**(4), Summer.

Harris, P. (1979) The unhappy world of the expatriate, *International Management*, July.

Harvey, M.C. (1982) The other side of foreign assignments: dealing with the repatriation dilemma, *Columbia Journal of World Business*, Spring.

Harvey, M.C. (1985) The executive family: an overlooked variable in international assignments, *Columbia Journal of World Business*, Spring.

Heijltjes, M., van Witteloostuijn, A. and Sorge, A. (1996) Human resource management in relation to generic strategies: a comparison of chemical food and drink companies in the Netherlands and Great Britain, *International Journal of Human Resource Management*, **7**(2), May, 383–412.

Heller, J.E. (1980) Criteria for selecting an international manager, *Personnel*, May/June.

Holmes, W. and Piker, F. (1980) Expatriate failure – prevention rather than cure, *Personnel Management*, December.

Howard, C.G. (1984) How relocation abroad affects expatriates' family life, *Personnel Administration*, November.

Lanier, A. (1979) Selecting and preparing personnel for overseas transfers, *Personnel Journal*, March.

Mahoney, T.A. and Deckop, J.R. (1986) Evolution of concept and practice in personnel administration/human resource management, *Journal of Management*, **12**(2), Summer.

Miller, E. (1972) The selection decision for an international assignment: a study of decision-maker's behaviour, *Journal of International Business Studies*.

Ohmae, K. (1990) *The Borderless World*, Collins, London.

Ondrack, D.A. (1985) International transfers of managers in North American and European MNEs, *Journal of International Business Studies*, Fall.

Perlmutter, H.V. (1984) Building the symbolic societal enterprise: a social architecture for the future, *World Futures*, **19**(3/4), 271–284.

Porter, M.E. (1986) *Competition in Global Business*, Harvard University Press, Boston.

Reynolds, C. (1979) Career paths and compensation in multinational corporations, in: Davis, S. (ed.), *Managing and Organizing Multinational Corporations*, Pergamon Press, New York.

Sieveking, N., Anchor, K. and Marston, R. (1981) Selection and preparing expatriate employees, *Personnel Journal*, March.

Thompson, J.L. (1993) *Strategic Management – Awareness and Change*, Chapman & Hall, London.

Tobiorn, L. (1982) *Living Abroad: Personal Adjustment and Personnel Policy in the Overseas Setting*, John Wiley, New York.

Toyne, B. and Kuhne, R.J. (1983) The management of the international executive compensation and benefits process, *Journal of International Business Studies*, Winter.

Tung, R.L. (1981) Selection and training of personnel for overseas assignments, *Columbia Journal of World Business*, Spring.

Tung, R.L. (1982) Selection and training procedures of US, European and Japanese multinationals, *California Management Review*, Fall.

Tung, R.L. (1984) Strategic management of human resources in the multinational enterprise, *Human Resource Management*, Summer.

Tung, R.L. (1988) *The New Expatriates: Managing Human Resources Abroad*, Ballinger, Cambridge, MA.

Tung, R.L. and Miller, E.L. (1990) Managing in the twenty-first century: the need for global orientation, *Management International Review*, **1**(90).

Van Den Bulcke, D. and Halsberghe, E. (1984) *Employment Decision-Making in Multinational Enterprises: Survey Results from Belgium*, ILO, Geneva.

Walker, J.W. (1992) *Human Resource Strategy*, McGraw-Hill, London.

Young, S., Hood, N. and Hamill, J. (1985) *Decision-Making in Foreign-Owned Multinational Subsidiaries in the United Kingdom*, ILO Working Paper, No. 35.

Zeira, Y. (1975) Overlooked personnel problems of multinational corporations, *Columbia Journal of World Business*.

GLOBAL TECHNOLOGY MANAGEMENT

10

CHAPTER

LEARNING OBJECTIVES

After studying this chapter, students should be able to:

- describe the linkages between technology and strategy;
- explain how technology can be defined and employed as a strategic asset;
- describe how technology can be used to enhance competitive advantage;
- describe how technology needs to be managed to enable it to be used to enhance global competitive advantage;
- explain what ICT is, how it has stimulated globalization and how it can be used in a company's technology strategy.

Introduction

The scope of what we refer to as 'technology' is too large to be considered in detail in a single chapter of a book of this type. The many ways in which the word is used is testimony to the plethora of ways in which it can impact upon business strategy. Technology can be found in electronics, chemicals, aerospace, telecommunications, design, production, logistics and many other fields – and in most cases, one technology is highly interconnected with other types. So whilst we might think of technology as describing computers and robots (which it certainly does), we should not forget that the same management skills required in these sectors are also required in every other area of technology: in pharmaceuticals, petrochemicals, automobiles and in hundreds of other contexts.

This chapter seeks to explain the key themes of technology strategy as it relates to international business. Much of the literature in this field has stressed the growing influence of technology on the competitiveness of international business. Harris *et al.* (1984) focused upon the influence of 'technology driven events' causing a lack of competitiveness in US industry. They correctly forecast that technology would continue to trigger major market shifts. Hence, the need for transnational businesses to adroitly manage technology is difficult to overstate.

Technology and strategy

> A powerful force drives the world toward a converging commonality, and that force is technology. It has proletarianized communication, transport and travel. It has made isolated places and impoverished peoples eager for modernity's allurements. Almost everyone everywhere wants all the things they have heard about, seen, or experienced via the new technologies. (Levitt 1983)

> Technology is, without doubt, one of the most important contributory factors underlying the internationalization and globalization of economic activity. (Dicken 1998)

The impact of technology on strategy

Theodore Levitt's (1983) prescient paper on market homogenization captured the enormous impact that technology has and will continue to have on markets and businesses. Although other authors (e.g. Douglas and Wind 1987) have pointed out weaknesses in Levitt's arguments, we can now look back and see how right he was to highlight the significance of technology in shaping the markets that the transnational deals with as well as the way in which the company is organized.

The effects of technology have, however, sometimes been different to those which Levitt discussed. For example, while communication technologies such as satellite television have continued to encourage a convergence of demand, flexible manufacturing technologies have enables businesses to offer a much greater variety of product designs without sacrificing economies of scale. Similarly, while the dramatic improvements in information technologies have enabled businesses to operate on a global scale, they have also enabled a move away from the old style multinational corporation with central control to the transnational with information shared throughout the organization.

Technology is one of the major factors behind the increased turbulence in the environment of many business sectors. The shortening of the new product design cycle through, for example, sophisticated CAD/CAM technologies has increased the rate of product obsolescence. Businesses have less time to respond to new developments and must make strategic decisions where the future becomes less and less predictable. The emergence of new, competing technologies and the acquisition of existing technologies by competitors can also increase the complexity of the environment. This complexity is even greater for the transnational facing both global and local competitors.

The general impact of technology on the macroenvironment has already been discussed in Chapter 5. The purpose of this chapter is to examine how the transnational can 'manage' technology as part of its corporate strategy. To do this we shall firstly consider the role of technology as a strategic asset and how it differs from more conventional assets; secondly we shall review the elements of a technology strategy – how the business responds to the challenges and opportunities posed by new technology; finally we shall examine the special cases of information and communication technologies (ICT) and their impact on the strategy and operations of the transnational.

Technology as a strategic asset

Defining technology

'Technology' is a word that is often used but not often explained. In this chapter we shall use the dictionary definition of the application of science to industry or commerce. There is an important distinction here; by 'science' we mean the results of fundamental academic investigations whilst by 'technology' we mean the *application* of science. This distinction is important when we consider how businesses acquire new technologies.

The importance of technology to a business lies in the fact that possession of a technology can give a competitive advantage. Technology can be therefore regarded as a strategic asset. Furthermore, we can also say that a business's ability to manage and exploit its technology can represent a core competence. There is also a close link between a company's ability to manage technology and its capacity to innovate. We shall now examine more closely how technology can give a competitive advantage through its products and production processes. The contribution that information and communication technologies can make to a business's operations will be discussed later in the chapter.

Technology and products

Technology can enhance a company's product portfolio in a number of ways.

New functions

A new product can be developed which allows the user to perform tasks that were hitherto not possible or else very difficult. An example of this is the development of the satellite telephone which allows the user to communicate from almost anywhere on the Earth's surface. Some customers are willing to pay high prices to own such a product. Such products are likely to be highly innovative requiring major investments in new technology.

New features

An existing product can be modified to make it more useful while the basic function remains the same; for example the development of compact satellite telephones which require almost no setting up. Companies continually seek innovations to differentiate their products from those of competitors. Although such innovations may be minor, over time these can add up to represent a significant advance in technology.

Greater reliability

As the technology becomes more mature, product reliability becomes a key factor in product differentiation. Design improvements and different assembly techniques will focus on performance and quality. For example, increased use of specialized integrated circuits can make the product easier to assemble and more robust.

Lower costs

As the product matures, the technology development focuses more on cost reduction. The use of specialized integrated circuits, mentioned above, which are expensive to design but in mass production offer huge cost advantages over discrete components, offers a tremendous advantage to the businesses which can master this technology.

Technology is one of the underlying reasons for the existence of a product life cycle. Product performance tends to follow an 'S' shaped curve as shown in Figure 10.1. When the technology is new, developments are rapid and product performance rises quickly. As the technology becomes mature, the rate of change of performance tends to level off as the technological limits are reached. At some point, a new technology may be developed and incorporated in the product. At first, product performance is lower than that of the existing technology. But as the invading technology is developed, product performance overtakes that of the current technology; eventually the old product/technology becomes obsolete.

As an example, consider the technology in wristwatches. The basic mechanism of the wristwatch was established around 1765. By the early twentieth century the watch was a sophisticated piece of precision mechanical engineering but there was relatively little rate of improvement in accuracy. When the electronic quartz movement was developed in the 1970s, the inherent accuracy was much greater than conventional mechanical movements. Since the quartz movement was also much cheaper to mass produce, the old mechanical technology was soon obsolete, with dramatic effect in the Swiss watch industry. The lesson here is that the invading technology can come from other industry sectors and other countries – and the time between initial launch and annihilation of the current product/technology can be quite rapid.

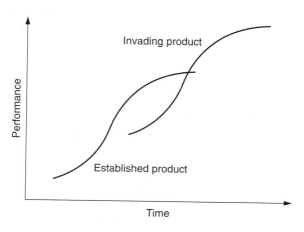

FIGURE 10.1   Performance of invading product compared to that of established product (source: Abernathy and Utterback 1978)

Technology and production

The section above has indicated that product design is a major factor in production cost. However the technologies used in the production process itself can lead to competitive advantage.

Shorter lead times
The use of CAD/CAM systems has dramatically reduced lead times from initial design to full-scale production. In many industries, components can be designed on computer and a prototype generated within a few hours. After testing is complete the computer-generated design can be used directly in the manufacturing process. Design information can be electronically transferred from one location to another.

Increased quality
The use of automated assembly, with robots as a leading example, can not only increase throughput but can reduce errors in complex, repetitive processes. Automation can also increase production flexibility; changes to a process can be introduced by reprogramming, which is faster and cheaper than hardware changes.

Reduced cost
The higher throughput and increased reliability offered by new technologies can also lead to reduced unit costs. With flexible manufacturing techniques large production runs are no longer required to keep unit costs low.

An example of technological change was the development by Pilkington Brothers of the float glass process. The traditional method of manufacturing flat glass was to pass molten glass through a series of rollers until it was the correct thickness; the glass has then to be polished on both sides. In the float process the glass flows in a continuous process across a bath of molten tin and emerges as a perfectly flat sheet at the other end with no rolling or polishing required. Although the development of the new process required a huge financial outlay it revolutionized the economics of flat glass production and put Pilkington in an unassailable competitive position.

Patterns of technological innovation

The pattern of technological innovation outlined above has been shown to apply to many product types. Abernathy and Utterback (1978) described a model of innovation summarized in Figure 10.2.

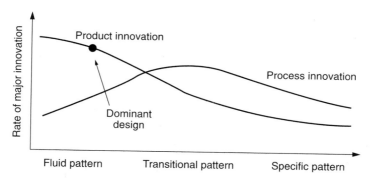

FIGURE 10.2   Patterns of innovation (source: Abernathy and Utterback 1978)

In the early stages of the product's life cycle, innovation dominates. The emphasis of technological development is on improving product performance, stimulated by information on user needs. The product design is 'fluid' with frequent major changes, together with flexible and inefficient production. Organizational control tends to be informal and entrepreneurial.

At some point a 'dominant design' emerges which all manufacturers adopt as a basic standard. The emphasis moves towards process innovation with the objective of reducing costs and improving quality. Changes are incremental and cumulative; products tend to be very similar. Production processes are efficient and capital intensive. Organizational control tends to be based on structure, goals and rules.

The significance of this for any business is that the nature of technological development and how it is managed changes greatly over the life of a product.

Differences between technology and other assets

Like other assets (except for some fixed assets), technology can be transferred from one location to another; it can be acquired and it can be considered as having value. The difference from other assets is that the *form* which the technology takes can vary. The clearest distinction is that between *tangible* and *intangible* technology. We can illustrate this difference in one way by considering how the technology appears to the user of the company's products.

Tangible technology

In the example mentioned above of the satellite telephone, the technology is embodied in the product itself and made available to the user. It would be possible for the user to 'reverse engineer' the telephone and acquire the company's technology to design and build its own telephones. Of course, reverse engineering complex integrated circuits and software is very difficult but most businesses make some attempt to examine their competitors' products to see if any secrets can be learned. The company must therefore find some means of protecting its technology.

Intangible technology

On the other hand, the user of glass manufactured by the float process would not be able to deduce from the product itself anything about the manufacturing process. The technology is not embodied in the product; this helps the company to protect its secrets from competitors. This technology in its purest form is intangible. The knowledge of how something is made may reside in the heads of a few key employees. It is much more difficult to talk about acquiring this kind of technology and even more difficult to value it. We shall consider this later in the section on technology transfer.

Technology and global competitiveness

Design technology

Many examples can be given of the link between technology and international competitiveness. In the consumer electronics industry, for example, international competitiveness depends to a significant extent on the continual introduction of new products incorporating new technology, e.g. VCRs; digital audio tapes; personal computers; electronic calculators; personal hi-fi systems; remote control and flat screen TVs etc. Similarly, in the pharmaceutical industry, the development and introduction of new drugs is a major determinant of transnational competitiveness – as in the case of Glaxo with its anti-ulcer drug Zantac and Hoffman-La-Roche with its anti-depressant drugs Valium and Librium.

Process technology

International competitiveness is also closely linked to new process developments, with one of the earliest examples being the pioneering of mass production technology by Ford. In the textile and clothing industry, producers in developed countries have responded to the flood of low-cost textile imports from developing countries by introducing increasingly automated production techniques.

Some businesses are more capable of generating a stock of proprietary information than they are of achieving commercial success. Others discover that their technology is more readily exploited by others who learn from their errors. In other cases, the company's international investment is largely motivated by the desire to acquire technology skills as a basis for a future stream of innovations.

Technology strategy

The components of a technology strategy

In order to exploit the opportunities and counter the challenges posed by technology, many transnational companies develop a technology strategy. Many businesses have some sort of 'IT strategy' which is rather limited in scope; here we suggest that this should be linked with a wider strategic approach to managing technology as a strategic asset. As with any other functional strategy (such as a human resource strategy), a technology strategy should be consistent with the overall corporate strategy and the objectives underlying that strategy.

The components of the strategy will vary from one business to another but in general will include:

- technology audit;
- sourcing new technology;
- exploiting technology;
- protecting the competitive advantage.

We consider each of these components in turn.

Technology audit

This activity is similar to the general internal analysis of the business described in Chapter 3. The purpose of such an audit (also known as an *innovation* audit) is to identify the specific technological competences within the business and match these against the opportunities the business intends to pursue in its corporate strategy. The outcome of the audit should be an estimate of the potential of the business to obtain a competitive advantage from the technology in one or more of the ways described earlier in this chapter. The audit should also identify technology 'gaps' which have to be filled. This information will be used to determine the level of investment in technological development required to meet corporate objectives and where that investment should be directed.

Goodman and Lawless (1994) described three systematic approaches to carrying out an audit which, when taken together, can present a useful picture of the business.

Technological innovation process audit

The aim of this is to construct a risk profile for existing and new projects by assessing the length and depth of the company's experience in its chosen technologies, its markets, project organization, the far environment and the industry structure. This can assist management in deciding which technological areas are more likely to be successful and which should perhaps be avoided as the risk of failure may be considered unacceptable.

Innovative comparison audit

This is an analysis of the business's innovative abilities compared to competitors. It requires an examination of the company's track record in new products, R&D staff capabilities, R&D performance, idea generation, time to commercialize (i.e. time to market), costs/benefits of R&D and relationships between R&D and other key functional areas.

Technological position audit

This reviews the technologies needed by the business and places them in one of four categories as shown in Table 10.1. For each category, the table shows a suggested level of investment that might be appropriate.

Sourcing new technology

Development or transfer?

Having identified weaknesses or gaps in its technology capabilities, management has a number of options to build new capabilities. The basic decision is to develop in-house or look externally. Some authors have discussed how the decision should be made; one example is the discussion in Roberts and Berry (1985). The key variable is the familiarity of the company with the technology, ranging from already making some use of the technology to simply being aware of the technology but without

Table 10.1   Technology categories (source: adapted from Goodman and Lawless 1994)

Category	Description	Investment level
Base	Technological foundation of business; widely available to competitors	Needs little
Key	Technologies with the greatest impact on competitive performance	Systematically built
Pacing	Technologies in early development which have the demonstrated potential to alter the basis of competition	Selective investment
Emerging	Technologies with long-term promise to alter the basis of competition	Monitored

any practical experience. Figure 10.3 summarizes the recommended approaches.

Roberts and Berry (1985) noted that joint ventures were often between a large business with an established market position and a small business with a new technology seeking entry to market. It is interesting to note that acquisition is not a recommended method when the company is unfamiliar with the technology – failure rates tend to be high in such circumstances.

For most large transnationals (especially those operating in technology intensive industries), new technology emerges mainly from the results of internally generated research and development. It is important to be aware, however, that there are a range of alternative sources of technology available to a business where a distinction is made between internal and external sources, both domestic and foreign. While large transnationals may rely mainly on internal R&D, smaller and non-dominant transnationals may focus on external sources of technology transfer and accumulation, since these will reduce the high capital expenditures involved.

Recent years have seen a rapid growth in the use made of these alternative forms of technology acquisition and development given the pace

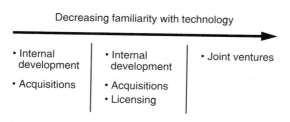

FIGURE 10.3   Optimum entry methods for new technologies (source: adapted from Roberts and Berry 1985)

of technology change, shortening product life cycles and the intensity of global competition. For example, foreign acquisitions of US companies have increased rapidly (in both number and value) since the late 1970s. Although motivated mainly by the need to gain access to US markets and existing distribution outlets, many US acquisitions have been motivated (at least in part) by the desire to acquire US technology (Hamill 1988). Similarly, recent years have seen the growing importance of joint government/industry sponsored research initiatives, mainly in the electronics industry and in various forms of international collaboration between organizations of different nationalities, including strategic alliances.

While the objectives of these various options are similar (i.e. technology development and transfer), the management implications of internal and external forms of technology acquisition differ significantly.

Some of the major management decisions which need to be taken in the case of internally generated R&D include:

- the level of R&D expenditure;
- the focus of R&D effort;
- the location of R&D, i.e. the centralization/decentralization issue;
- the nature of R&D undertaken at subsidiary level;
- the transfer and diffusion of R&D results throughout the global network.

External forms of technology involve partnerships and collaboration between unrelated concerns. The major managerial issues involved, therefore, relate to the planning, negotiation and organization of collaborative agreements (this issue is examined in more detail in Chapter 14).

Problems with technology transfer
The problems associated with the successful transfer of technology into an organization are closely related to those in any merger or acquisition and require careful management. We have already mentioned that technology can exist both as a tangible and intangible asset. Simply acquiring a few product samples and manufacturing drawings does little more than permit the company, at best, to manufacture a copy of the original product. If the acquiring business is unfamiliar with the technology, it is also necessary to acquire the underlying knowledge that went into the design of the product. Only then can the business expect to be able to continue the product and process innovations discussed earlier that are an essential part of achieving

a sustainable competitive advantage. The business therefore needs to have available the key technologists in the source organization either as new employees of the business or on some kind of consultancy basis to educate the current employees.

Another problem can be caused by the acquiring company not having the appropriate expertise to manufacture the product in a reliable way. Once again the acquirer may have to go through a substantial learning period. The difficulties may be increased if the source company is small and entrepreneurial; as we have already seen, production processes in such companies may be inefficient and poorly documented.

A further problem in technology transfer is caused by the nature of technology itself – something between science and its practical application. The relationship is shown schematically in Figure 10.4.

The nature, location and timescales of the three types of activity can be very different. Acquisition of a technology which is still in the experimental stage is risky; there may be culture clashes between the technologists in the business and the scientists who carried out the original research. The problems are similar to the clashes that may occur between technologists in an R&D department and the engineers in a manufacturing department. All parties need to have a good understanding of each other's needs and problems for the transfer to be successful.

Exploiting new technology

The process of technology development and acquisition (discussed in the previous section) represents only the first stage in effectively managing technology within the transnational business. There are many companies

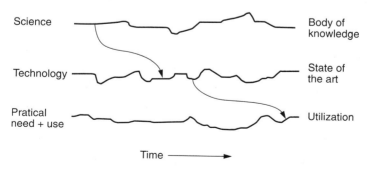

FIGURE 10.4   Science, technology and the utilization of their products (source: Allen 1984)

that have successfully generated new proprietary technology, but that have failed to exploit such know-how commercially. In order to commercially exploit new technology know-how, two other stages need to be covered in the company's technology strategy.

First, effective organizational channels need to be established for transferring technology throughout the transnational network. Second, the organization needs to determine the most effective foreign market entry and development strategy for exploiting the newly acquired technology know-how. This (second point) involves an assessment of the relative merits of exporting, licensing, joint-ventures, FDI etc. (see Chapter 7).

The two key issues relating to the process of technology diffusion within the transnational are the location of R&D activity and the organizational structure.

Location of R&D activity

Most transnationals adopt a qualified policy of centralization in R&D. Where decentralization does occur, overseas R&D units tend to take the form of technology transfer units to assist in the transfer of technology from parent to foreign subsidiary (Hakanson 1983; Ronstadt 1977, 1978). The importance of these units is that technology can rarely be transferred without some form of modification. There is evidence (Davidson 1980) to suggest that the speed, rate and extent of technology transfer have accelerated over time, reflecting the transnational's need to apply new technology throughout the international network almost immediately in order to obtain (even a brief) competitive advantage. In these circumstances, the transnational's competitive position is enhanced if its key subsidiaries have some development capability and can handle much of their own adaptation. As a result, this is perhaps one of the strongest motivations for a measure of R&D decentralization in recent years.

Structure and technology exploitation

The organizational structure of the transnational plays an important role in its ability to transfer technology. Davidson (1983), for example, found that the transfer performance of companies organized along matrix lines was superior to those with alternative organizational structures, especially those with global product divisions. He argued that, in this context, accumulated experience and information is better exploited in more centralized structures. Thus, global matrix companies tend to transfer new products more rapidly and more extensively to foreign subsidiaries.

Systems to support technology exploitation

There have been a number of attempts to address the question of appropriate systems for the management and transfer of technology within the business. One of the earliest and most comprehensive by Burns and Stalker (1961) noted the need to move from mechanistic to organic models of organization of work in the transfer into new technologies. Many transnationals are frequently, if not constantly, in that change process. Gresov (1984) captured this position quite effectively for transnationals. Recognizing that the successful management of technology involves the two distinct processes of innovation and implementation, he observes two organizational dilemmas. Where the business is centralized, implementation is usually improved at the expense of innovation; with a complex organizational design, the converse is true.

Similarly with an organization's culture: a homogeneous culture favours implementation at the cost of innovation, with the reverse holding true for a heterogeneous organizational culture. Gresov (1984) suggested that it may, for instance, be possible to compensate for the poorer adoptive capacity of the centralized structure by encouraging and promoting cultural heterogeneity. Similarly, by extending aspects of the homogeneous organizational culture, the implementation weaknesses of the complex structural form might be improved. The resulting trade-off may produce a solution which improves the company's overall capacity to manage its technology.

Protecting the competitive advantage

If possession and application of one or more key technologies give a business a significant competitive advantage, the business needs to consider how it can ensure that such technologies remain proprietary for as long as possible. We mentioned earlier that it is easier for process technologies to be kept secret than for technologies which are embedded within the final product. Even so, the company would be wise to consider how it can maintain the value of its intellectual property. The business has two main courses of action: it can apply for a patent or it may choose to keep the technology as a trade secret.

Patents

If the technology and its application are considered sufficiently novel, the company may be granted a patent which gives the company the exclusive rights to the benefits of the technology for a certain period (20 years in the USA). There are, however, some disadvantages in gaining a patent.

- In return for the patent, the company must publish openly a detailed explanation of the technology and its application. This information is freely available to competitors who may use it to develop alternative forms of technology which they themselves can patent. Once the patent expires no further protection is possible.
- Although 20 years may seem a long time the actual time during which the company can profit from the technology may be much less. For example it can take several years after the patent is filed for new compounds developed by pharmaceutical companies to enter the market.
- If the patent is contested by another company the cost of patent litigation can be rather high.
- The cost of filing an application and keeping the patent in force in several countries can be quite high; however for a transnational of any size this should not be a serious problem.
- Different countries have different patent systems so each patent application may have to be adapted. This problem is being reduced by the increasing co-operation between governments; for example only one application is necessary for protection in all members of the EU.
- It is not possible to gain such protection in some countries so competitors there are free to sell goods using the technology in such countries.

However, the benefits in owning a patent are considerable. The protection offered by the patent means that it has measurable *value*. This means that it can be used as an instrument of negotiation; for example the company may grant a licence to a competitor allowing it to use the technology in return for royalty payments. This was the approach used by Pilkington after it developed the float glass technology in the 1960s. The company received substantial payments from competitors throughout the world for many years without itself having to make substantial capital investments. However this approach was later criticized as being too risk averse (Stopford and Turner 1985).

Trade secrets
If the company believes that it can keep the technology secret for a substantial length of time then it can obtain the benefits of the technology

without the drawbacks of the patent approach. This approach is particularly useful when the company can bring the product to market rapidly so that even if competitors can copy the technology the company still has a substantial lead. However, the company should maintain certified records to prove that it developed the technology first to prevent a competitor obtaining a patent for themselves.

Comparisons of transnational technological performance

Comparing US and Japanese performance

Transnationals have differential rates of success in maintaining technological advantage. Over recent years there has been much discussion about different levels of innovation and their influence on competitiveness. Much of this has been motivated by the decline in US and European competitiveness in many fields and by the growth of Japanese exports. While some of the explanations for these changes lie at the macro level, managers of transnationals are increasingly sensitive to company-specific dimensions.

On national comparisons, Johnson (1984) compared the R&D strategies of Japanese and US companies to determine whether differences in these had contributed to different competitive positions. He noted that Japanese businesses:

- invested more heavily in applied research and product development (and less in basic research projects);
- invested more on building on pre-existing products and technologies developed by other companies in the same or related industries, rather than in the development of new, unproven products or technologies;
- tended to follow the products or technologies of other businesses, rather than trying to be first.

This pattern of difference is by now well established, of course, and Johnson showed that over the period 1965–1981, Japanese companies pursuing such strategies had a substantially higher private rate of return than their US counterparts. In seeking explanations for this, he emphasized the importance of differential government subsidiaries and tax incentives for R&D in the two countries. He also indicated that the US government's strict enforcement of the patent system has deterred many US companies from taking advantage of opportunities to build on the products and technologies of their foreign competitors.

Commentary on different home nation support environments for technology has become an increasingly important dimension of this debate. Daneke (1984), for example, contrasted the US/Japanese policy approaches by illustrations from the biotechnology industry. Japanese businesses have benefited from their government's policy of making biotechnology a national priority, providing direct public financing for private sector R&D and the commercialization of its output, compared to the (less effective) US motivation of tax incentives. Daneke believes that the US governmental policy will effectively drive a wedge between the successful and entrepreneurial aspects of biotechnology, allowing Japanese and European transnationals to take the lead.

Learning good practice

Another important aspect of comparative work has inevitably been that of the identification of lessons from practice at a corporate level. Here again there are illustrations from the literature. Maidique and Hayes (1984) examined a large sample of US high-technology companies, including many transnationals, in an endeavour to trace the origins of their successful technology management.

They found that five themes emerged and while no one of the companies showed excellence in all areas at any one time, neither were the less successful deficient in all of them.

- *Business focus*. This was clearly related to success, with the examples of IBM, Boeing, Intel (integrated circuits) and Genentech (genetic engineering) being cited as among those whose sales were largely in single or clearly related product groups.
- *Adaptability*. Having a long-term focus, but also with the capability for rapid change. Not strategically immobile.
- *Organizational cohesion*. Widely regarded as critical in successful high-technology companies. Reflected for example, in Hewlett-Packard's 50 divisions; Texas Instruments with some 30 divisions and 250 tactical action programmes.
- *Sense of integrity*. Desire to maintain positive stable associations with all interest groups.

- *'Hands-on' top management.* Deep involvement in the assessment process of technological advance.

Information and communication technologies

The effects of ICT

Technological change, particularly the development of information and communications technology (ICT), has been among the most important driving forces behind globalization. While developments in transport have played a major role in internationalizing industries and markets, by making it possible to transfer resources and goods between countries and continents, it is ICT, probably more than any other single factor, which has caused globalization. Developments like satellite television have helped to bring about convergence of customer wants and needs. ICT has had an even more significant impact on the ability of businesses to co-ordinate value-adding activities across national boundaries in remote geographical locations while still permitting local responsiveness when and where it may be required.

The key to successful global strategy can often be found in ICT. The technology is important because of the role that it plays in the processes of organizational learning and in knowledge management (Stonehouse and Pemberton 1999). ICT is both a powerful competitive weapon and a major integrating force for the business. ICT can assist in building and leveraging core competences, in reducing costs and in differentiating products. The impact of ICT has not, however, been entirely positive and it is cited as a major cause of hypercompetition and environmental turbulence (Chakravarthy 1997).

Ironically it is ICT, in the context of organizational learning and knowledge management, which offers the best hope to businesses seeking to acquire and sustain competitive advantage in turbulent environments (Stonehouse and Pemberton 1999). This section examines the changes which have taken place in information and communications technology and their impact on the global strategies of transnationals.

Developments in ICT

ICT alone has not driven the globalization of business activity but without recent developments in ICT it is difficult to see how globalization could have developed to such an extent. For many years, the level of technology was a major factor inhibiting those businesses seeking to achieve superior performance through their distinctive global architecture and co-ordination. According to Dicken (1992), 'both the geographical and organizational scale at which any human activity can occur is directly related to the available media of transport and communication'. The physical barriers to the movement of materials and products have been substantially reduced by the improvements in transport technology. They have revolutionized logistics and resulted in global shrinkage, opening up the possibility of new configurations to transnationals.

Of even greater significance to the globalization of business activity have been the developments in ICT. In this context, 'convergent IT' (Hall and Preston 1988), or the integration of computers and telecommunications into a unified system for the processing and interchange of business information, has been of singular importance. This convergence has opened new opportunities to transnationals for the acquisition of global competitive advantage.

The two most important contributions to the development of convergent IT have been in the areas of computing power and connectivity. There has been a 'radical change in information architecture' (Laudon and Laudon, 1991). There has been a move from centralized to distributed processing via PCs and workstations. Most of these have processing, display and storage capabilities well in excess of some of their mainframe predecessors. Helms and Wright (1992) predicted that 'By the year 2000, over 15 million personal computers will be installed in businesses with 40% connected through far-reaching networks'. In fact, this figure was greatly exceeded, such is the pace of change in ICT. The average personal computer has immeasurably more processing power and speed than the most powerful mainframe in the 1970s and at a tiny fraction of the cost. Thus, not only has computing power increased beyond recognition in the last thirty years, but information and knowledge have become relatively cheap and far more accessible as resources.

Accompanying developments in software have the potential to empower individual managers and at a price which is no longer prohibitive. Spreadsheets, databases, word processors and the like have made powerful business software accessible to all managers. One of the major problems faced by managers in international enterprises is the volume and complexity of data which has to be analysed before decisions can be made. In this respect, Decision Support Systems (DSS), Expert Systems, Neural

Networks, Multimedia, Intelligent Databases and Artificial Intelligence all have an important role to play. Parsaye (1989) stated that 'The implementation of intelligent databases was inconceivable prior to the implementation of hypermedia systems, advanced microcomputer workstations and expert systems. Now that these technologies have matured, intelligent databases can be used to respond to the needs of data rich and information poor users'. Software developments, allied to hardware, are at the root of Executive Information Systems (EIS) and Strategic Information Systems (SIS). From complex, conflicting and incomplete data such systems help to produce the information and knowledge which support improved decision making and enhance organizational responsiveness in increasingly chaotic and hypercompetitive environments.

The value of this individual power has been augmented by developments in connectivity. Local Area Networks and Wide Area Networks are the basis of this connectivity. Developments in telecommunications, like satellite and cable links, have drastically improved inter- and intra-company communications. They have made possible increased co-ordination of geographically dispersed organizations. Equally, they have improved linkages in the value chain between businesses, their suppliers and distributors. It is these developments which have made possible the development of the internet which has already had a dramatic impact on business activity, particularly on the links between businesses and their customers.

ICT and transnational strategy

The technological developments in ICT, particularly those which have improved networking and connectivity, have important implications for the architecture of transnational organizations, for the management of knowledge and for co-ordination of activities and for flexibility and responsiveness. According to Frankovich (1998), 'Any business seeking to globalize its operations has a major IT challenge on its hands. Never has the intelligent application of technology been more important to improving business performance'.

In Chapter 6 we identified several potential sources of global competitive advantage centred on the core competences, generic and transnational strategies of the organization. Knowledge and information have become the major resources underpinning competitive advantage (see Chapter 15). ICT plays a vital role in the collection of information, its manipulation, analysis, storage and interpretation and in the generation of new organizational knowledge which forms the basis of core competences. ICT has provided the infrastructure needed to support network organizational structures which can be important to both organizational learning and transnational business (Bartlett and Ghoshal 1995; Stonehouse and Pemberton 1999).

Core competences can be based upon knowledge of customers and their needs, knowledge of technology and how to employ it in distinctive ways, knowledge of products and processes etc. Microsoft's core competences are based upon its knowledge of how to build and market operating systems and software. Equally, Microsoft's competitive advantage is based upon its knowledge of computer hardware and networking, and its knowledge of the companies that produce those products. Microsoft has leveraged its competences in personal computer operating systems and software, and also built new associated competences in order to build competitive advantage in computer networking and internet software. Such competence building and leveraging is largely knowledge-based.

ICT has also assisted the process of building collaborative business networks which are also a valuable source of competitive advantage. Network members can concentrate on their individual core competences and, by pooling them together in network activities, synergy is created. ICT has made it possible to integrate network activities far more effectively and efficiently, leading to the development of what are often called *virtual corporations* (Davidow and Malone 1992). In the airline industry, alliances use ICT to co-ordinate and integrate flight schedules, bookings and prices.

As we saw in Chapter 6, according to Porter's model of global strategy (Porter 1986a, 1990) competitive advantage is viewed as arising from the *configuration of organizational activities* (i.e. where, and in how many nations each activity in the value chain is performed) and *co-ordination* (how dispersed international activities are co-ordinated). ICT has transformed the ability of transnationals to co-ordinate their activities in geographically remote locations. This has increased the range of alternative configurations of activities available to them, thus making it possible to gain global competitive advantage by choosing distinctive configurations for value-adding activities. In addition, ICT has made it possible to achieve co-ordination and integration at the same time as maintaining a high degree of flexibility and responsiveness.

Configuring ICT for transnational business

According to Frankovich (1998), IT in global business is typically configured in four basic ways:

- *Centralized:* strong control from headquarters;
- *Replicated:* identical country systems;
- *Autonomous:* dissimilar and unco-ordinated country systems;
- *Integrated:* compatible and co-ordinated systems.

There is no ideal configuration for ICT and the configuration chosen will depend upon the transnational strategy of the organization. The globalization drivers (Yip 1992) will dictate the extent to which local responsiveness is required. A centralized configuration will suffer from lack of flexibility and is likely to hinder responsiveness. A replicated configuration will include unnecessary duplication. When responsiveness is the priority, an autonomous configuration may well be chosen but this will hinder the co-ordination of global activities. A truly transnational strategy is likely to be associated with an integrated configuration where there is co-ordination combined with a degree of local variation to allow for local responsiveness.

REVIEW AND DISCUSSION QUESTIONS

1. Define what is meant by the word 'technology'.
2. How can technology make products more competitive?
3. Explain how technology can assist in making production more competitive.
4. What is a technology audit and what does it contain?
5. Define and distinguish between technology development and technology transfer.
6. When might a company, having made a technological innovation, use a patent and when might it keep its development secret?
7. What is included in ICT and how has it contributed to globalization?
8. What is convergent IT and why has it been a major cause of globalization?

References and further reading

Abernathy, W.J. and Utterback, J.M. (1978) Patterns of industrial innovation, *Technology Review*, June/July, 40–47.

Allen, T.J. (1984) *Managing the Flow of Technology*, MIT Press, Cambridge, MA.

Andrews, F.J. (1954) The learning curve as a production tool, *Harvard Business Review*, Jan/Feb, 1–11.

Argyris, C. (1977) Double loop learning in organizations, *Harvard Business Review*, September/October, 115–125.

Argyris, C. (1992) *On Organizational Learning*, Blackwell, Cambridge, MA.

Argyris, C. and Schon, D. (1978) *Organization Learning: A Theory of Action Perspective*, Addison Wesley, Reading, MA.

Avishar, B. and Taylor, W. (1989) Customers drive a technology-driven company: an interview with George Fisher, *Harvard Business Review*, November/December.

Bagchi, P.K. (1992) International logistics information systems, *International Journal of Physical Distribution and Logistics Management*, **22**(9), 11–19.

Barber, C.E., Pemberton, J. and Stonehouse, G.H. (1993) Airline developed computer reservation systems: a turbulent course ahead?, *European Business and Economic Development*, **2**(3), 30–35.

Barber, C. (1998) *CRS Information and Competitive Advantage in the Airline Industry*, Unpublished PhD Thesis, University of Northumbria, Newcastle.

Bartlett, C.A. and Ghoshal, S. (1995) *Transnational Management: Text, Cases and Readings in Cross-Border Management*, R.D. Irwin, Homewood.

Beaumont, J.R. and Sutherland, E. (1992) *Information Resource Management*, Butterworth Heinemann, Oxford.

Beaumont, J.R. and Walters, D. (1991) Information management in service industries: towards a strategic framework, *Journal of Information Systems*, **1**(3), 155–172.

Behrman, J.N. and Fischer, W.A. (1980) Transnational corporations: market orientations and R&D abroad, *Columbia Journal of World Business*, **15**.

Benjamin, R.I. and Blunt, J. (1992) Critical IT issues: the next ten years, *Sloan Management Review*, Summer, 7–19.

Bjornsonn, H. and Lundegard, R. (1992) Corporate competitiveness and information technology, *European Management Journal*, **10**(3), 341–347.

Brown, J.K. and Elvers, L.M. (eds.) (1983) *Research and Development: Key Issues for Management*, The Conference Board, New York.

Burns, T. and Stalker, G.M. (1961) *The Management of Innovation*, Tavistock Publications, London.

Camillus, J.C. (1984) Technology-driven and market-driven life cycles, *Columbia Journal of World Business*, Summer, 56–60.

Caves, R.E. (1982) Multinational enterprises and technology transfer, in: Rugman, A.M. (ed.), *New Theories of the Multinational Enterprise*, Croom Helm, London, pp. 254–293.

Chakravarthy, B. (1997) A new strategy framework for coping with turbulence, *Sloan Management Review*, Winter, 69–82.

Clark, K.B. (1989) What strategy can do for technology, *Harvard Business Review*, November/December.

Cravens, D.W., Greenley, G., Piercy, N.F. and Slater, S. (1997) Integrating contemporary strategic management perspectives, *Long Range Planning*, **30**(4), 493–506.

Cravens, D.W., Piercy, N.F. and Shipp, S.H. (1996) New organizational forms for competing in highly dynamic environments: the network paradigm, *British Journal of Management*, **7**(3), September.

Daneke, G.A. (1984) The global contest over the control of the innovation process, *Columbia Journal of World Business*, Winter, 83–87.

Davidow, W.H. and Malone, M.S. (1992) *Structuring and Revitalising the Corporation for the 21st Century – The Virtual Corporation*, Harper Business, London.

Davidson, W.H. (1980) *Experience Effects in International Investment and Technology Transfer*, UMI Research Press.

Davidson, W.H. (1983) Structure and performance in international technology transfer, *Journal of Management Studies*, **20**, 453–465.

De Meyer, A. and Ferdows, K. (1985) Integration of information systems in manufacturing, *International Journal of Operations and Production Management (UK)*, **5**(2), 5–12.

Demarest, M. (1997) Understanding knowledge management, *Long Range Planning*, **30**(3), 374–384.

Dicken, P. (1992) *Global Shift – The Internationalization of Economic Activity*, Paul Chapman Publishing, London.

Dicken, P. (1998) *Global Shift – Transforming the World Economy*, Paul Chapman Publishing, London.

Douglas, S. and Wind, Y. (1987) The myth of globalization, *Columbia Journal of World Business*, Winter.

Earl, M.J. (1980) *Management Strategies for Information Technology*, Prentice Hall, Englewood Cliffs.

Frankovich, J. (1998) The techno-world, in *Mastering Global Business*, PriceWaterhouseCoopers/FT, Pitman, London.

Galliers, R.D. (1990) Pinstripes at the terminals, *Times Higher Education Supplement*, 29 June, p. 26.

Gamble, P.R. (1992) The virtual corporation: an IT challenge, *Logistics Information Management*, **5**(4), 34–37.

Ghoshal, S. and Butler, C. (1992) *Kao Corporation*, INSEAD-EAC, Fontainebleau, France.

Gomery, R.E. (1989) From the 'Ladder of Science' to the product development cycle, *Harvard Business Review*, November/December.

Goodman, R.A. and Lawless, M.W. (1994) *Technology and Strategy*, Oxford University Press, Oxford.

Grant, R.M. (1997) The knowledge-based view of the firm: implications for management practice, *Long Range Planning*, **30**(3), 450–454.

Gresov, C. (1984) Designing organizations to innovate and implement, *Columbia Journal of World Business*, **19**(4), 63–67.

Hakanson, L. (1983) R&D in foreign-owned subsidiaries in Sweden, in: *Governments and Multinationals, The Policy Control Versus Autonomy*, Goldberg, W. (ed.), Oelgeschlager, Gunn and Hain, Cambridge, MA, pp. 163–176.

Hamill, J. (1988) British acquisitions in the US, *National Westminster Bank Quarterly Review*, August.

Hall, P. and Preston, P. (1988) *The Carrier Wave: New Information Technology and the Geography of Information, 1846–2003*, Unwin Hyman.

Harris, I.M., Shaw, R.W. and Sommers, W.P. (1984) The strategic management of technology, in: *Competitive Strategic Management*, Lamb, R.B. (ed.), Prentice Hall, Englewood Cliffs.

Helms, M.M. and Wright, P. (1992) External considerations: their influence on future strategic planning, *Management Decision*, **30**(8), 4–11.

Hilgard, E.R. and Bower, G.H. (1967) *Theories of Learning*, Appleton, New York.

Hirschey, R.C. and Caves, R.E. (1981) Internationalization of research and transfer of technology by multinational enterprises, *Oxford Bulletin of Economics and Statistics*, **42**, May, 115–130.

Hopper, M.D. (1990) Rattling sabre: new ways to compete on information, *Harvard Business Review*, **68**(3), 118–125.

Inkpen, A.C. and Crossan, M.M. (1995) Believing is seeing: joint ventures and organization learning, *Journal of Management Studies*, **32**(5), 595–618.

Jackson, T. (1993) *Organizational Behaviour in International Management*, Butterworth-Heinemann, Oxford.

Jelinek, M. and Golhar, J.D. (1983) The interface between strategy and manufacturing technology, *Columbia Journal of World Business*, Spring.

Johnson, S.B. (1984) Comparing R&D strategies of Japanese and US firms, *Sloan Management Review*, **25**(3), 25–34.

Kamoche, K. (1997) Knowledge creation and learning in international human resource management, *International Journal of Human Resource Management*, **8**(3), April, 213–225.

Kay, J. (1993) *Foundations of Corporate Success*, Oxford University Press, Oxford.

Keen, P.G.W. (1987) An international perspective on managing information technologies, an ICIT briefing paper, International Center for Information Technologies, Washington DC.

Kolb, D.A., Rubin, I.M. and Osland J. (1991) *Organizational Behaviour: An Experiential Approach*, Prentice Hall, Englewood Cliffs.

Laudon, K.C. and Laudon, J.P. (1991) *Management Information Systems – A Contemporary Perspective*, Macmillan, London.

Levitt, T. (1983) The globalization of markets, *Harvard Business Review*, May/June.

Liao, W.M. (1979) Effects of learning on resource allocation decisions, *Decision Sciences*, **10**(1), January, 116–125.

Maidique, M.A. and Hayes, R.H. (1984) The art of high technology management, *Sloan Management Review*, **25**(2), 17–31.

Mansfield, E., Teece, D.J. and Romeo, A. (1979) Overseas research and development by US-based firms, *Economica*, **46** (May), 187–196.

Martin, J. (1984) *An Information Systems Manifesto*, Prentice Hall, Englewood Cliffs.

Martin, J. (1990) *Information Engineering*, Vols 1–3, Prentice Hall, Englewood Cliffs.

Martin, N. and Hough, D. (1990) The open systems revolution: opportunities for the logistics industry, *Logistics Information Management*, **5**(3), 19–23.

McMaster, M. (1997) Organizing for innovation; technology and intelligent capacities, *Long Range Planning*, **30**(5), 799–802.

Parsaye K. (1989) *Intelligent Databases*, John Wiley, New York.

Parsons, G.L. (1983) Information technology: a new competitive weapon, *Sloan Management Review*, **25**(1), 3–13.

Pavitt, K. (1984) Technology transfer amongst the industrially advanced countries: an overview, in: *International Technology Transfer*, Rosenberg, N. (ed.), Wiley, Chichester.

Pavitt, K. (1986) Technology, innovation and strategic management, in: *Strategic Management Research*, McGee, J. and Thomas, A. (eds), Wiley, London, pp. 171–190.

Porter, M.E. (1985) *Competitive Advantage*, The Free Press, New York.

Porter, M.E. (1986a) Changing patterns of international competition, *California Management Review*, **28**(2), Winter, 9–40.

Porter, M.E. (1986b) *Competition in Global Business*, Harvard University Press, Boston.

Porter, M.E. (1990) *The Competitive Advantage of Nations*, The Free Press, New York.

Porter, M.E. and Millar, V.E. (1985) How information gives you competitive advantage, *Harvard Business Review*, **63**(4), 149–160.

Prahalad, C.K. and Doz, Y.L. (1997) The multinational mission: balancing local demands and global vision, The Free Press, New York.

Prahalad, C.K. and Hamel, G. (1989) Strategic intent, *Harvard Business Review*, 63–76.

Prahalad, C.K. and Hamel, G. (1990) The core competence of the corporation, *Harvard Business Review*, May/June, 79–91.

Quinn, J.B. (1992) *The Intelligent Enterprise*, Free Press, New York.

Quintas, P. and Lefevre, P. (1997) Knowledge management: a strategic agenda, *Long Range Planning*, **30**(3), 385–397.

Roberts, E.B. and Berry, C.A. (1985) Entering new businesses: selecting strategies for success, *Sloan Management Review*, Spring, 3–17.

Rogers, D.S., Daugherty, P.J. and Stank, T.P. (1993) Enhancing service responsiveness: the strategic potential of EDI, *Logistics Information Management*, **6**(3), 27–32.

Ronstadt, R. (1977) *Research and Development Abroad by US Multinationals*, Praeger, New York.

Ronstadt, R. (1978) International R&D: the establishment and evolution of research and development abroad by US multinationals, *Journal of International Business Studies*, **9**, 7–24.

Sanchez, R. and Heene, A. (eds) (1997) *Strategic Learning and Knowledge Management*, John Wiley, New York.

Senge, P. (1990a) Building learning organizations, *Sloan Management Review*, Fall.

Senge, P. (1990b) *The Fifth Discipline: the Art and Practice of the Learning Organization*, Century Business, London.

Severn, A.K. and Laurance, M.M. (1974) Direct investment, research intensity and profitability, *Journal of Financial and Quantitative Analysis*, **9**, March, 181–190.

Steele, L.W. (1975) *Innovation in Big Business*, Elsevier, New York.

Stonehouse, G.H. and Pemberton, J. (1999) Learning and knowledge management in the intelligent organization, *Participation and Empowerment: An International Journal*, **7**(5), 131–144.

Stopford, J.M. and Turner, L. (1985) *Britain and the Multinationals*. John Wiley, New York.

Teece, D.J. (1977) *Technology Transfer by Multinational Firms*, Ballinger, Cambridge, MA.

Tsurumi, U. (1976) *The Japanese are Coming: A Multinational Spread of Japanese Firms*, Ballinger, Cambridge, MA.

Turner, I. (1996) Working with chaos, *Financial Times*, 4th October.

Volberda, H.W. (1997) Building flexible organizations for fast-moving markets, *Long Range Planning*, **30**(2), 169–183.

Whitehill, M. (1997) Knowledge-based strategy to deliver sustained competitive advantage, *Long Range Planning*, **30**(4), 621–627.

Wilson, I. (1986) The strategic management of technology: corporate fad or strategic necessity, *Long Range Planning*, **19**(2), 21–22.

Wiseman, C. (1985) *Strategy and Computers: Information Systems as Competitive Weapons*, Dow Jones, Irwin, Homewood.

Wyman, J. (1985) SMR forum technological myopia – the need to think about technology, *Sloan Management Review*, **26**(4), Summer.

Yelle, L.E. (1979) The learning curve: historical review and comprehensive survey, *Decision Sciences*, **10**(2), April, 302–328.

Yip, G.S. (1992) *Total Global Strategy – Managing for Worldwide Competitive Advantage*, Prentice Hall, Englewood Cliffs, NJ.

Zuboff, S. (1988) *In the Age of the Smart Machine*, Heinemann, London.

GLOBAL AND TRANSNATIONAL MARKETING MANAGEMENT

11

CHAPTER

LEARNING OBJECTIVES

After studying this chapter, students should be able to:

- understand the role of marketing in global strategy and global competitiveness;
- explain the alternative global marketing strategies available to global businesses;
- describe the importance of global market segmentation and positioning strategies;
- describe the important issues arising in the global management of marketing mix variables;
- understand the links which exist between global marketing management and the overall global strategy of the business;
- describe the impact of the internet on global marketing.

Introduction

Global marketing strategy is primarily concerned with the global scope and co-ordination of marketing activities and the extent of standardization and adaptation of products, brands, and promotion and advertising. A global and transnational marketing strategy does not imply global standardization of all aspects of the strategy. Rather it implies a global perspective, seeking to combine the benefits of global and local features. Marketing strategy is based upon the appropriate global segmentation and positioning strategies, accompanied by a global marketing mix which is based upon a global perspective of products, brands, advertising and promotion combined with local adaptation where it gives marketing advantages.

Global marketing strategy is based upon analysis of the extent of globalization of various aspects of the market environment like similarities and differences in consumer tastes, cultural similarities and differences, technical standards, levels of income, legislation, and availability of advertising media.

The internet has an increasingly important role to play in the marketing strategy and operations of global business organizations. It has the potential to transform relationships with customers, suppliers, agents and distributors on a worldwide basis.

The role of marketing in global and transnational strategy

Marketing and strategy

The study and practice of marketing have broadened considerably, from an emphasis on marketing as a functional management issue, to a wider focus on the strategic role of marketing in overall corporate strategy. This broadening of the marketing concept, to include strategic as well as operational decisions, has resulted in an overlap between marketing and strategic management; and has generated considerable controversy over the role and position of marketing in corporate strategy.

One view of strategy argues that strategic planning is the reserve of directors and corporate planners who can take a broad-based view of the company's operations. In this context, marketing is seen as only one of several functional management areas providing important inputs into the strategic planning process. The primary role of marketing is to provide marketing information as an input into planning and the development of the tactical marketing mix.

Not surprisingly, the leading marketing authors dispute this view, arguing for a more central role for marketing in the determination of corporate strategy. For example, Baker (1985), argued for the adoption of a strategic marketing orientation.

It is my belief that while general managers do not see themselves as marketing managers, they should be just that, in the sense that they ought to subscribe to the philosophy of business encapsulated in the marketing concept ... Similarly, corporate strategists must be marketing strategists, for without a market there is no purpose for the corporation and no role for a corporate strategist. (Baker 1985, p. 29)

Toyne and Walter's (1993) perspective

The controversy regarding the role of marketing in corporate strategy has also emerged in global business. Toyne and Walters (1993), in their book *Global Marketing Management: A Strategic Perspective*, adopted a traditional view of marketing as a functional management area providing important inputs into the strategic planning process (and this despite the subtitle of the book 'A Strategic Perspective').

Marketing is seen as fulfilling the following roles in the overall global strategy of the business:

- identifying and making recommendations about future trends and opportunities in the markets where the company is already active;
- identifying and making recommendations about new marketing opportunities;
- providing estimates of the marketing resources (budget and staff) needed to exploit these opportunities;
- developing and implementing marketing strategies which are consistent with the overall strategic direction of the company in global markets.

Global marketing co-ordination

The second main perspective on the role of marketing in global strategy emphasizes the competitive advantages which can be derived from co-ordinating marketing on a global basis. Michael Porter's (1986) work on the global configuration and co-ordination of value-added activities was reviewed in Chapter 6. Within the framework adopted, marketing is seen as an important source of value-added which performs three significant roles in the overall global strategy of the business.

- marketing configuration, which refers to the location of various marketing activities through the world (geographically concentrated or dispersed);
- marketing co-ordination, which refers to the extent of standardization or adaptation of the marketing mix globally;

- the strategic role of marketing, especially the link between marketing and the other value-added activities of the company, e.g. design, technology development, manufacturing etc.

Marketing and competitive advantage

According to Takeuchi and Porter (1986), significant competitive advantages can be achieved in each of these areas. Taking the first, the need to perform marketing in all countries implies a high level of geographical dispersion of activity. Important competitive advantages can be derived, however, by concentrating certain marketing activities globally, when conditions permit, including the production of promotion material; central sales force; central service support; centralized training; and global advertising.

There are a number of ways in which geographically-dispersed marketing activities can be co-ordinated to gain competitive advantage including:

- performing marketing activities using similar methods across countries;
- transferring marketing know-how and skills from country to country;
- sequencing of marketing programmes across countries;
- integrating the efforts of various marketing groups in different countries.

Finally, the greatest leverage from taking a global view of marketing is its links to other upstream and support activities in the value chain. In particular, global marketing can allow significant economies of scale and learning in production and research and development, through uniform products for global markets.

The work of Takeuchi and Porter (1986), therefore, suggests a more central role for marketing in global business strategy. While recognizing its importance, marketing is seen as only one of several sources of competitive advantage and the hypotheses concerning the role of marketing are secondary to the main argument concerning global configuration and co-ordination of all value chain activities.

Ohmae's (1989) view of marketing

This can be contrasted with the work of Ohmae (1989), who argued that marketing is the core of any global strategy. Three distinct phases in the evolution of global business are identified.

Incremental multinational expansion

In the initial phase of multinational expansion, foreign markets were entered incrementally (according to Vernon's (1966) international product life cycle model) through clone-like subsidiaries of the parent company in each new country of operation. These subsidiaries repatriated profits to the parent company, which remained the dominant force at the centre.

Competitor-focused expansion

This model of multinational expansion gave way by the early 1980s to a competitor-focused approach to globalization, associated mainly with the work of Michael Porter. According to Ohmae, this competitor-driven phase of globalization has been superseded by a customer-driven phase.

Customer-driven expansion

The needs and preferences of customers have globalized; that is why businesses need to globalize. Delivering value to customers, rather than pre-empting competitors, is the only legitimate reason for thinking global. Yip (1992) contended that global marketing can bring about four major benefits:

1. enhanced knowledge of customer preferences;
2. increased competitive leverage;
3. improved product quality;
4. cost reduction.

To summarize these views, global marketing strategy is an essential element of an overall transnational strategy. It will be both customer- and competitor-based and will be both globally and locally orientated.

Globalization of markets and marketing research

Customer needs, and therefore markets, are becoming increasingly global for many goods and services, but the extent of globalization varies considerably from market to market. Even in a market where customer needs are similar on a global basis there may be elements of the marketing mix (this being the considerations over product design, price, place, i.e. segment, and promotion) which must be varied locally.

A global marketing strategy and the associated marketing mix must take account of the following factors in the market environment:

- *customer needs* – the extent to which they are global or to which there are specific local needs;
- *culture* – the products, brand names or advertising may have to be varied on a local basis to account for regional cultural differences;
- *language* – may require local variations in packaging, labelling, brand name and advertising;
- *technology* – the level of technology in a country or differing technical standards may require variations in product;
- *legal factors* – may demand variations in packaging, advertising, product features and so on.

In addition, analysis using Yip's globalization drivers (Chapter 4) will give an indication of which aspects of marketing strategy can be global and which must be varied locally. Global marketing research will indicate the extent to which aspects of marketing strategy can be standardized or the extent to which local variations must be introduced. The impact of these various factors on a global and transnational marketing strategy are explored further in the remainder of this chapter. Finally, marketing strategy (along with all other 'functional' strategies) must be an integral part of the overall transnational strategy of the organization.

Global marketing strategies

Different perspectives

Chapter 6 examined a number of approaches to global and transnational strategy which had been developed by different authors, from both a competitor- and customer-orientated perspective. Global marketing strategy must also adopt to these perspectives. Drawing upon Porter (1986a), a global marketing strategy must incorporate an appropriate degree of co-ordination and integration of geographically dispersed or concentrated marketing activities.

Although developed from a competitor-orientated perspective, Porter's view has important implications for global marketing. Hamel and Prahalad (1985) attributed the success of Japanese companies in global markets to their long-term strategic intent of global brand domination. Doz (1986) analysed the extent of global product standardization vs adaptation and found that success depends to a large extent on the type of global strategy adopted – multinational integration; national responsiveness; or multifocal strategies.

In the same way that aspects of global marketing strategy have been developed from a competitor-orientated perspective, other authors have developed perspectives more closely based on a customer-orientation. This section examines three such typologies based on the work of Douglas and Craig (1989), Leontiades (1986), and Toyne and Walters (1993).

Douglas and Craig's (1989) typology

An important feature of global marketing strategy is the co-ordination and integration of marketing on a worldwide basis in the pursuit of global competitive advantage. The importance of co-ordination and integration issues were emphasized by Douglas and Craig (1989), who related global marketing to the evolution of global strategy over time. They identified three main phases in the evolution of global marketing with each stage presenting new strategic challenges and decision priorities to the firm.

Phase one
Phase one represents the initial stage of international market expansion where the main strategic decisions facing the business include the choice of country to enter, the mode of entry adopted (see Chapter 7) and the extent of product standardization or adaptation.

Phase two
Once the company has established a 'beachhead' in a number of foreign markets, it then begins to seek new directions for growth and expansion, thus moving to phase two of internationalization. The focus in this stage is mainly on building market penetration in countries where the company is already located. In consequence, the expansion effort is mainly directed by local management with marketing strategy being determined on a country-by-country or nationally responsive basis.

Phase three
It is the third evolutionary phase which is the most important in the context of global marketing. In phase three the business moves towards a global orientation. The country-by-country approach to marketing is replaced by one in which markets are viewed as a set of interrelated and interdependent entities. These are increasingly integrated and interlinked worldwide and

co-ordination and integration of global marketing becomes essential to fully exploit the competitive advantages to be derived from the company's global scope. According to Douglas and Craig (1989) there are two key strategic thrusts in phase three.

First, the drive to improve the efficiency of worldwide operations through co-ordination and integration. This will cover both marketing activities such as product development, advertising, distribution and pricing; but also related production, sourcing and management. Standardization of product lines globally, for example, will facilitate the development of a globally integrated production and logistics network (see Chapter 8).

The second key strategic thrust is the search for global expansion and growth opportunities. This will involve a range of activities including opportunities for transferring products, brand names, marketing ideas, skills and expertise between countries; the identification of global market segments and target customers; and worldwide product development aimed at global markets.

Leontiades's (1986) perspective

While Douglas and Craig (1989) focused on the evolution towards global marketing, Leontiades (1986) focused more on the competitive marketing strategies of international businesses, identifying four generic international competitive marketing strategies (Figure 11.1).

Global high share strategies
These strategies involve pricing, promotion, product and other elements of the marketing mix being geared towards high volume segments of global markets. The essence of global high share strategies is the worldwide co-ordination of company resources behind global objectives. The global

		High	Low
Scope	*Global*	Global high share strategy	Global niche strategy
	National	National high share strategy	National niche strategy

Configuration of activities

FIGURE 11.1   Four generic international marketing strategies (source: Leontiades 1986)

scope of marketing creates opportunities for competitive advantage through lower costs and economies of scale; providing a global service; international sourcing; experience transfers; promoting an international corporate image; global resource focus; and improving the risk/return characteristics of the company's international business portfolio.

Global niche strategies
These involve specialization by product, technology, stage of life cycle, market segment etc. and avoid head-on competition with companies pursuing global high share strategies.

National high share strategies
These involve the use of nationally based competitive advantages, with marketing and production geared towards achieving high volume and lower costs relative to other national competitors.

National niche strategies
These involve specialization on a national scale to avoid competition with both global and national high share companies.

Only the first two of these marketing strategies can be classified as being global. While Leontiades (1986) focused on the overall generic strategies of companies in global markets, Toyne and Walters (1993) provided a more comprehensive coverage of the main components of global marketing.

Four stages in global marketing strategy

The development of a global marketing strategy involves four main stages:

- defining the global marketing mission;
- the global segmentation strategy;
- the competitive-market positioning strategy;
- the global marketing mix strategy.

Global marketing mission
The global marketing mission defines the major target markets to be attacked, the way these markets are to be segmented and the competitive position to be adopted in each market. In other words, the mission establishes the general parameters within which global marketing strategy decisions are made.

Segmentation strategies

In terms of global segmentation strategies, the three main alternatives identified are:

- *global market segments* – where markets are segmented according to variables which largely ignore national boundaries, e.g. demographic, buying practices, preferences etc. The strategy concentrates on identifying similarities in customer needs across countries rather than emphasizing country/cultural differences. Some techniques for achieving this are examined in the next section;
- *national market segments* – which involves serving the same market segments in multiple markets but on a national basis. Segmentation is on the basis of geography/nationality which emphasizes cultural differences rather than similarities between countries;
- *mixed market segments* – which is largely a combination of the first two. Some national markets may be of a sufficient size to warrant individualization. Others may be clustered into similar market segments.

Deciding on competitive position and marketing mix

Once the broad segmentation strategy has been established, the global company must decide on its competitive position within each market and its marketing mix strategy (see marketing mix strategy below).

Yip's (1992) view is that a global marketing strategy must be part of a global business strategy. A global strategy will be appropriate when customer needs are globally common, there are global customers and channels, and when marketing is globally transferable. In addition, cost drivers are likely to favour a global approach to marketing by creating economies of scale and scope. There are also competitive advantages of global marketing, through, for example, global branding. Yip did not advocate a marketing strategy which is global in every detail, rather one which is global where there are evident advantages and local where necessary:

> So global marketing is not a blind adherence to standardization of all marketing elements for its own sake, but a different, global approach to developing marketing strategy and programs that blends flexibility with uniformity. (Yip 1992)

In essence, then, a global or transnational marketing strategy is concerned with devising a strategy which is global in scope and which is globally co-ordinated. The extent of globalization of each element of the

Table 11.1 Potential advantages and limitations of global marketing strategy (source: derived from Toyne and Walters 1993, and Yip 1992)

Advantages of global marketing	*Comments*
Unit cost reduction	Consolidation of the global marketing function, economies of scale, experience curve economies, dilution of R&D and other fixed costs etc.
Improved quality of products and programmes	Through concentration on key marketing activities, uniform products etc.
Enhanced customer preferences	Through global customer knowledge of products, global availability, global serviceability etc.
Increased competitive leverage	By focusing resources and unifying the approach to competition
Risk reduction	Through reduced dependency on local demand, wider access to capital
Global knowledge and information transfers	Transfer of experience, practice, etc.
Limitations of global marketing	
Company-specific factors	For example, lack of resources, lack of global orientation, higher costs of co-ordination
Environment factors	Linguistic, cultural, technological and legal factors
Market factors	Customer need differences, channel differences etc.
Product factors	Over-standardization can result in products which satisfy nobody
Responsiveness	Over-centralization reduces responsiveness

strategy will be dependent upon the transnational strategy of the organization, the relative advantages of globalization or localization based on factors such as customer needs (Table 11.1).

Global market segmentation and positioning strategies

The key to successful global co-ordination and integration of marketing is effective market segmentation and product positioning strategy. If the globalization hypothesis of Levitt (1983) and its 'converging commonality' of customer needs were accepted, then it could be seen as removing the need for market segmentation and product positioning strategies, in that completely standardized products could be sold worldwide. Yet it is evident that there remain important national differences between markets which require segmentation and positioning.

Segmentation bases

The traditional approach to international marketing segmentation was to segment a market on a country basis to take account of national differences in demand conditions. Kale and Sudharsham (1987), however, suggested a different approach for segmenting international markets which is more compatible with the requirement for global marketing co-ordination. The approach makes customers and their needs the basis for segmentation. It has the advantage of being consumer orientated, while allowing global co-ordination of marketing, since it focuses on similarities rather than differences across groups of consumers in different countries. The basis of this approach is the 'strategically equivalent segmentation' (SES) of consumers. This is the identification of transnational segments of consumers, with similar needs, who will respond similarly to a given marketing mix. Four main stages are involved in identifying SES:

1. *the criteria to be used in segmenting markets* – develop qualifying and determining dimensions;
2. *country screening* – using qualifying dimensions to narrow down the list of countries as viable entry candidates;
3. *identifying market segments in each country* – develop microsegments in each qualified country;
4. *measuring segments* – develop factor score representation of microsegments and clustering analysis for SES.

The initial stage is the identification of qualifying criteria for identifying market segments (e.g. age, sex, income etc.). This is followed by country screening to identify the relative size of the segments in each country. After these filtering processes to identify which segments in which countries are to be targeted, the target market segment is then aggregated across countries to provide the total market. The major advantage of this approach is that it permits a business to adopt a global marketing strategy in strategically equivalent segments without assuming the complete cultural convergence of countries. Examples of products which are offered in strategically equivalent segments across the world include Nike trainers, Calvin Klein jeans and Ferrari cars.

Market positioning

A useful review of the issues involved in global marketing positioning can be found in Perry (1988). Two main types of positioning are identified.

First, market positioning which refers to the competitive position of a product in the market, for example, market leader; strong number two etc. Second, product positioning which refers to the attributes of a product in comparison with other products or to consumer needs. These two types of positioning can occur at two levels; first, the marketplace and second, in the consumer's mind. The first emphasizes the importance of competition; the second, customer orientation. A combination of these alternatives gives the model shown in Table 11.2. The importance of this to global marketing is that different positioning strategies can be adopted in different country markets in terms of market and product position.

There are advantages in having a common global perception of positioning. Nissan Motors, for example, is seen as a producer of good quality, reliable, reasonably-priced products on a global basis. This is also linked to many standardized aspects of its marketing mix. There are, however, occasions when companies adopt different positions globally. Stella Artois is regarded as a standard beer in Belgium but in some other markets it is positioned as a premium lager. In each case the advantages of uniform position have to be weighed against the advantages of differentiated positioning. Businesses adopting the same positioning strategy in all markets have adopted a *global positioning strategy* while those that vary position across markets are said to have adopted a *mixed positioning strategy*.

Table 11.2 Positioning concepts and their meaning (source: derived from Perry 1988)

	Market position (competitive standing)	Product position (profile attributes)
Measurements – marketplace Consumer's mind Possible positions	Market share Reputation Leader (lion) Challenger (tiger) Leaper (frog) Nicher (groundhog) Follower (ant) Imitator (mouse)	Comparison of attributes Image (perceptual map) Product category Price/quality vector Main features
Possible strategies	Enlarge Concur Advance Protect Withdraw	Reinforce Reposition

Global marketing management

The adoption of global marketing strategies involving co-ordination and integration of worldwide marketing raises a large number of important issues concerning global management of the marketing mix. These are examined in this section covering global products, pricing, promotion and distribution. It should be noted that the issues involved are complex and varied and all that can be attempted in the confines of this section is to present a brief overview of issues, together with a slightly more detailed discussion of some of the more important topics. Readers requiring a more comprehensive coverage should consult the further reading references at the end of the chapter.

Marketing mix strategy

Toyne and Walters (1993) identified four main categories of marketing mix strategy based upon the global segmentation and positioning strategy of the business (Figure 11.2).

The four options for marketing strategy are:

- *ideal global marketing strategy* – the marketing of a standard product to a global market segment using uniform marketing programmes;
- *ideal national marketing strategy* – the marketing mix is specifically tailored to meet the requirements of each national market;
- *hybrid I marketing strategy* – the standardization of products but the adaptation of other elements of the marketing mix to reinforce the product strategy;
- *hybrid II marketing strategy* – the standardization of one key element of the marketing mix but the adaptation of others.

		National market segments	Global market segments
Product strategy	*Global product*	Hybrid I marketing strategy	Ideal global marketing strategy
	National product	Ideal national marketing strategy	Hybrid II marketing strategy

Segmentation strategy

FIGURE 11.2 The global marketing strategy mix matrix (source: adapted from Toyne and Walters 1993)

Yip (1992) argued the case that *any* elements of the marketing mix can be standardized or varied as part of a global marketing strategy, according to the requirements of the global market.

The following sections consider the impact of alternative global or transnational marketing strategies on elements of the marketing mix. The emphasis of global marketing, however, remains focused upon the identification of similarities between customer needs in particular market segments across countries rather than emphasizing differences. Thus the strategy of companies like McDonald's is centred on a core formula for its restaurants and food products but a degree of customization is allowed to meet different needs. For example, alcohol is served in McDonald's stores in some countries but not in others. The extent of standardization and customization of marketing strategy will depend upon the competences of the business, the nature of its products, the nature of its markets and the importance of cultural, legal, technological and other factors.

Global products

The importance of product decisions

Product decisions are probably the most important element of a company's marketing mix. They can have a major impact on performance of the whole business in global markets. Products represent the most visible aspect of the company in foreign markets. Product design, quality, performance etc. have a very significant effect on the global image and reputation of the company. In addition, other elements of the global marketing mix (pricing, promotion and distribution) need to be designed and developed on the basis of product decisions.

> To a very important degree, a company's products define its business. Pricing, communication, and distribution policies must fit the product. A firm's customers and competitors are determined by the products it offers. Its research and development requirements depend upon the technologies of its products. Indeed, every aspect of the enterprise is heavily influenced by the firm's product offering. (Keegan 1980)

Decisions on product strategy

A wide range of decisions need to be taken in the area of global product policy including:

- *product range decisions* concerning the number, range and type of product sold throughout the world;
- *new product development* for global markets including the process of research and development;
- *global product diffusion and adoption* concerning the rate of transfer and acceptance of new products in different markets;
- *managing the international product life cycle* which may be at different stages in different markets;
- *product standardization or differentiation* questions;
- *generic product strategies* which may be based on core competences and associated cost leadership, differentiation, hybrid or focus;
- *packaging, branding, after-sales service* etc. decisions.

It is not possible to consider all of these issues in detail in this section. Indeed, two of these decisions, standardization vs differentiation, and global market segmentation and positioning, were examined in the previous section. The remainder of this section focuses in more detail on one of the most important global product decisions facing any company, namely that of global branding.

Global branding

A brand was defined by Thomas (1986) as 'a name, term, sign, symbol, mark, lettering or design (or any combination thereof) intended to differentiate a product from its competitors'. Successful branding strategies can be an important source of competitive advantage in some marketplaces by differentiating the product from those of competitors, maintaining product quality and image, achieving strong brand loyalty and sustained consumer commitment, and erecting barriers to entry. Brands tend to be most important in consumer rather than industrial or intermediate markets. Whereas brands tend to cultivate confidence amongst consumers in FMCG (fast-moving consumer goods) or consumer durables sectors, intermediates such as petrochemicals, energy, aggregates and other industrial goods tend to be bought much more on the basis of technical specification or price.

The advantages of successful branding will be particularly important in global marketing given the intensity of the competitive environment in consumer goods sectors. One of the most important issues in branding for global markets is the choice between global or multiple country brands, that is whether a standardized global brand is sold worldwide or whether the brand is adapted to local market differences. The world's top brands are shown in Table 11.3.

It is noteworthy that few names appear in all four lists. Coca-Cola is one of the few names which does. There are some interesting omissions from the list, including Nike, Reebok and some others. These brands are undoubtedly well recognized on a global basis, particularly among groups of consumers in the global market segments which they serve. It is therefore a mistake to assume that global brands are insignificant. There are few people in the global consumer groups who purchase training shoes who are not aware of the Nike and Reebok brand names.

Advantages and constraints

There are several advantages to be gained from a global brand name. Brand names are often associated with consumer perceptions of quality, reliability, performance and other positive product features. Perhaps the most important advantage, therefore, is the positive perception that consumers have of products associated with the brand name. Other major advantages to be derived from global branding are marketing efficiency through economies

Table 11.3   The world's top 20 brands by triad region and world (source: Owen 1993)

World	USA	Europe	Japan
Coca-Cola	Coca-Cola	Coca-Cola	Sony
Sony	Campbell's	Sony	National
Mercedes-Benz	Disney	Mercedes-Benz	Mercedes-Benz
Kodak	Pepsi-Cola	BMW	Toyota
Disney	Kodak	Philips	Takashimaya
Nestlé	NBC	Volkswagen	Rolls Royce
Toyota	Black & Decker	Adidas	Seiko
McDonald's	Kellogg's	Kodak	Matsushita
IBM	McDonald's	Nivea	Hibachi
Pepsi-Cola	Hershey's	Porsche	Suntory
Rolls Royce	Levi's	Volvo	Porsche
Honda	GE	Colgate	Kirin
Panasonic	Sears	Rolls Royce	Hotel New Otani
Levi's	Hallmark	Levi's	Fuji TV
Kleenex	Johnson & Johnson	Ford	Snow Brand Milk
Ford	Betty Crocker	Jaguar	Imperial Hotel
Volkswagen	Kraft	Fanta	Coca-Cola
Kellogg's	Kleenex	Nescafé	Mitsukoshi
Porsche	Jell-O	Black & Decker	Japan Travel Bureau
Polaroid	Tylenol	Esso	Disney

of scale, promotion of a global image and reputation, and global consumer loyalty.

The extent of global branding, however, is constrained by several factors including:

- *legal constraints* – in some developing countries, for example, foreign brands may be either banned or taxed more heavily;
- *language and cultural factors* – which may lead to misleading connotations of certain brand names, requiring brand adaptation. In the automobile industry, for example, manufacturers have long tailored their product/ brand names to individual countries or regions. The Volkswagen Golf is standard throughout most of Europe, Asia and Africa. In the USA, Latin America and the Caribbean, however, it is known as the Rabbit;
- *consumer homogeneity* – the extent to which global branding is possible obviously depends on the extent of consumer homogeneity between markets – or to use Levitt's (1983) terminology, the extent of 'converging commonality';
- *counterfeiting* – this is one of the most serious problems faced by global branders. Pirating of video films, computer software, music recordings and designer clothing cost global business millions of dollars each year (see Kotabe and Helsen, 1998, for a detailed discussion).

Key branding decisions
The strategic decisions facing companies in global branding have been examined by Onkvisit and Shaw (1983). Four main strategic decisions are discussed, namely:

1. *whether to brand or not to brand* – which depends on whether the product has salient attributes which can be differentiated;
2. *whether to use the manufacturer's own brand or the distributor's/retailer's private brand*;
3. *whether to use global or local brands* – which depends on the extent of inter-market differences;
4. *whether to use single or multiple brands* in the same market.

These decisions are summarized in Figure 11.3. The main advantages and disadvantages of each of these strategic options are listed in Table 11.4. The figure and table should be considered in conjunction with each other as they assist in the brand decision making process. Particular attention

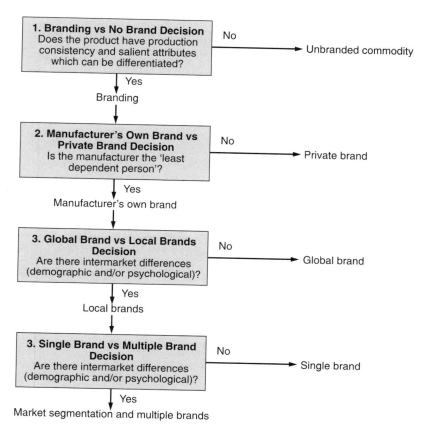

FIGURE 11.3   Branding decisions – from a manufacturer's perspective (source: Onkvisist and Shaw 1983)

should be paid to the advantages and disadvantages of worldwide branding. The framework can be used as the basis of analysis of the branding strategy of a particular business in global markets.

Some research (Landor Associates 1990, Rosen *et al.* 1989, Kashani 1997a) has cast doubts on the significance of brand names as a means of attracting customers. Some of the doubts are the result of research which targeted general consumers rather than consumers from the segments where brands are known. Kashani (1997a) argued that successful brands can still be built and that brand building must involve:

- *getting lean* – pruning weak brands and concentrating resources on successful and potentially successful brands;

Table 11.4 Branding perspectives (source: Onkvisit and Shaw 1983)

Advantages		Disadvantages
Lower production cost Lower marketing cost Lower legal cost Flexible quality and quantity control	*No brand*	Severe price competition Lack of market identity
Better identification and awareness Better chance of product differentiation Possible brand loyalty Possible premium pricing	*Branding*	Higher production cost Higher marketing cost Higher legal cost
Better margins for dealers Possibly of larger market share No promotional problems	*Private brand*	Severe price competition Lack of market identity
Better price – greater price inelasticity Better bargaining power Better control of distribution	*Manufacturer's brand*	Difficult for small manufacturers with unknown brand or identity Requiring brand promotion
Market segmented for varying needs Creating competitive spirits Avoiding negative connotation of existing brand Gaining more retail shelf space Not hurting existing brand's image	*Multiple brands (in one market)*	Higher marketing cost Higher inventory cost Loss of economies of scale
Marketing efficiency Permitting more focused marketing Eliminator of brand confusion Good for product with good reputation (halo effect)	*Single brand (in one market)*	Assuming market homogeneity Existing brand's image hurt when trading up/down Limited shelf space
Meaningful names Local identification Avoidance of taxation on international brand Quick market penetration by acquiring local brand Allowing variations of quantity and quality across markets	*Local brands*	Higher marketing cost Higher inventory cost Loss of economies of scale Diffused image
Maximum marketing efficiency Reduction of advertising costs Elimination of brand confusion Good for culture-free product Good for prestigious product Easy identification/recognition for international travellers Uniform worldwide image	*Worldwide brands*	Assuming market homogeneity Problems with black and grey markets Possibility of negative connotation Requiring quality and quantity consistency LDC's opposition and resentment Legal complications

- *investment* – particularly in product innovation;
- *listening* – to consumers and understanding their needs.

It is evident that the decision to brand globally or locally is not simple. Many businesses therefore adopt a hierarchy of global, regional and local brands (Kotabe and Helsen 1998) to combine the benefits of global and local branding. The Swiss company Nestlé has, for example:

- 10 global corporate brands including Nestlé, Carnation, Perrier;
- 45 global strategic brands including Kit Kat, Polo, Smarties, After Eight;
- 140 regional strategic brands including Macintosh, Vittel Contadina;
- 7500 local brands including Texicana, Rocky etc.

Global pricing

Pricing decisions

Like branding and advertising, *price* is an important element of a global marketing strategy. While price is heavily influenced by the overall strategy of the business, there is a need to ensure that it is sensitive to local market conditions. Price determination in international marketing is significantly more complex than in domestic marketing as a result of factors such as variations in market demand and competitive conditions abroad, transport and distribution costs, tariffs and other government price controls, exchange rate fluctuations etc. The need to integrate pricing with global strategy suggests that there should be global co-ordination of pricing policy, but the need to be locally responsive suggests variation in pricing. This section examines co-ordination and integration issues in relation to global pricing. Two of the most important issues in this respect are the locus of decision-making regarding price determination and transfer pricing.

One of the most important price-related decisions in global marketing is the need for pricing policy to be developed within the context of the company's overall strategic objectives in global markets and this is a powerful argument in favour of centralized co-ordination of pricing decisions. At the same time, however, prices need to be responsive to local environmental and market conditions in different countries and this favours a decentralized approach, with pricing decisions being the responsibility of foreign subsidiaries. Decentralizing pricing decisions, on the other hand, may lead to inter-subsidiary price competition.

Toyne and Walters (1993) identified three major groups of factors affecting international pricing:

- *company-specific factors* – these include the transnational strategy of the company, local variations to its strategy, research and development costs, marketing and distribution costs;
- *external, market-specific factors* – these include consumer tastes and behaviour, government regulations, the competitive environment, market structure and exchange rate fluctuations;
- *product-specific factors* – the stage of the international product life cycle etc.

Becker (1980) identified four main factors as affecting international pricing:

- *costs* which establish a 'price floor';
- *demand and market factors* which set a 'price ceiling';
- *market structure and competition* which help to set a 'realistic price';
- *environmental constraints* such as government price controls.

Yip (1992) made the point that 'Charging the same absolute price can be very difficult because of inherent international differences in market price levels, laws, and the role of price, as well as differences in the business's market position and delivered costs'.

As an alternative to charging the same absolute price, businesses can opt to charge 'the same prices relative to their competitors in each market' (Yip 1992). This, Yip argued, can help the business to maintain a consistent position in its markets.

Keegan (1980) identified three alternative pricing policies in global marketing.

- *The extension/ethnocentric pricing policy* involving the uniformity of prices worldwide.
- *The adaptation/polycentric pricing policy* where prices are determined by local subsidiaries and are responsive to local market needs.
- *The invention/geocentric pricing policy* with prices determined in relation to the company's overall global marketing strategy.

The advantages and disadvantages of alternative pricing strategies are important to consider. Highly decentralized pricing has the advantage of being fully responsive to local market conditions. The main disadvantage is that decentralized prices may not be consistent with the overall global market objectives of the company and may encourage inter-subsidiary price competition. This, in turn, may lead to opportunities for arbitrage and 'grey market' activities. The main advantage of centralized pricing is the consistency with global strategy. The main disadvantage is that centrally determined prices may not take adequate account of local market conditions.

There are two intermediary situations between the two extremes of centralized, uniform pricing and decentralized, local market pricing. First, centralized pricing policy with decentralized price determination. Under this strategy each national subsidiary is responsible for determining its own prices, but overall pricing policy is determined centrally. This may include decisions regarding rates of return to be achieved; market share and product positioning objectives etc. Second, prices may be determined decentrally but only within clearly defined limits laid down by the corporate centre.

Cross-subsidization is an important and controversial issue in global pricing. This occurs when a transnational or global company uses profits made in one country to subsidize prices elsewhere to gain market share. Thus, some Japanese companies have been accused of using surplus profits made in the protected Japanese market to subsidize prices on entry into the US and European markets leading to accusations of 'dumping' (such as in the case of some semiconductors).

Toyne and Walters (1993) identified three alternative approaches to global pricing (Table 11.5).

- *Standard world pricing* – uniform pricing throughout the world.
- *Market differentiated pricing* – prices are customized for each market.
- *Dichotomous pricing* – standardized foreign prices separate from the domestic market price structure.

Toyne and Walters (1993) went on to argue that, subject to central co-ordination, a market differentiated approach should be adopted in many cases, because:

Table 11.5 Pros and cons of different pricing strategies (source: adapted from Toyne and Walters 1993)

	Advantages	Disadvantages
Standardized world pricing	Simple Equitable Removes possibility for arbitrage	Lack of responsiveness to local economic and demand conditions
Market differentiated pricing	Market responsiveness	Creates opportunities for arbitrage and 'grey marketing'
Dichotomous pricing		Worst of both worlds

- environmental factors affecting prices often vary significantly from market to market;
- pricing policy should be used proactively to achieve local market goals;
- the advantages of price uniformity are generally small;
- many of the drawbacks of price differentiation can be anticipated and managed.

Differentiated pricing can, however, create significant problems as it did in the late 1990s within the European Union where supermarket chains have used the 'grey market' to obtain and sell designer goods at lower prices. At the same time, many American products are sold in Europe for higher prices than in the USA.

Transfer pricing

The question of transfer pricing is an important and controversial one in global marketing. Transfer prices are the prices charged on intra-group trade. It occurs when there is a movement of parts, components, machinery, technology etc. from one part of the global business network to another. The flow of goods and services is one-way; the flow of payment for these goods/services is the other way. The question then arises – what price is to be charged on such intra-group trade?

At this stage, it is worth pointing out the importance of the transfer pricing issue since between 35 and 40 per cent of all international trade takes the form of intra-company trade. The internal prices set for such trade can have a major effect on the value of exports and imports and, hence, on the balance of payments accounts of host and home countries.

Keegan (1980) identified four main approaches to transfer pricing:

- transfer at direct cost;
- transfer at direct cost plus apportioned overhead and margin;
- transfer at a price derived from end market prices;
- transfer at an 'arm's-length price', i.e. a price which would have been negotiated by unrelated parties.

The crucial issue here is that international business can derive a number of benefits from the manipulation of internal transfer prices. These include reduced tax liability; circumventing restrictions on profit repatriation; reducing exchange risk; and avoidance of import tariffs. The global tax liability of the business can be reduced by shifting declared profits from high tax to low tax countries. One way of achieving this is to manipulate transfer prices in order to increase the profits of subsidiaries in low tax countries. Similarly, restrictions on profit repatriation may be overcome by 'overcharging' subsidiaries for goods and service transfers. Thus, money may be remitted from the country as payment for goods and services rather than as profits. In the same way, foreign exchange risk can be mitigated by manipulating transfer prices to siphon funds from countries where local currency depreciation is expected. Finally, where import tariffs are charged as a proportion of the value of goods, these can be reduced by artificially reducing the value of imports to subsidiaries through manipulating transfer prices.

Transfer pricing is also important in relation to management of exchange rate risk. This issue is discussed in Chapter 12 on global finance.

Pricing decisions – a summary

The major issues in global pricing are:

- factors affecting global pricing;
- co-ordination of pricing;
- standardized vs differentiated pricing;
- transfer pricing;
- exchange rate risk and pricing.

Global pricing must be consistent with transnational strategy and with other elements of marketing strategy. Just as other elements of strategy can be standardized or localized, so can pricing. This allows the benefits of global strategy to be combined with those of local flexibility.

Global promotion

Marketing communications

Global promotion is defined here to include all forms of marketing communications that seek to influence the buying behaviour of existing and potential customers including advertising, personal selling, direct mail, point-of-sale displays, literature, publicity and word of mouth communications (Keegan 1980). Marketing texts have referred to these promotions as above-line (media promotions), below-line (more focused non-media promotions) and direct selling.

The major objectives of global promotion, as with domestic marketing, are, 'to enhance the company's image vis-à-vis its competitors and/or to inform, educate, and influence the attitudes and buying behaviour of the individuals, companies, institutions, and/or government agencies that make up a target market' (Toyne and Walters, 1993).

Despite sharing the same objectives, global promotion is far more complex than domestic promotion due to the complexity of the global environment. This section explores:

- The extent of standardization of global promotion
- The ways in which global promotion is organized and controlled (centralization versus decentralization)
- Management of global promotional campaigns
- The role and growth of global advertising agencies

Standardization of global promotion

A concise summary of the arguments for and against the standardization of global advertising can be found in Mooji and Keegan (1991); and these are summarized in Table 11.6. One of the most important factors constraining global advertising standardization is the relationship between the centre and subsidiary managers. This point was reinforced by Peebles (1989) who argued that the main obstacle to global advertising and the reason so many global campaigns fail is not because of cultural differences around the world, but rather because of inter-personal relationships between foreign subsidiaries and corporate headquarters, i.e. the 'not invented here'

Table 11.6 Global advertising standardization (source: derived from Mooji and Keegan 1991)

Arguments in favour of standardization	Arguments against standardization
Costs savings through economies of scale in promotion	The heterogeneity of countries in terms of culture, mentality and product usage
Promotion of uniform brand and corporate image	The 'not invented here' syndrome, i.e. the desire of each country to create its own campaign
Utilization of global media	Differences in the media scene
Simplified promotional planning through uniform objectives and simplified co-ordination and control	Legal and regulatory constraints
Maximum use of good ideas, transmission of know-how and continuous exchange of ideas	Competitive position in different markets
The tendency for global business to be centrally managed	Product may be at different stages of its life cycle in different countries
Better use of management abilities and resources	Danger of being regarded as a foreign enterprise
Universal guidelines and quality standards	Higher co-ordination costs which need to be balanced against economies of scale
Better access to stored know-how and experience of other countries and improved ways of identifying global opportunities	

syndrome which can create subsidiary opposition to centrally-designed campaigns.

Organization and control of promotions

Organization and control issues, therefore, are central to the debate on global advertising and they have been well covered in the literature. Centralization of advertising decisions allows for greater co-ordination and integration of worldwide promotion with the associated benefits listed in Table 11.6. Decentralization, on the other hand, will allow greater flexibility and responsiveness to local market needs.

The extent to which a business standardizes global promotion is governed by several external and internal factors. The major external factors are:

- *language differences* which may affect the translation of the advertising message and the appropriateness of trade names, brands, slogans etc.;

- *cultural differences* which may affect behaviour patterns, values, tastes, fashions etc.;
- *social differences* especially the general attitude of society towards advertising;
- *economic differences* including the stage of development of the country and its effects on education, levels of literacy, possession of radio, TV etc.
- *competitive differences* and the promotional campaigns of competitors;
- *promotion infrastructure differences* – the relative importance of different promotion channels can vary significantly between countries as between TV, radio and the media;
- *legal and regulatory controls* including codes of practice and legislation can vary considerably.

The most important internal factors are the overall global strategy of the business and the relationship between headquarters executives and foreign subsidiary management. The scope for global promotion is far greater when transnational strategy places greater emphasis on co-ordination of activities rather than when a locally responsive approach is adopted. Similarly, the greater the degree of centralized control, the greater the standardization of promotion. When decision-making power is decentralized then there is greater scope for local variations in promotion.

The choice of promotional strategy is, of course, not a simple choice between total standardization and complete local adaptation. As with other aspects of transnational strategy, it is more likely that a company will adopt an approach which combines a high degree of uniformity with local variations. Yip (1992) quoted the example of the Coca-Cola 'little boy gives Coke to sports hero' campaign. In the USA the hero was 'Mean' Joe Green of the Pittsburgh Steelers, in Latin America it was Diego Maradona so as to give an element of local appeal. At the same time, however, the major theme of the advertisement was globally consistent.

Toyne and Walters (1993) and Mooji and Keegan (1991) identified three broadly similar alternative options in relation to the decision as to the extent to which promotion should be centralized or decentralized:

- *the centralized organization* – centralization of all promotional decision-making at corporate headquarters;
- *the decentralized organization* – decentralization of promotional decision-making;

- *the mixed organization* – combining elements of centralized and decentralized promotional decision-making.

Several factors will influence the choice between these three alternatives:

- *corporate and marketing objectives* – where global objectives predominate, promotion will tend to be centralized;
- *the uniformity of the product* – the greater the uniformity of the product, the greater the centralization of promotion;
- *the appeal of the product or brand* – where this is widespread, decentralization will be increased;
- *legal constraints* – decentralization may be necessary to take account of different national regulations;
- *cultural aspects* – may dictate decentralization;
- *socio-economic conditions* – different tastes, habits and preferences may require decentralization;
- *the competitive situation* – where this differs from country to country promotional decisions will need to be at least partially decentralized.

Existing decision-making processes in global businesses vary considerably. Companies adopting global strategies (e.g. Coca-Cola, IBM, Sony etc.) will be significantly more centralized in promotional decision-making than nationally responsive ones. Generally speaking, however, the two extremes of complete centralization or complete decentralization are rare in practice, with most businesses adopting a variation of the mixed organization.

Generally, corporate (at the centre) staff are responsible for developing the core promotional objectives and core campaigns; and for providing advice and expertise to foreign affiliates. Decisions regarding the detailed implementation of core campaigns in foreign markets are often best left to subsidiary managers to achieve local flexibility. Certain local decisions, however, may still require the ultimate approval of the parent company.

The role of corporate headquarters in global advertising was examined in detail by Mooij and Keegan (1991) where a distinction was drawn between the professional and management role. The former refers to the role of headquarters in creating and placing advertising. The latter refers to the importance of ensuring co-operation between headquarters and subsidiary and for evaluating campaign effectiveness. The role of corporate headquarters in these two areas is summarized in Figure 11.4

(a) Professional Role
- Positioning
- Strategy development
- Creative concept development and judgement
- Assisting local management in selecting the right target groups
- Giving an insight into the degree to which specific products and product attributes must be emphasized in local campaigns or in adapted campaigns
- Providing an insight into what kind of advertising is most effective in which country
- Selecting the media types to be used, both locally and internationally
- Drawing up procedures for reporting and internal communication between subsidiaries and head office
- Cultivating a feeling for cultural differences and thus increasing the possibilities of standardizing a creative approach
- Evaluating international media
- Co-ordinating advertising research and measurement of effect

(b) Management Role
- Providing worldwide planning systems including worldwide production outlines or guidance
- Organizing worldwide co-ordination of local advertising plans
- Setting global budgets, dividing them according to region or country, evaluating country budgets and checking whether they meet the company's requirements
- Assisting with the selection of local advertising managers
- Developing documentation systems for registering successful multinational campaigns in order to help local subsidiaries developing their own campaigns
- Selecting advertising agencies (local, multinational or global)
- Evaluating agency relationships and remuneration arrangements

FIGURE 11.4   The role of corporate headquarters in global advertising (source: derived from Mooij and Keegan 1991)

The role of corporate headquarters in global advertising was also examined by Quelch and Hoff (1986). The main responsibilities of the centre included product/brand positioning and effect measurement. Foreign subsidiaries, on the other hand, were mainly responsible for media planning and media buying. Decisions which were jointly determined by both headquarters and foreign subsidiaries included advertising agency selection; concept development; execution; and marketing research.

The management of global promotional campaigns

Toyne and Walters (1993) distinguished between strategic issues in promotion planning and management issues. The six main strategic issues are:

- *the market segment* at which the promotion is directed – in global marketing this refers mainly to the territorial boundaries or geographical scope of the campaign whether national, regional or global;

- *the objectives of the promotion campaign* – where a distinction can be made, for example, between building a global brand and increasing market share in a particular country;
- *the message(s)* communicated and whether this should be the same across countries;
- *the allocation of expenditure* to the campaign and the total budget;
- *the allocation of the total budget* across promotional mix elements – media, geographical areas, products and over time;
- *procedures for monitoring the performance* of the campaign.

The major managerial issues involved in implementing a campaign include:

- *the organization and control dimension* – as discussed in the previous section;
- *choosing an advertising agency* – where alternatives include using a domestic agency; using an agency with branches overseas; using local agencies in foreign markets; or some combination of these alternatives. The choice between these alternatives will be influenced by three broad categories of factors including:
    (a) corporate factors such as the extent of the company's internationalization, organizational structure, and standardization policy;
    (b) market-specific factors such as sociocultural, economic and legal differences; and
    (c) characteristics of the agency itself including its market coverage, quality and reputation.

Mooij and Keegan (1991) identified 10 steps in planning worldwide advertising.

1. *Situation analysis* – analysis of the forces influencing promotional decisions including organizational structure, brand portfolio, the extent of standardization, market share abroad and brand positioning.
2. *Marketing communications strategy and objectives* – whether a brand is to be developed globally or multi-locally.
3. *Deciding on the target groups* – identifying similar market segments in each country (see the previous discussion of Strategically Equivalent Segments).
4. *Setting the total communications budget* – whether it is set centrally or locally, determine the basis upon which the budget is determined, e.g. based on past experience, objectives etc.

5. *The message* – the choice between standardized and locally varied.
6. *The means of communication and their integration* – choices on sales, promotion, PR, media advertising, sponsorship and the interrelationships between these methods.
7. *Centralized or decentralized control of the means of communication* – decisions governing who controls promotion.
8. *Budget allocation* – between different promotional media and communications channels.
9. *Organization and implementation* – of the strategy including managing agency arrangements.
10. *Control and evaluation* – measuring the effectiveness of the campaign in each country.

Choosing an advertising agency.

The globalization of business and the attention focused on the opportunities for global promotion has resulted in a rapid internationalization of the advertising industry itself. Most of the early international advertising agencies originated from the USA, with expansion abroad being a gradual process in response to the internationalization of client companies. Since the mid-1980s, internationalization of the advertising industry has accelerated at an unprecedented rate, with the emergence of a number of global, 'mega'-agencies. This has mainly been a consequence of the wave of cross-border mergers and acquisitions which have swept the industry in recent years.

The rapid internationalization of the advertising industry and the emergence of global, 'mega'-agencies can be attributed to three main causes.

1. *Globalization* – some agencies have explicitly adopted the globalization hypothesis of Levitt (1983). Indeed, Theodore Levitt was appointed to the board of Saatchi and Saatchi in 1986. Once the premise of 'converging commonality' has been accepted, the opportunities for global promotion become apparent. To exploit such opportunities, agencies have established geographically dispersed subsidiaries throughout the world – sometimes through establishing new branches, but more commonly through mergers and acquisition.
2. *The benefits of size* – closely related to the advantages of globalization, are the benefits of size. Global, 'mega'-agencies, due to their size and geographical scope, can exert considerable influence over media groups, and can achieve considerable economies of scale in operations.

3. *Synergy* – a third factor in the emergence of global, 'mega'-agencies has been the view that substantial benefits can be derived from the provision of an integrated marketing communications service to clients. Thus, most of the rapidly expanding agencies have diversified their operations to include not only advertising and promotion but also other services including public relations, market research, consultancy, design, executive recruitment etc.

Jaben (1994) suggested that 'think globally, act locally' is still the 'dominant strategy of international advertisers but with a slight revision: "think globally, act regionally"'. This implies that global headquarters has a central role to play in ensuring a globally consistent message while regional managers must have the autonomy to adapt advertising to local markets.

ICT and global marketing

It has been claimed that 'commercialization of the WWW will revolutionize the study and practice of international marketing' (Hamill 1997). Certainly the Internet has the potential to revolutionize many aspects of global marketing and strategy. Hamill (1997) identified three main strategic applications of the internet in the context of internationalization:

- *a communications tool* supporting network relationships with overseas customers (actual and potential), agents, distributors, suppliers etc.;
- *a low cost export market research resource*;
- *a global marketing and promotions tool* through the design and effective marketing of company web sites and the development of integrated Internet supported strategies.

The Internet is potentially useful to both large and small companies operating in or wishing to enter global markets. It is a valuable tool for communicating both with customers and with other businesses. It is inexpensive to use and is therefore of particular value to small and medium sized enterprises wishing to operate internationally. Table 11.7 summarizes the most significant effects of the internet on global marketing strategies.

Table 11.7   Ten effects of the internet on global marketing (source: adapted from Hamill and Gregory 1997)

Effect	Comment
1. Improved global communications with customers	The web allows businesses greater opportunity to communicate directly with their customers all over the world
2. Improved global communications with other businesses	Suppliers and distributors all over the world can be contacted electronically. Materials etc. can be globally sourced via the web at low cost
3. Improved internal communications	The internet can be used to provide cheap and quick worldwide internal communications within a global business
4. Improved corporate image	The web site of a business can be used to present its corporate image
5. Finding new global customers	New customers can be attracted by the company's web site. Additionally new customers can be approached directly via the web on a worldwide basis
6. Reduced market entry costs for small businesses	Small businesses were often deterred from entering global markets on the basis of the costs of market research, agents charges etc. The internet has reduced these costs substantially
7. Global price standardization	Marketing on the internet increases the advantages of and need for global price standardization
8. Global market niche strategies	Niche markets can be accessed through groups on the web. Customers are also more able to access specialist services and products by searching the web
9. Global marketing research tool	Access to information sources available on the internet
10. Reduced importance of traditional marketing intermediaries	Agents etc. will be of less value to businesses entering international markets

One thing is certain: the impact of the internet on global marketing has increased and will increase further, particularly amongst small- and medium-sized enterprises. As we have seen, it is likely to influence global promotion, pricing, logistics and distribution and, indeed, permeates most aspects of global marketing. Managers in global businesses must assess the potential role of the internet in their global marketing strategies.

THE INTERNET AND GLOBAL MARKETING – AXIS COMMUNICATIONS INC. A CASE STUDY EXAMPLE

Axis communications has its headquarters at Lund in Sweden. It develops and manufactures a range of products designed to support network centric computing. The company's flagship products, the StorePoint CD Network CD-ROM Server and the NetEye 200 Network Camera, are part of the first wave of network and web appliances designed to increase productivity by enabling users to access and share computer resources more efficiently. The company, which currently employs 200 people, has experienced an average annual sales growth of 43 per cent since its foundation in 1984. In 1995/96 its sales were US$49 million and it had an installed base of 50 000 products worldwide. Major customers include 'Fortune 500' companies such as Ford, GM, AT&T, Pepsi, ABC News, Microsoft, GE and Boeing and many more smaller organizations worldwide.

The rapid growth of the company has been, to a large extent, dependent on the establishment of 'strategic technology relationships' with customers and with leading hardware vendors and software developers such as Hewlett Packard, IBM, Canon, Fujitsu, Sony, Xerox, Microsoft, Netscape, Oracle and Sun. Maintaining good relationships and communications with their existing customer base is vital for Axis.

Despite its success, Axis remains a relatively small company in global terms and this has created two major challenges: how to support its existing global customer base and how to achieve greater global brand awareness and sales volume on a small promotion budget compared to major global competitors. Axis sees the internet as providing a low-cost solution to both problems and one which is highly relevant to the changing nature of procurement in the IT industry.

Axis' web site has become central to its global marketing strategy. It contains full and comprehensive product information, sales contacts by region, corporate news, new product developments and a jobs vacant section. The site is fully interactive and the company relies heavily on e-mail to support existing customers and to develop relationships with new ones. An innovative feature of the Axis website is the Axis electronic newsletter which is widely accessible and provides new product information to existing and potential customers around the world. The ultimate aim of the site is to create a virtual community of customers, distributors, resellers and suppliers in order to supply the Axis brand globally.

REVIEW AND DISCUSSION QUESTIONS

1. Explain what you understand by the term 'global marketing'. What are the major potential advantages and drawbacks of adopting a global marketing strategy?

2. Why are many markets becoming more global? How is the extent of globalization of a market assessed?

3. Choose a market with which you are familiar. Assess the extent to which it is globalized and the extent to which it is localized.

4. What is meant by a 'Strategically Equivalent Segment'? How can one be identified?

5. Select a product which is globally available. What are the limitations on its standardization?

6. Why are global products often not sold at a globally standardized price? What are the major factors affecting the pricing decisions of a global business?

7. What factors affect the extent of globalization of promotion of a good or service? What are the relative advantages and disadvantages of global promotion?

8. Explain the growth and importance of global advertising agencies.

9. Discuss the impact of the Internet on global marketing.

References and further reading

Aaker, D.A.(1992) *Strategic Market Management*, John Wiley, New York.

Akhter, S.H. and Laczniak, G.R. (1989) The future US business environment with strategic marketing implications for European exporters, *European Journal of Marketing*, **23**(5).

Ayal, I. and Zif, J. (1979) Market expansion strategies in multinational marketing, *Journal of Marketing*, **43**(2).

Baker, M.J. (1985) *Marketing Strategy and Management*, Macmillan, London.

Barnard, P. (1982) Conducting and co-ordinating multicountry quantitative studies across Europe, *Journal of Market Research Society*, **24**(1), January.

Bartlett, C.A. and Ghoshal, S. (1989) *Managing Across Borders: The Transnational Solution*, Harvard Business School Press, Boston.

Bartlett, C.A. and Ghoshal, S. (1990) Matrix management: not a structure, a frame of mind, *Harvard Business Review*, July/August.

Becker, H. (1980) Pricing: an international marketing challenge, in: Thorelli, H. and Becker, H. (eds), *International Marketing Strategy*, Pergamon Press, New York.

Becker, H. and Thorelli, H. (eds) (1980) Strategic planning in international marketing, in: *International Marketing Strategy*, Pergamon Press, New York.

Benjamin, R. and Wigand, R. (1995) Electronic markets and virtual value chains on the information superhighway, *Sloan Management Review*, Winter, 62–72.

Boddewyn, J.J., Soehl, R. and Picard, P. (1986) Standardization in international marketing: is Ted Levitt in fact right?, *Business Horizons*, Nov/Dec.

Bolt, J.F. (1988) Global competitors: some criteria for success, *Business Horizons*, January/February.

Cavusgil, T.S. and Nevin, J.R. (1981) State-of-the-art in international marketing: an assessment, in: Enis, B.M. and Roering, K.J. (eds), *Review of Marketing 1981*, American Marketing Association, Chicago.

Chakravarthy, B.S. and Perlmutter, H.V. (1985) Strategic planning for a global business, *Columbia Journal of World Business*, Summer.

Chan, P.S. and Justis, R.T. (1991) Developing a global business strategy vision for the next decade and beyond, *Journal of Management Development*, **10**(2).

Czinkota, M.R. and Ilkka, A. (1992) Global marketing 2000: a marketing survival guide, *Marketing Management*, **1**(1), 36–45.

Daniels, J.D. (1987) Bridging national and global marketing strategies through regional operations, *International Marketing Review*, **4**(3).

Day, E., Fox, R.J. and Huszagh, S.M. (1988) Segmenting the global market for industrial goods: issues and implications, *International Marketing Review*, **5**(3), Autumn.

Diamantopoulos, A. and Schlegelmilch, B.B. (1987) Comparing marketing operations of autonomous subsidiaries, *International Marketing Review*, **4**(4), Winter.

Douglas, S.P. and Craig, C.S. (1989) Evolution of global marketing strategy: scale, scope and synergy, *Columbia Journal of World Business*, Fall, pp. 47–59.

Doyle, F.P. (1990) People power: the global human resource challenge for the '90s, *Columbia Journal of World Business*, Spring/Summer.

Doz, Y. (1986) *Strategic Management in Multinational Companies*, Pergamon Press, New York.

Edwards, F. and Spawton, T. (1990) Pricing in the Australian wine industry, *European Journal of Marketing*, **24**(4).

Espey, J. (1989) 'The big four': an examination of the international drinks industry, *European Journal of Marketing*, **23**(9).

Fayerweather, J. (1981) Four winning strategies for the international corporation, *Journal of Business Strategy*, **1**(2), Fall.

Glaum, M. (1990) Strategic management of exchange rate risks, *Long Range Planning*, **23**(4).

Going Global (1986) selected excerpts from a Conference organized by the Economist Conference Unit, *European Management Journal*, **4**(1).

Gregson, J. (1987) How Cadbury Schwepped into worldwide markets, *Financial Weekly*, March.

Hamel, G. and Prahalad, C.K. (1985) Do you really have a global strategy? *Harvard Business Review*, July/August.

Hamill, J. (1992) Global marketing, in: Baker M.J. (ed.), *Perspectives on Marketing Management*, **2**, John Wiley, New York.

Hamill, J. (1997) The internet and international marketing, *International Marketing Review*, September.

Hamill, J. and Gregory K. (1997) Internet marketing in the internationalization of small and medium sized enterprises, *Journal of Marketing Management*, January.

Henzler, H. and Rall, W. (1986) Facing up to the globalization challenge, *McKinsey Quarterly*, Winter.

Herbert, I.C. (1988) How Coke markets to the world, *Journal of Business Strategy*, September/October.

Howard, D.G. and Ryans, J.K. (1989) Advertising executives' perceptions of satellite TV's potential impact on the European market, *European Journal of Marketing*, **23**(5).

Huszagh, J.D., Fox, R.J. and Day, E. (1986) Marketing: an empirical investigation, *Journal of World Business*, **20**(2).

Jaben, J. (1994) For business, global arena is greatest show on earth, *Business Marketing*, **79**(8).

Jatusripitak, S., Fahey, L. and Kotler, P. (1985) Strategic global marketing: lessons from the Japanese, *Columbia Journal of World Business*, **20**(1), Spring.

Jeelof, G. (1989) Global strategies of Philips, *European Management Journal*, **7**(1).

Kahani, K. (1997) Why marketing still matters, in: Dickson, T. (ed.), *Financial Times Mastering Management*, Pitman, London.

Kale, S.H. and Sudharsham, D. (1987) A strategic approach to international segmentation, *International Marketing Review*, Summer.

Kashani, K. (1990) Why does global marketing work – or not work?, *European Management Journal*, **8**(2), June.

Kashani, K. (1997a) A new future for brands in: Dickson, T. (ed.), *Financial Times Mastering Management*, Pitman, London.

Kashani, K. (1997b) Why marketing still matters, in: Dickson, T. (ed.), *Financial Times Mastering Management*, Pitman, London.

Keegan, W.J. (1980) Five strategies for multinational marketing, in: Thorelli, H. and Becker, H. (eds), *International Marketing Strategy*, Pergamon, New York.

Keown, C.F., Synodinus, N.E. and Jacobs, L.W. (1989) Advertising practices in Northern Europe, *European Journal of Marketing*, **23**(3).

Killough, J. (1980) Improved payoffs from transnational advertising, in: Thorelli, H. and Becker, H. (eds), *International Marketing Strategy*, Pergamon, New York.

Kotabe, M. and Helsen, K. (1998) *Global Marketing Management*, John Wiley, New York.

Kreutzer, R.T. (1988) Marketing-mix standardization: an integrated approach in global marketing, *European Journal of Marketing*, **22**(10).

Lancioni, R.A. (1989) The importance of price in international business development, *European Journal of Marketing*, **23**(11).

Landor Associates (1990) *The World's Most Powerful Brands*, San Francisco.

Larreche, J.C. (1980) The international product/market portfolio, in: Thorelli, H. and Becker, H. (eds), *International Marketing Strategy*, Pergamon, New York.

Leontiades, J. (1985) *Multinational Corporate Strategy: Planning for World Markets*, Lexington Books, Lexington.

Leontiades, J. (1986) Going global – global strategies vs national strategies, *Long Range Planning*, **19**(6).

Levitt, T. (1983) The globalization of markets, *Harvard Business Review*, May/June.

Luqmani, M., Yavas, U. and Quraeshi, Z. (1989) Advertising in Saudi Arabia: content and regulation, *International Marketing Review*, **6**(1).

Mahmoud, E. and Rice, G. (1988) Use of analytical techniques in international marketing, *International Marketing Review*, **5**(3), Autumn.

Main, J. (1989) How to go global – and why, *Fortune*, 28th August.

Martenson, R. (1987) Is standardization of marketing feasible in culture-bound industries? A European case study, *International Marketing Review*, **4**(3).

Mayer, S. (1978) Multinational marketing research: methodological problems, *European Research*, **6**, March.

Mooij, M.K. and Keegan, W.J. (1991) *Advertising Worldwide: Concepts, Theories and Practice of International, Multinational and Global Advertising*, Prentice Hall, Englewood Cliffs, NJ.

Moyer, R. (1968) International market analysis, *Journal of Marketing Research*, **5**.

Naylor, T.H. (1985) The international strategy matrix, *Columbia Journal of World Business*, Summer.

Ohmae, K. (1985) *Triad Power: The Coming Shape of Global Competition*, Free Press, New York.

Ohmae, K. (1989) Managing in a borderless world, *Harvard Business Review*, **??**, May/June.

Ohmae, K, (1990) *The Borderless World: Power and Strategy in the Interlinked Economy*, Collins, London.

Onkvisit, S. and Shaw, J.J. (1983) An examination of the international product life cycle and its application within marketing, *Columbia Journal of World Business*, **18**(3), Fall.

Onkvisit, S. and Shaw, J.J. (1989) The international dimension of branding: strategic considerations and decisions, *International Marketing Review*, **6**(3).

Owen, S. (1993) The London image power survey[R]: a global assessment of brand strength, in: Aaker, D.A. and Biel, A.L. (eds), *Brand Equity and Advertising: Advertising's Role in Building Strong Brands*, Hillsdale, NJ.

Papavassiliou, N.K. (1989) The involvement model in advertising consumer product abroad, *European Journal of Marketing*, **23**(1).

Peebles, D.M. (1989) Don't write off global advertising: a commentary, *International Marketing Review*, **6**(1).

Perlmutter, H.V. (1969) The tortuous evolution of the multinational corporation, *Columbia Journal of World Business*, January/February.

Perry, A.C. (1990) International versus domestic marketing: four conceptual perspectives, *European Journal of Marketing*, **24**(6).

Perry, M. (1988) Conceptual overview and applications of international marketing positioning, *European Management Journal*, **6**(4), Winter.

Pitts, R.A. and Daniels, J.D. (1984) Aftermath of the matrix mania, *Columbia Journal of World Business*, Summer.

Porter, M.E. (1986a) *Competition in Global Industries*, Harvard Business School Press, Boston.

Porter, M.E. (1986b) Changing patterns of international competition, *California Management Review*, **28**(2), Winter.

Quelch, J.A. and Hoff, R.J. (1986) Customizing global marketing, *Harvard Business Review*, May/June.

Raffée, H. and Kreutzer, R.T. (1989) Organizational dimension of global marketing, *European Journal of Marketing*, **23**(5).

Ratnatunga, J., Hooley, G.J. and Pike, R. (1990) The marketing–finance interface, *European Journal of Marketing*, **24**(1).

Rau, P.A. and Preble, J.F. (1987) Standardization of marketing strategy by multinationals, *International Marketing Review*, Autumn.

Rosen, B.N., Boddewyn, J.J. and Louis, E.A. (1989) US brands abroad: an empirical study of global branding, *International Marketing Review*, **6**(1).

Sanders, P. (1989) Global managers for global corporations, *Journal of Management Development*, **7**(1).

Schmittlein, D. (1997) Customers as strategic assets, in: Dickson, T. (ed.), *Financial Times Mastering Management*, Pitman, London.

Shulman, J.S. (1980) Transfer pricing in the multinational firm, in: Thorelli, H. and Becker, H. (eds), *International Marketing Strategy*, Pergamon, New York.

Sims, C., Phillips, A. and Richards, T. (1992) Developing a global pricing strategy, *Marketing and Research Today*, **20**(1), 3–15.

Spawton, T. (1990) Development in the global alcoholic drinks industry and its implications for the future marketing of wine, *European Journal of Marketing*, **24**(4).

Takeuchi, H. and Porter, M.E. (1986) Three roles of international marketing in global strategy, in: Porter, M.E. (ed.), *Competition in Global Industries*, Harvard Business School Press, Boston.

Terpstra, V. (1987) The evolution of international marketing, *International Marketing Review*, Summer.

Thomas, M. (1986) *Pocket Guide to Marketing*, Economist Publications, London.

Toyne, B. and Walters, P.G.P. (1993) *Global Marketing Management: A Strategic Perspective*, Allyn and Bacon, Boston.

Tuncalp, S. (1988) The marketing research scene in Saudi Arabia, *European Journal of Marketing*, **22**(5).

Turnbull, P.W. and Doherty-Wilson, L. (1990) The internationalization of the advertising industry, *European Journal of Marketing*, **24**(1).

Vernon, R. (1966) International investment and international trade in the product cycle, *Quarterly Journal of Economics*, **80**.

Yip, G. (1992) *Total Global Strategy*, Prentice Hall, Englewood Cliffs.

GLOBAL FINANCIAL MANAGEMENT

12
CHAPTER

LEARNING OBJECTIVES

After studying the chapter, students should be able to:

- understand the basic concepts of international financial management and relate these to earlier chapters;
- understand the role of finance management in global competition;
- understand the various components of financial strategy (i.e. financing foreign operations, capital budgeting, remittance strategy and operational policies);
- describe how political risk and exchange rate fluctuation can be managed by international companies.

Introduction

The purpose of the chapter is to discuss the major financial issues faced by a global business and to relate these to other aspects of international management reviewed elsewhere in this book. It is assumed that the reader is familiar with basic finance topics which can be found in many elementary textbooks. Readers who wish to learn in detail about the international monetary system, foreign exchange markets and how businesses can reduce the associated risks should consult an up-to-date textbook on international finance such as Eiteman *et al*. (1998).

Finance, as one of the key resources-under-management of a global or transnational business, is one of the key strategic areas to address in the implementation of strategy and in internal analysis. Financing investments and working capital can be complicated in domestic business but for international companies, factors such as political uncertainty and exchange rate fluctuations mean that certainty can be even more elusive. This has implications for all parts of international business strategy because operational investments and changes to the stock of fixed assets all require significant input from the financial function.

Finance management and the global enterprise

The key issues in international financing

In other parts of this book we have seen that all functions within a business are affected by the overall strategy of the business in international markets. Lessard (1986) examined some international finance activities within a business to show how they would differ between a US-based business following an export/import strategy, a multidomestic strategy and a pure global strategy (Table 12.1).

Investment evaluation

Whilst the business following a multidomestic strategy can take decisions in one country which have little or no effect on its operations in another country, the global company is faced with a complex and interdependent set of choices. For example, the decision to locate a plant in China to take advantage of low labour (and hence production) costs must also take into account the associated logistical costs of shipping to other markets as well as strategic issues such as locating in that country before competitors and the potential for organizational learning.

Funding operations

A global enterprise has (by definition) access to a wide range of sources of finance with lower costs than domestic sources as well as opportunities to reduce taxation through the use of 'creative' transfer pricing. Access to lower cost of capital can be a source of competitive advantage but the company may be restricted by the degree of choice available to it. Host government legislation, for example, may prevent the use of resources from other parts of the business in other countries. While this may not be a significant drawback for the multidomestic company, it does limit the ability of the global company to achieve the lowest possible costs of capital.

Table 12.1 Global competitive strategy and international finance functions (source: Lessard 1986)

Function	Export/Import	Multidomestic	Global
Investment evaluation	Domestic perspective; few 'foreign' considerations	Yes/no decision to enter market or change mode to serve local market	Mutually exclusive global choices; currency and tax issues central
Funding operations	Meet domestic norms	Meet local norms	Match global competitors' cost of capital
Exchange risk management	Focus on exposure of foreign currency contracts	Focus on exposure of converting foreign profits into dollars	Focus on exposure of home and foreign profits to competitive effects of exchange rate shifts
Output pricing Responses to exchange rate movements	No change in home currency price	No change in local currency price	Change in home and local price to reflect global competitive position
Performance measurement	Measure all operations in dollars at actual exchange rates	Measure foreign operation in local currency	Measure all operations relative to standards that reflects competitive effects of exchange rate changes

Exchange risk management: output/pricing responses to exchange rate movements
Changes in the exchange rate for a country will affect the operating costs and the revenues of the company's subsidiary in that country. Lessard (1986) pointed out that for the company following a multidomestic strategy, the costs and revenues move together because most of the value-adding costs are locally incurred and the revenues are locally generated. Thus, profits move in simple proportion to the exchange rate. On the other hand, the sourcing costs, value-adding activities and revenues of the global enterprise may be associated with a number of countries. Thus a change in the exchange rate of one country will have a much more complex effect on the profits of the global business.

Performance measurement
The financial performance of a global or transnational company can be measured in terms of the host country currency or the currency of the parent's country. Operational performance can be partly masked by

exchange rate changes during the accounting period making it difficult for the global enterprise to compare performance in different countries. Global strategic financial targets and control systems are usually therefore set up in such a way as to permit the effect of rate changes to be removed thus exposing the underlying financial performance. Lessard and Lorange (1977) advocated a system where budgets are established based on the projected exchange rate over a period and performance is tracked using the same projected rate. This does not shield the business from unexpected exchange rate changes but does at least provide a fair measure of the effectiveness of the operating managers.

Centralization versus decentralization of the finance function

Different approaches to decentralization

As with all the functions of an international business, a compromise has to be found between the need for global co-ordination (implying centralization) and local responsiveness (implying decentralization) of the finance function. The above discussion of multidomestic and global strategy helps us to understand how the function should be organized depending on the strategy the company is pursuing. According to Asheghian and Ebrahimi (1990) there are three approaches used (based on the EPRG framework – see Chapter 2).

Polycentric approach
Decision making is decentralized to the subsidiaries with the parent company's role limited to decisions on financing new projects. This is most likely to be used by companies following a multidomestic strategy.

Ethnocentric approach
Strategic decision making and operational control are centralized and remain the responsibility of the parent company. This is the approach adopted by the business following a purely global strategy. While this approach can optimize the financial performance of the company as a whole, it can have an adverse effect on the apparent performance of individual subsidiaries. This approach can also create difficulties with meeting local financial reporting requirements.

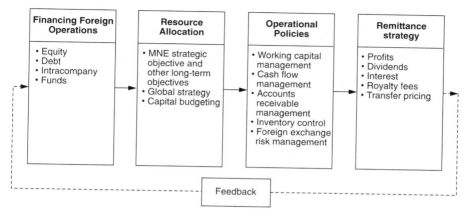

FIGURE 12.1 Fundamental decisions in financial strategy (source: Asheghian and Ebrahimi 1990)

Geocentric approach

Each subsidiary is treated differently according to factors such as the local financial environment, the quality of local management and the nature of the business. This approach could be compared to the transnational strategic approach in that the centre is permitting some adaptation to suit local conditions while maintaining a degree of central co-ordination. In practice, as suggested by Table 12.1, different parts of the financial function tend to be centralized (e.g. capital budgeting) while other parts tend to be decentralized. In order to look more closely at the different elements of the financial strategy of an international business, we will examine the four fundamental decision areas (see Figure 12.1).

Decision area 1: financing foreign operations

The options

The global or transnational business, like any other business which wants to grow, needs access to funds to finance land, plant and equipment as well as the additional working capital required for the day-to-day operations of the business. The three main sources of funds are:

- equity capital raised by selling shares on the stock exchange;
- debt capital raised by borrowing from a lender;
- internal funds generated through the normal operation of the business (retained profits).

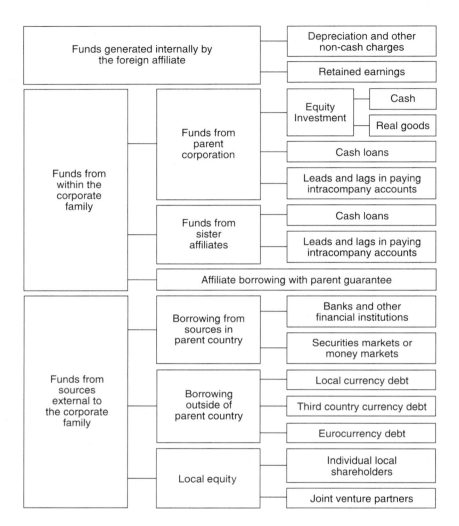

FIGURE 12.2   Potential sources of capital for financing foreign operations (source: Eiteman *et al.* 1998)

The options of sources of funds to choose from are summarized in Figure 12.2.

Equity capital

The international company has the opportunity to raise capital not only on its home stock exchange but also thorough crosslisting, that is listing its shares on other stock exchanges. The underlying objective of listing on additional stock exchanges is to lower the weighted average cost of capital. The main drawback to obtaining additional listings is that other stock exchanges, in particular the New York Stock Exchange, may require the company to disclose much more detail about its financial operations that its home stock exchange requires. An alternative approach is to raise capital by selling shares directly to foreign investors. This can include the sale of rights issue stock to a joint venture partner based in the host country in which the company wishes to invest. Table 12.2 summarizes the advantages and disadvantages of raising equity capital through the parent company and through host country sources.

Debt (or loan) capital

There are a number of possible sources of debt capital for foreign investment (Asheghian and Ebrahimi 1990).

Development banks and government agencies in the host country
These sources are most relevant for developing countries. There are often restrictions on what may be purchased, for example the subsidiary may be constrained to source from local suppliers.

Investment and commercial banks in host countries
The interest rate chargeable on debt capital varies between countries and it can sometimes be preferable to borrow locally if monetary pressure is lower

Table 12.2   Advantages and disadvantages of different sources of equity capital for international companies (source: Davidson 1982)

Sources of equity financing	Advantages	Disadvantages
Parent company	Possibility of enhancing debt capacity of overseas subsidiaries Higher parental controls on subsidiary operations	Higher foreign exchange exposure risks Higher risks for remittance of earning and repatriation of invested capital Higher risks for expropriation and nationalization
Host country	Lower foreign exchange exposure risks Stronger identity with host country and local interest groups	Less parental control on overseas operations

Table 12.3 Advantages and disadvantages of home versus host sources of funding for financing (source: Davidson 1982)

Source of debt financing	Advantages	Disadvantages
Home base (parent company, home country)	Tax deductions on interest paid Ease in remittance and repatriation Access to low cost funds	Higher foreign exchange exposure risks
Host country	Low political risk Tax deduction on interest paid Elimination of foreign exchange exposure risks Possibility of establishing a good relationship with local businesses and other financial institutions	Availability of capital Less control over subsidiary operations

in the host country. One of the advantages of international development is the ability to borrow in a range of countries depending on the attractiveness of interest rates at the time the finance is needed.

Financial markets

There is a wide rages of sources for finance as well as a wide range of instruments through which the loan may be raised. The three major sources of funding are *international bank loans*, the *Euronote market* and *the international bond market*. The last of these 'sports a rich array of innovative instruments created by imaginative investment bankers, who are unfettered by the usual controls and regulations governing domestic capital markets' (Eiteman *et al.* 1998).

Table 12.3 summarizes the advantages and disadvantages of domestic and host country sources of debt financing for international businesses. From this we can see that a company has to balance the opposing factors of exchange rate risks and political risks.

Decision area 2: resource allocation and capital budgeting

Uncertainties constraining the certainty of choice

Any business needs to plan how it is going to invest its capital in order to meet its long-term objectives. New opportunities for investment may come from a variety of sources inside and outside the business. One of the key activities of the finance function is to evaluate the financial aspects of each proposal to determine, firstly, if they meet company set criteria for the return generated and, secondly, to rank the proposals so that the most attractive can be identified. The standard tools used in such evaluations include calculation of the net present value (NPV) or the internal rate of return (IRR). A company using the latter approach will specify a 'hurdle rate' for all investment decisions; any project with an IRR below this rate will not be considered further.

Investment decisions for international businesses are made in a similar way to those for domestic companies; differences are mainly caused by the greater complexity present in the international environment. Asheghian and Ebrahimi (1990) identified the following causes of this additional complexity:

- political risks are higher and more varied;
- variations in the sources and forms of financing;
- foreign exchange rate fluctuations;
- restrictions on capital, exchange and profit flows in many countries;
- differences in taxation systems between home and host countries;
- differences in the economic systems and conditions between countries;
- differences in inflation rates;
- varying interest and discount rates;
- uncertainty in the estimation of salvage value (the value of project assets at the end of the project).

Because investment appraisal for international business can be more complex than for purely domestic decisions, a number of 'softer' criteria are sometimes applied to the decision. Non-financial criteria can be applied to an investment proposal and such tools as impact analysis and cost-benefit analysis can provide information as useful as the financial calculations that are often based upon unreliable projections of revenue flows.

The conclusions reached by these three approaches could be different. Multiple evaluations do not necessarily make decision-making any easier but at least the final decision should be made on the basis of a wider range of information than the basic NPV approach. A further important factor in the decision is how the company is able to address the risks posed by political and exchange rate uncertainties – problems very commonly encountered by global and transnational businesses.

Political risk

The political environment has already been discussed in Chapter 5. Political factors vary by country, by industry and by individual business. The greatest risk that any international business faces is the expropriation, without compensation, of assets held in a foreign country. This threat is a major deterrent to investment in late developing countries. There are other ways in which host governments can directly influence the operations of global companies; the imposition of currency restriction introduced by the Malaysian government in 1998 following the collapse of the 'tiger' economies is a dramatic example of this.

Kobrin (1982) defined two different types of political risk:

1. country-specific (macro) risks which apply to all foreign businesses in that country;
2. company-specific (micro) risks which apply to an industry, a particular company or even a particular project.

Figure 12.3 summarizes the various components of political risk.

Assessing and forecasting political risk

Two different types of risk have to be assessed – macro-risk and micro-risk.

Macro-risk
The international business will need to know the degree of political stability in a host country and the current attitude of the various political forces towards foreign investors. Some estimates of this can be gained from

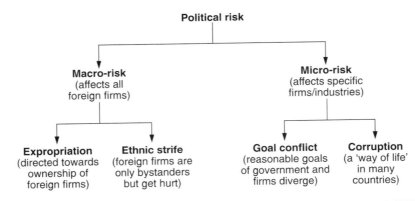

FIGURE 12.3   Macro-micro decomposition of political risk (source: Eiteman *et al*. 1998)

examining the country's history as well as sources such as radio, television and newspapers. However in countries where the media is controlled by political forces, an incomplete or (at worst) totally misleading picture may be gathered. Alternative sources of information are professional analysts, recent visitors and business contacts within the country. The problem is that political change can be very sudden and overwhelming, as events such as the break-up of the USSR demonstrated.

Micro-risk

Even if some degree of accuracy can be made in forecasting political events, the impact of these on specific companies or industries may be even harder to predict. Eiteman *et al.* (1998) suggested that international companies with significant exposure to micro-risk are likely to employ in-house political analysts who understand the industry well and can focus their attention on each country. Knickerbocker (1973) suggested that in many cases, international companies make little attempt to make independent risk assessments but instead will tend to watch what other companies do and then copy them.

Dealing with political risk

It is demonstrably obvious, then, that political risk cannot be avoided. For companies seeking to expand in other countries, strategy formulation is more concerned with finding appropriate approaches to dealing with the risk. An obvious way to minimize such risk is to invest only in those countries which have a historically low level of risk. Unfortunately this may deprive the company the opportunity to invest in many countries where the potential returns are very high. An alternative approach is to accept that risks are present and plan investment and operations in such a way that the consequences of unexpected political changes can be minimized.

Such plans might include:

- *negotiating investment agreements* with the host country government covering as many aspects as possible. The implication here is that a compromise must be reached which offers acceptable benefits for the investor *and* the host country government. This does not, of course, eliminate the possibility of a new government ignoring agreements made with its predecessor;

- *adapting to host country goals and cultural norms*, so that the investor is seen as a benefit to the country rather than an exploiter;
- *planning disinvestment* so that ownership of the project will be acquired by the host government after an agreed period of time;
- employing *operating strategies* such as local sourcing, keeping ownership of key technologies, building market control, investing using funds sourced from the host country etc. to strengthen the company's bargaining position.

Decision area 3: operational policies

Working capital and cash flow management

Working capital is the value of assets required for the normal operations of the business. In practice, this means the value of stock, creditors (including trade creditors and short-term debts), debtors and cash-in-hand. Businesses need working capital to ensure that the day-to-day operations of the business are properly financed. There is usually a lag between the purchase of the inputs and the recovery of the added value through payment by customers for the final product.

Businesses will hold cash balances (and other liquid assets) in order to fund the normal day-to-day operations of the business (*transaction* motive) and as a buffer against unexpected variations in cash requirements (*precautionary* motive). However, all working capital is an asset tied up in the business which is not earning a useful return (the opportunity cost of working capital). Thus, the purpose of cash flow management is to ensure that while the business has sufficient cash to cover the transaction and risk motives, it does not hold excess cash which might be better employed elsewhere in the system and in another form.

All businesses, whether domestic or international, engage in some form of cash flow management. The international business must deal with a more complex situation because of the additional uncertainties posed by exchange rate changes, government restrictions on the flow of funds in and out of the country, differences in tax systems and the costs and other difficulties involved in transferring funds across national boundaries. It may not, therefore, be able to make the maximum use of opportunities such as transfer of cash into stronger currencies or into areas with more favourable tax systems.

Eiteman *et al.* (1998) summarized the main differences between domestic and international business cash management.

Planning

An international business usually prepares three cash budgets – one for each individual national entity, one for each currency used within the system and one for the parent company as a whole. In order for the last of these budgets to be prepared, the company must use a forecast set of exchange rates.

Collection

Delays between customer payment and the cash being actually available to the company should be minimized. The availability of a multinational banking system with a presence in each host country can facilitate this process.

Repositioning

Funds collected have to be transferred to where they are of most use to the business. The international business may face restrictions (see above) in its ability to do this to maximum effect. A variety of direct and indirect techniques may be used to effect transfers and reduce restrictions, including intra-company transfer pricing.

Disbursement

This is similar to the collection of cash; the aim is to keep the cash within the business for as long as possible while ensuring that it reaches the recipient at the agreed time. Again, the selection of an appropriate banking system is important.

Covering cash shortages

Cash shortage at a subsidiary can be covered either by the subsidiary itself borrowing locally or by an internal transfer of funds from another part of the parent company. The opportunity here is that some parts of the business may be able to borrow at much more favourable rates of interest than others.

Investing surplus cash

The various parts of an international business may hold cash in local currency which represents a surplus generated from normal operations.

Subsidiaries may have responsibility for managing this surplus themselves, but many companies accumulate these surpluses into a 'pool' and may then set up a financial subsidiary to manage the pool effectively.

Foreign exchange exposure

There are three main types of risk associated with unexpected foreign exchange rate movements that are faced by an international company with subsidiaries in several countries. One of the objectives of the finance department is to estimate the potential of such movements to affect the profitability and other key measures of financial performance (in other words gain an estimate of the company's *exposure*) and to take steps to ensure that these key measures are maximized.

Transaction exposure
If the company agrees to some sort of financial transaction where payment will be made some time after the agreement then the value of the transaction will change as the exchange rate changes. For example, a British company may agree to purchase machinery from an American supplier for US$150 000 with delivery in six months. If the exchange rate at the time of the agreement is £1 = US$1.50 then the value of the transaction is £100 000. If in six months the rate rises to £1 = US$2.00 then the value of the transaction will be only £75 000 which is a significant saving. On the other hand, if the rate drops to £1 = US$1.00, the value of the transaction will rise to £150 000 which would make the deal much less attractive. Thus, transaction exposure arises from cash flows generated by current financial obligations.

Operating exposure
This is also related to cash flows but in a much wider sense; unexpected changes in exchange rates will affect not only a company but also its suppliers, customers and competitors. This, in turn, could affect the company's international competitiveness, future sales and costs. Thus, operating (or economic) exposure is a measure of how much the present value of the company is altered by unexpected rate changes.

Translation exposure
A global or transnational business with subsidiaries in several countries must prepare consolidated accounts in its domestic currency. In order to

accurately report in the financial statements, all figures must be translated into the domestic currency. Exchange rate changes may, therefore, have a significant effect on the value of the shareholders' equity. Note that this is only an accounting change and not a realized gain or loss.

Reducing exposure

There are many methods which can be used to reduce the exposure of a business to exchange rate changes; the reader is referred to any standard textbook on international finance for details. One technique that is commonly used to reduce risk is *hedging*. If we return to the example above, the business may consider the risk of the sterling price increasing to £150 000 unacceptable. It may therefore buy US$150 000 immediately the deal is agreed. The drawback with this is the opportunity cost of tying up this amount of capital for six months.

An alternative is to buy US$150 000 in the forward market for delivery in six months at the six month forward rate – say £1 = US$1.20. The company's capital is not tied up during this time and it knows exactly how much it will have to pay for the machinery. Thus, hedging places an upper limit on the detrimental effect that adverse changes of exchange rates will have on the company's cash flows. One drawback is that the business cannot benefit from favourable exchange rate movements. It is up to the finance function to determine which method(s) of managing the company's exposure are most appropriate.

Decision area 4: remittance strategy

Types of funds transfer

In the above discussion on operational policies, we referred to the movement of cash between different parts of an international company. A remittance strategy refers to the company's polices and procedures for implementing the flow of funds around the business, and in particular, the repatriation of funds to the parent company.

Table 12.4 summarizes the conduits that an international business has for moving funds.

Table 12.4   Conduits for moving funds (source: Eiteman *et al*. 1998)

Type of funds flow	Methods of performing the flow
Flows as compensation for invested capital	Payment of dividends, interest payment on intercompany loans, principal repayment on intercompany loans
Flows for goods and services received	Payment for purchased materials and components, payment for purchase or services, royalty payments, licence fees, management fees, overhead compensation
Flows for both categories	Leading or lagging of payments

Problems with transferring funds

Unlike a purely domestic company the global or transnational company may face a number of restrictions which impede its ability to freely transfer funds around the organization.

Political constraints

Just as an exporter may face tariff and non-tariff barriers to trade, so an internationalized business may be subject to direct and indirect constraints. The currency may become unconvertible or else the government may impose a fixed exchange rate which makes conversion to the home country's currency impossible or not economically viable. Governments may also place limits on the total amount of funds that may be transferred out of the country. Less obvious limitations may be present through the imposition of complex and time consuming processes which must be followed in order to gain permission to transfer funds.

Tax constraints

In addition to foreign exchange losses, the international company can be subject to taxation in the host country and any other country whose borders the funds cross. Even within countries there may be regional taxation in addition to national taxation which causes extra complexity. The threat by the State of California to tax local subsidiaries of foreign-based companies on the profits of the parent rather than the subsidiary is an interesting example of this. Some companies establish subsidiaries in tax havens in order to defer the payment of taxes.

Transaction costs

Even when exchange rates themselves are not a constraint, the conversion from one currency to another incurs a cost. Although for a single conversion the cost is only a small percentage of the total value of the transaction, these costs can become significant if funds are repeatedly converted. The effects can be reduced by planning funds flow so that instead of going from subsidiaries to the parent then back to subsidiaries, the funds flow directly between subsidiaries. Another approach is to use *netting*. Instead of several unconnected exchanges of funds between a parent and a subsidiary, the transactions over a period are grouped together so that only one transfer of funds, representing the net value of all the transactions, is required.

Liquidity needs

We mentioned above the need for each subsidiary to hold funds for transaction and precautionary motives. The level of funds held by the subsidiary will vary from one country to another due to local conditions and may sometimes have to be somewhat higher than the optimum level for the company as a whole.

Blocked funds

If exchange or other controls severely restrict the normal movement of funds out of a country then the business may still be able to effect a transfer through indirect means. Eiteman *et al.* (1998) described a number of alternatives.

'Unbundling' services

Instead of repatriating profits the company can split the transfers up into a number of categories as shown in Table 12.4. Host governments may be more willing to permit at least some of these payments.

Transfer pricing

If a parent company wishes to relocate funds from a subsidiary, it can charge artificially high prices for goods and services purchased from the parent by the subsidiary. This may, however, results in additional tax complications.

Leading and lagging payments

The parent can delay payments to the subsidiary (lag) but accelerate some payments by the subsidiary to the parent (lead). This has the effect of a temporary transfer of funds to the parent but some countries set limits on the timings that may be used.

Reinvoicing centres

This could be viewed as a method of implementing the first three approaches. Intracompany transfers of goods and services are all made through a reinvoicing centre, a separate corporate entity which buys from the supplier in the supplier's home currency and then resells to the buyer in the buyer's home currency. The main use of this technique is to mange the company's exposure to movements in exchange rates. Where there are restrictions on fund transfers, the reinvoicing centre can handle the unbundling, transfer pricing and lead/lag methods discussed above with the added benefit of masking the ultimate destination of funds transferred out of the subsidiary.

Fronting loans

Loans from a parent to a subsidiary are made through a financial intermediary (usually a large international bank) and interest payments from the subsidiary are made to that intermediary. The idea is that foreign governments are less likely to restrict payments to a large international bank than to the parent.

Unrelated exports

The blocked funds are used to pay for goods or services used by other parts of the business and provided by the host country. Eiteman *et al.* (1998) gave the example of an international company's employees using the host country's state airline for international flights. The tickets are paid for in the host country's currency using the blocked funds. Other more sophisticated techniques such as bartering and countertrade (Hennart 1990) have also been used. The underlying theme is finding ways to improve the host country's economy whose poor state was the original cause of the block.

REVIEW AND DISCUSSION QUESTIONS

1. When might a decentralization of financial decision making be preferable to centralization?

2. What are the options available to international companies seeking to find finance for foreign investment?

3. Describe the pros and cons of the three options for financing foreign investment.

4. Why might an international company have an advantage over a domestic business when raising debt finance in an overseas country?

5. Why is an international company more vulnerable to political risks than purely domestic producers?

References and further reading

Aharoni, Y. (1966) *The Foreign Investment Decision Process*, Harvard University Press, Boston.

Asheghian, P. and Ebrahimi, B. (1990) *International Business, Economics, Environment, Strategies*, Harper and Row, New York.

Brigham, E. and Gapenski, L.C. (1985) *Financial Management: Theory and Practice*, 4th edn, Dryden Press.

Buckley, A. (1986) *Multinational Finance*, Philip Allan.

Chakravarthy, B.S. and Perlmutter, H.V. (1985) Strategic planning for a global business, *Columbia Journal of World Business*, Summer, 3–10.

Davidson, W.H. (1982) *Global Strategic Management*, John Wiley, New York.

Eiteman, D.K., Stonehill, A.I. and Moffett, M.H (1998) *Multinational Business Finance*, 8th edn, Addison Wesley, Reading, MA.

Fayerweather, J. (1978) *International Business Strategy and Administration*, Ballinger Publishing Company, Cambridge, MA.

Hennart, J.-F. (1990) Some empirical dimesions of countertrade, *Journal of International Business Studies*, second quarter, 243–270.

Knickerbocker, F.T. (1973) *Oligopolistic Reaction and Multinational Enterprise*, Harvard Business School Press, Boston.

Kobrin, S.J. (1979) Political risk: a review and recommendations, *Journal of International Business Studies*, Spring/Summer, 69–80.

Kobrin, S.J. (1982) *Managing Political Risk Assessment: Strategic Response to Environmental Change*, University of California Press, Berkeley.

Lessard, D.R. (1986) Finance and global competition: exploiting financial scope and coping with volatile exchange rates, in: M.E. Porter (ed.), *Competition in Global Industries*, Harvard Business School Press, Boston.

Lessard, D.R. and Lorange, P. (1997) Currency changes and management control: resolving the centralization/decentralization dilemma, *Accounting Review*, July, 628–637.

Murrenbeeld, M. (1975) Economic factors for forecasting foreign exchange rate changes, *Columbia Journal of World Business*, Summer, 81–95.

Robbins, S. and Stobaugh, R. (1973) *Money in the Multinational Enterprise*, Basic Books.

Robock, S.H. (1971) Political risk: identification and assessment, *Columbia Journal of World Business*, July/August, 6–20.

Robock, S.H. and Simmonds, K. (1989) *International Business and Multinational Enterprises*, 4th edn, Homewood, Irwin.

Rummel, R.J. and Heenan, D.A. (1978) How multinationals analyze political risk, *Harvard Business Review*, January/February, 67–76.

Shapiro, A. (1984) *Multinational Financial Management*, 2nd edn, Allyn and Bacon, Boston.

ORGANIZATIONAL STRUCTURE AND CONTROL IN GLOBAL AND TRANSNATIONAL BUSINESSES

13

CHAPTER

LEARNING OBJECTIVES

After studying this chapter, students should be able to:

- describe two key variables that distinguish forms of organizational structure from each other;
- explain the contingency and configuration approaches to determining structure;
- explain the types of structure adopted by international and global businesses;
- describe the routes by which structures develop, particular into complex forms; such as matrix structures;
- describe the influences behind, and forms of, transnational structures;
- describe the issues surrounding decision making and control in transnational structures;
- explain how performance measures can be used to appraise the performance of transnational businesses.

Introduction

This chapter is important to the main themes of the book since it provides the link between global strategies, global management, strategy implementation and global competitiveness. There are particularly strong links, therefore, between this chapter and those on global strategy, human resource management and networks. The chapter explores the determinants of organizational structure, summarizes the alternative organizational structures available to international organizations, introduces recent alternative configurations, and examines the important links which exist between global strategies and organizational structure and control.

The essence of a global and transnational strategy is the co-ordination and integration of geographically-dispersed operations in the pursuit of global competitive advantage. This chapter examines the complex inter-relationships between global strategy and the organization and control issues associated with its implementation.

Some essentials of organizational structure

Key variables

Organizational structure concerns the shape adopted by the business in the pursuit of its strategic objectives. For international businesses, the importance of structure is brought into focus because of the distances between the various parts and the need to co-ordinate activities between them.

Structures are usually distinguished according to two variables:

1. the height and width of the structure;
2. the extent to which hierarchical management is observed.

Before we begin our discussion of the importance of structure in global and transnational businesses, we will review these three key themes in general terms.

'Height' and 'width' of structures

Height of structures
It is perhaps obvious to say that different organizations adopt different 'shapes'. 'Height' refers to the number of layers that exist within a structure. Larger organizations are higher than smaller ones. The guide to how high an organizational structure should be depends upon the complexity of the tasks that a proposed strategy entails. A small, single-site manufacturer will typically be involved in competing in one industry, sometimes with a single product type. This scenario is much less complex than a transnational chemical company that competes in many national markets, in several product types and with a high dependence on research and legal regulations.

Height facilitates the engagement of specialist managers in the middle of an organization who can oversee and direct the many activities that some large organizations are involved in. Not all organizations have this requirement and it would be more appropriate for such organizations to have a flatter structure. Companies with a high requirement for specialist professional staff often have several layers of management (thus increasing their height) and accordingly, civil engineering consultancies, accountancy firms, chemical and specialist engineering companies often have this feature.

Width of structures

The 'width' of organizational structures refers to the extent to which the organization is centralized or decentralized. A decentralized organizational structure is one in which the centre elects to devolve some degree of decision-making power to other parts of the organization (see the EPRG framework in Chapter 2). A centralized organization is one in which little or no power is devolved from the centre. In practice, a continuum exists between the two extremes along which the varying extents of decentralization can be visualized (see Figure 13.1). Transnational businesses tend towards the right-hand side of the continuum.

As with the height of structures, there is a trade-off between the costs and benefits of width. The advantages of centralization are mainly concerned with the ability of the centre to maintain tighter direct control over the activities of the organization. This is usually more appropriate when the organization is smaller and engages in few product or market segments. Some degree of decentralization is advantageous when the organization operates in a number of markets and localized specialized knowledge is an important determinant of overall success.

Hierarchical configuration of structures

It would be wrong to assume that all organizations observe a strict form of structural hierarchy. Strict hierarchy is not always an appropriate form of

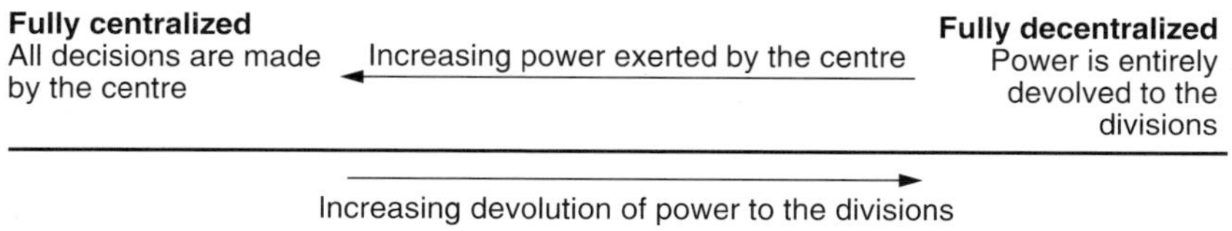

Fully centralized
All decisions are made
by the centre

Increasing power exerted by the centre ◄————

Fully decentralized
Power is entirely
devolved to the
divisions

————► Increasing devolution of power to the divisions

FIGURE 13.1   The centralization–decentralization continuum

organization, especially when it cannot be automatically assumed that seniority guarantees superior management skill.

In some contexts, formal hierarchy is entirely appropriate in implementing strategy. In others, however, allowing employees to act with some degree of independence can in fact enable the organization to be more effective in its various spheres of activity. The use of matrix structures, for example, can result in the organization being able to carry out many more tasks that a formal hierarchical structure (see later). Many companies go 'half way' in this regard by seconding employees into special task forces or cross-functional teams that are not part of the hierarchical structure, and which act semi-independently in pursuit of their brief.

Determinants of organizational structure

Mintzberg's determinants

According to Mintzberg (1979) and Mintzberg *et al.* (1998) there are two basic approaches to the formation of organizational structure, the contingency approach and the configuration approach.

According to the contingency approach, the structure of an organization will depend upon factors like the nature of its business and its strategy, its size, the geographical span of its activities, its age and history and the nature of its environment. Mintzberg argued that rather than adopting a contingency approach, it is sometimes better to base structure on a configuration approach. Factors like spans of control, the need for formalization, centralization or decentralization, and planning systems should be logically configured into internally consistent groupings.

Peters and Waterman (1982) argued that 'excellent' organizational performance depends upon strategy, systems, culture (shared values), skills, leadership, staff and structure (drawing upon what has become known as the McKinsey 7 S framework). As these organizational features are interdependent, each was thought to play an important part in determining the others so that structure will be affected by strategy, systems, culture etc. Equally, structure will help to shape strategy, culture and systems. It is therefore evident that there are many complex factors shaping the structure of organizations.

The contingency approach

Contingency theory (as it relates to organizational structure) suggests that the most important determinants of organizational structure will include a number of factors. The key point with contingency theory is that the structure adopted will *depend*. This is in contrast to the configuration approach which seeks to proactively determine.

The structure that an organization adopts (which may be a domestic or internationalized business) will depend upon several determining factors:

- the nature of the business;
- the environment of the organization;
- the global strategy of the business;
- the age and history of the organization;
- the size of business and limitations of span of control;
- the level of technology in the organization;
- the geographical span of activities;
- the culture of the organization;
- leadership and leadership style.

We will briefly consider each of these determining factors in turn.

The nature of the business
Businesses whose value-adding activities are largely repetitive, and which may be centred on a production line, are likely to adopt hierarchical structures with centralized decision making. Hierarchical structures are better suited to standardization of procedures. Organizations whose activities are diverse, creative or innovative are more likely to be based upon flatter structures which encourage horizontal communication and devolve decision making powers.

The environment of the organization
The more dynamic, turbulent and complex the environment, the more adaptable the organization will usually need to be. In these circumstances, decision making is likely to be decentralized so as to increase responsiveness. On the other hand, Mintzberg (1979) argued that organizations will tend to centralize decision making under conditions of extreme environmental hostility. In the international environment, a market which is globally homogeneous will permit greater centralization of authority

while diversity of market conditions will increase the need for local responsiveness and will require decentralized decision making.

The global strategy of the business

When a business has a globally standardized strategy its structure will tend to concentrate power at the centre as this facilitates global co-ordination and integration of activities. A strategy which is centred upon local responsiveness will require devolution of power to local managers. A transnational strategy, combining global co-ordination with local responsiveness, will require a complex structure allowing a degree of global control to be combined with the ability to respond locally. Developments in information and communications technology have made possible new organizational structures designed to achieve these dual, but somewhat conflicting, objectives (see Chapter 10).

The age and history of the organization

Mintzberg (1979) found that older organizations and businesses in mature industries tended to have more formalized structures. Few structures are designed 'from scratch' and consequently, most structures evolve alongside the business itself. Accordingly, a small, new organization will have little need for a formal or complex structure but as an organization grows, the need for formalization and the observance of hierarchy increases.

The size of business and limitations of span of control

Larger organizations have more formalized and complex structures with greater specialization of tasks and clearly defined methods of communication. Tasks will be clustered into related groupings and the relationships between these groupings will be well established. The size of any cluster of activities will be dictated by the limitations of a manager's effective span of control (i.e. the number of subordinates he or she can directly control). Activities are often typically grouped by functional area so that marketing- and sales-related activities will be grouped together, and activities like recruitment, training and payroll are often grouped under the banner of human resources management.

The level of technology in the organization

Information and communications technology (ICT) has widened the potential span of control of an individual manager, making possible flatter organizational structures. Similarly, ICT makes it possible to centrally co-ordinate activities while simultaneously allowing decentralization of decision making assisting local responsiveness. Before the advent of ICT, most international businesses operated on a multinational basis — allowing considerable autonomy to national subsidiaries because it was almost impossible to co-ordinate activities across boundaries with such constraints upon effective communication.

The geographical span of activities

The greater the geographical span of an organization's activities, the greater the need for formalization and complexity of structure. Again, ICT has increased the ability of organizations to increase the geographical span of their activities. Developments in telecommunications, like satellite and cable technology, have been critical in allowing businesses to integrate and manage their activities on a worldwide basis.

The culture of the organization

The values, attitudes and beliefs of the members of the organization will play an important part in moulding organizational structure. Thus a creative organization like a software house or an advertising agency will often have a flexible structure (less observance of hierarchy) whereas a production-based manufacturing company is likely to have much more precisely defined and formalized groupings of activities with a much firmer observance of hierarchy. Organizational culture also often has its origins in the national culture of the country of origin of the business. The organizational culture of many Japanese businesses, for example, is often strongly influenced by values, attitudes and beliefs like loyalty and obedience which are prominent features of traditional Japanese society.

Leadership and leadership style

Larger organizations with strong leadership will tend to adopt structures which concentrate power at the centre of the organization. Smaller organizations have structures which spread from the leader at the centre. There will also be a close relationship between leadership style and organizational culture.

The configuration approach to organizational design

Although the factors discussed in the previous section contribute to understanding of how organization structures evolve, Mintzberg (1979) and Mintzberg *et al.* (1998) proposed a 'configuration approach' to organization design. The configuration of an organization (according to Mintzberg) must take account of the following design parameters:

- *job specialization* – to logically divide up the tasks of the organization;
- *behaviour formalization* – standardization of work processes;
- *training* – instructional programmes to provide employees with the skills and knowledge to do their jobs;
- *indoctrination* – to inculcate organizational norms in workers;
- *unit grouping* – according to (i) business function (e.g. marketing, finance, production etc.) and (ii) market served. These may conflict with each other as grouping by business function centres on the efficiency of the processes of the organization while grouping by market increases organizational flexibility but encourages duplication (so, in turn, reducing efficiency);
- *unit size* – the number of positions contained in a single unit of the business;
- *planning and control systems* – used to plan and control the activities of the organization;
- *liaison and integrating devices* – devices like task forces and committees can integrate the units of the business. The logical conclusion of such devices is a matrix structure (see later);
- *the need for centralization or decentralization* – the extent to which it is necessary or desirable to diffuse decision making power.

In addition, it is important to consider both horizontal and vertical communication requirements and systems within the organization. In an international business unit grouping, planning and control systems, integrating devices, the need for centralization or decentralization and indoctrination are particularly important. The way in which units are grouped is one of the most significant decisions to be made in the design of international organizations. It is not simply a decision between grouping by functional area or by market, but rather how to integrate the two. The structures of global organizations must also take account of the need to co-ordinate and integrate geographically dispersed activities, at the same time as making possible local responsiveness where and when it is required. The matrix and the transnational (Bartlett and Ghoshal 1987) are alternative forms of organization which attempt to resolve these conflicting requirements.

There is no ideal organizational structure. There are several commonly found types of structure which incorporate the parameters above and which reflect the range of internal and external factors influencing the evolution of organization structure.

Types of international organizational structure

International businesses can theoretically choose from a range of alternative organizational structures as summarized in Table 13.1. Each structure has its own inherent strengths and weaknesses.

Table 13.1 Types of transnational organizational structure

International structures	*Characteristics*
Export department	Responsibility for foreign sales transferred from domestic product divisions to a separate export department reporting directly to the Group CEO
Mother–daughter structure	Parent company acts as holding company for largely autonomous foreign subsidiaries. Subsidiary management report directly to CEO, but on an informal and personal basis. Subsidiaries are granted substantial operating freedom subject to satisfactory performance evaluation
International divisional structure	Responsibility for all foreign operations transferred to a separate international division based at the corporate centre. Foreign subsidiaries report directly to the international centre
Global structures	
Functional	Responsibility for foreign operations allocated to functional line managers at the centre. Foreign subsidiaries report directly to functional executives at the centre (production; marketing; human resources; finance etc.)
Product	Responsibility for foreign operations allocated to product divisions based at the centre. Foreign subsidiaries report directly to product divisions
Geographic/regional	Responsibility for foreign operations allocated to area executives. Foreign subsidiaries report directly to geographic/regional division based at the centre or abroad
Matrix	Responsibility for foreign operations divided between product and geographic divisions. Foreign subsidiaries report directly to both product and geographic centres

International structures

Export departments

The establishment of a separate export department to control and co-ordinate foreign sales is most frequently found in companies in the early stages of internationalization where foreign production is minimal and foreign markets are supplied mainly through domestic production and exports. The creation of a separate export department allows a greater degree of control and co-ordination of the export drive by concentrating knowledge of foreign markets in a single department and by ensuring that foreign sales are included in the planning process.

Export departments, however, suffer from two main weaknesses. First, conflicts of interest may arise between domestically-orientated product divisions and the export department regarding the relative importance of foreign as opposed to domestic sales. The export department will be dependent on domestic product divisions for both products and technology. Since the latter are mainly concerned with domestic sales, less attention may be devoted to enhancing foreign markets. Second, export departments are ill-suited to further foreign market expansion through licensing, subcontracting and FDI because of the lack of expertise in managing foreign operations as opposed to foreign sales. Largely because of the second of these disadvantages, most export departments are relatively short-lived. Continued foreign market expansion through FDI has led most international businesses to replace their export departments with international divisions, or, in the case of some European businesses, with mother–daughter structures.

Mother–daughter structures

This type of structure is particularly suited to two types of international enterprise. First, new foreign investors, where foreign operations are not of crucial importance to the parent company. Second, businesses with extensive foreign direct investments, but limited central resources, as with some European businesses. The main advantage of the mother–daughter structure is that it encourages subsidiary innovation and motivation by substituting subsidiary autonomy for centralized control. Its main disadvantage, on the other hand, is the lack of global planning and co-ordination of activity.

International divisional structures

The majority of US businesses (and some European and Japanese businesses) have used this type of structure at some stage in their internationalization. The strengths and weaknesses of the international division are similar to those of export departments. Thus, the international division provides a focal point for the growing foreign involvement of the company (through FDI) by concentrating international knowledge and expertise in a single division. This allows greater control and co-ordination of foreign operations as well as ensuring that the interests of foreign subsidiaries are taken into account in the corporate planning process. On the negative side, however, the same conflict of interest evident between domestic product divisions and export departments will also exist in the relationship between the former and the international division. International divisions are also usually short-lived in most international companies. Indeed, the very success of the international division in stimulating FDI may sow the seeds of its own destruction. The continued foreign expansion of the company through FDI will result in the need for closer control and planning of foreign activities by the parent company. This has led most international organizations to replace their international divisions with global structures aimed at providing a greater degree of co-ordination and integration of their worldwide activities. Such global structures may be organized on functional, product or geographical lines of responsibilities.

Global structures

Functionally-based structures

Global organization along functional lines is rare among US companies, although it has been used successfully by some European and US international businesses with extremely narrow product lines (e.g. oil companies). The global functional organization allows tight control over specific functions worldwide, which may be of particular importance to businesses whose competitive strengths lie in superior technology, marketing or personnel practices. Such advantages, however, are often outweighed by the disadvantages of this type of structure. First, co-ordination of functions is difficult, leading to the potential separation of, for example, production and marketing. Second, subsidiaries will be reporting to several different divisions at the corporate centre, resulting in the duplication of effort and a possible breakdown of communications. Finally, the structure is unsuitable for multi-product or geographically dispersed organizations. As a consequence of such disadvantages, most international companies have incorporated functional responsibilities within global divisions based on product or geographical lines.

Product-based structures

Under the global product organizational structure, product divisions at the corporate centre are given worldwide responsibilities for their own products and services, including both functional and geographical responsibilities. The global product structure is particularly suited for global businesses with diverse product lines, when products go to a variety of end-users, and when a high degree of technology capability is required. Organization by product may also permit significant economies of scale to be achieved through the co-ordination and integration of production in different countries. It also allows the business to respond quickly to the actions of competitors. The principal weaknesses of global product divisions relate to the lack of emphasis placed on international or geographical planning. Global product divisions may be staffed by executives with particular product expertise but with limited knowledge of international/geographic markets. Thus, the emphasis of the division may be on the domestic market to the detriment of foreign markets. Similarly, the lack of international knowledge may create difficulties in assessing changes in environmental and political conditions in overseas markets, leading to lost opportunities for expansion. Finally, co-ordination and integration of the subsidiary companies in a particular geographical area is difficult to achieve under global product divisions.

Geographic/regionally-based structures

The problems associated with the lack of regional co-ordination can be overcome by adopting global regional/geographic structures. Under this structure, subsidiary companies (regardless of product line) report directly to corporate executives responsible for a particular geographical area. Each area division has both product line and functional responsibilities for all operations within its area. Such area divisions may be based at the centre. More commonly, however, separate regional headquarters will be established in the relevant areas. Many US companies, for example, have established separate regional headquarters based in Europe.

A survey by Daniels (1986) identified various reasons for the establishment of such offices, including:

- *pooling of resources* – the provision of specialist staff support to operating divisions;
- *product rationalization* – the management of product integration on a European basis;
- *size of reporting structures* – to reduce the number of subsidiaries reporting directly to the parent company;
- *day-to-day control* – to exert greater operating control over subsidiaries than is possible from a distant parent company;
- *management development* – the regional headquarters is used to develop a cadre of highly trained managers with global orientations;
- *unification of external relations* – the consolidation of public relations efforts.

The global regional/geographic structure is particularly suited for international companies with narrow product lines but with geographically dispersed operations. The structure allows co-ordination and integration of activities within particular regions, as well as allowing greater responsiveness to local or regional market conditions. The concentration of knowledge of particular regions within a separate division may allow scope for the further development of the organization's operations in that area. Many global businesses have established separate regional head offices for Europe since the development of the single market in 1993. The weaknesses of the global regional/geographic structure relate to the lack of integration of product lines and the possible duplication of functional and product specialists at each regional headquarters.

Matrix structures
In order to preserve the strengths of each of these international structures and to overcome their disadvantages, many global businesses adopted global matrix structures which attempted to co-ordinate and integrate worldwide functional, product and area responsibilities. Under this structure, responsibility for foreign operations is divided between global product and regional divisions with subsidiary managers reporting to two bosses (thus confusing the hierarchy of the organization). Co-ordination and integration of product and area responsibilities is achieved through frequent interchanges between the product and regional divisions and through the CEO. The drawbacks of the global matrix structure are that it can be difficult to manage because of conflicts of interest between product and regional groupings. Decision-making procedures are also

complex because decision-making is a group process. The advantages and disadvantages of global matrix structures are examined in more detail later.

The development of global and transnational matrix structures

Stimuli to matrix development

The link between corporate strategy and corporate structure has become firmly established in the literature since the pioneering work of Chandler (1962) who showed that as a company's product/market strategy changed so too did its organizational structure to support implementation of the new strategy. The work of Stopford and Wells (1972) established patterns of development found in the structures of many multinational businesses. When only a limited range of products are sold abroad, and when foreign sales are only a small proportion of sales, many companies initially manage their overseas activities through an international division. Organizations which then broaden the range of products offered abroad tend to establish a worldwide product division. Those which expand sales abroad without broadening product range will often do so by establishing an area division structure. When sales abroad reach a high percentage of total sales and a broad range of products are offered for sale then businesses often opt for a matrix structure. These developments in structure are illustrated in Figure 13.2 which shows Stopford and Wells' 'International structural stages model' (1972).

FIGURE 13.2   International structural stages model (source: adapted from Stopford and Wells 1972)

According to the Stopford and Wells model, development through path 1 or path 2 will culminate in the development of a global matrix structure. The extent to which global matrix structures provide a solution to the complex organization and control problems of transnationals has been the subject of extensive debate which is explored below.

Global matrix structures

At some point in the internationalization process, the introduction of global structures becomes necessary to achieve co-ordination and integration of geographically dispersed activities. One possible approach to this situation is the global matrix structure which is one means of achieving global co-ordination and local responsiveness.

Benefits of matrix structures
One of the key benefits of a matrix structure is that co-ordination and integration of activity on a global scale can be achieved through global product divisions. Local responsiveness can be achieved through global regional or geographic structures. Thus, global matrix structures, which combine both product and geographic divisions, can achieve both global co-ordination and national responsiveness simultaneously. The main advantage of matrix compared to strict hierarchical structures is that they are able to accommodate managers with worldwide (product) responsibilities for particular businesses and country managers responsible for specific area markets.

Disadvantages of matrix structures
Bartlett and Ghoshal (1995) observed that many companies which had previously adopted matrix structures like Dow Chemical and Citibank have now abandoned them. This is because of the problems inherent in managing through such structures which include:

* overlapping responsibilities;
* reporting duplication with managers reporting to two or more bosses, often with conflicting objectives;
* survival of the fittest with one decision-making centre emerging as dominant;
* excessive time spent on reaching compromise decisions;
* duplication of information, communications and activities;
* increased administrative costs.

The development of the transnational organizational structure

National influences on structural form

The weakness of traditional organizational structure in an international and global context gave rise to Bartlett and Ghoshal's (1995) view that 'formal structure is a powerful but blunt instrument of strategic change'. They argued that to 'develop multidimensional and flexible strategic capabilities, a company must go beyond structure and expand its fundamental organizational capabilities'. Bartlett and Ghoshal (1987, 1988, 1989, 1992, 1995) developed the concepts of the transnational business and transnational management which are explained in this section.

European businesses

A company's organizational structure is shaped by its tasks, its environment and its administrative heritage or the history which, in turn, has shaped its culture (Bartlett and Ghoshal 1995). European businesses, which expanded abroad in the 1920s and 1930s in a time of protectionism and limited transport and communications technology, developed as *decentralized federations*. Within these federations, headquarters provided capital investment while national subsidiaries were integrated business units with considerable management autonomy.

American businesses

American businesses which experienced their greatest period of growth in the 1950s and 1960s, based on technological superiority, developed as *co-ordinated federations* where knowledge was passed to subsidiaries, structures were rigid and centralized planning prevailed. Subsidiaries were allowed limited freedom to modify products to reflect local market differences.

Japanese businesses

Japanese companies, internationalising in the 1970s, grew as *centralized hubs* because their strategies depended upon cost advantages requiring tight centralized control of activities.

Limitations of the three forms

Each of these solutions to the problems of international structure has disadvantages. The decentralized federation achieved local responsiveness but at the cost of duplication of activities and a failure to gain the efficiencies possible with international co-ordination of activities. At the other extreme, centralized hubs realized the advantages of co-ordination but at the expense of local responsiveness. The failure of the matrix to reconcile these problems meant that an alternative solution had to be sought.

'Anatomy' and 'physiology'

As global and transnational strategies became more sophisticated, the problem became one of organizational incapacity to implement such sophisticated strategies. In other words, strategic thinking has far out-distanced organizational capabilities. The main problem facing global companies is not one of designing appropriate global strategies. Rather, it is one of organizational incapability to implement complex strategies. Matrix structures provide no solution since they can sometimes result in excessive conflict and confusion.

The key organizational task, therefore, is not to design ever more elegant and complex structures but to capture individual capabilities and motivate the entire organization to respond co-operatively to a complicated and dynamic environment. To achieve this, Bartlett and Ghoshal (1995) suggested a reversal in the traditional organizational sequence which emphasizes organizational anatomy (formal structure), physiology (communications and decision processes), and psychology (corporate beliefs and norms that shape managers' perceptions and actions).

Rather than searching for the 'ideal' organizational anatomy (structure), the first task is to alter organizational psychology; then to enrich communications and decision processes through improvements in organizational physiology. Only then should these changes be consolidated and confirmed by realigning organizational anatomy through changing the formal structure. The companies which respond most successfully to the complexities of the global business environment are those which emphasize the need to change organizational psychology in the broad corporate beliefs and norms that shape managers' perceptions and actions. These changes can be reinforced by changing organizational physiology by enriching and clarifying communications and decision processes. Only then should these be consolidated by realigning organizational anatomy (i.e. the formal structure) (Figure 13.3).

Features of transnational structures

Bartlett and Ghoshal (1995) made the case that industries have changed from being international, multinational or global to being 'transnational'.

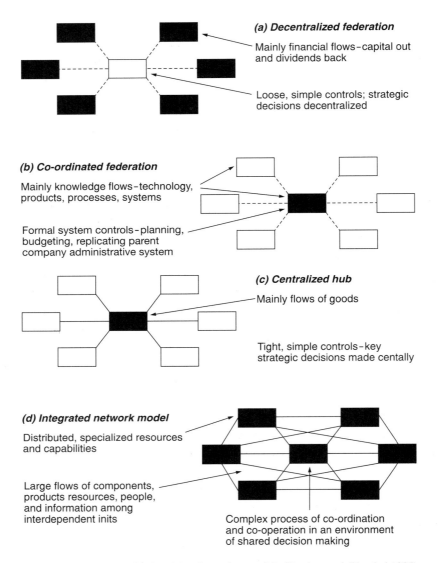

FIGURE 13.3   Organizational configuration models (Bartlett and Ghoshal 1995)

In such an environment, organizations themselves must become transnational. According to Bartlett and Ghoshal (1995), successful international corporations must 'optimize efficiency, responsiveness and learning simultaneously in their worldwide operations'. The difficulty is achieving 'a three way balance of organizational perspectives and capabilities among product, function and (geographical) area' (Bartlett and Ghoshal 1987).

The issue is not whether to be globally integrated *or* locally responsive but how to be *both* simultaneously. Authoritative global corporate management is required to integrate activities and ensure global efficiencies are obtained. Corporate managers must determine the overarching strategy of the organization, stress the interdependence of its functional and geographical parts, and co-ordinate its activities. The development and transfer of core competences requires capable functional management. Functional managers must facilitate learning and innovation within each domain of the business. Strong geographical management is required to ensure local responsiveness to national and regional markets. Local managers, in turn, must develop locally-determined competences which must then contribute to company-wide competences. Only a multidimensional organization can provide these three strands of management simultaneously.

Accordingly, the transnational is multidimensional by ensuring that:

- tasks are systematically *differentiated* by treating different businesses, functions and areas differently and by allowing them to be organized differently;
- relationships between the different parts of the business are based on *interdependence* rather than independence;
- *co-ordination and co-option* of differentiated and interdependent organizational units are achieved through shared vision and integrative mechanisms.

The transnational model

Bartlett and Ghoshal (1995) gave several examples of organizations which were, at that time, becoming transnational:

- Unilever adopted differentiated organization of tasks. In Europe, activities were closely integrated (recognizing the similarities between national markets), whilst in Latin America there was greater local autonomy to cater for greater market diversity. In other words, Unilever moved from being an organization which is symmetrical to one which is differentiated in terms of product, function and geography;
- NEC developed co-ordination of its activities through a clearly communicated global vision and strategy rather than through tight management controls.

In both of these cases, creating a transnational is more concerned with creating a organizational culture based on a global vision, emphasizing differentiation and co-ordination, rather than a specific structure which incorporates tight controls.

Bartlett and Ghoshal (1995) developed the transnational model further by suggesting that transnationals possess integrated networks with three major characteristics:

1. multidimensional perspectives;
2. distributed, interdependent capabilities;
3. flexible integrative processes.

We will briefly consider each of these characteristics.

Multidimensional perspectives
The cultural diversity and increasing volatility of the international business environment have increased the need for organizations to sense and respond to environmental changes. This depends on developing strong global, subsidiary and functional management without domination by any one of these groups. Strong *subsidiary management* is required to identify the changing needs of local customers. Strong *global management* is required to respond to the global strategies of competitors and to co-ordinate an appropriate response. Strong *functional management* is required to provide focus for areas of organizational knowledge and to ensure its transfer among units of the organization.

Distributed, interdependent capabilities
In devising its response to changes in the environment, a transnational seeks to avoid the problems of other international configurations. The global centralized hub makes it difficult to respond to diverse local demands while the decentralized federation results in duplication, inefficiency and barriers to organizational learning. Within a transnational it is not seen as necessary to centralize activities which require global scale or specialized knowledge. Global scale can be achieved by making a local plant into a global production centre serving all the company's worldwide markets. A particular research and development centre can become the centre of excellence for the whole business. A local marketing group with proven expertise may be given the role of developing a global marketing strategy for a particular product. In this way the company becomes

an *integrated network* [Figure 13.3(d)] of distributed but interdependent capabilities which benefit the whole organization.

Flexible integrative processes

Once the network of distributed and integrated capabilities has been created alongside the management groups which represent the multiple perspectives of the organization's environment, then flexible integrative management processes are required which integrate these diverse perspectives and capabilities. These processes must be flexible to allow differentiated operating relationships, adaptable operating relationships and functional decision-making roles which can change over time in response to changing circumstances.

This flexible integration is achieved by three separate but interdependent management processes.

- *Centralization* – which is sensitive to the groups within the organization but allows senior management to intervene in certain decisions to ensure co-ordination.
- *Formalization* – which allows different parts of the organization to have influence on key decisions.
- *Socialization* – which is a set of cultural norms and procedures which provides the framework for delegated decision making in the context of the overall organization.

There is no prescribed structure for a transnational. Rather there are a set of principles which guide the managers of global businesses in the design and configuration of their organizations. These principles assist in achieving simultaneous global co-ordination and local responsiveness, alongside organizational learning and competence building.

Decision-making and control in international business

Decentralization and control

The issue of decision-making within the transnational is closely related to the discussion of organizational structures presented above. In traditional multinationals, for example, decision-making is largely decentralized at the level of the foreign subsidiary. In global structures, on the other hand, greater centralization of decision-making may be expected although this will vary between different businesses and across functional areas. In a transnational corporation the issue is how to combine centralization and decentralization so as to achieve global co-ordination and local responsiveness.

Too much centralization may prevent the utilization of local initiative and have an adverse effect on the motivation of local management. Over-centralized decision-making may also result in a lack of adaptation to local market needs and may create political problems with host country governments. Decentralizing certain decision-making to the local subsidiary may overcome many of these difficulties. By granting subsidiary autonomy the transnational may encourage the use of local initiative and the flexibility of the subsidiary to changes in local market conditions. Pressures on the corporate centre are also reduced as are the potential tensions with host country governments. The identification of a 'local' image may also be important in a number of industries. National units can develop new products and new techniques locally which can then be used throughout the transnational.

Centralization of some decision-making may be necessary to achieve the benefits of global co-ordination through global economies and efficiencies. In the transnational model this centralized decision-making would include representation of different local, functional and business areas rather than only central management. Typically the centre of any organization is concerned with establishing its overall vision, mission and its broad strategy. At the same time, within a transnational the centre plays an important role in co-ordinating activities, improving efficiency through benchmarking and setting standards, promoting innovation, and encouraging a learning and interdependent culture.

Empirical studies

Several studies have investigated the centralization/decentralization of decision-making within transnationals (Brooke and Remmers 1976; Goehle 1980; Hedlund 1981; Young *et al*. 1985). The general conclusion emerging from these studies is that the locus of decision-making varies significantly across functional areas and between different transnationals.

A survey of 154 foreign-owned subsidiaries operating in the UK highlighted the variation in decision making procedures across functional areas, with financial decisions being the most centralized, and personnel decisions the most decentralized (Young *et al*. 1985). Production and marketing decisions generally fell within these two extremes, with strategic production/marketing decisions being more centralized than operational decisions. Research and development decisions were also closely controlled by the parent company in a large proportion of the sample companies. Such variations in the locus of decision-making across functional areas can be explained in terms of the relative importance of each decision to the parent company. Decisions that draw on or directly affect central resources (e.g. most financial decisions), decisions which constitute long-term obligations for the transnational (e.g. the introduction of new products and the entry into new markets) and decisions which attempt to standardize and establish a common framework of organizational routines and procedures (e.g. the setting of financial targets and rates of return on investment) are the most likely to be centralized.

In addition to establishing appropriate organizational structures and decision-making procedures, transnationals must also establish evaluation and control procedures for assessing subsidiary performance and ensuring the conformity of the subsidiary to corporate objectives. Internal benchmarking of performance is an important feature of a transnational organization. It is one means by which best practice can be spread throughout the organization from one geographical area to another and from one functional area to another.

Evaluating performance

Performance evaluation within the transnational serves a number of functions (Hedlund and Zander 1985):

- ensuring the co-ordination and integration of strategy. Global and local strategy are integrated;
- assisting in the internal benchmarking of performance. This acts as a mechanism to spread best practice throughout the organization;
- ensuring a realistic level of profitability. Performance of parts of the organization may be measured against some target variable (e.g. actual profit, return on investment etc.);
- early identification of problems. Failure to meet targets provides early warning system in order that corrective action may be taken;
- resource allocation. Limited resources channelled into areas of highest return;
- information. The performance evaluation system provides essential information on the operations of the different parts of the business;

- long-run planning. Information acts as an input into strategic planning;
- motivation. Performance evaluation used to motivate management in different parts of the organization;
- communications. Performance evaluation stimulates discussion between different parts of the organization regarding performance, problems, long-run trends etc.

While each of these functions may be important, surveys by the BIC (1982), Hedlund and Zander (1985), covering both US and European transnationals, showed that the three most important functions performed by the evaluation procedure are:

1. ensuring subsidiary profitability;
2. identifying potential problems;
3. facilitating resource allocation.

Hedlund and Zander (1985) also suggested that the importance of these three objectives varies with the nature of the international involvement of the company. Large, geographically-dispersed, transnationals emphasized the problem identification and resource allocation roles, while early internationalizers emphasize profitability as an objective.

In terms of the actual performance measures used, the transnational has the same alternatives available as a domestic company including return on investment, income/profit contribution, market share, cash flow measures etc. The use of these measures, however, is usually more difficult in an transnational due to exchange rate variations, differences in accounting procedures, variations in national inflation rates and tax rates, transfer pricing and restriction on remittances (see Chapter 12).

Global and transnational strategies, organization and control

Several references have already been made in this chapter to the link between corporate strategy and the internal management and control of the transnational. This final section examines this relationship in more detail by linking the discussion in this chapter to Chapter 6 on global strategy.

Many factors influence the internal management and control systems adopted by transnationals. The most important are:

- the global or transnational strategy of the organization;
- the strategic predispositions and value systems of the transnational as identified in the EPRG profile (see Chapter 2, p. 41);
- the geographical extent of its operations;
- the nature of its international business environment.

The influence of strategy on structure and control systems

According to Porter's (1986, 1990) classification of international strategies, the organizational and control challenge facing the transnational is the need to balance the conflicting forces of country responsiveness and global direction. The relative importance of these and the impact on organization and control will vary with the type of international strategy. Thus, country-centred strategies (geographically-dispersed operations with minimum co-ordination) imply an organizational structure which is country-responsive, such as a geographic divisional structure, with considerable decision-making autonomy being devolved to the local subsidiaries. Performance evaluation within international businesses with country-centred strategies will normally be confined to ensuring subsidiary profitability.

In geographically-dispersed but highly co-ordinated businesses, on the other hand, the need for global planning and co-ordination will be reflected in the organizational structure which will be based on factors like global product, geographic or matrix systems. This, in turn, will depend on the company's product range and its geographical spread of activities. Similarly, authority over a range of both strategic and operational decisions will be transferred to a higher level in the organization which has a global perspective. Decision-making, therefore, will be highly centralized, with a hierarchical chain of command between subsidiary and parent. Finally, performance evaluation within such organizations will serve several functions relating to resource allocation, problem spotting and planning, in addition to the short-run measurement of subsidiary profitability.

In Yip's (1992) model of 'total global strategy' and the model of transnational strategy presented in this book, co-ordination and responsiveness are *both* viewed as essential to the achievement of competitive advantage. In this context it is necessary to build an organization which is 'transnational'. This will imply, as discussed in the previous sections of this chapter:

- strong global, subsidiary and functional management and multidimensional perspectives;
- distributed, interdependent capabilities;
- flexible integrative processes.

REVIEW AND DISCUSSION QUESTIONS

1. Discuss the contributions made by contingency theory and the configuration approach to our understanding of organizational structures.
2. Discuss the major organizational and control problems specific to international businesses.
3. Explain the international structural stages model (Stopford and Wells 1972). Is the matrix structure the inevitable outcome of the process?
4. Why are export departments and international divisions unlikely to be structures permanently adopted by an international business?
5. What are the problems inherent in simply adopting a global functional or product division structure?
6. To what extent does a geographical structure solve the problems inherent in a global functional or product division structure?
7. Explain the relative advantages and disadvantages of: the decentralized federation; the co-ordinated federation; the centralized hub; the integrated network.
8. Explain what Bartlett and Ghoshal meant by the 'transnational solution'. What are the main characteristics of a transnational? What are its advantages and disadvantages compared to a global matrix structure? Give examples in support of your answer.
9. Explain the functions of performance evaluation systems in transnationals.
10. What is the relationship between global and transnational strategy and organizational structure?

References and further reading

Bartlett, C.A. (1981) Multinational structural change: evolution versus reorganization, in: Otterbeck, L. (ed.), *The Management of Headquarters–Subsidiary Relationships in Multinational Corporations*, Gower, London.

Bartlett, C. and Ghoshal, S. (1987) Managing across borders: new organizational responses, *Sloan Management Review*, Fall, 45–53.

Bartlett, C. and Ghoshal, S. (1988) Organizing for a worldwide effectiveness. The transnational solution, *California Management Review* **30**, 54–74.

Bartlett, C. and Ghoshal, S. (1989) *Managing Across Borders: The Transnational Solution*, Harvard Business School Press, Boston.

Bartlett, C.A. and Ghoshal, S. (1990) Matrix management: not a structure, a frame of mind, *Harvard Business Review*, **22**(4), July/August, 138–145.

Bartlett, C.A. and Ghoshal, S. (1992) What is a global manager?, *Harvard Business Review*, **70**(5), 124–132.

Bartlett, C.A. and Ghoshal, S. (1995) *Transnational Management: Text, Cases and Readings in Cross-Border Management*, R.D. Irwin, Homewood.

Brooke, M.Z. and Remmers, H.L. (1976) *The Strategy of Multinational Enterprise*, Pitman, London.

Business International Corporation (BIC) (1981) *New Directions in Multinational Corporation Organization*, BIC.

Chandler, A. (1962) *Strategy and Structure*, MIT Press, Cambridge, MA.

Daniels, J.D. (1986) Approaches to European regional management by large US multinational firms, *Management International Review*, **26**(2).

Davidow, W. and Malone, M. (1992) *The Virtual Corporation*, Harper Business, London.

Franks, L.G. (1976) *The European Multinationals*, Harper and Row, New York.

Ghertman, M. (1984) *Decision-Making in Multinational Enterprises: Concepts and Research Approaches*, ILO Working Paper, No. 31.

Goehle, D.G. (1980) *Decision-Making in Multinational Corporations*, UMI Research Press, Ann Arbor.

Hedlund, G. (1981) Autonomy of subsidiaries and formalization of headquarters–subsidiary relationships in Swedish MNCs, in: Otterbeck, L. (Ed.), *The Management of Headquarters–Subsidiary Relationships in Multinational Corporations*, Gower, London.

Hedlund, G. (1984) Organization in-between: the evolution of the mother–daughter structure of managing foreign subsidiaries in Swedish multinational corporations, *Journal of International Business Studies*, Fall.

Hedlund, G. and Aman, P. (1983) *Managing Relationships with Foreign Subsidiaries – Organization and Control in Swedish MNCs*, Sveriges Mekunforbund, Stockholm.

Hedlund, G. and Zander, U. (1985) *Formulation of Goals and Follow-Up of Performance for Foreign Subsidiaries in Swedish MNCs*, Stockholm School of Economics, Institute of International Business, RP 85/4.

Hulbert, J.M. and Brandt, W.K. (1980) *Managing the Multinational Subsidiary*, Holt, Rinehart and Winston, New York.

Jarillo, J.C. (1993) *Strategic Networks: Creating the Borderless Organization*, Butterworth Heinemann, Oxford.

Jennings, D. and Seaman, S. (1994) High and low levels of organizational adaptation; an empirical analysis of strategy, structure and performance, *Strategic Management Journal*, **15**(6), 459–475.

Johnson, G. and Scholes, K. (1999) *Exploring Corporate Strategy*, Prentice Hall, Englewood Cliffs.

Journal of International Business Studies (1983) Journal of International Business Studies, Special issue on management and culture in the transnational, Fall.

Miller, D. (1987) The genesis of configuration, *Academy of Management Review*, **12**(4), 686–701.

Miller, D. (1990) Organizational configurations: cohesion, change and prediction, *Human Relations*, **43**(8), 771–789.

Mintzberg, H. (1979) *The Structuring of Organizations*, Prentice Hall, Englewood Cliffs.

Mintzberg, H. (1983) *Power in and around Organizations*, Prentice Hall, Englewood Cliffs.

Mintzberg, H. (1984) *Mintzberg on Management: Inside Our Strange World of Organizations*, The Free Press, New York.

Mintzberg, H., Quinn, J.B. and Ghoshal, S. (1998) *The Strategy Process* (Revised European Edition), Prentice Hall, Englewood Cliffs.

Mullins, L. (1996) *Management and Organizational Behaviour*, Pitman, London.

Naylor, T.H. (1985) The international strategy matrix, *Columbia Journal of World Business*, **20**(2), Summer.

Otterbeck, L. (Ed.) (1981) *The Management of Headquarters–Subsidiary Relationships in Multinational Corporations*, Gower, London.

Perlmutter, H.V. (1969) The tortuous evolution of the multinational corporation, *Columbia Journal of World Business*, January/February.

Peters, T. and Waterman, R. (1982) *In Search of Excellence*, Harper and Row, New York.

Pitts, R.A. and Daniels, J.D. (1984) Aftermath of the matrix mania, *Columbia Journal of World Business*, **19**(2), Summer.

Porter, M.E. (1986) Changing patterns of international competition, *California Management Review*, **28**(2), Winter.

Porter, M.E. (1990) *The Competitive Advantage of Nations*, The Free Press, New York.

Prahalad, C.K. and Doz, Y.L. (1986) *The Multinational Mission: Balancing Local Demands and Global Vision*, The Free Press, New York.

Rugman, A.M., Lecraw, D.J. and Booth, L.D. (1985) *International Business: Firm and Environment*, McGraw-Hill, London.

Stopford, J.M. and Wells, L.T. (1972) *Strategy and Structure of Multinational Enterprise*, Basic Books, London.

Yip, G.S. (1992) *Total Global Strategy – Managing for Worldwide Competitive Advantage*, Prentice Hall, Englewood Cliffs.

Young, S., Hood, N. and Hamill, J. (1985) *Decision-Making in Foreign-Owned Multinational Subsidiaries in the United Kingdom*, ILO Working Paper, No. 35.

MANAGING GLOBAL MERGERS, ACQUISITIONS AND ALLIANCES

14

CHAPTER

LEARNING OBJECTIVES

After studying this chapter, students should be able to:

- define and distinguish between the portfolio and core competence perspectives on integrations and alliances;
- describe the main types and 'directions' of integrations and alliances;
- define and distinguish between a merger, acquisition, strategic alliance and joint venture;
- explain the motivations behind and potential problems with mergers and acquisitions;
- describe the factors behind successful integrations;
- explain the motivations for forming strategic alliances and describe the various types of alliance;
- explain the concept of the 'focal' business in the management of successful international alliances.

Introduction

Sirower (1997) made the point that 'The 1990s will go down in history as the time of the biggest merger and acquisition wave of the century'. At the same time as this boom in mergers and acquisitions, there was a similar increase in the numbers of strategic alliances and collaborative business networks involving international organizations. In this chapter we begin by explaining the motivations which underlie international mergers and acquisitions and collaborative business networks. We then explore the reasons for the success and failure of such ventures before considering how global managers can seek to increase the chances of successful integration or collaboration.

An overview of integrations and alliances

Perspectives on external growth

De Wit and Meyer (1998) presented an interesting review of the factors underlying merger and collaborative activity from two opposing perspectives: *the portfolio perspective* and *the core competence perspective*.

The portfolio perspective
The portfolio perspective stresses that the major benefits of integration are the leveraging of financial resources, entry to new businesses and markets and the spreading of risks. Successful management of a diversified business will, accordingly, depend upon responsiveness. There is, therefore, an emphasis on devolving responsibility for strategy to each of the strategic business units which comprise the corporation so as to increase their ability to respond flexibly to changes in the environment.

The core competence perspective
The core competence perspective is based on the view that mergers, acquisitions and alliances improve performance by creating synergy between the businesses involved. This synergy arises from the leveraging of resources and core competences between the businesses. For example, the reputation or brand name of a company can produce shared benefits. The involvement of the German Volkswagen Group in Skoda of the Czech Republic helped to improve the latter's reputation. Similarly, the sharing of Volkswagen's knowledge, skills and technology improved Skoda's productivity, quality, and products. De Wit and Meyer (1998) listed the other potential sources of resource leveraging as increased bargaining power in relation to customers and suppliers, improved linkages to distributors, shared marketing, shared finance etc.

From a core competence perspective, a successful merger or collaborative agreement must create greater value through synergy and co-ordination than the value lost through reduced responsiveness. In fact, it is not the case that increased co-ordination will necessarily result in decreased responsiveness. In the case of horizontal or diversified integration and alliances, there may well be some resultant loss of responsiveness to the business. Vertical integration or alliances between a business and its suppliers and distributors is likely to increase responsiveness due to more reliable access to inputs and outlets (this being a major factor in many just-in-time alliances between businesses and their suppliers). The advent of information and communications technology and its impact on organizational learning (Stonehouse and Pemberton 1999) has further enhanced the ability of networks of collaborating or integrated organizations to sustain responsiveness at the same time as achieving synergy through co-ordination.

Types of integrations and alliances

A major factor in the boom in the 1990s in integrations and collaborative ventures was their increasing importance in the global and transnational strategies of many businesses. Despite the potential benefits of competence leveraging and synergy, improved co-ordination and responsiveness, cross-border deals suffer from a very high failure rate (20–50 per cent according to some empirical studies). It is, therefore, important to consider the possible reasons for the success and failure of integration and collaboration.

Although there are many similar concerns in the setting up and management of integrations (mergers and acquisitions) and alliances, there are also many differences. These arise from the fact that alliances involve collaboration between two or more organizations that may continue to compete in one form or another as well as collaborating in global markets (Figure 14.1). Integration and collaboration can be split into four distinct categories.

Vertical backward or upstream integration or collaboration

Such integrations and alliances take place when a business engages with its suppliers. The major motivations for vertical backward integration or upstream collaboration are mainly related to resource leveraging by improving access to and control of resources and better supply chain linkages. Many motor vehicle manufacturers, for example, are involved in vertical alliances with suppliers. Collaboration with suppliers improves access to materials and parts. This, in turn, allows greater control of quality and delivery.

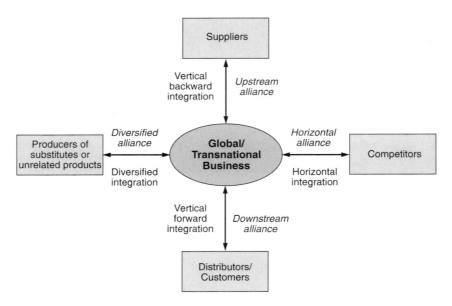

FIGURE 14.1   A categorization of integration and collaboration

Vertical forward or downstream integration or collaboration
This form of integration or alliance takes place when a business engages with its distributors or customers. Collaboration with distributors provides improved access to customers and allows greater marketing synergies between a business and its distributors.

Horizontal integration or collaboration
When two companies at the same stage of the supply chain or value system collaborate or integrate it is horizontal in direction. Thus the collaboration between Honda and Rover or the later acquisition of Rover by BMW are classified as horizontal collaboration and a horizontal acquisition, respectively. Here the major advantages relate to synergy rather than responsiveness. There are opportunities for competence leveraging through brand names, shared finance etc.

Diversified integration or collaboration
Diversified integrations and collaborative ventures take place between a business and other businesses in other industries. Here the major advantages also relate to leveraging of brand names and access to finance.

Transnational mergers and acquisitions

The key definitions

It is important to begin by understanding the terms *merger*, *acquisition* and *integration*. In a *merger*, two organizations agree to join together and pool their assets in a new business entity. Both of the previous entities 'disappear' into the new organization. Shares in the previous entities are commuted into new stock, usually revalued to account for the new market value. In practice, the two partners in a merger are usually of comparable size and importantly, they are entered into willingly by both parties.

An *acquisition* is a joining of unequal partners. A large organization purchases all (or a controlling share interest in) a smaller business and then subsumes it into its structure. Acquisitions can be either agreed or hostile, depending upon the attitude of the smaller company.

- An *agreed acquisition* is one where the directors of the target company accept that the offer for the shares is in the best interests of the shareholders and they accordingly recommend that shareholders accept the price offered.
- A *hostile acquisition* (sometimes called a hostile take-over in the press) is an attempt to acquire a controlling share holding in a public limited company which is not recommended by the target company's directors. In this case, acceptance of the offer price by shareholders represents a difference of opinion between directors and shareholders and questions are often raised as to the extent to which directors are or are not acting in the shareholders' best interests.

Whichever of these routes is taken, the result is a larger and more financially powerful company. The word integration is the collective term used to describe these growth mechanisms.

Motivations for transnational mergers and acquisitions

Transnational mergers and acquisitions are motivated by a range of business considerations and will depend upon the strategic intent and transnational strategy of the business. The more common motivations include:

- market entry – mergers and acquisitions (M&As) are often used as a method for entering and servicing a new national market;

- market share – M&As can increase market share by combining the market shares of the two businesses. In addition the selling power of the two businesses is likely to be increased resulting in further increases in market share (especially in the case of horizontal integrations);
- product and market portfolio – M&As can be used to increase an organization's product portfolio thus rendering the business more robust in the event of trauma in one or more of its product or market sectors;
- reduction of competition – competition can be reduced if the integration target is a competitor;
- leveraging of core competences – control can be gained of key inputs and brand names can be leveraged;
- access to supply or distribution channels – backward and forward integration can improve access to resources and customers, respectively;
- product development – new products can often be acquired more rapidly than could be achieved by the internal R&D function;
- technology acquisition – new technology can be acquired such as that employed in production or IT applications;
- economies of scale and scope – these can be achieved especially if the integration involves an increase in capacity;
- resource utilization – resources can be successfully and fruitfully deployed, such as underused cash deposits;
- reputation enhancement – reputation can be enhanced if the acquisition or merger is with a business of some repute in a key market or with a key stakeholder group.

Each separate integration will have its own specific objectives at the strategic level. For many transnationals the major motivations are access to new markets or to resources, competences and skills.

Synergy is intended to facilitate an enhancement in the value-adding capability of the business. Kay (1993) made the point that 'Value is added, and only added, [in an integration] if distinctive capabilities or strategic assets are exploited more effectively. A merger adds no value if all that is acquired is a distinctive capability which is already fully exploited, as the price paid will reflect the competitive advantage held'. Accordingly, integrations that do not enable the 'new' organization to produce higher profits or consolidate a stronger market position are usually deemed to have been relatively unsuccessful.

Problems with integration

A number of academic studies have been undertaken with regard to the successes and failures of external growth and the balance of evidence is that more fail than succeed (see for example Kay 1993; Porter 1985; Ravenscraft and Scherer 1987). Many acquisitions ended in subsequent disposal because performance of the post-integration organization was not as hoped. Of those integrations that did survive, Kay (1993) found that when profitability before and after the integration were compared, a 'nil to negative effect' was achieved.

What causes failure?
We suggest that there are six reasons why some integrations fail to add value and become subject to subsequent 'divorce'.

1. *Lack of research* into the internal and external environmental features of the target company (and hence incomplete knowledge).
2. *Cultural incompatibility* between the acquirer and the target – especially important when the two parties are in different countries.
3. *Lack of communication* within and between the two parties.
4. *Loss of key personnel* in the target company after the integration.
5. *Paying too much for the acquired company* and hence over-exposing the acquiring company to financial risk.
6. *Assuming that growth in a target company's market will continue indefinitely.* Market trends can fall as well as rise.

A seventh reason for failure, albeit one which is outside the control of the organization, is legislative or regulatory frameworks that prevent the integration from happening or from fully performing as it might. Most developed economies have frameworks in place to regulate merger and acquisition activity. Article 86 of The Treaty of Rome 1957 (the primary legislation of the European Union) is one such instrument. It enables the European Commission to review proposed mergers or acquisitions resulting in a combined national market share of 25 per cent or when the combined turnover in European Union markets exceeds a certain financial figure (which at 1998 was ECU 250 million). The UK has similar legislation (The Fair Trading Act 1973).

Successful mergers and acquisitions

The high failure rate of mergers and acquisitions (Sirower 1997) obviously indicates that managers of transnationals must evaluate potential mergers and acquisitions carefully before entering into them. Once the decision to merge or acquire has been taken, it is then necessary to plan the integration process carefully.

The chances of successful integration are increased when seven 'success factors' are observed:

1. find a suitable target partner;
2. fully evaluate the target's competitive position;
3. fully evaluate the target's management and culture for compatibility with the initiator;
4. investigate the compatibility of the two companies' structures;
5. ensure that key resources (including key human resources) can be locked in after the integration;
6. ensure the price paid for the target's stock is realistic;
7. plan the post-merger process carefully.

(Sources: Based on Sirower 1997, Payne 1987, Shelton, 1988).

Each of these success factors is discussed below.

Finding a suitable target
First, success depends upon the identification of a suitable 'target' candidate with which to merge or acquire. This is often problematic as the initiating organization – with specific strategic intentions in mind – may have to wait for many years or consider international M&A in order to find such a partner. In practice, some compromise is necessary.

Evaluation of the target's competitive position
Second, a preparation for an approach should involve a detailed evaluation of the target company's competitive position. This would typically comprise a survey of its profitability, its market share, its product portfolio, its competitiveness in resource markets etc. Key success factors are identified and the core competences of key competitors are addressed.

Cultural compatibility
Third, consideration should be given to the compatibility of the two companies' management styles and cultures – a process that may require significant pre-integration discussions. As integrations often involve the

merging of the two boards of directors, it is usually important that the directors from the two companies are able to work together. In addition, the cultures, if not identical in character, should be able to be brought together successfully.

Structures

Fourth, there should be the possibility of a successful marriage between the two corporate structures. Integrations work best where the two structures in question are comparably decentralized and have similar 'height' and 'width'.

Locking in resources

Fifth, any key resources that the target company has must be guaranteed to still be available post-integration. Key resources that helped to build the target's core competences must be locked in so that their use can be continued after the integration. In many organizations, these key resources will be human but in others, they may also be key locations, processes, patents, brands or sources of finance.

Valuing the stock price

Sixth, the initiating company will need to be certain that its valuation of the target company is reasonable insofar as it will enable a satisfactory return to be made on the investment. This is one of the most difficult matters to sort out in advance of an integration. Whilst the balance sheet value of a company can be easily ascertained, attention will need to be given to the value of the target's *goodwill* – a figure over and above the balance sheet value to take account of its future prospects and a valuation of its intellectual resources (brands, patents, licences etc.). For large acquisitions, the value of goodwill is often the matter of intense debate between the parties. Accordingly, the importance of detailed information gathering before the integration cannot be over-emphasized. The acquisition of Wellcome plc by Glaxo (Holdings) in the mid-1990s was one in which the majority of the price paid was goodwill. Although Wellcome's balance sheet value was ca £2.5 billion, Glaxo paid around £9 billion for the target company. Whilst some of this £6.5 billion difference can be accounted for by asset revaluation, the majority was goodwill reflecting Wellcome's capabilities in promising pharmaceutical areas such as virology and its product range, which contained some of the most important drugs in the world.

Planning the integration

Finally, the post-merger process must be carefully planned. Ollie's (1990) study identified poor integration of merged businesses as the major cause of poor performance. Obstacles to successful integration were found to include: resistance to change; a focus on personal security rather than organizational goals; culture shock; and resentment of management. Ollie concluded that even when a merger was initially flawed then it could be made successful by effective management of the post-merger process.

Collaborative ventures and strategic alliances

What are collaborative ventures and strategic alliances?

The terms *collaborative venture* and *strategic alliance* are used to describe a family of arrangements between two or more organizations to collaborate across organizational boundaries with the express purpose of gaining mutual competitive advantage. Conventional models of business behaviour have tended to emphasize the role of the individual business in gaining competitive advantage. Some core competence theorists (Heene and Sanchez 1997) identified collaboration between businesses as an important potential source of competitive advantage.

According to Contractor and Lorange (1988a) it is important to view a transnational business as a member of various open and shifting coalitions, each with a specific strategic purpose, rather than as a closed internalized system which straddles national boundaries. Competitive advantage can result from the effective management of such international and global coalitions.

As we saw in Chapter 6, resource-based strategy theory argues that superior performance is based upon the development and deployment of core competences and distinctive capabilities. Quinn *et al.* (1990) suggested that it is best for a company to concentrate on activities which are directly related to its core competences and that other non-core activities can be outsourced to other businesses for which those activities are core. According to Quinn *et al.* (1990) 'outside vendors can supply many important corporate functions at greatly enhanced value and lower cost. Thus many of those functions should be outsourced'. Consequently, outsourcing is often associated with collaborative behaviour.

Porter (1986, 1990) stressed the importance of *configuration* of business activities and their *co-ordination* to achieving global competitive advantage. Collaboration has made it possible for businesses to adopt new configurations which are difficult for competitors to emulate and which can also sometimes enhance organizational responsiveness.

In broad terms, then, the acquisition of competitive advantage through collaborative ventures and strategic alliances will require:

- identification of the core competences of the organization;
- identification and focus upon activities which are critical to the core competence of the organization and outsourcing those which are not to collaborating businesses;
- achieving the internal and external linkages in the value/supply chain which are necessary for effective co-ordination of activities and which permit responsiveness.

The remainder of the chapter explains the different categories of alliance which exist, the motivations behind them and how such alliances can be best managed.

Motivations for forming strategic alliances

It is possible to identify several rationales for collaboration (Contractor and Lorange, 1988a):

- the sharing of different but linked core competences;
- international expansion and market entry;
- vertical quasi-integration – access to resources, skills, materials, technology, labour, capital, distribution channels, buyers, regulatory permits;
- sharing of risks;
- the acquisition of economies of scale and scope;
- access to complementary technologies and technology development;
- the blocking or reduction of competition;
- overcoming government mandated investment or trade barriers.

The second of Contractor and Lorange's motivations is the most important in the context of this book. As organizations seek out new markets for their products, many recognize skill or knowledge deficiencies where an in-depth knowledge of a foreign market is required. The need to develop local knowledge is increased if overseas production (with an overseas alliance partner) is being considered to meet market demands. While local knowledge can be hired (say through a local importing agent), it is often quicker and more reliable to seek assistance from an already established producing organization of the host country. It should also be noted that a legal requirement of many countries is that foreign organizations must have host partners before they can trade, thus making a collaborative agreement a prerequisite for market entry.

Types of strategic alliance and collaborative venture

Directions of alliances

Like mergers and acquisitions collaborative ventures can be categorized as vertical backward (or upstream), vertical forward (or downstream), horizontal or diversified. Vertical backward or upstream alliances are between a business and its suppliers. Vertical forward or downstream alliances are between a company and its distributors or customers. Horizontal alliances are between a business and other companies at the same stage of the value system, while diversified alliances are between companies in industries which are not closely related to each other. Collaborative ventures are always entered into willingly and all participating parties expect the alliance to work towards their own specific strategic purposes. They vary from highly formal, long-term agreements linking two or more organizations, to short-term consortia of organizations engaged together in a relatively short-term project.

The legal status of an organization need not be a barrier to its participation in an alliance. Whilst many are between two business organizations, many countries have witnessed an increase in alliances between governmental bodies and privately-owned companies. In the UK, for example, the Private Finance Initiative (PFI) has been responsible for collaboration in the building of roads, hospitals and other public sector investments. The channel tunnel between Britain and France was constructed by a number of companies working together in an alliance referred to as a *consortium*. In some circumstances, collaboration between companies can result in the creation of a new and jointly-owned enterprise. Cellnet, for example, was founded as a jointly-owned mobile telephone business by two British companies, BT and Securicor.

Strategic alliances can therefore assume a number of different forms depending upon the participants' structures, the mechanism of decision-making, the nature of the capital commitment, the apportionment of profit and the legal status of the venture. Some exist for a particular project only and are short-term in time-scale whilst others are more permanent. The choice of arrangement will depend upon the specific objectives that the participants have at the time.

Horizontal networks and alliances

Alliances between businesses at the same stage of the value system are generally intended to strengthen the participating companies against outside competition. Partners in such alliances can benefit from:

- shared skills and competences;
- shared technologies;
- access to some new market segments;
- reduced risks;
- reduced costs, particularly development costs;
- increased entry barriers and reduced danger from new entrants;
- forces which create synergy;
- advantages in vertical relationships – for example, a voluntary retail group can obtain discounts from suppliers for bulk buying.

The company must always retain control of its core strategic assets and activities but can outsource other activities to partners. From a portfolio perspective, this form of alliance gains synergy through leveraging shared financial resources.

Diversification alliances

Alliances between businesses in unrelated areas are often used by one or more of the businesses to take them into a new competitive arena. This form of alliance is viewed as important from a portfolio perspective insofar as the key advantage of diversification is to broaden product and market portfolio in order to reduce the risk of trauma in any one sector.

Vertical networks and alliances

These can be upstream in the supply chain towards suppliers or downstream towards distributors and customers (see Figure 14.1).

These alliances produce the following potential benefits:

- the ability for each collaborating business to concentrate on its own core competence while at the same time benefiting from the core competences of the other businesses in the alliance, creating synergy;
- improved responsiveness if just-in-time management techniques are employed;
- creation of new barriers to entry;
- production of logistical economies of scale;
- generation of superior information on activities at all stages of the supply chain;
- tying in of suppliers, distributors and customers to the business.

The extent and time scale of collaboration

There are several other methods which can be used to distinguish alliances.

The extent of co-operation – focused and complex alliances
It is possible to distinguish alliances by where they are positioned in respect to how many areas the parties co-operate with each other in. Some alliances are set up between businesses in order to collaborate in only one area of activity such as joint purchasing, shared research or shared distribution. A continuum exists between the two extremes of fully-focused (collaboration in one activity only) and complex (collaboration in all activities – the parties act in concert to the point where they appear to be one single organization). As with all continua, the majority of real life cases fall somewhere between the two extremes.

Time scales of the collaboration
The second way in which we can sub-divide strategic alliances is by asking how long they are intended to last. Some are set up for a specific project only and we tend to refer to these as 'joint ventures' – time limited arrangements for the joint accomplishment of a shared aim or project. Others can last for many years and are intended to enable both (or all) parties to intensify the strength of their strategic position on an ongoing basis. Longer-term alliances tend to be more common when the partners are from different countries as the interpenetration of markets can take many years to achieve and consolidate.

Consortiums

One particular type of (usually) short- to medium-term alliance is the consortium. Consortiums are often created for time-limited projects such as civil engineering or construction developments. The channel tunnel was constructed by a number of construction companies in a consortium which was called Trans Manche Link (TML). TML was dissolved upon the completion of the project. Camelot, the first UK National Lottery operator, is another example of a consortium.

Choosing the most appropriate type of alliance

The form of alliance chosen by the parties will depend upon several factors. The complexity of the alliance will depend upon the objectives that the two parties are pursuing. Alliance partners tend to seek co-operation on the minimum number of areas that are needed in order to avoid over-exposure to the risk of one of the parties leaving abruptly or 'finding out too much'. The selection of partners for a consortium will depend upon matching the resource and skill requirement of the project with those organizations that are willing to contribute to the effort. Organizations with previous experience of projects of the type proposed will obviously be among the most in demand as consortium participants.

Successful alliances

The success of an alliance is attributed to a number of factors, some of which are similar to the factors present in a successful integration (mergers and acquisitions). The failure of an alliance often results from problems like incompatibility of objectives, the ending of the basis for the collaboration as a result of competitive, environmental or organizational change, cultural differences, and problems of co-ordination.

Faulkner (1995) suggested that the following factors are critical to the success of collaborative ventures:

- complementary skills and capabilities of the partners;
- the degree of overlap between the parties' markets be kept to a minimum;
- a high level of autonomy, with strong leadership and commitment from the parent organizations (if appropriate);

- the need to build up trust and not to depend solely on the contractual framework of the relationship;
- recognizing that the two partners may have different cultures.

Researchers in this area have noted that alliances seem to work best when the partners are from related industries (or the same industry) or when the objective of the alliance is the development of a new geographical region. Success is further enhanced when the parties are of a similar size and are as equally committed (in resource terms), to the alliance. Strict adherence to the initial objectives of the alliance can often limit its success, as modification of the original purpose may become necessary if the business environment changes. There is thus a need to continually reappraise the parameters of the agreement. Reve (1990) argued that alliances are more likely to succeed when a *behavioural approach* is adopted which emphasizes the value of the relationship to the parties and which places a high value on trust and personal contacts. An *economic approach*, emphasizing only a profit motive, is likely to create a much less stable alliance.

Brouthers *et al.* (1993) advanced a more succinct version of Faulkner's success factors in the '3 Cs' of successful alliances. The two parties should have:

- complimentary skills;
- compatible goals;
- co-operative cultures.

The termination of an alliance should, of course, not always lead us to conclude that it has been a failure. For fixed-term alliances such as joint ventures for the purposes of a research or marketing project, the conclusion date may have been set at the start of the alliance. Similarly, consortium partners such as those that form an alliance for a large civil engineering project, will dissolve the alliance upon the successful completion of the project.

The success of the venture should be judged in terms of the extent to which it improves the performance of the partner businesses over its life time. Similarly, not all partners in an alliance will benefit from it equally. Nevertheless, it can be viewed as successful if they realize benefits from the alliance in terms of improved performance.

The strategic management of networks and alliances

The concept of the 'focal' business

Many collaborative networks are centred on what can be regarded as a *focal business*. Toyota, for example, is at the heart of a network of suppliers and distributors and can be regarded as the focal business in its arrangements. It is the strategy of the focal business which will have the greatest influence in determining the overall strategy of the network and the other businesses which will comprise it.

According to Reve (1990), the focal business will have three major elements to its strategy. The first element is the strategic core which consists of core skills which are high in specificity and are managed internally. Such activities are central to the core competences of the organization and are managed via internal contracts and organizational incentives. The second element of strategy consists of the strategic alliances in which the focal business is involved. These are used to acquire complementary skills of medium asset specificity but which are not viewed as central to core competencies. Such activities are managed by external contracts governed through alliances. Finally, all assets of low specificity are obtained through the appropriate markets.

Strategic management within a network or alliance is therefore concerned with:

- determining which activities and assets are core and should therefore be carried out by the focal business;
- determining which activities are of medium specificity and should be obtained via alliances and outsourcing;
- determining which activities are of low specificity and should be obtained through the market;
- co-ordination and integration of core and alliance activities;
- management and operation of the alliance.

Information and communications technology has played an important role in improving the management of collaborative networks (see Chapter 10) by improving co-ordination and responsiveness and by facilitating learning across organizational boundaries. As network relationships change over time, the survival of a strategic alliance will depend upon its ability to co-ordinate activities and adapt relationships.

REVIEW AND DISCUSSION QUESTIONS

1. Define and distinguish between a merger, an agreed acquisition and a hostile acquisition.
2. What is the difference between the horizontal and vertical directions for integrations and alliances?
3. What is a consortium?
4. Explain the strategic reasoning behind a horizontal integration and a forward vertical arrangement.
5. What pre-integration practices, if adopted, might reduce the failure of the integration?
6. Why is the identification of the focal business important in understanding alliances?

References and further reading

Alexander, M. (1995) Managing the boundaries of the organization, *Long Range Planning*, **30**(5).

Bengtsson, A.M. (1992) *Managing Mergers and Acquisitions: A European Perspective*, Gower, Aldershot.

Bishop, M. and Kay, J. (1993) *European Mergers and Merger Policy*. Oxford University Press, Oxford.

Bleek, J. and Ernst, D. (1993) *Collaborating to Compete*, John Wiley, New York.

Bowerson, D.J. (1990) The strategic benefits of logistics alliances, *Harvard Business Review*, **90**(4), 36–47.

Brooke, M.Z. (1986) *International Management: A Review of Strategies and Operations*, Hutchinson, London.

Brouthers, K.D., Brouthers, L.E. and Wilkinson, T.J. (1993) Strategic alliances: choose your partners, *Long Range Planning*, **28**(3), 18–25.

Buckley, A. (1975) Growth by acquisition, *Long Range Planning*, August.

Buckley, P.J. and Casson, M. (1988) A theory of co-operation in international business, in: Contractor, F.J. and Lorange P. (eds), *Competitive Strategies in International Business*, Lexington Books, Lexington.

Buckley, P.J., Pass, C.L. and Prescott, K. (1990) Foreign market servicing by multinationals – an integrated treatment, *International Marketing Review*, **7**(4), 25–40.

Buckley, P.J., Pass, C.L. and Prescott, K. (1992) Foreign market servicing strategies of UK retail financial service firms in continental Europe, in: Young, S. and Hamill, J. (eds), *Europe and the Multinationals: Issues and Responses for the 1990s*, Edward Elgar, Aldershot.

Business International (1987) Acquisition strategy in Europe, Business International Research Report.

Business International (1988) Making acquisitions work: lessons from companies' successes and mistakes, Business International Research Report.

Chai, T. and McGuire, D.J. (1996) Collaborative ventures and value of learning: integrating the transaction cost and strategic option perspectives on the choice of market entry modes, *Journal of International Business Studies*, **27**(2).

Contractor, F. and Lorange, P. (1988a) Why should firms co-operate? in: *Co-operative Strategies in International Business*, Lexington Books, Lexington.

Contractor, F.J. and Lorange, P. (1988b) Competition vs. cooperation: a benefit/cost framework for choosing between fully-owned investments and cooperative relationships, *Management International Review*, **28**, Special Issue, 88.

Davidson, K.M. (1990) Mergers and acquisitions: anatomy of the fall, *Journal of Business Strategy*, **11**(5), 48–51.

Davidson, K.M. (1991) Mergers and acquisitions: innovation and corporate mergers, *Journal of Business Strategy*, **12**(1), 42–45.

De Noble, A.F., Gustafson, L.T. and Hergert, M. (1988) Planning for post-merger integration – eight lessons for merger success, *Long Range Planning*, **21**(110), 82–86.

De Wit, B. and Meyer, R. (1998) *Strategy – Process, Content, Context, An International Perspective*, International Thomson Business Press.

Devlin, G. and Bleackley, M. (1988) Strategic alliances – guidelines for success, *Long Range Planning*, **21**(5), 18–23.

Doz, Y.L., Hamel, G. and Prahalad, C.K. (1986) Strategic partnerships: success or surrender? The challenge of competitive collaboration. Paper presented at *Joint Academy of International Business/European International Business Association Conference*, London, November.

Faulkner, D. (1995) *Strategic Alliances: Cooperating to Compete*, McGraw Hill, New York.

Firth, M. (1991) Corporate takeovers, stockholder returns and executive rewards, *Managerial and Decision Economics*, **12**.

Foot, R., Robinson T.M. and Clarke-Hill, C.M. (1993) The entry of UK firms into the former East German market through acquisitions in the Treuhand: a case approach, *European Business and Economic Development*, **2**(3), November.

Franck, G. (1990) Mergers and acquisitions: competitive advantage and cultural fit, *European Management Journal*, **8**(1).

Franks, J. and Harris, R. (1989) Shareholders wealth effects of corporate takeover: the UK experience 1955–1985. *Journal of Financial Economics*, **23**.

Gall, E.A. (1991) Strategies for merger success, *Journal of Business Strategy*, **12**(2), 26–30.

Geroski, P.A. and Vlassopoulos, A. (1990) Recent patterns of European merger activity, *Business Strategy Review*, Summer.

Ghoshal, S. and Bartlett, C.A. (1990) The multinational corporation as an interorganizational network, *Academy of Management Review*, **15**, 603–625.

Glaister, K. (1993) UK joint venture formation in Western Europe, *European Business and Economic Development*, **2**(3), November.

Glaister, K.W. and Buckley, P. (1994) UK international joint ventures: an analysis of patterns of activity and distribution, *British Journal of Management*, **5**.

Gogler, P. (1992) Building transnational alliances to create competitive advantage, *Long Range Planning*, **25**(1), 90–99.

Gulati, R. (1998) Alliances and networks, *Strategic Management Journal*, **19**, 293–317.

Hamel, G., Doz, Y.L. and Prahalad, C.K. (1989) Collaborate with your competitors – and win, *Harvard Business Review*, January/February, 133–139.

Hamill, J. (1988a) British acquisitions in the US, *National Westminster Bank Quarterly Review*, August.

Hamill, J. (1988b) US acquisitions and the internationalization of British industry, *Acquisitions Monthly*, November.

Hamill, J. (1991a) Strategic restructuring through international acquisitions and divestments, *Journal of General Management*, **17**(1), Autumn.

Hamill, J. (1991b) Changing patterns of international business: crossborder mergers, acquisitions and alliances, *Proceedings of the UK Region, Academy of International Business Conference*, London, April.

Hamill, J. and Crosbie, J. (1989) Acquiring in the US food and drink industry, *Acquisitions Monthly*, May.

Hamill, J. and El-Hajjar, S. (1990) Defending competitiveness, *Acquisitions Monthly*, April, 36–39.

Haspeslagh, P. and Jemison, D. (1991) *Managing Acquisitions: Creating Value Through Corporate Renewal*. Free Press, New York.

Heene, A. and Sanchez, R. (Eds.) (1997) *Competence-Based Strategic Management*, John Wiley, New York.

Hennart, J.F., Roehl, T. and Zietlow, D.S. (1999) Trojan horse or workhorse? The evolution of US–Japanese joint ventures in the United States, *Strategic Management Journal*, **20**, 15–29.

Jain, S.C. (1987) Perspectives on international strategic alliances, *Advances in International Marketing*, JAI Press, Greenwich, pp. 103–120.

Jarillo, J.C. (1988) On strategic networks, *Strategic Management Journal*, June/July.

Jarillo, J.C. and Stevenson, H.H. (1991) Cooperative strategies – the payoffs and pitfalls, *Long Range Planning*, **24**(1), 64–70.

Jemison, D.B. and Sitkin, S.M. (1986a) Corporate acquisitions: a process perspective, *Academy of Management Review*, **11**(1).

Jemison, D.B. and Sitkin, S.M. (1986b) Acquisitions: the process can be a problem, *Harvard Business Review*, March.

Johanson, J. and Mattson, L.G. (1992) Network positions and strategic action, in: Axelsson, B. and Easton, G. (eds), *Industrial Networks: A New View of Reality*, Routledge, London.

Kay, J. (1993) *Foundations of Corporate Success*, Oxford University Press, Oxford.

Khanna, T., Gulati, R. and Nitin, N. (1998) The dynamics of learning alliances: competition, cooperation and relative scope, *Strategic Management Journal*, **19**, 191–209.

Kitching, J. (1974) Why acquisitions are abortive, *Management Today*, November.

Lorange, P. (1988) Cooperative strategies: planning and control considerations, *Centre for International Management Studies*, WP-512.

Lorange, P. and Roos, J. (1991) Why some strategic alliances succeed and others fail, *Journal of Business Strategy*, **12**(1), 25–31.

Lorange, P. and Roos, J. (1992) *Strategic Alliances: Formation, Implementation and Evolution*, Basil Blackwell, Oxford.

Lorenzoni, G. and Baden-Fuller, C. (1995) Creating a strategic center to manage a web of partners, *California Management Review*, **37**(3).

Love, J.H. and Scouller, J. (1990) Growth by acquisition: the lessons of experience, *Journal of General Management*, **15**(3), Spring.

Luostarinen, R. (1979) *The Internationalization of the Firm*, Acta Academic Oeconumicae Helsingiensis, Helsinki.

Lyons, M.P. (1991) Joint ventures as strategic choice – a literature review, *Long Range Planning*, **24**(4), 130–144.

Malekzadeh, A.R. and Nahavindi, A. (1990) Making mergers work by managing cultures, *Journal of Business Strategy*, **11**(3), 55–58.

Medcof, J.W. (1997) Why too many alliances end in divorce, *Long Range Planning*, **30**(5).

Meeks, G. (1977) *Disappointing Marriage: A Study of the Gains from Mergers*, Cambridge University Press, Cambridge.

Morgan, N.A. (1988) Successful growth by acquisition, *Journal of General Management*, **14**(2), Winter.

Morris, D. and Hergert, M. (1987) Trends in international collaborative agreements, *Columbia Journal of World Business*, Summer.

Ohmae, K. (1989) The global logic of strategic alliances, *Harvard Business Review*, March/April.

Ollie, R. (1990) Culture and integration problems in international mergers and acquisitions, *European Management Journal*, **8**(2), June.

Oman, C. (1984) *New Forms of International Investment in Developing Countries*, Paris, OECD.

Payne, A.F. (1987) Approaching acquisitions strategically, *Journal of General Management*, **13**(2), Winter.

Pearson, M. (1985) *Managing Acquisitions*, British Institute of Management, London.

Perlmutter, H.V. and Heenan, D.H. (1986) Cooperate to compete globally, *Harvard Business Review*, March/April.

Porter, M.E. (1980) *Competitive Strategy*, Free Press, New York.

Porter, M.E. (1985) *Competitive Advantage*, Free Press, New York.

Porter, M.E. (Ed.) (1986) *Competition in Global Industries*, Harvard Business School Press, Boston.

Porter, M.E. (1990) *The Competitive Advantage of Nations*, Macmillan, London.

Porter, M.E. and Fuller, M.B. (1987) Coalitions and global strategy, in: Porter, M.E. (ed.), *Competition in Global Industries*, Harvard Business School Press, Boston.

Preece, S. (1995) Incorporating international strategic alliances into overall firm strategy: a typology of six managerial objectives, *The International Executive*, **37**(3), 261–277.

Quinn, J., Dooley, T. and Paquette, P. (1990) Technology in services: rethinking strategic focus, *Sloan Management Review*, Winter.

Ravenscraft, D.J. and Scherer F.M. (1987) *Mergers, Sell-offs and Economic Efficiency*, Brooking Institution, Washington, DC.

Reve, T. (1990) The firm as a nexus of internal and external contracts, in: Aoki, M., Gustafsson, M. and Williamson, O.E. (eds), *The Firm as a Nexus of Treaties*, Sage, London.

Shelton, L.M. (1988) Strategic business fits and corporate acquisitions: empirical evidence, *Strategic Management Journal*, **9**.

Shleifer, A. and Vishny, R. (1986) Large shareholders and corporate control, *Journal of Political Economy*, **94**, 461–488.

Shleifer, A. and Vishny, R. (1991) Takeovers in the '60s and the '80s: evidence and implications, *Strategic Management Journal*, **12**.

Sirower, M.L. (1997) *The Synergy Trap: How Companies Lose the Acquisition Game*. Free Press, New York.

Stonehouse, G.H. (1995) International collaborative business networks and the virtual corporation, *Conference Paper British Academy of Management*, Sheffield.

Stonehouse, G.H. and Pemberton, J. (1999) Learning and knowledge management in the intelligent organization, *Participation and Empowerment: An International Journal*, **7**(5), 131–144.

Sudarsanam, P.S. (1995) *The Essence of Mergers and Acquisitions*, Prentice Hall, Englewood Cliffs.

Walsh, J. and Ellwood, J. (1991) Mergers, acquisitions and the pruning of managerial deadwood, *Strategic Management Journal*, **12**.

GLOBAL BUSINESS – PRESENT AND FUTURE TRENDS

15

CHAPTER

LEARNING OBJECTIVES

After completing this chapter, students should be able to:

- identify the key themes in future trends in the global business environment;
- explain the impact of such changes on transnational businesses;
- identify future potential sources of global competitive advantage;
- describe the principles of knowledge management;
- describe the potential of e-commerce in global business;
- explain what a 'virtual' corporation is and the benefits of such a concept to competitive strategy.

Introduction

In the future, global strategy will continue to be centred upon new sources of competitive advantage for transnational organizations. The acquisition of competitive edge will depend upon the ability of businesses to build and leverage new competences in the context of a rapidly changing global business environment. This chapter therefore examines potential developments in the forces which shape the global environment, their effect upon transnationals and the means by which they compete. First, the future of globalization and its limitations are explored before potential new sources of competitive advantage including knowledge, collaborative networks and e-commerce are considered.

The global business environment – limits of globalization

The real state of homogenization

Levitt (1983) presented his seminal vision of a 'global village', characterized by standardized products and services, and global strategies built upon economies of scale and scope. There are a growing number of industries and markets which display some of the characteristics thought to typify a global market. At the same time, Segal-Horn (1992) argued that there is actually little evidence of homogenization of markets, rather 'the differences both within and across countries are far greater than any similarities which may exist'.

The question for the future is whether the differences which currently exist between national markets will continue or whether there will be ultimate convergence into a series of global markets for goods and services. Parker (1998) presented a discussion of factors which he argued will always inhibit, and indeed prevent, convergence of markets. His argument is based upon physioeconomic theory.

Physioeconomic theory

Physioeconomic theory dates back to the eighteenth century and the work of Adam Smith (1723–1790) and the French philosopher Montesquieu (1689–1755). Its roots are in natural history, which recognizes that there is a hierarchy of phenomena. For example, solar climate precedes and determines physical climate whilst the natural resources that a country possesses place a theoretical limit to its ultimate wealth. As Parker (1998) put it, 'Each level in the hierarchy is a necessary condition for the next: culture depends upon the existence of terrestrial life, which depends upon the existence of marine life, which depends on a particular climate'. Physioeconomic theories use both physiological and physiographic (physical-geographic) factors to explain differences between cultures, tastes and needs. To put this another way, similarities and differences in human behaviour will depend upon similarities and differences in climatic conditions, terrain, and endowments of natural resources which will help to predetermine culture, political and economic conditions.

According to Parker (1998), 'solar climate alone ... has a stronger correlation than income per head with many economic behaviours that are usually thought of as "development driven"'. Milk, cereal, flour, coffee and cigarette consumption per head are better explained by solar climate than by income per head. People in colder climates consume more alcohol than those in warmer climates. Furthermore, 'Physiological adaptations across populations affect dietary preferences . . . , housing preferences (heating, insulation, architecture) and clothing preferences . . . ; overall they influence 30–50% of total household consumption in developed economies and up to 90% in less developed economies' (Parker 1998). Climatic differences also explain differences in consumption of psychological products like entertainment products which are more strongly demanded in colder climates.

In essence, physioeconomic theory suggests that although countries with similar physioeconomic characteristics, like climate, terrain and natural resources, will tend to converge in economic and social terms, those facing different physioeconomic conditions will preserve many of their differences. Thus, although cultures may converge in some respects, physioeconomic factors will ensure that differences between many national markets persist. There are therefore natural limitations to globalization.

Challenging the presuppositions

As well as forces beyond the control of humankind, there are other factors which challenge some of the assumptions upon which globalization is based. For Levitt (1983), organizations must sell high volumes of standardized products on a global scale so as to enjoy the benefits of economies of scale. Yet, 'Developments in factor automation allowing flexible, lower cost, lower volume, high variety operations are challenging the standard assumptions of scale economy benefits by yielding variety at lower costs' (Segal-Horn 1992). When this is coupled to the fact that consumers in many markets are becoming increasingly fickle, some of the perceived benefits of globalization to business seem to disappear. According to Martin (1997) the increasing volatility of markets means that there may be advantages in dispersion of manufacturing activities rather than concentration. Having a manufacturing facility located near to a market increases responsiveness and, while concentration of activities may bring the benefits of economies of scale, it may be at the cost of local adaptability.

Even some of the supposed benefits of globalization are not so great as might be assumed. While the OECD argued in 1996 that globalization 'gives all countries the possibility of participating in world development and all consumers the assurance of benefiting from increasingly vigorous competition between producers', the argument fails to take into account that consumers are also producers. From the viewpoint of producers, increased competition drives down prices, wages, and potentially, employment.

Further, Elliot (1996) made the point that 'Liberalization and globalization in industrial countries have not resulted in increased growth, nor are they likely to do so'. In fact, it is often the case that those countries which have prospered most in recent years have been those with high levels of government intervention (such as Germany, Japan and Korea). Professor Alit Singh of Cambridge University made the point in Elliot's (1996) article that records for growth, employment, living standards and investment were much poorer in the period from the mid-1970s to the mid-1990s than they were between 1945 and 1973 when interventionism based upon the Keynesian economic model was common practice.

At the level of the individual business there are also drawbacks in being global. Global companies are sometimes blamed for many of the world's ills. Jackson (1997) gave the examples of oil companies like Exxon being blamed for the world's pollution problems after the Exxon Valdez tanker sinking in 1989, McDonald's for rain forest destruction and Nike for exploiting child labour. These accusations are often unjust but arise because the names of these businesses are known globally.

A global approach to strategy and management?

There have been various attempts to make the case that the management philosophy and techniques of one country or region are superior to those of others. For example, American and Japanese techniques are often held up as examples of good practice. If this were the case then it might be reasonable to assume that some form of global approach to management might develop. There are certainly global trends in management theory like total quality management, knowledge management and others, but there remain fundamental differences in approach between managers.

Doyle (1996) argued that the focus of international management varies from country to country. American and British managers emphasize seeking to maximize 'shareholder value' which is achieved when an attractive rate of return on capital expenditure is achieved. This differs from Japanese, German and Korean companies, which tend to place greater emphasis on achieving market leadership by seeking to build customer satisfaction with their products. There are therefore important differences in the way that strategy is determined in businesses in these two groups. In the Anglo-American group, the approach adopted focuses on arriving at the financial budget necessary to achieve the target return on capital employed. This has been criticized as representing a short-term approach to business strategy. In the other group, businesses emphasize the importance of R&D, innovation, brand building and supply chain management so as to increase customer satisfaction. In other words, it is patently obvious that there is not a single global approach to management and strategy in businesses around the world.

Martin (1997) pointed out that 'Going global is not the only possible approach to the 21st century business challenge. It is also feasible to build a company strategy around defending a home market'. For the transnational business, the strategic challenge of the 21st century is to combine global scope with the responsiveness and flexibility necessary to compete with local domestic producers. Further, it is necessary to balance the pressures for globalization resulting from the benefits of economies of large-scale production against the need to respond flexibly to increasingly erratic customer preferences. On the other hand, companies which choose to defend their domestic positions rather than going global will only do so successfully if they remain alert to the changes taking place at a global level.

There are many examples of global players facing successful local competitors. In the global fast-food market McDonald's faces strong local competition in France and Belgium from Quick and in Greece from Goody's, which holds a significant share of the market but is by no means a global competitor. Similarly, Coca-Cola and Pepsi-Cola face competition in Scotland from Barr's Irn Bru soft drink which holds a 25% market share but which is virtually unknown outside of the UK. It may therefore be necessary to make local variations to strategy to cope with local competitors.

Global competitive advantage in the future

The increasingly turbulent and hypercompetitive business environment has made it correspondingly difficult to generate and, even more importantly, sustain competitive advantage. Companies must develop and leverage core competences which meet the realized and unrealized needs of customers. At the heart of such core competences is organizational learning. To put this another way, core competence is normally founded upon organizational knowledge. The pace of change means that knowledge changes rapidly over time so that organizations must 'learn' in order to build new knowledge. Organizations must become 'intelligent' and remain focused upon the creation and management of knowledge which forms the basis of competitive advantage (Stonehouse and Pemberton 1999).

Knowledge-based strategy: the intelligent organization

As the pace and unpredictability of change in the global business environment increase, flexibility and adaptability become more and more critical to sustaining a competitive edge. Responsiveness and proactivity are dependent upon the ability of both individuals and organizations to learn more quickly than their rivals. Organizations must become 'intelligent' by actively attempting to learn about their internal and external environments and the relationships between them. In order to learn more quickly than competitors, it is necessary to develop understanding of the nature and processes of organizational learning and knowledge management.

Stonehouse and Pemberton (1999) developed a model of knowledge management and organizational learning (Figure 15.1). As organizational

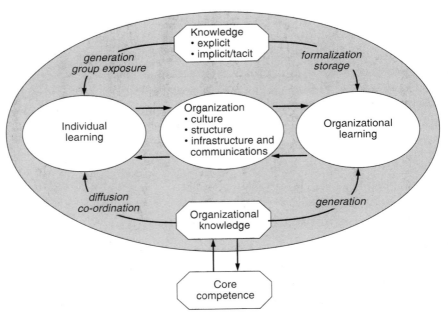

FIGURE 15.1 The intelligent organization – knowledge management and organizational learning loops (source: Stonehouse and Pemberton 1999)

learning is not linear (Argyris 1977, 1992), it is represented in a series of loops. Organizational learning and knowledge are based upon individual knowledge which must be formalized and stored in appropriate formats for dissemination and diffusion throughout the organization. Knowledge management in an 'intelligent organization' will be founded upon a culture, structure and infrastructure which encourage and support the creation and development of knowledge.

Types of knowledge

Organizational knowledge can be defined 'as a shared collection of principles, facts, skills, and rules which inform organizational decision-making, behaviour and actions', forming the basis of core competences. Raising the level of knowledge in the organization will increase its competitiveness. Knowledge can be either explicit or implicit.

Explicit knowledge is knowledge whose meaning is clearly stated, details of which can readily be recorded and stored. *Implicit or tacit knowledge* (Demarest 1997) is often unstated and is based upon individual experience. It is difficult to record and store but is often a vital source of competitive edge. One of the major challenges of knowledge management is the transformation of individual and tacit knowledge into organizational knowledge. A second major challenge is creating an organizational context which encourages and facilitates the development of new knowledge through organizational learning. The process of knowledge management is highly contingent upon organization culture, structure and infrastructure. An important factor to be borne in mind when attempting to build a learning organization through knowledge management is that 'knowledge is . . . one of the few assets that grows most – usually exponentially – when shared' (Quinn 1992). For this reason an intelligent organization must create a context in which learning and sharing of knowledge throughout the organization are supported.

Managing knowledge in an intelligent organization

Knowledge management is therefore concerned with the following processes:

- *the generation of knowledge* – individual and organizational learning;
- *the formalization of knowledge* – development of principles, rules and procedures which will allow knowledge to be shared;

- *the storage of knowledge* – determining the appropriate medium for storage which permits sharing;
- *the diffusion of knowledge* – sharing of knowledge within the organization and limiting sharing across organizational boundaries;
- *the co-ordination and control of knowledge* – ensuring that organizational knowledge is coherent and applied consistently.

The organizational context of such activities is vital to effective knowledge management. This context consists of:

- *organizational culture* – this must encourage experimentation, the sharing of ideas and must place a high value on learning and knowledge;
- *organizational structure* – this must allow experts to share ideas but must also be holistic allowing ideas to be shared across the whole organization. It favours a network structure or the use of project teams and task groups (see Chapter 13 where organizational structure is discussed);
- *organizational infrastructure and communications* – this will depend upon the efficient and effective use of information and communications technology, particularly networks (internal and external, the Internet), expert systems, neural networks and multimedia. ICT has an important role to play in the storage and diffusion of knowledge (see Chapter 10 where technology strategy is discussed).

Core competences and knowledge
Core competences must be distinctive, complex, difficult to imitate, durable and adaptable if they are to be a source of sustained superior performance. Knowledge can be an important source of these characteristics. Knowledge, particularly tacit or implicit knowledge, is both complex and difficult to imitate. Organizational learning can make knowledge a durable and adaptable source of competitive advantage. There are numerous examples of the ways in which knowledge acts as the foundation for competence building and leveraging. Microsoft's competitive advantage in the software sector, for example, is largely knowledge-based (Stonehouse and Pemberton 1999).

The number of organizations seeking to become 'intelligent' by fostering organizational learning through knowledge management is increasing. Grant (1997) pointed out that 'companies such as Dow Chemical, Andersen Consulting, Polaroid and Skania are developing corporate wide systems to track, access, exploit and create organizational knowledge'.

The distinctive features shared by these organizations are that they encourage questioning and creativity, and place a high value on trust, teamwork and sharing. At the same time, they have created infrastructures which support learning, which assist in the storage and controlled diffusion of knowledge, and which co-ordinate its application in creating and supporting core competences.

The idea of knowledge as an important source of competitive advantage is not new but renewed interest in it is partly due to rapid change in the macroenvironment, turbulence and hypercompetition. Collectively, these factors mean that organizations must learn more quickly than their rivals if they are to stay ahead in the competitive game. Knowledge, which is distinctive, is vital to the building and leveraging of core competences. In these circumstances it is inevitable that managers in transnational businesses will be seeking better ways of fostering learning through knowledge management.

The 'virtual' corporation

The 1990s witnessed an increase in interest in the potential of collaboration between businesses, coupled with the use of information and communications technology (ICT) as a potential source of competitive edge. This interest is again linked to the rise of the core competence school of thought in strategic management. The development of core competences within an organization requires a degree of specialization so as to focus the development of knowledge and skills which are relevant to a particular form or aspect of business. Collaboration allows businesses to share knowledge and core competences so as to create synergies and new sources of competitive advantage. The development of ICT and e-commerce has further increased possibilities for collaboration both between businesses and between businesses and their customers.

Davidow and Malone (1992) were among the first to highlight the role of information and ICT in the management of collaborative activities, stressing the improved service, flexibility and responsiveness made possible by the sharing of information. Since their article in 1992, the rapid expansion of the internet and developments in e-commerce have sparked a revolution in the use of technology to support business in general and collaboration in particular. For these reasons, information technology is hailed as having given birth to the virtual corporation.

The virtual corporation can be viewed as a collaborative network comprising of a focal business, its suppliers and customers whose activities are integrated and co-ordinated by the extensive use of information and communications technology. There are several key characteristics which may be viewed as essential to the existence of a virtual corporation:

- a network of collaborative businesses and customers centred on a focal business;
- concentration upon core business activities by individual network members;
- shared complementary goals;
- alignment of network business strategies;
- integration of business and information strategies;
- shared technology which often includes computer networks, satellite or cable communications, common software standards, and electronic data interchange.

The truly virtual corporation will be centred on a focal business which shows a high degree of integration of internal activities with considerable blurring between functional business areas. The external linkages of the focal organization will also demonstrate a high degree of integration both upstream, with suppliers, and downstream, with customers and distributors, in the value system.

The potential benefits to the network include more effective co-ordination of activities, reduced costs, greatly enhanced responsiveness, ability to compete more effectively on the basis of time and, equally as importantly, information which leads to superior knowledge of customers, products and markets. Thus ICT, while usually not the major underlying motivation for a network, has the ability to transform its competitive performance from the acceptable to the exceptional.

REVIEW AND DISCUSSION QUESTIONS

1. Discuss the potential for further globalization of business activity. What limitations are there on globalization?
2. What impact might limitations on globalization have on the strategies of transnational organizations?
3. Why is there increasing interest in knowledge as a source of competitive advantage?

4. What factors must be taken into account in building an intelligent organization?

5. Explain the main features of a virtual corporation

References and further reading

Argyris, C. (1977) Double loop learning in organizations, *Harvard Business Review*, September/October, 115–125.

Argyris, C. (1992) *On Organizational Learning*, Blackwell, Cambridge, MA.

Argyris, C. and Schon, D. (1978) *Organization Learning: A Theory of Action Perspective*, Addison Wesley, Reading, MA.

Chakravarthy, B. (1997) A new strategy framework for coping with turbulence, *Sloan Management Review*, Winter, 69–82.

Davidow, W.H. and Malone, M.S. (1992) *Structuring and Revitalizing the Corporation for the 21st Century – The Virtual Corporation*, Harper Business, London.

Demarest, M. (1997) Understanding knowledge management, *Long Range Planning*, **30**(3), 374–384.

Doyle, P. (1996) The loss from profits, *Financial Times*, 25th October.

Elliot, L. (1996) Putting trade in its place, *The Guardian*, 27th May.

Financial Times (1997) *Financial Times*, 27th September.

Graham, G. (1997) The difficulty of banking on the world – is there a life for the non-global?, *Financial Times*, 29th October.

Grant, R.M. (1997) The knowledge-based view of the firm: implications for management practice, *Long Range Planning*, **30**(3), 450–454.

Hilgard, E.R. and Bower, G.H. (1967) *Theories of Learning*, Appleton.

Inkpen, A.C. and Crossan, M.M. (1995) Believing is seeing: joint ventures and organization learning, *Journal of Management Studies*, **32**(5), 595–618.

Jackson, T. (1993) *Organizational Behaviour in International Management*, Butterworth Heinemann, Oxford.

Jackson, T. (1997) Facing up to challenging opposition, *Financial Times*, 31st October.

Kamoche, K. (1997) Knowledge creation and learning in international human resource management, *International Journal of Human Resource Management*, **8**(3), April, 213–225.

Kolb, D.A., Rubin, I.M. and Osland, J. (1991) *Organizational Behaviour: An Experiential Approach*, Prentice Hall, Englewood Cliffs.

Levitt, T. (1983) The globalization of markets, *Harvard Business Review*, May/June.

Martin, P. (1997) A future depending on choice – the global company in the 21st century, *Financial Times*, 7th November.

McMaster, M. (1997) Organising for innovation; technology and intelligent capacities, *Long Range Planning*, **30**(5), 799–802.

Parker, P. (1998) Why markets will not converge, *Mastering Marketing*, Financial Times, London.

Parsaye, K. *et al.* (1989) *Intelligent Databases*, John Wiley, New York.

Quinn, J.B. (1992) *The Intelligent Enterprise*, Free Press, New York.

Quintas, P. and Lefevre, P. (1997) Knowledge management: a strategic agenda, *Long Range Planning*, **30**(3), 385–397.

Rushde, D. and Oldfield, C. (1999) E-mania, *Sunday Times*, 19th September.

Sanchez, R. and Heene, A. (eds) (1997) *Strategic Learning and Knowledge Management*, John Wiley, New York.

Segal-Horn, S. (1992) Global markets, regional trading blocs and international consumers, *Journal of Global Marketing*, **5**(3).

Senge, P. (1990) Building learning organizations, *Sloan Management Review*, Fall.

Stonehouse, G.H. and Pemberton, J.D. (1999) Learning and knowledge management in the intelligent organization, *Participation and Empowerment: An International Journal*, **7**(5), 131–144.

Turner, I. (1996) Working with chaos, *Financial Times*, 4th October.

Volberda, H.W. (1997) Building flexible organizations for fast-moving markets, *Long Range Planning*, **30**(2), 169–183.

Whitehill, M. (1997) Knowledge-based strategy to deliver sustained competitive advantage, *Long Range Planning*, **30**(4), 621–627.

THE CASES

Case Study 1

AIRTOURS PLC

Nigel Evans

University of Northumbria

An entrepreneurial beginning

David Crossland's introduction to the business world was not very promising. On leaving Burnley Grammar School in 1963 he took a job as a coffee boy in a local travel agent and it was difficult to imagine that he would in time become the chairman of what became one of the world's leading travel companies and rank 86th in *The Sunday Times* 'Rich List' of Britain's wealthiest 1000 people.

During the 1970s Crossland joined with his brother in law, Tom Trickett to form Pendle Travel. Entry costs were at the time relatively low and the powerful multiple chains were far less the threat to the independent travel agency business that they later became. Trickett backed Crossland in 1972 with an £8000 investment in the first travel agency, and he remained a large shareholder in the Airtours business until the mid-1990s. The Airtours name originated in 1978 when Pendle Travel launched a tour operations division within the successful travel agency business. When the first tours took to the air the company was operating from a tiny office above a travel agency in the small Lancashire village of Haslingden. The initial specialization of the company was low-cost package holidays to Malta which found a ready market in the north-west of England. The speed of development of the tour operating business outstripped that of the travel agency chain and the competitive pressures on independent travel agents were becoming ever greater with 'the march of the multiples' as it was later termed.

From 1985, Crossland, recognizing that the development of the business required professional inputs from others, started to draw around him a strong management team to help him build the business. The sale of the 22-branch chain to Hogg Robinson (which operated a nationwide branch network) was concluded in 1986 and in that year, Airtours carried 300 000 holidaymakers. This period culminated the following year with a major step in the company's strategic development. The company was floated on the London Stock Exchange to become a public limited company, making it one of a very small number of tour operators to have a full stock market listing at that time.

After flotation

As Airtours plc, the management could raise capital for investment allowing opportunities for expansion, but this also imposed financial disciplines on the management team. The company had to deliver satisfaction to customers, shareholders and bankers – and balancing these competing demands is not always easy. Still based in its north-west England heartland (the company today has its corporate headquarters in the Manchester suburbs and operates its core UK tour operating from a converted mill in the small town of Helmshore), Airtours established a reputation throughout the travel industry for its relatively low staffing costs and the loyalty it has been able to engender in its staff. 'They stay a long time because they are determined that one day they will get to the office before me' Crossland jokes. This may prove to be something of a long-term challenge to staff since he regularly arrives at 5.30 am.

Despite developments elsewhere in the business, tour operations remained at the core of the group's activities with both the airline and distribution networks developing largely to service its needs rather than as business interests in themselves. The Aspro brand was positioned at the value for money or price-led end of the market whilst Airtours was positioned as the main market brand with particular appeal to families. A large number of different brochures were produced in the UK using the Airtours name and representing a variety of holiday types. The brochures included: Summer Sun, Far and Away, Turkey, Greece, Florida, Fly-Drive USA, Cruises, Florida and Caribbean Cruise and Stay Holidays (featuring Carnival Cruises), All-Inclusive, Suncenters, City and Short Breaks, and Lakes and Mountains. The Tradewinds brand offered more exclusive and exotic holidays, mainly utilizing scheduled flights to destinations all over the world.

In 1990 Airtours introduced EuroSites by establishing a subsidiary operating the self-drive holidays with pre-arranged camping locations. By the late 1990s, EuroSites was the second largest company in its sector (after Eurocamp). EuroSites offered tent and mobile home holidays across Europe, selling since its launch in the UK and more recently in the Dutch and German markets. Further capacity was added progressively from one season to the next through the adding of capacity at sites and by adding additional camp sites to its portfolio. Demand for the product has proved to be strong with a good levels of profitability, high levels of customer satisfaction and high levels of repeat business. During 1990 'The Cottage Directory' product selling UK country cottages was also developed. However, sales levels achieved were lower than forecast and the product proved operationally difficult, involving as it did close liaison with a large number of property owners. After the end of its first season, an offer for the business was received and accepted thereby incurring a relatively limited loss overall.

Throughout the 1990s, the UK outbound tour operating sector was characterized by intense competition and was highly seasonal and cyclical in its booking patterns. A number of factors combined to create a substantial imbalance between supply and demand for summer 1995. Tour operators had anticipated the arrival of the much talked about 'feel-good factor' in the UK economy and sales in the pre-Christmas selling period were encouraging. However, this did not continue into the peak booking months of January–March and all operators maintained capacity in the expectation of an upturn in demand. Several companies also declared their aim of gaining market share in 1995. Onto this market position was added the effect of the excellent, record-breaking UK weather during the summer months. With supply greater than demand in the late sales market, many prices fell to unprofitable levels across the industry and discounting was substantially higher than in recent years. The alternatives indicated by the 1995 market were straightforward. The industry could either downsize by offering fewer holidays at realistic margins or continue on the same basis as 1995 with higher and higher late sales discounts giving customers little incentive to book early.

Launched ahead of schedule on 18 March 1991, Airtours International was set up, unlike some other charter carriers, solely to serve the group's tour operations. Its capacity was fully utilized on Airtours business and was not dependent upon third party customers. The growing needs of the tour operations required assurance that sufficient seat capacity could be acquired at the right price and be of a consistent quality. The airline's growth has, however, been determined by Airtours' winter tour operations with the airline providing over 90 per cent of the winter tour operations flying programme, dropping to between 60 and 70 per cent for the summer programme.

Airtours' northern roots were emphasized by its utilization of Manchester airport. In 1986, 76 per cent of Airtours bookings were for Manchester departures and although growth from the airport continued after that time in terms of absolute numbers, its relative position has declined since it represented only 46 per cent of UK departures in 1991. This proportion has subsequently fallen further. The company's in-house airline, Airtours International, has from its inception in 1991 been based at Manchester airport.

In September 1992 Airtours re-entered the UK retail travel agency business with the purchase of 335 branches of the third largest retail chain, Pickfords. This was followed by the purchase in June 1993 of 210 branches acquired from Hogg Robinson, moving the group to second position behind Lunn Poly in UK retail distribution. The branches served as outlets for the distribution of Airtours products and provided market intelligence on customer preferences and market trends. A major re-branding exercise took place during December 1993 when the retail division was re-launched under the Going Places name. Within seven days every one of the company's 545 retail shops had been fitted out with new facias, signage and stationery. Later in the year the 40-strong Winston Rees chain was added to the Airtours network.

The merging of large retail networks resulted in a degree of duplication with some shops being closer to others than would be considered ideal. The company found that there was little merit in closing branches despite the close proximity of a second Going Places outlet as long as each shop continued to make a satisfactory contribution to central overhead. Nevertheless, the profitability of each shop remained under constant review and while many new sites were subsequently developed by Going Places, several poorly performing shops were closed. In 1995 Going Places had over 650 branches operating in the UK compared to 795 operated by the market leader, Lunn Poly. Late Escapes, a telephone sales business specializing in the sales of holidays within eight weeks of departure, was purchased in 1994. Late Escapes, based in north-east England, made extensive use of the teletext information services for the marketing of its services directly to customers in their homes.

In January 1993 Airtours launched a hostile take-over bid for Owners Abroad (another large tour operator which served many of the same destinations). The acrimonious battle fought over several months and widely reported by the media led to a narrow defeat for Airtours and incurred costs of some £9 million.

International expansion

After 1994, the group expanded internationally, most significantly in Scandinavia and then in North America. The acquisition from Scandinavian Airways in June 1994 of the Scandinavian Leisure Group (SLG) gave the group ownership of the largest leisure travel company in Scandinavia, albeit one that serves many of the same destinations as Airtours in the UK market. SLG operates the Ving, Always and Saga brands, with particular strengths in Norway and Sweden. Seventy per cent of its sales are made directly to the public either by 'direct sell' methods or through dedicated retail outlets with the remaining 30 per cent of bookings effected via third party travel agents.

During the winter of 1994/95 SLG undertook a major restructuring exercise of its operations which, together with an improvement in the Scandinavian economies, resulted in a greatly enhanced performance by this division. SLG carried 915 000 customers in 1995 increasing to 1 028 000 in 1996. The acquisition of the Spies group, Scandinavia's third largest tour operator during 1996, added a further 397 000 customers under the Spies and Tjaerborg brands. The Spies group was extensively reorganized and re-focused after its acquisition with most administrative functions being integrated into SLG's Stockholm headquarters and respective overseas resort offices being rationalized. Following its major expansion SLG gained approximately 50 per cent of the Scandinavian market with the leading position in each of the Scandinavian countries. The acquisition of Spies gave Airtours full control of Premiair, Scandinavia's largest charter airline.

The Scandinavian acquisitions brought with them hotel and holiday complex portfolios – 16 properties in the case of SLG and 25 properties in the case of Spies – located in many of the principal resorts served by the group's tour operations. Accommodation ownership allowed the retention within the group of a higher proportion of resort expenditure and allowed the company to monitor customer tastes and preferences. By limiting hotel ownership to less than 20 per cent of total accommodation requirements within any one area, the group is able to ensure high occupancy levels. Distinct accommodation brands were developed in order to satisfy the differing demands of the group's tour operations. The successful Sunwing brand was primarily designed for Scandinavian customers, whilst the Suncenter product was marketed through Airtours Holidays and catered largely for the needs of the UK market. Suncenters offer families an action packed home-from-home with many activities, lots of entertainment and children's clubs.

The acquisition of Sunquest Vacations in August 1995 established Airtours' presence in the North American market through its tour operating businesses in Ontario and western Canada. This was followed by the acquisition of Alba, another significant Canadian tour operator, in August of the following year. Airtours also made its first foray into the vast US market during 1996 deciding that the most cost effective entry vehicle would be through a greenfield start-up operation capitalizing on the Sunquest brand name. Accordingly Sunquest Holidays was formed under the leadership of John Trickett, who had previously held management positions within the Airtours Group in the UK prior to moving to California in 1989 where he had subsequently worked for other tour operators. The company operated its first programme of holidays flying largely from California from April 1997 focusing on Mexico, the Caribbean and Hawaii, all of which are also served by existing tour operations within the Airtours group. By 1996, Airtours' North American Leisure Group had built a business carrying almost 500 000 customers.

Cruising as a holiday choice grew in popularity during the 1990s in most western economies. The UK cruise market remained relatively small (representing about 500 000 customers in 1994) due to its image of high cost, exclusivity and older age group appeal, but the market experienced significant growth in the latter half of the decade. In Europe, the potential for growth was also there as the percentage of customers opting for a cruise as their main package holiday was still around 2 per cent in the late 1990s. The North American market developed in a different way with rapid growth, a much younger customer base, specialist targeted cruise programmes and a product that offered high standards at competitive prices.

In 1994 Airtours announced its intention of creating a cruise product, Sun Cruises, for the UK market at a price level which would appeal to its existing customer base and two ships containing a total of 1900 berths were purchased to facilitate the product launch during the following year. Under the package arrangement, passengers fly from local airports in the UK, Scandinavia or North America to their point of embarkation (mainly in traditional Mediterranean resort areas and the Caribbean). The operational management of the ships is sub-contracted to an experienced cruise operator. Utilizing many of the services of the group's tour operating businesses and taking advantage of its distribution network substantially reduces costs and enables a high quality product to be offered at prices significantly below those offered by traditional cruise operators. In only its second year of operation Sun Cruises achieved load factors approaching 100 per cent and a UK market share of 18 per cent.

The principal risks usually perceived by external observers of the travel industry for a group such as Airtours are those of under-utilized aircraft and excess hotel accommodation for which payment has already been made. Airtours, in common with other major tour operators, designed in considerable flexibility in its contracting of both of these services. The company negotiated aviation contracts with third party suppliers that had a variety of cancellation options, exercisable once booking patterns had been established. This provided a margin of comfort when coupled with the way in which Airtours' in-house flying capacity was tailored to provide 60–70 per cent of expected summer requirements. With regard to accommodation, only 10 per cent of Airtours' requirements were booked on an irrevocable basis.

Along with many other businesses dealing with international conditions, Airtours had to find a way of accommodating changes in exchange rates, local interest rates and fluctuations in the price of aviation fuel. Airtours developed a policy of 'hedging' against all major risks on the financial and commodity markets prior to each brochure launch. Specifically, the group developed the practice of negotiating a range of forward contracts and options. In this way the costs of hedging these risks were built into the brochure selling prices.

The holiday business has traditionally been able to benefit from substantial cash flows as customers traditionally pay in advance and the holiday companies pay their suppliers in arrears. There is a degree of seasonality to this cash flow but even at its lowest point substantial cash balances are usually held by Airtours. Effective 'cash management' of these balances is therefore a very important part of managing the business and interest receivable, as with other tour operators, represents a significant source of income. Surplus funds are placed on deposit with established international banks, but other investment opportunities are examined at times of falling interest rates.

Management, staff and systems

The transition from its single business core of tour operating into an integrated international travel business was rapid, but placed considerable demands on management, staff and systems. Considerable resources were devoted to staff recruitment, management training and the procurement of the necessary computer hardware and software in order to enhance the group's competitive position. The Airtours group is now managed on a decentralized basis with a small head office team and a separate Board of Directors for each of the principal Divisions: UK Tour Operations, UK Retail, Scandinavian Leisure Group, North American Leisure Group, Aviation Division and Cruise and Hotels Division.

Such rapid development has not always run smoothly. The integration of the UK's seventh largest tour operator (Aspro, a budget holiday brand based in Cardiff), proved to be somewhat difficult. Legal action was taken against its former owners alleging that the representation of its true trading position had been overstated resulting in an overpayment by Airtours for the business. Airtours has long been a favourite target for attack by sections of the media, attracting poor ratings by reports emanating from The Consumers' Association, and attracting more than its share of press criticism over quality standards.

Over recent years Airtours has made strenuous efforts to ensure that customers know what they are buying and get what they have been promised. Each of the group's divisions operates its own quality control initiatives relying heavily on customer feed-back, and though still an area for some concern relative to competitors, a marked reduction in the percentage of complaints has occurred in recent years

Appendices

Appendix 1. Airtours plc group structure

	Scandinavia	United Kingdom	North America
Distribution	Spies Shops Tjaerborg Shops Ving Shops	Going Places Late Escapes	
Tour operations	Ving Always Saga Spies Tjaerborg	Airtours Aspro Tradewinds EuroSites	Sunquest Vacations Sunquest West Sunquest Holidays Alba
Aviation	Premiair	Airtours International	
Cruise and hotels	Hotels Sun Cruises	Hotels Sun Cruises	Sun Cruises

Appendix 2. Interview with David Crossland

I certainly can't claim that I sat down 20 years ago and created a master plan for a travel business, but I did always believe that if you really wanted to achieve something you could. In the earliest days, I wanted to give holidaymakers a good value-for-money product and believed that if I did so they would come back for more. That desire is something that has not changed and it has something which proved to be correct. To this day the only people I really worry about are those who buy our products, the end users. I care passionately about them.

Initially, Airtours was very much a family business. I had very little capital and knew the only way the company would grow was through reinvestment and hard work. Today it is a big organization, but the management and staff all share that original commitment towards our passengers and they work extremely hard, showing great loyalty. My enthusiasm seems to be infectious and rubs off on them. It is still a family business, but now it has become the Airtours family rather than the Crossland family.

Personally, I believe I only really have one talent and that is the ability to appoint managers who are far cleverer than I, who are extremely professional and absolute experts in their field. The success of the company has a great deal to do with them. Another key to our success is that we believe in our product. We believe we have a really good product, that our brochures are clear, clean and easily understood, and that our advertising is effective. We have grown and changed, but our roots are in travel retailing and we understand, from inside knowledge, just how retailers work.

The travel industry is being forced to become far more professional and proactive and further changes are still to come. Airtours has become a major player within the travel trade and recognizes its responsibilities. It is a major public company in the leisure sector which has had considerable successes in the past and looks forward to continued successes in the future.

Source: *Travel Weekly* 1992

Appendix 3. Statement from Airtours 1996 report and accounts

Three years ago we concluded that in order to maintain our rate of growth we would need to develop our business overseas. At that time we stated our objectives of achieving, in the medium term, an even split of profits between UK and overseas businesses.

In a short period of time, Airtours has transformed itself from a purely UK-based company into an internationally diversified leisure group which is now the largest air inclusive tour operator in the world. The growth of the group continues to produce economies of scale and by managing capacity across our different markets we obtain the maximum utilization of our aircraft, cruise ships and hotels.

For future growth we shall seek to develop or acquire businesses operating in markets which we understand, where we can add value and where the acquired business has high quality management or alternatively can be readily integrated into our existing management infrastructures. We believe that there will be significant opportunities for further expansion which we shall exploit as they arise. One such business where we believe that we can add value is timeshare development. Subject to the success of our recently announced first venture in Orlando, Florida, we will extend this business into other principal destination areas.

In April 1996, Carnival Corporation of the USA acquired 29.54 per cent of the ordinary share capital of the Company. This was achieved by means of a partial offer to existing shareholders and a subscription for new ordinary shares which, after the deduction of expenses, raised new capital of £97.9 million. Carnival are the world leaders in the cruise industry.

Appendix 4. Airtours aircraft fleet

	Premiair	*Airtours International*	*Total Fleet*
Airbus A300/A320's	9	10	19
Boeing 757/767's	–	8	8
McDonnell Douglas DC10's	4	–	4
Totals	13	18	31

Appendix 5. Airtours – financial statements (1986–1996)

Airtours – turnover/profits/dividends/employees (£M)

	1996	1995	1994	1993	1992	1991	1990	1989	1988	1987	1986
Turnover	1717.9	1317.8	971.7	615.6	405.6	289.5	183.0	155.6	102.5	68.3	55.0
Profit before tax	86.8	59.1	75.8	45.6	36.5	27.5	6.3	5.2	4.1	2.0	2.0
Earnings per ordinary share	45.63p	32.76p	41.79p	29.22p	24.47p	24.68p	6.69p	5.12p	17.43p	8.55p	8.53p
Dividends per ordinary share	16.00p	14.00p	12.00p	9.00p	7.25p	5.75p	2.03p	1.72p	6.25p	n/a	n/a
No of employees											
Total	12198	9896	6337	3819	1349	946	571	389	310	212	283
Tour operating and other	7548	5899	3188	1763	1349	946	571	389	310	212	283
UK travel retailing	4650	3997	3149	2056	–	–	–	–	–	–	–

Airtours plc business segment analysis £(M)

Turnover

	96	95	94	93	92	91
United Kingdom						
Tour Operating Continuing	794.2	788.5	701.5	482.9	405.6	289.5
Tour Operating Acquisitions	–	–	–	56.4	–	–
Retail Continuing	157.1	135.0	118.8	–	–	–
Retail Acquisitions	–	–	–	76.3	–	–
Scandinavia						
Continuing	484.6	386.8	–	–	–	–
Acquisitions	236.7	–	151.4	–	–	–
Canada						
Continuing	102.5	7.5	–	–	–	–
Acquisitions	4.8	–	–	–	–	–
Inter Company Elimination	−62.0	–	–	–	–	–

Profit Before Tax*

	96	95	94	93	92	91
United Kingdom						
Tour Operating Continuing	41.7	27.8	55.6	41.1	36.5	27.5
Tour Operating Acquisitions	–	–	–	–	–	–
Retail Continuing	8.8	7.1	6.5	0.0	–	–
Retail Acquisitions	–	–	–	4.5	–	–
Scandinavia						
Continuing	31.5	25.1	–	–	–	–
Acquisitions	3.0	–	13.7	–	–	–
Canada						
Continuing	2.3	−0.9	–	–	–	–
Acquisitions	−0.5	–	–	–	–	–
Inter Company Elimination	–	–	–	–	–	–

Net Assets

	96	95	94	93	92	91
United Kingdom						
Tour Operating Continuing	111.7	45.4	98.4	72.0	55.1	41.8
Tour Operating Acquisitions	–	–	–	–	–	–
Retail Continuing	–	–	–	–	–	–
Retail Acquisitions	–	–	–	–	–	–
Scandinavia						
Continuing	91.2	70.5	47.0	–	–	–
Acquisitions	–	–	–	–	–	–
Canada						
Continuing	4.5	3.1	–	–	–	–
Acquisitions	–	–	–	–	–	–
Inter Company Elimination	–	–	–	–	–	–

Note: *Net group interest receivable – 91 = 4.8, 92 = 8.1, 93 = 10.9, 94 = 7.6, 95 = 9.1, 96 = 10.0

Balance sheets Airtours (£M) (1991–1996)

		1996	1995	1994	1993	1992	1991
Fixed Assets	Tangible	256.4	197.9	109.1	38.2	24.8	10.9
	Intangible	0	0	0	0	0	0
	Investments	6.5	5.0	2.8	0	0	0
	TOTAL	262.9	202.9	111.9	38.2	24.8	10.9
Current Assets	Stock	6.8	3.6	2.7	0	0	0
	Debtors	38.2	27.9	24.4	46.0	38.6	9.9
	Investments	9.7	4.8	4.7	0	0	0
	Bank & Deposits	425.6	304.5	291.9	220.6	155.6	103.3
	Prepayments	197.7	140.7	139.1	59.5	4.5	3.1
	TOTAL	678.0	481.5	462.8	326.1	198.7	116.3
Current Liabilities	Creditors	−211.3	−189.1	−138.0	−164.8	−106.6	−36.9
	Loans/Overdraft	−35.2	−35.3	−20.1	0	0	
	Other	−341.5	−221.2	−226.1	−90.3	−60.4	−47.9
	TOTAL	−588.0	−445.6	−384.2	−275.1	−167.0	−84.8
Non Current Liabilities		−145.5	−119.8	−45.1	−17.2	−1.4	−0.4
Total Assets Less Liabilities		207.4	119.0	145.4	72.0	55.1	41.8
Shareholders Funds	Share Capital	23.6	21.6	21.5	19.4	9.2	2.2
	Reserves	183.8	97.4	123.9	52.6	45.9	39.6
	TOTAL	207.4	119.0	145.4	72.0	55.1	41.8

Appendix 6. Major competitors – financial statements

Leading tour operators – turnover/profits/employees (£M)

		1995	1994	1993	1992	1991
Turnover	Thomson	1503.9	1455.8	1359.9	1245.3	1162.7
	First Choice	934.6	821.8	710.2	772.0	643.6
	Unijet	213.2	180.3	127.1	95.3	81.5
Profit Before Tax	Thomson	75.9	106.1	84.8	72.5	68.8
	First Choice	1.3	16.3	5.8	25.5	31.6
	Unijet	4.5	4.4	3.9	1.7	2.4
No of Employees	Thomson	Not stated	Not stated	Not stated	Not stated	Not stated
	First Choice	3564	3314	2812	2932	2248
	Unijet	288	267	245	204	165

Leading tour operators — balance sheet Thomson Travel Group (£M)

		1995	1994	1993	1992	1991
Fixed Assets	Tangible	589.9	573.6	549.1	464.3	453.1
	Intangible	100.3	82.3	49.1	50.6	52.1
	Investments	0.4	0.4	0.3	1.9	2.2
	TOTAL	690.6	656.3	598.5	516.8	507.4
Current Assets	Stock	11.1	9.3	8.3	13.2	13.8
	Debtors	37.9	43.0	33.3	41.8	34.5
	Investments	0	0	0	0	0
	Bank & Deposits	221.6	290.4	311.4	250.6	238.8
	Prepayments	126.8	84.9	74.6	71.6	55.4
	TOTAL	397.4	427.6	427.6	377.2	342.5
Current Liabilities	Creditors	−425.0	−440.3	−436.5	−405.7	−331.5
	Loans/Overdraft	0	0	0	0	0
	Other	0	0	0	0	0
	TOTAL	−425.0	−440.3	−436.5	−405.7	−331.5
Non Current Liabilities		−268.8	−239.9	−212.0	−227.7	−265.3
Total Assets Less Liabilities		394.2	403.7	377.6	260.6	253.1
Shareholders Funds	Share Capital					
	Reserves					
	TOTAL	394.2	403.7	377.6	260.6	253.1

Thomson Travel Group business segment analysis (£M)

	Turnover					Profit before tax*					Net Assets				
	95	94	93	92	91	95	94	93	92	91	95	94	93	92	91
Tour Operating	1277.3	1260.7	1144.3	1021.6	953.4	15.7	43.2	24.2	21.5	37.5	13.5	8.9	9.1	15.8	—
Airline Operations	605.5	595.7	564.3	522.9	466.2	42.7	52.0	47.4	31.8	28.9	218.1	257.4	265.3	187.4	—
Travel Retailing	118.4	119.2	107.4	92.8	70.2	13.0	15.0	17.0	24.0	6.0	28.5	31.7	32.6	28.9	—
Holiday Property Letting	17.6	2.4				5.6	0.4				23.0				
Corporate & others	5.0	5.2	4.1	5.0	5.0	-1.1	-4.5	-3.8	-4.8	-3.6	111.1	105.7	70.4	28.5	—
	2023.8	1983.2	1819.8	1642.3	1494.8	75.9	106.1	84.8	72.5	68.8	394.2	403.7	377.6	260.6	—
Intra Group	-519.9	-527.4	-459.9	-397.0	-332.1										
	1503.9	1455.8	1359.9	1245.3	1162.7	75.9	106.1	84.8	72.5	68.8	394.2	403.7	377.6	260.6	—

Note: *Net group interest receivable 91 = 14.5, 92 = 12.8, 93 = 7.3, 94 = 12.8, 95 = 14.5

Leading tour operators – balance sheet First Choice plc

		1995	1994	1993	1992	1991
Fixed assets	Tangible	105.9	102.3	62.6	68.9	62.5
	Intangible	0	0	0	0.2	29.1
	Investments	1.4	0	5.2	5.6	5.9
	TOTAL	107.3	102.3	67.8	74.7	97.5
Current assets	Stock	0	0	0	0	0
	Debtors	158.2	116.7	140.4	150.4	162.0
	Investments	0	0	0	0	0
	Bank & Deposits	101.0	131.6	100.3	98.4	72.7
	Prepayments	127.3	80.4	4.4	1.8	1.8
	TOTAL	386.5	328.7	245.1	250.6	236.5
Current liabilities	Creditors	−54.0	−15.4	−77.7	−85.8	−68.1
	Loans/Overdraft	−5.5	−23.8	0	0	0
	Other	−313.6	−256.1	−134.3	−137.6	−137.6
	TOTAL	−373.1	−295.3	−212.0	−223.4	−205.7
Non current liabilities		−62.1	−79.6	−39.3	−32.8	−31.3
Total assets less liabilities		58.6	56.1	61.6	69.0	97.1
Shareholders funds	Share Capital	7.1	7.1	7.1	7.1	7.2
	Reserves	51.5	49	54.6	61.9	89.9
	TOTAL	58.6	56.1	61.6	69.0	97.1

Leading tour operators – balance sheet Unijet plc

		1995	1994	1993	1992	1991
Fixed assets	Tangible	4.2	4.2	4.6	4.2	3.5
	Intangible	0	0	0	0	0
	Investments	1.2	1.6	1.6	1.5	1.2
	TOTAL	5.4	5.8	6.2	5.7	4.7
Current assets	Stock	0.9	0.9	0	0	0
	Debtors	3.7	2.9	3.8	3.3	9.3
	Investments	0	0	0	0	0
	Bank & Deposits	29.5	23.2	0	0	11.4
	Prepayments	19.3	14.0	30.3	15.3	0
	TOTAL	53.4	41.0	34.1	18.6	20.7
Current liabilities	Creditors	−11.1	−8.9	−12.0	−7.6	−17.8
	Loans/Overdraft	−3.0	−0.8	0	−0.1	
	Other	−28.7	−24.3	−18.3	−9.3	−1.1
	TOTAL	−42.8	−34.0	−30.3	−17.0	−18.9
Non current liabilities		−0.1	−0.2	−0.2	−0.2	−0.3
Total assets less liabilities		15.9	12.6	9.8	7.1	6.2
Shareholders funds	Share Capital	0.6	0.6	0.6	0.6	0.6
	Reserves	15.3	12.0	9.2	6.5	5.6
	TOTAL	15.9	12.6	9.8	7.1	6.2

Case Study 2

THE UK OUTBOUND TOUR OPERATIONS INDUSTRY

Nigel Evans
University of Northumbria

The package concept

Tourists travelling abroad can purchase each separate component of a holiday as individual items (i.e. transportation, activities, ground handling etc.) and some travellers do take this option. During the 1960s, however, the foreign inclusive tour or 'package' holiday became established in western Europe and brought with it a substantial expansion in the numbers of tourists venturing abroad.

A 'package' can be defined as a pre-arranged combination, sold or offered for sale at an inclusive price, of not fewer than two of the following three elements:

- transport;
- accommodation;
- other tourist services not ancillary to transport or accommodation and accounting for a significant part of the package.

The growth of the package has been a major cause of the increase in the holiday market since the 1950s. The role of the package company goes beyond that of the wholesaler, in that they not only purchase or reserve the separate components in bulk but, in combining these components into an 'inclusive tour', they also become producers into the holiday market. The traditional appeal of the tour operators' product has been to offer a complete holiday package at the lowest price to a population often lacking the linguistic knowledge or the knowledge and confidence to organize independent travel with the result that tour operation has become the dominant feature of the holiday market not only in the United Kingdom but in most tourist-generating countries.

The growth of UK outbound tour operations

Vladimar Raitz, a Russian émigré, is widely credited with operating the first inclusive air tour charter to Corsica in 1950 at an inclusive price of £32.10. Part of his original company, Horizon, continues to this day as a trading name of Thomson. Others who pioneered air inclusive tours (AITs) during the 1950s in the UK were Captain Ted Langton, who set up Universal Skytours which was also later to become part of Thomson; Joe and Syril Shuman, founders of Global Holidays; Christopher and Stephen Lord whose Lord Brothers firm was later absorbed by Laker Airways; George Jackman and Wilf Jones, who built up Cosmos; and Harry Chandler, whose family continues to control The Travel Club of Upminster (founded in 1936).

Some companies missed out on the early market opportunities. Thomas Cook never achieved the market leadership in air holidays that it had in rail holidays, whilst British European Airways (BEA), a forerunner of British Airways, was slow to react to the threat posed by the charter airlines. In the 1950s, foreign travel remained a luxury, within the reach of only a privileged few who had both plenty of free time and considerable purchasing power. The market changed during the 1960s from that of a privileged 'niche' market to a 'mass' tourism market as a result of innovations in aircraft technology, changes in labour legislation (which provided for paid holidays), and changes to the structure of the tour operating industry itself. Large companies had begun buying into tour operating as early as 1956 when Great Universal Stores acquired Global, but the industry remained highly fragmented during the 1950s and early 1960s.

The industry of the early 1960s was also beset by a number of company failures, including the failure in 1964 of Fiesta Tours, a major tour operator of the period. The Association of British Travel Agents (ABTA), which had been formed in 1950, had to step in to rescue customers stranded abroad and in the aftermath, calls were made for statutory controls of the burgeoning tour operating sector. ABTA responded in November 1966 with the introduction of the so-called 'Stabilizer Resolution'. Stabilizer was an attempt by ABTA to regulate the UK travel industry whereby ABTA member agents could sell only the foreign inclusive tours of ABTA tour operators, while ABTA tour operators could only sell through ABTA agents (or direct). It consequently became impossible to build up a major market presence without belonging to ABTA. Stabilizer did indeed help to stabilize the industry as the rate of failures reduced after its introduction. Stabilizer remained in force until 1993, when ABTA relinquished the requirement upon the introduction of the EC Directive on package travel, one effect of which was to require tour operators to provide financial protection to customers under law.

New entrants and consolidation

The entry into the market of The International Thomson Organization (ITO) in 1965 proved to be a major turning point for the industry. It coincided with the beginning of a period of consolidation within the industry which continued until the late 1980s, and the entry to UK tour operations of a large, sophisticated and diversified international group of companies. During the summer of 1965 Thomson had around 100 000 holidays on offer.

The air inclusive tour (AIT) market (which is regulated in the UK by the Civil Aviation Authority (CAA) through the Air Travel Organizers' Licences (ATOLs) it issues each year) grew enormously during the period, but detailed figures are only available from 1976. Although many operators do not use their full ATOL allocation, the licences issued give an indication of the size of the total market and relative market shares.

The reasons for this rapid growth of the UK outbound AIT market and that of the operators that service it are inextricably linked, but perhaps two major factors stand out. Firstly, many UK residents travel abroad for their holidays in order to obtain reliable sunshine and warmth. The UK's island location has necessitated the development of well-organized, packaged transportation to service this need. Secondly, UK residents give holidays and travel a high priority in terms of their discretionary expenditure even in times of relative economic hardship. Again, a highly sophisticated holiday travel industry has developed to service these needs.

Relatively low barriers to entry and continual striving among operators for increased market share led to price wars (particularly in the early 1970s and the mid-1980s), which resulted in a highly volatile record of profitability over the period. The price wars, low margins and the vulnerability of the travel industry to external economic and political factors inevitably took their toll on operators. For example, Clarkson's, which had expanded rapidly in the late 1960s, was losing money by 1971 and was taken over by the Court Line Group. The group had invested heavily in jet aircraft, but the 1973 oil crisis (when oil prices rose rapidly as a result of war in the Middle East) and economic recession led to the collapse of the company at the height of the summer season in August 1974. Parallels can be drawn between Clarkson's and The International Leisure Group (ILG), which, when it failed in March 1991, was Britain's second largest tour operator. The downturn in business at the time of The Gulf War in 1990-91, exposed ILG's strategy of using strong tour operating cash flows to diversify into scheduled air services through its airline Air Europe.

During the 1970s and 1980s, the large tour operators came to increasingly dominate the AIT market, as mass market operators were determined to increase their market share and to reap the anticipated rewards of market dominance. Thomson, the market leader, had, since its inception, faced major challenges to its market leadership position, but had hitherto always successfully defended its position. A number of major competitors had disappeared from the scene: Clarkson's collapsed in 1974; ILG collapsed in March 1991. Thomson's major challengers in the current market are of more recent prominence. Owners Abroad, (now re-named First Choice) was founded in 1972, and was a 'seat-only' specialist serving the needs of expatriate overseas property owners, and Airtours started in 1978 as Pendle Airtours, a small operating division of David Crossland's travel agency Pendle Travel. The demise of ILG removed from the industry a privately held company that had targeted Thomson through aggressive pricing in a bid for an ever greater share of the market. Both Airtours (since 1989) and First Choice are public limited companies. Their status as plcs necessitated the targeting of profitability rather than market share as the primary objective of the two companies and as a result competition since 1991 has focused on matching supply much more closely to demand and thereby avoiding damaging price wars.

By 1990 a marked polarization had occurred in the industry dividing the industry into a relatively small number of 'mass' tour operators and a much larger number of 'independent' operators, largely serving specialized niche markets. The term 'independent' tour operator has become widely used in the UK but it has no precise meaning. The term is often used loosely to describe any operator that is not one of the largest mass tour operators. In the UK the term 'independent' tour operator also has a more precise meaning, in that it can refer to those companies that are members of The Association of Independent Tour Operators (AITO). AITO was formed in 1976 in the wake of the Clarkson's crash primarily to represent the views of smaller tour operators during the setting up of the CAA's bonding scheme. The association has grown to represent about 150 members which collectively carry some 1 500 000 customers per annum.

AITO members range from those carrying fewer than 500 customers per year to those carrying in excess of 100 000. The membership includes well-known companies that are part of the second tier of operators such as Manos, Balkan Holidays and Panorama Holidays and less well-known names such as Sunvil Villas. The membership also includes many tour operators that predominately use cars and ferries as means of transport. These companies, particularly a large number of French specialists, include well-known names such as Eurocamp (which has the status of a public limited company and carries over 200 000 customers a year), but do not appear in the ATOL listings, which solely cover AITs.

Benefits of the package concept

Many predictions have been made that the package holiday product may be set to decline, but the popularity owes much to a number of key advantages:

- the convenience of purchasing all the elements of the product in one purpose designed 'bundle';
- delivery of product quality assurance, reliability and protection;
- perceived good value prices.

Although the future of the package seems assured at least in the medium-term, changes in consumer preferences and changes in the environment in which tour operating products are provided are changing the characteristics of these packages which will in turn have an effect on the future structure of this industrial sector. The tour operating industry as a whole (and the independent sector in particular) is facing a number of pressures which have led to a marked differences in recent performance.

Influences on the future of UK tour operating

One of the reasons often cited for ever greater concentration by a few large suppliers of activities for an industry is that larger companies enjoy the advantages to be derived from economies of scale. These economies clearly exist in tour operating, in terms of (for example) marketing and purchasing economies, but there is evidence that the benefits of such economies may be declining. The trend away from standard 'summer sun' packages towards a more diverse range of package options in the UK means that such economies are harder to achieve. Tour operators are increasingly being forced to respond to a much more complex holiday market than has hitherto existed, through diversification, narrower market segmentation, independently minded travellers and increasingly experienced customers. All of these trends reduce, to some extent, the advantages to be derived from economies of scale.

Furthermore, although no empirical evidence exists, it is by no means clear that economies of scale are great beyond a certain size threshold in the industry. The increasing bureaucracy, expense of systems and the inflexibility of a larger scale of operations can lead to diseconomies of scale resulting in higher not lower unit costs. The tour operating industry may well have many of the same characteristics as the airline industry. In the USA, the lowest cost 'producer' that other airlines seek to emulate is not one of the major carriers, but a medium-sized airline called Southwest.

The three largest tour operating companies have become vertically integrated in recent years, that is to say, they own both inputs to the operating process and control a part of the distribution channels for their products. To this end, Thomson, Airtours and First Choice own the airlines Britannia, Airtours and Air 2000, respectively. Thomson and Airtours also own the country's first and second largest travel agency chains, Lunn Poly and Going Places (an amalgamation and re-branding of the former Pickfords and Hogg Robinson chains). The larger travel agency chains (which have themselves expanded their share of the total travel agency market) have increasingly favoured the larger operators which are able to offer bulk capacity and sufficient brochures to 'rack'. This trend has intensified as vertical integration has led to travel agencies favouring the operating brands of their owners, and operators seek preferential terms with agents. In the UK, the Monopolies and Mergers Commission (MMC) recently investigated vertical integration in the travel industry and its effect upon consumer choice. Its findings were that further regulation was not necessary because the vertical integration had not resulted in any significant diminution of competition in the industry.

Tour operators in the UK have played an important part in the development of computerized bookings for tour packages. The investment in on-line interactive view data systems (during the 1970s and 1980s) has resulted in the majority of the larger tour operators relying on this technology for most of their bookings. Other smaller operators have chosen not to automate and rely instead on using conventional telephone calls as the main vehicle for bookings. This has worked to the advantage of the larger tour operators as travel agents have endeavoured to reduce telephone call charges and improve efficiency.

The development of new technologies may, however, reduce somewhat the advantages of the larger operators. Foremost amongst these new technologies is the development of Computerized Reservation Systems (CRS). CRS systems were first developed in the USA in the 1960s and 1970s as databases and booking systems for US airlines. They have continued to develop and now include vast amounts of information on other transport providers, hotels, car hire provision, local tourist attractions and so on. In addition, the reach of systems such as Amadeus and Gallileo has expanded throughout the developed world as non-US airlines have forged partnerships with the US instigators of the systems.

In the USA, 96 per cent of travel agents are linked to a CRS system. Potentially, CRS systems give travel agencies the ability to flexibly package together exactly what the consumers want, thereby undermining the role of the traditional mass market tour operator (by combining hotels, flights, car hire and so on using the CRS database). However, the role of the CRS in a British 'leisure traveller' context should not be overstated. There is a marked polarization of business and leisure travel agencies with a low level of CRS penetration in the leisure travel agency sector. Many leisure travel agents are owned by tour operators which have invested heavily in their own view-data technology, and therefore have a vested interest in delaying the development of CRS systems in the leisure travel agent sector. Other technological developments are also important. Future distribution options may include home shopping, point of sale multi-media booths, mail order and booking through the internet.

The EC Directive on Package Travel, Package Holidays and Package Tours was adopted on 13 June 1990 (Council Directive 1990) and member states were required to implement its measures prior to 31 December 1992. The main provisions of the directive were as follows:

- Article 2, Definitions – The directive covers 'packages' which are defined as a pre-arranged combination of not fewer than two of three elements: transport; accommodation; and other tourist services
- Article 3, Descriptions and advertising – The directive does not impose a legal obligation to provide a brochure, but where one is available it must contain in a legible, comprehensive and accurate manner both the price and adequate information concerning certain specified items such as the itinerary and the meal plan
- Article 4, The package travel contract – Certain information is specified, such as information relating to passport and visa requirements, that the tour operator and/or the travel agent must provide to the consumer prior to travelling
- Article 5, Liability – The tour operator becomes responsible for ensuring that all services under the package are rendered effectively and efficiently (whether rendered directly or by a third party)
- Article 7, Financial security – The tour operator must provide evidence of security for the refund of money paid over and for repatriation of the consumer in the event of insolvency.

The goal of the directive was to codify and harmonize existing EC legislation relating to package travel. In so doing, much of the detailed implementation of the directive was left to the discretion of member states. In the UK, The Department of Trade and Industry took the view that it wanted to place a minimum of additional burdens on the industry and consequently opted for a self-regulating system. As a result, bonding in the UK is now undertaken by a number of 'approved' schemes including those operated by ABTA, AITO, The Federation of Tour Operators (FTO) and the CAA. One effect of the implementation of the directive in the UK has been to include surface transport, and domestic packages as 'packages' requiring financial protection for the first time. A possible effect of the directive in the longer term could be to raise the entry barriers to the tour-operating industry in Europe, and to force some of the smaller, specialized tour operators out of business.

Mass tourism can be seen as a phenomenon of large-scale packaging of standardized leisure services at fixed prices for sale to a mass clientele. Clearly such tourism remains central to the outbound tourism product of the UK and several other north European countries, but underlying trends towards a new type of more independent and experienced traveller have been discerned.

'New' tourists and their motivations

These 'new tourists' are: 'consumers who are flexible, independent and experienced travellers, whose values and lifestyles are different from those of mass tourists' (Poon 1993). Six key attributes are characteristic of these 'new' tourists.

- They are more experienced.
- They have changed values.
- They have changed lifestyles.
- They are the products of changing population demographics.
- They are more flexible.
- They are more independent.

New consumers are more experienced

In the UK the proportion of adults who *had ever been on holiday* abroad rose sharply from the 1960s through to the mid-1980s, reaching 67 per cent in 1985. The figure has stayed close to this level ever since. 'In other words first time buyers with sufficient income to enter the market had been captured and future growth (or decline) would reflect the motivations of experienced travellers' (Middleton 1991). More experienced travellers are more knowledgeable and consequently more quality and value conscious. They demand greater choice and flexibility and are more certain of what they want and what they find unacceptable

New consumers have changed values

Values of conservation, health and nature are being reflected in the tour operators' products and there are growing signs that the fashion for the sun is beginning to fade.

New consumers have changed lifestyles

The factors that have motivated people have changed over the course of several decades such that today's holiday makers are quite different in their lifestyles to those of some years ago. We can identify three broad 'phases' of lifestyle emphasis since the industrial era began. The first, called *live to work* is in contrast to those who *work to live*. The third, more in evidence today than at any other period in history, is one in which people have found a balance between work and leisure – both being important in a balanced life.

These changes in the role of travel and leisure in society have implications for the travel industry. People who *live to work* have simple holiday and travel motivations while people who *work to live* view leisure as the counterweight to everyday life. Those seeking *unity* of everyday life want to reduce the polarity between work and leisure and are looking for fulfilment throughout all sectors of life – during working time, through humanized working conditions, and at home through more habitable cities and a more colourful everyday life. The varying motivations of these three groups are summarized below:

People who live to work motivations for travel	People who work to live motivations for travel	People seeking a unity between work and leisure motivations for travel
To recover To recuperate To rest To be served To switch off	To experience something different To explore To have fun To play To be active To relax without stress To enjoy proximity to nature	To do as one pleases To broaden their horizons To learn something new To encourage introspection and communication with other people To discover the simple things in life and nature To foster creativity To experiment To take personal risks

Source: Adapted from Krippendorf (1986)

FIGURE CS2.1

New consumers are the products of changing population demographics

Population demographics in the tourism generating countries are changing. In particular, the population in many parts of Europe is ageing. These demographic changes will have profound effects upon buyer behaviour in tourist generating countries. The years surrounding the turn of the millennium, for example, witnessed a slight growth in the proportion of elderly people over 65, a large growth in the middle age categories and a relative decline in the 18–35 age category.

A significant European demographic trend is the rise of the 'baby boomers', that is a rise in births in the years immediately after the second world war. The 'baby-boomers' generation are now at the peak of their earning and spending potential and this has a knock-on effect in many industries, including the tour operating industry. The majority take wealth (or at least financial comfort) for granted, have higher expectations of the products and services that they buy and are likely to buy such products and services for their intrinsic qualities rather than for their status.

New consumers are more flexible

Consumers are becoming 'hybrid' in nature in that they may consume in a non-predictable way making the traditional stereotypical categories of rich, poor or middle-income people no longer sufficient to segment holiday markets. Some consumers may, for instance, take the cheapest charter flight available but stay in the most luxurious accommodation available at the destination. Other consumers may stay in relatively modest accommodation but partake in the most expensive sporting activities such as heli-skiing or hot air ballooning. Another aspect of the flexible consumer is the spread of impulse buying to the travel industry. There are shorter lead times before booking and paying for holidays, a changing consumer preference which partially explains the growing number of shorter and more frequent breaks.

New consumers are more independent

Increasingly consumers are asserting their individuality and independence, and seeking more flexible and custom-made travel and leisure options and resisting the standardized product options. This trend towards independence, individuality and more experimentation in travel and leisure is clearly underpinned by the value, lifestyle and demographic changes. Such changes are likely to manifest themselves in the continuing demand by consumers for the core advantages provided by packaged travel products relating to pricing, convenience, reliability and easy access. However, consumers are likely to increasingly reject some of the traditional drawbacks of packaged travel products relating to the inflexibility of products, and resistance to travelling in organized groups.

The future of 'independent' tour operators

Using a Delphi technique to assess the views of 28 leading industry practitioners, Ryan (1991) found that the major tour operators can establish subsidiary companies to offer specialist products. These companies can then benefit from economies of scale in administration and transport. In such a situation, even though the market may be shifting towards niche marketing, smaller specialist companies and greater customer awareness, there is nothing to inhibit growing supplier concentration ratios.

However, Ryan's respondents identified three main constraints on further increases in market (supplier) concentration:

- If competition is based on quality of product rather than price, small tour operators can compete;
- Anti-monopoly legislation may act as a deterrent;
- The large tour operators may be unable to think small and flexible in a way that maintains quality for clients (Ryan 1991).

Appendices

Appendix 1. Total ATOL capacity

Year	Total ATOL capacity (000s)
1976	8345
1977	7424
1978	8578
1979	5303
1980	6164
1981	6661
1982	7067
1983	7938
1984	8623
1985	8647
1986	9843
1987	12 598
1988	14 567
1989	13 982
1990	13 065
1991	10 061
1992	13 575
1993	14 545
1994	17 136
1995	18 813
1996	21 995

Source: CAA, various

Appendix 2. The largest 30 tour operators' turnover and profitability

Year	Turnover (£M)	Profits/(losses) (£M)
1972	206	(8.9)
1973	245	(0.4)
1974	226	(3.0)
1975	278	12.9
1976	326	11.7
1977	355	7.9
1978	530	34.4
1979	695	37.3
1980	906	43.8
1981	1019	52.2
1982	1299	27.7
1983	1407	55.3
1984	1799	55.3
1985	1841	60.7
1986	2132	35.6
1987	2791	(24.8)
1988	3005	15.5
1989	3048	(0.1)
1990	2731	40.3
1991	2743	104.8
1992	3621	100.6
1993	3826	99.1
1994	4434	85.6
1995	5073	(9.9)

Source: CAA, various

Appendix 3. Largest tour operator's capacity

Year	Five largest tour operators capacity (000s of places)	Tour operators in order of market share
1976	1553	Thomson, Cosmos, Silverwing, Laker Air, Horizon-Midlands
1977	1502	Thomson, Cosmos, Silverwing, Horizon-Midlands, Laker Air
1978	1521	Thomson, Cosmos, Silverwing, Horizon-Midlands, Laker Air
1979	1875	Thomson, Silverwing, Cosmos, Horizon, Laker Air
1980	2165	Thomson, Silverwing, Horizon, Cosmos, Owners Services
1981	2263	Thomson, Silverwing, Horizon, Cosmos, Owners Services
1982	2913	Thomson, Silverwing, Intasun, Horizon, Cosmos
1983	3142	Thomson, British Airways, Intasun, Horizon, Rank
1984	3076	Thomson, Horizon, Intasun, British Airways, Rank
1985	3456	Thomson, Horizon, Intasun, Rank, British Airways
1986	5041	Thomson, Horizon, Intasun, Rank, British Airways
1987	8493	Thomson, ILG, Bass, British Airways, First Choice
1988	8985	Thomson, ILG, Horizon, Redwing, First Choice
1989	10 022	Thomson, ILG, First Choice, Redwing, Airtours
1990	8899	Thomson, ILG, First Choice, Airtours, Yugotours
1991	6088	Thomson, First Choice, Airtours, Yugotours, Sunworld
1992	8353	Thomson, First Choice, Airtours, Cosmos, Sunworld
1993	8600	Thomson, First Choice, Airtours, Cosmos, Sunworld
1994	10 719	Thomson, Airtours, First Choice, Cosmos, Sunworld
1995	11 799	Thomson, Airtours, First Choice, Cosmos, Sunworld
1996	10 253	Thomson, Airtours, First Choice, Cosmos, Unijet

Source: CAA, various

Note: tour operator figures are for the group of companies, where an operator has more than one operating brand.

Appendix 4. Largest tour operator's capacity

Tour operator	May 1990 ATOL capacity (000s)	May 1991* ATOL capacity (000s)	May 1992 ATOL capacity (000s)	May 1993 ATOL capacity (000s)	May 1994 ATOL capacity (000s)	May 1995 ATOL capacity (000s)	May 1996 ATOL capacity (000s)
Thomson	4348	3015	3326	3488	3801	4281	4032
ILG	1798	a	a	a	a	a	a
First Choice	1798	1621	2275	1939	2042	2373	2029
Airtours	635	828	1488	1692	2438	2946	2671
Cosmos	b	b	822	1081	1805	1453	831
Yugotours	320	340	b	b	b	b	b
Sunworld	b	284	442	400	633	746	b
Unijet	b	b	b	b	b		690
Total	8899	6088	8353	8600	10719	11799	10253
Largest 5 Total	13065	10061	13575	14545	17136	18813	21995
All Tour Operators							

Source: CAA, various

Notes:

a   ILG was placed in receivership in March 1991.

b   Not placed in the top five tour operators.

Airtours' 1994 and 1995 figures include Aspro which was acquired in June 1993.

* Gulf War.

Appendix 5. Actual carryings

Tour operator	1991 carryings (000s)	1992 carryings (000s)	1993 carryings (000s)	1994 carryings (000s)	1995 carryings (000s)	1996 carryings (000s)
Thomson	2850	3247	3481	3950	4208	3657
First Choice	1658	2094	1878	1915	1928	1992
Airtours	993	1437	2135	2427	2720	2488
Cosmos	600	864	1135	1562	1091	931
Sunworld	239	461	429	661	705	649
Unijet	a	a	a	a	a	a
1st Tier Sub Total	6340	8103	9058	10 515	10 652	9717
2nd Tier Sub Total	1944	2739	2949	3444	3929	4563
3rd Tier Sub Total	2096	2068	2203	2631	3013	2629
TOTAL	10 380	12 910	14 210	16 590	17 594	16 909

Source: CAA, various

Notes: Figures relate to 'fully bonded' licences for 12-month periods to the end of September.

a   Not placed in the top five tour operators.

Since 1990 the Civil Aviation Authority (CAA) has published data on the actual carryings of the total AIT market and from 1991 this data has been broken down to itemize the actual carryings of individual ATOL holders. The CAA data on actual carryings can be categorized in order to distinguish between three groupings of tour operators:

- first tier operators – consisting of the largest 5 tour operators;
- second tier operators – consisting of the top 40 tour operators, (excluding those in the first tier);
- third tier operators – which include all remaining actual carryings by ATOL holders.

In the summer 1992 season, scheduled packages sold by ATOL holders were covered by licences for the first time. This factor accounts for a substantial (but not precisely quantifiable) proportion of the growth between 1991 and 1992. The Gulf War had a depressing effect on Winter 90/91 and Summer 1991 carryings.

Following the introduction of new ATOL regulations in May 1995, three kinds of business are specified in licences. These are:

- 'fully bonded' – scheduled or charter-based inclusive packages and seat-only travel on charter flights (1406 Licences December 1996);
- 'lower bonded' – scheduled seat-only tickets covered by a bond. These are bonded at a lower level than packages and charters, usually 5 per cent (186 Licences December 1996);
- 'agency' – scheduled seat-only tickets where an airline guarantees the business of a consolidator and provides a 'Deed of Undertaking' to the CAA (63 Licences December 1996).

The introduction of Lower Bonded and Agency ATOLs from 1995 accounts for a large (although not precisely quantifiable) part of the increase in ATOL capacity between 1995 and 1996.

Appendix 6. Number of ATOL holders

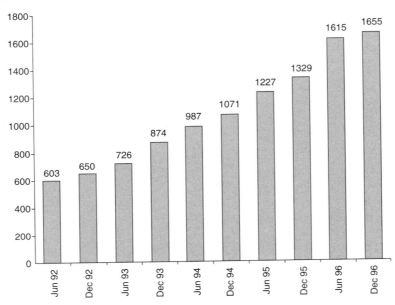

Source: CAA, various

Appendix 7. Average prices

1992	1993	1994	1995	1996
£333	£346	£355	£358	£379

Source: CAA, various

Note: table shows actual average prices charged by tour operators for 12 months to September.

References

European Commission, *Council Directive of June 13 1990 on Package Travel*, Package Holidays and Package Tours (90/314/EEC).

Krippendorf, J. (1986) Tourism in the system of industrial society, *Annals of Tourism Research*, **13**(4).

Krippendorf, J. (1987) *The Holidaymakers: Understanding the Impact of Leisure and Travel*, Heinemann, London.

Middleton, V.T.C. (1991) Whither the package tour? *Tourism Management*, September.

Poon, A. (1993) *Tourism Technology and Competitive Strategies*, CAB International, Wallingford, UK.

Ryan, C. (1991) UK package holiday industry, *Tourism Management*, March.

Case Study 3

BRITISH AIRWAYS PLC

Tony Purdie
University of Northumbria

Introduction

In May 1997 British Airways (BA) announced pre-tax profits of £640 million against revenue of £8359 million. The British Airways Group, which included the Deutsche BA and Air Liberté subsidiaries, carried a record total of 38.2 million passengers during the year 1996/97. With the most visible performance measures showing regular year on year growth, chief executive Bob Ayling could justifiably claim that British Airways was the world's largest passenger airline as well as being one of the most successful. Yet in August 1999, the airline announced first quarter profits of just £23 million and some analysts were suggesting that the company might even record a full-year loss. BA was experiencing some turbulence as it journeyed towards its stated goal of being 'truly global'; as the share price descended from a high of 692p to 391p shareholders wondered whether or not Ayling would be able to steer the company back onto its original flight plan.

The growth of international competition

The origins and development of British Airways are similar to those of other European and American airline companies. However, there are some key differences between Europe and America which have had a significant impact on world airline development.

In all major European countries (and even a few minor ones) commercial aviation developed soon after the end of the first world war. With a well-developed rail and road infrastructure within Europe, air transport initially offered little advantage over surface travel. On the other hand, governments welcomed the opportunity to develop links with their colonies spread around the world. By the early 1930s and after a period of consolidation, the pattern of European flag carriers that we recognize today had emerged. Each airline had a characteristic international route structure which reflected that country's colonial past. Furthermore, these airlines were usually required to use aircraft built by that country's aircraft industry. Thus, most European airlines functioned as a *de facto* arm of each national government.

In order to protect each airline from competition from other national airlines, governments created a system of bilateral agreements. In order to operate commercial services between London and Paris for example, an airline had to hold a licence for that route. Only the state airlines of each country were permitted to hold the licence and the two airlines usually co-operated and shared the profits. These airlines were known as the designated *flag carriers*. Thus by the 1950s, European commercial aviation operated in a highly regulated environment, usually with each country having a single flag carrier, and with prices set by national agreements.

The evolution of the airline industry in the USA was rather different. The first key difference was that all USA-based airline companies were privately owned. Instead of direct government subsidies, there was a substantial *indirect* subsidy in the form of profitable mail carrying contracts which exceeded the direct subsidies paid to European airlines. The second key difference was that due to the large geographical size of the country, a strong, viable route network could be established without crossing national boundaries. Thus the US airline industry was built on a domestic base while the European industry was built on an international base.

In the early days, the US industry was unregulated. However in 1938, the Civil Aeronautics Board (CAB) was established to regulate the number of carriers between destinations and fix fares. Although this seems at first sight to be identical to the type of regulation in Europe, the reasoning behind the regulation was subtly different. In Europe, regulation was designed to protect national flag carries from competition. In America it was argued that in order to counter the oligopolistic nature of the industry which could lead to either collusion and excess profits or else instability caused by price wars (neither of which would benefit the customer) – some form of control was necessary. Accordingly, until 1978 both the US and European industries were subject to government regulation.

In the US, the CAB could only regulate interstate routes. Within states there was no regulation and by the 1970s there was a marked disparity between intrastate and interstate fares even for similar journey lengths. The view that regulation was keeping fares artificially high led to the 1978 Airline Deregulation Act. The aim of the Act was to permit the entry to the market of new carriers and thus create much greater competition and hence cheaper fares. This is exactly what happened in the first two or three years after deregulation but what was not foreseen was that the established carriers were able to react quickly to the new competition by reducing costs and using aggressive pricing and similar tactics to counter the threats. During the mid-1980s many of the new entrants were either forced to leave the industry or were taken over by the established carriers. This concentration left the industry marginally more oligopolistic than immediately before deregulation and US air fares rose proportionately faster than average consumer prices.

The internationalization of the US industry began in 1927 with the award of a government air mail contract from Florida to Cuba. This was a deliberate policy of the US government which was concerned at the growing presence of European airlines serving Latin America. The new service was operated by Pan American Airways, a newcomer to the industry led by the entrepreneurial Juan Trippe. Within five years Pan American was the designated US flag carrier on routes to Latin America and across the Pacific. By 1937, Pan American services extended to Hong Kong and Trippe began planning a transatlantic service – the next step in his vision of a global airline. But before such a service could be established Trippe had to overcome two barriers; the resistance from the British and French governments and the fact that other than lighter-than-air machines there were no suitable passenger carrying aircraft able to cross the Atlantic Ocean non-stop. The latter problem was removed when Boeing developed the giant Type 314 flying boat in 1939. Europe had nothing to counter this threat and it delayed permission for Pan Am to start direct services to northern Europe until the outbreak of war removed the possibility of normal commercial transatlantic traffic.

Aircraft and navigation technology

If the development of the airline industry has been linked on the one hand to government regulation then on the other hand, the development of new aircraft has had an even more significant effect in the industry. The first world war gave the first real impetus towards the design of aircraft that were more than toys for daredevil pilots. The single most successful aircraft between the wars was the American DC-3 which dominated commercial aviation in the 1930s. By the second world war, aircraft had become much larger, faster and more reliable and were used as a principal means of transporting passengers and cargo. Huge numbers of aircraft were built between 1939 and 1945 – 125 000 in the UK and over 300 000 in the USA. With the end of the war, aircraft could be purchased very cheaply – less than one-tenth of the cost before 1939. America had a virtual monopoly in building transport aircraft and new designs became available rapidly. The newest aircraft had pressurized cabins so were able to cruise at altitudes above rough weather. By 1947 aircraft such as the Douglas DC-6 and the Lockheed Constellation could fly from New York to European capitals and land at conventional airfields. The era of the flying boats had come to an end.

For the first time European Airlines were faced with new, aggressive competitors led by entrepreneurs of great vision, using aircraft that were considerably more advanced than those being manufactured by the European aircraft industry. In order to compete on the prestigious and profitable transatlantic routes, BOAC and Air France were forced to abandon the 'buy national' policy and purchase American aircraft. Worse still, none of the European aircraft manufacturers had the resources available to design and build anything comparable to the Americans. The reason for this was simple; since most European airlines were compelled to buy aircraft manufactured in their own country, no manufacturer could expect to receive a large enough volume of orders to justify the investment required. In America, these new aircraft were based on military designs which had been paid for by the US Government and once in the lead, Boeing and Lockheed could expect orders from both US and European airlines.

The UK, however, had technical leadership in one area – the design of jet engines which potentially offered much higher power and smoother, quieter operation than conventional piston engines. The Vickers Viscount (a turboprop) proved highly attractive on short haul flights following its first flight in 1948 and in 1952, BOAC launched the world's first scheduled service in a turbojet aircraft when the Comet 1 flew from London to Johannesburg. With longer range variants of the Comet able to cross the Atlantic, Europe seemed to have a lead over the Americans. This lead proved short-lived when three Comets crashed mysteriously in 1953/54. Investigations showed that the aircraft had broken up in flight due to metal fatigue induced by repeated pressurization and

depressurization. The jet age entered a period of lull until the technology to build suitab
airframes was developed.

The aircraft that really launched the jet age was the Boeing 707 derived from a milita
transport prototype first flown in 1954. Boeing gambled heavily on this aircraft and t
design work and prototype manufacture went ahead with no secured orders. Boei
learned from the Comet disasters and the 707 proved to be a highly successful and reliab
aircraft. Although a redesigned Comet 4 entered transatlantic service in 1958 around t
same time as the Boeing 707 it was the American aircraft which was successful with ov
800 sold in the 1970s and 1980s. Although some European-designed short/medium-ha
aircraft were moderately successful, no-one was able to challenge the dominance of t
Americans until the 1980s. In the early 1960s US and European thinking were moving
opposite directions. American airlines discovered that the long haul market was very pri
elastic; demand increased when cheaper fares were offered. In order to make a profit, t
airlines sought larger and larger aircraft. In Europe, the belief was that the future lay
faster aircraft able to offer a premium service at high price. This divergence led to differe
design approaches. In 1969 the first prototype of the Boeing 747, with a capacity of over 4
passengers, made its maiden flight. One month later Concorde, a joint venture betwe
Britain and France with a capacity of 100 passengers and able to cruise over twice as fast
the 747, made its maiden flight. Although a technical success, Concorde was a commerc
failure; only 14 aircraft were manufactured. The aircraft, although still in service offering
premium service at very high prices, did not revolutionize air transport. The Boeing 7
and its variants have since become the most successful commercial transport aircraft fe
lowing its entry into service in 1970. The greatly reduced costs per passenger mile allow
airlines to charge fares that were within reach of a much larger number of people and t
generated a large increase in the number of passengers flying to long-haul destinations.

There have been a large number of advances in aircraft technology since 1969 but the
are mostly incremental in nature. Aircraft have become safer, more reliable and cheaper
operate but even the most up-to-date models are based on the technology developed in t
1950s. Until a radically new form of propulsion becomes commercially viable, it see
unlikely that the nature and economics of air travel will change significantly. In a simi
manner, navigation systems have improved immeasurably since the pioneering days of
travel. The two most important developments have been inertial (more recently satelli
navigation systems which allow an aircraft to follow a route with great accuracy witho
requiring ground-based aids and radar which allows air traffic controllers to accurate
monitor flights en route and near airports. Such developments have enabled the growth
air traffic with increased safety and reliability, but no dramatic changes to the industry a
expected from this direction for the foreseeable future.

Company history 1924–1987

The origins of British Airways can be traced back to the early 1920s. At the end of the fi
world war the UK, like several European countries, possessed the technology to bu
aircraft able to carry passengers in reasonable safety and comfort; with experienced aircre
to fly them and suitable airfields to operate from. A number of commercial passeng
services began. In 1924 a number of these operators amalgamated to form Imper

Airways. The new airline, although privately owned, received regular government subsidies as it built up a route structure which stretched to the eastern and southern extremities
of the British Empire – India, South Africa and Australia. Imperial Airways could be seen
as representing Britain and the British government.

In the early 1930s, the main aircraft used by the airline were the Short flying boats (which
had the useful merit of not requiring airfields) and the Handley Page HP42 (which did).
Although photographs of the time showed elegant passengers being served meals to
restaurant standards, it is easy to forget how primitive aircraft and other equipment
were compared to today. The aircraft were slow (90 knots for the HP42), noisy and, as
they flew at low altitudes, subject to variations in weather. Navigation was very basic, with
very few radio navigation aids. Flying was a luxury, available only to the wealthy and
government officials.

While Imperial Airways concentrated on routes to the colonies, another airline, British
Airways Ltd, was formed in 1935 from a merger of three smaller companies. The new
company operated mail and passenger services to destinations in northern Europe. In 1939,
following a review of the two airlines, the government decided to nationalize and merge
them in order to form a single airline which would better serve national/government
interests and be strong enough, through government subsidy, to withstand growing
competition from other national airlines. The new company, the British Overseas
Airways Corporation (BOAC), began operations in 1940 and almost immediately came
under the control of the Royal Air Force and remained so until after the second world war
(1939–45).

In 1946 the Labour Government under Prime Minister Clement Attlee published the
Civil Aviation Act which redefined the role and structure of the state airline. Two separate
airlines were formed: BOAC would be the flag carrier for intercontinental routes while
British European Airways (BEA) would be the flag carrier for domestic and European
routes. A third airline, BSSA, was soon reabsorbed into BOAC. There were two key
elements of the 1946 Act that affected the operations and development of both airlines:

- they were granted monopoly rights on profitable routes and were encouraged to cross-
  subsidize unprofitable ones;
- they should, wherever possible, use British-built aircraft.

This arrangement continued with only minor modifications to the monopoly status until
1971 when the British Airways Board was created to oversee the management of the two
airlines. In 1974, BOAC and BEA were merged to form British Airways (BA) (although
still under state ownership). At the same time, the government formally designated the
privately owned British Caledonian Airways (BCal) as the second force carrier offering
some competition to BA. However real integration of long-haul and short/medium-haul
operation did not begin until 1979. The inevitable culture clashes and job losses which
followed contributed to a difficult period as the company adjusted to the changes.

The changes of the early 1980s were driven by the Conservative government led by
Prime Minister Margaret Thatcher. Unlike the previous Labour governments, Thatcher
was ideologically opposed to state-owned monopolies and accordingly, her government
encouraged greater competition from the private sector. Thatcher also sought to sell off
state-owned companies to the private sector, partly to raise capital but also because she

believed that these companies would be better managed in a normal commercial environment. However, BA in the late 1970s was not an attractive candidate for privatization so Thatcher brought in Sir John (later Lord) King, an experienced and tough industrialist, as chairman in 1980. King carried out a major rationalization of the company's operations which resulted in over 20 000 job losses.

In 1983 Colin Marshall was appointed chief executive and one of his major strategic thrusts was to redefine the brand name whilst also focusing on customer service. Marshall is credited with implementing the major cultural change within the company which was required to meet the company's new goals. By the time that BA was privatized in early 1987, it was well on the road to becoming the world's most profitable airline with high liquidity and an enviable international route structure.

International linkages

As with any business wishing to expand its international markets an airline may pursue a variety of methods. Although most of these can be directly compared to a conventional business there are some additional factors which have to be taken into account in selecting the best option. As BA has pursued most of these options we shall review some of them briefly.

Network development without a partner

This is the simplest form of expansion; the airline flies passengers to and from its domestic base to a larger number of foreign airports. With small numbers of passengers the airline may use an agent at the foreign airport but for very large numbers it may build its own terminal as BA has done at JFK, New York. The airline may have to obtain permission to operate the service from its own government as well as the foreign government.

Airlines tend to concentrate their international operations at one domestic airport; for example BA at London Heathrow and KLM at Amsterdam Schipol. Within their home country they can operate domestic feeder routes to convey international passengers to and from the main airport – a simple form of the 'hub and spoke' system used by US airlines for internal services. However, the opportunities to operate feeder services in the foreign country are normally very restricted. International agreements for air services are negotiated between governments within the framework of the Chicago Convention which defined five 'freedoms' which could be granted to an airline. These freedoms include rights to overfly a state, convey passengers to and from the state and convey passengers to another state via the first. A further freedom which lies outside the framework is the right to operate feeder services within a foreign state, also known as 'cabotage'. Very few states permit cabotage because of the potential competition with domestic airlines. Accordingly, although BA can fly passengers from London to Pittsburgh via Philadelphia, it is not allowed to pick up passengers in Philadelphia and fly them to Pittsburgh. On the return journey the ultimate destination of passengers who embark at Pittsburgh must be London, not Philadelphia. The airline therefore loses the opportunities both to fill empty seats in the internal US sector and generate more passengers for the international services. Although there is some relaxation of these restraints within the EU most other governments are reluctant to permit open competition.

Acquisition

At first sight this might seems a good alternative to international expansion without a partner. In practice it is difficult to implement. The simplest case is an airline based on one country acquiring another airline based in the same country. As already mentioned, the airline industry tends to be oligopolistic and governments may be reluctant to sanction such an acquisition if it is likely to significantly reduce competition in the domestic market even if the effect of concentration on a global scale is insignificant. This puts European carriers with their small domestic markets at a disadvantage to the much larger US carriers.

Most countries also have statutory restrictions on the degree of ownership of a national airline by a foreign airline which effectively prevents a controlling interest being acquired. Even if a controlling interest can be bought, the foreign government may still not permit cabotage as the acquired airline is under foreign control.

In view of these restrictions, airlines with large-scale international ambitions have pursued some kind of alliance with one or more partners with the aim of offering to their customers a much more extensive international network than is otherwise possible. Three of the most popular forms of alliance are pooling, franchising and codesharing.

Pooling is an agreement between two flag carriers operating on a single route to share capacity and revenue. The total number of seats and the prices that will be offered by each airline is agreed, and the total revenue is shared. The airlines do not attempt to compete with one another and can therefore enjoy orderly growth. This arrangement was very common in Europe in the early 1960s where most international routes were regulated and operation was restricted to two airlines. It became much less common after the partial European deregulation of the industry.

Under a franchising arrangement, one airline (the franchiser) gives another airline (the franchisee – usually a much smaller airline), the right to use the franchiser's name, aircraft livery and uniforms. The franchiser may or may not hold shares in the franchisee. Since to passengers it appears that he is flying with the franchiser, the franchiser appears to operate a larger network than it actually does with feeder services at foreign airports. The franchisee benefits because the franchiser normally markets the franchisee's services on behalf of both airlines.

Franchising is very well developed in the US and is becoming more popular in other countries. For the arrangement to be successful the franchisee must be able to offer standards of service, reliability and safety comparable to those of the franchiser.

Codesharing is an arrangement wherein two airlines agree that flights operated by one of them can use the flight number of the other and vice versa. Thus a flight operated by Sabena from Brussels to Paris may be known both as SN105 (a Sabena code) and DL2050 (a code used by Delta, one of Sabena's codesharing partners). Sabena also operates the passenger check-in and baggage handling services at Brussels for Delta. The airlines also agree to co-ordinate flight times. From an American passenger's point of view the ticket for a flight from the USA to Brussels then on to Paris will carry only the Delta codes, again giving the illusion that Delta operates a much more extensive network than it actually does. In contrast to franchising, the codesharing partners may be of similar size. Codesharing is very common in America and is becoming increasingly employed in Europe.

Computer reservation systems

The overwhelming majority of flights are booked through travel agents who use a computer reservation system (CRS) to display flight combinations which meet the customers requirements and make reservations. The first CRS was designed by IBM for American Airlines and installed in 1962. The system was known as the 'Semi-Automated Business Reservations Environment' or SABRE and cut the reservation process time from 45 minutes to 3 seconds. The system was extended to allow travel agents to sell tickets on other airlines; every time this was done, American Airlines received a fee. Thus SABRE became a major and highly profitable source of revenue for American Airlines.

Following deregulation, the competition between US airlines intensified and a useful benefit of the CRS to the owner airline became apparent. The CRS could be programmed to always display American Airlines flights before those of its competitors thus giving American Airlines a significant competitive advantage. In response, the other US airlines set up their own CRSs. Although regulations were introduced in the US and Europe to prevent airlines owning CRSs from gaining unfair advantages over other airlines, there is no doubt that owning or being part of a group of airlines owning a CRS is essential for international airlines. Within Europe the major systems are called Galileo and Amadeus.

BA after privatization

The flotation of BA in February 1987 was a triumph for the company, in particular the then chairman Lord King and chief executive Colin Marshall. It was also a great success for the Thatcher government; a business which 10 years before was an inefficient, consistent loss maker was now a profitable enterprise, able to compete with even the giant US airlines. The revenues from the flotation were used to pay off the large debts owed by BA, a classic 'debt for equity' swap on a grand scale. However, there was a contradiction at the heart of the privatization; as with many of the other privatized state companies such as British Telecom and the utilities, in competitive terms all that had happened was that a state-owned monopoly had been converted into a privately owned monopoly. In domestic terms, BA dwarfed its competitors and was very happy to use its size to beat off anything which might remotely threaten its dominant competitive position. The situation was remarkably similar to that in the USA during the early 1980s when the burst of free competition following deregulation gradually fizzled out as the smaller carriers either went out of business or else were acquired by the larger carriers.

The US pattern was repeated in the UK. The first casualty was BCal which had been officially designated as BA's main competitor. By the early 1980s it was clear that in order to survive BCal needed more international routes. This could only be achieved by the government taking them away from BA and giving them to BCal because of the restriction imposed by bilateral agreements permitting only one designated flag carrier on each route. The government decided against this as it did not want to risk any damage to BA as privatization approached. Within six months of the BA privatization, the merger of the two airlines was announced. Although the merger was referred to the Monopolies and Mergers Commission, the MMC approved it because BCal could no longer survive as an independent airline. In 1992, BA acquired Dan-Air, another UK independent airline. Once again the MMC approved the acquisition despite the fact that BA would now be the sole carrier on a large number of domestic routes.

Although the demise of BCal and Dan-Air reduced competition for BA, the relaxation of the regulatory climate permitted other UK-based airlines to compete with BA on its domestic and international routes. British Midland Airways' first major challenge to BA was in the Glasgow–London route in the late 1970s. This was BA's most important route which it operated as a 'shuttle' service. In its original form, passengers could neither pre-book nor prepay; instead the airline guaranteed that provided that a passenger checked in around 15 minutes before the scheduled departure time they were guaranteed a seat, even if a second or even third aircraft had to be used for the journey. Payment was made during the flight so that instead of serving drinks and food, the cabin staff wheeled around cash machines. BCal also operated from Glasgow to London, but it used Gatwick rather than Heathrow so as to avoid offering direct competition. When British Midland started its service between Glasgow and Heathrow it was a prebook, prepay service but with a good standard of catering. This service proved very popular, especially the early morning flights where passengers could enjoy a substantial breakfast *en route*. Eventually BA had to withdraw the 'pay on board' element of the shuttle and the cabin staff reverted to serving drinks and snacks.

Although British Midland had a very small international route structure compared to BA it made full use of codesharing to offer passengers easy access to a wide range of destinations. The airline could be classed as an 'irritant' to BA, particularly as its chairman, Sir Michael Bishop, constantly sought to influence public and government opinion in an effort to reduce BA's monopoly position.

On long-haul routes, BA's only real UK-based competitor is Virgin Atlantic Airways. Managed by Richard Branson, it started operations between London Gatwick and Newark, New Jersey, using refurbished Boeing 747s flown by a substantial proportion of ex-BA pilots in the late 1980s. Although the threat to BA's prestige Heathrow–JFK route was only indirect, the low price but good service offered by Virgin was successful at attracting economy class passengers who might otherwise have flown with BA. Furthermore, Virgin showed great ambition by starting other services across the North Atlantic and even to Far Eastern destinations which were some of BA's most profitable routes. What BA found even more threatening was that Virgin also began attracting business class passengers with its 'Upper Class' service and even succeeded in obtaining landing slots at Heathrow.

BA and Lord King greatly underestimated the threat posed by Virgin. King did not regard Branson as a serious businessman and assumed that Virgin would soon collapse, as Freddie Laker's undercapitalized airline had done ten years earlier. But although Branson was a highly unconventional owner the actual running of Virgin was carried out by experienced managers while Branson concentrated on publicity stunts which kept the brand name constantly in public view. Branson also had substantial capital available from the sale of other business interests. When it became apparent that Virgin would remain a serious and growing competitor, BA tried to lure the lucrative business class customers back by using what the courts later ruled to be illegal tactics. BA was forced to compensate Virgin and Lord King issued a public apology. Shortly after, in February 1993, Lord King retired as Chairman of BA in what many saw as a decision to take the blame for the mishandling of the Virgin threat.

The explicit link between the earlier incarnations of BA and the British aircraft industry have already been mentioned. This link was not explicitly broken until the late 1970s when the airline began to pursue a policy of standardizing on one manufacturer, Boeing. Appendix 3 shows the percentage of the long- and short/medium-haul fleets which were British.

In the period up to 1965 the only non-British aircraft in the short/medium-haul fleet were US DC-3s. When these were sold the fleet became 100 per cent British. There were some advantages in this; customers liked to 'fly British'. Although these aircraft were technically advanced in some ways (the Trident pioneered the use of automatic landing systems in commercial aircraft), they were considerably more expensive to run than American aircraft due to higher fuel and maintenance costs. As BA came under greater pressure to reduce costs, aircraft purchases from 1977 onwards were mainly from Boeing.

The long-haul fleet always had a smaller proportion of British aircraft because, apart from the Comet and the VC10 in the 1960s, there were no British aircraft capable of operating on transatlantic routes. From 1973 on, the Boeing 747 gradually became the dominant aircraft in the fleet and the small percentage of British aircraft from 1981 onward consisted of seven Anglo-French Concordes.

From the early 1980s onwards, the official policy of BA was to standardize on Boeing aircraft to reduce maintenance and pilot training costs and to take advantage of advantageous financial terms. Although it owned 10 Airbus 320 aircraft (from the European Airbus consortium) in 1997, these were acquired following the acquisition of BCal which had placed orders for them before the take-over. In 1999, however, BA announced that it would replace older Boeing 757s with smaller Airbus A319s and A320s as part of its revised fleet strategy to concentrate on higher yield markets. From BA's point of view, the operation of a modern, reliable and standardized fleet was a key component of its strategy to reduce costs and offer an attractive product as it attempts to compete on a global scale.

From international to global airline

In the years after privatization, BA set itself the target of becoming the world's best and most successful airline. In order to achieve this ambitious goal, the company believed that it had to become a global airline, able to operate services to and from destinations all round the world. Robert Ayling, the chief executive, stated that he expected that the industry would follow the pattern of several other service industries and become dominated by a small number of very large companies. Accordingly, it became BA's objective to be one of these. In this section we examine how BA developed after privatization, but we shall consider briefly one of the main sources of the airline's competitive advantage – its domination of London airports.

Heathrow Airport first opened for international commercial traffic in 1946 and BOAC immediately moved its operations there from Croydon with BEA following suit in the early

1950s. Between them these two carriers dominated the airport which steadily grew into the busiest international airport in the world. Heathrow has a pivotal position in international aviation because of its geographical position relative to North America and Europe and most major international airlines operate services through the airport. This position has been challenged in recent years by Amsterdam Schipol and even Manchester but with limited success.

As a result of this growth, the airport is so busy at peak periods that departures and landings have to be controlled through a process of slot allocation. Any new entrant has to obtain a slot; although the airport allocates a small number of slots each year to new entrants, BA has 'grandfather rights' to a large percentage of slots. Thus the only way for other airlines to increase market share is for the UK government to take slots away from BA. This has been done on a small scale to allow British Midland and Virgin Atlantic to build up a challenge to BA but the 1996 position where BA accounted for around 40 per cent of passenger movements has not altered very much and BA can always be relied upon to mount a spirited defence of its rights to retain control of as many slots as it can. Since privatization, BA has continued to invest heavily at the airport; as well as its own terminal for long-haul services the airline also owns substantial maintenance, training and cargo facilities.

Although in many ways Heathrow resembles the 'hub' airports dominated by large US airlines, the degree of domination by BA of Heathrow is somewhat less that that of, for example, American Airlines at Dallas/Forth Worth (70 per cent) and Delta at Atlanta (76 per cent). Flights are not co-ordinated in the way that Sabena operates at Brussels with a large number of flights arriving during a short period followed by a large number of departures soon after. BA essentially operates a linear route network with Heathrow as its main base.

Following the acquisitions of BCal and Dan-Air, BA acquired routes from Gatwick which had developed in the early 1960s as London's second airport. In more recent years, BA extended its operations at Gatwick and some of its franchise airlines were based there. Gatwick itself grew considerably and is forecast to be approaching capacity in the next few years unless a second runway is built. The airline also began operations at Stansted which has been designated as London's third airport, through its **go** subsidiary.

Building a global brand – a new strategic direction

There are two elements to the creation of a brand image for an airline; the first is the image of the airline itself and the second is the various levels of service that it offers and which can be marketed separately.

The BA image was somewhat tarnished by the late 1970s; the airline had acquired a (justified) reputation of mediocre service delivered by rather aloof and uncaring staff. The original Shuttle service between Glasgow and London discussed earlier exemplified this. One of the achievements of the new management in the 1980s was to change the culture of the company to customer focus. New livery for the aircraft and higher quality of service gradually transformed the competitive position of the airline.

The airline also established brand names for each of the classes of service that were provided making them more distinctive than the standard first, business and economy classes offered by other airlines. Indicative fares for each class of service are shown in Appendix 5.

- *Concorde*. Only two airlines fly Concorde, BA and Air France, giving both a unique form of competitive advantage which can be used to create a very positive image for the airline as a whole. The supersonic London–New York service arrives at New York at an earlier local time than the departure time allowing customers to carry out a full day's business before returning. Apart from luxurious standards of service on board, very rapid check-in and arrival facilities at either end of the journey maximize the time savings. As might be expected for such a unique service the price is high – some 15 per cent higher than first class.
- *First Class*. This is the brand name for the conventional top-class service. It is only available on intercontinental flights and offers a very high standard of on-board service (including beds) and facilities at departure and destination airports.
- *Club World, Club Europe*. The brand name for business class on intercontinental and European flights. Both brands offer exclusive check-in facilities and special lounges at airports. Service on intercontinental flights is of a high standard, while that on European flights is lower as flight times are shorter.
- *World Traveller, Eurotraveller*. The brand name for economy class. BA claims that the service offered is higher than on other airlines with more space and good catering.

In June 1997 BA announced what it called a major change to its corporate identity.

Based on what is believed to be the largest consumer research exercise in the history of the travel industry, the aim is to establish British Airways as the undisputed leader in world travel as it flies into the 21st century and to build on its British strengths.

The changes were explained in a speech by Robert Ayling.

Like every successful company, we need to grow and increase shareholder value. We cannot do this and cannot prosper as a company if we restrict ourselves to taking people to and from the UK.

Our existing livery has served us well. It helped transform our company in preparation for privatization. Now all of our research is telling us we must change again, to prepare for the exciting new era that the new millennium will bring.

We need a corporate identity that will enable us to become not just a UK carrier, but a global airline that is based in Britain. British Airways remains proudly British, but perhaps we need to lose some of our old fashioned Britishness and take on board some of the new British traits. Abroad, people see this country as friendly, diverse and open to other cultures. We must better reflect that.

The key element in this new strategic direction is summarized in the phrase 'a global airline that is based in Britain'. Before June 1997, a design incorporating elements of the Union flag were incorporated in the tail livery of all BA aircraft – a welcome sight for British ravellers in airports far from home. Now the company wanted to create a new image which would be recognizable and attractive to non-UK as well as UK travellers. A new range of designs was created by a design consultant with 50 'world images' based on ethnic art styles in a wide range of countries; these images would appear on aircraft, vehicles, tickets, baggage tags – anything that currently bore the BA name.

The reaction to the new designs, prominently featured on aircraft tailfins, was somewhat mixed. Passengers could no longer identify a BA aircraft at a distance and many UK travellers found the designs ugly and garish. Some practical problems emerged; air traffic controllers and other pilots had difficulties identifying BA aircraft on the ground, especially at night; if rudders needed changing the replacement did not match the design on the rest of the tail. Other UK airlines mocked the changes and the irrepressible Richard Branson announced that Virgin aircraft would in future carry a design in which the Union flag would be very prominent.

Although BA defended the new image vigorously it could not avoid some embarrassment when a newspaper revealed that Robert Ayling was colour blind and may not have realized how jarring the new designs were. During 1999, BA began a partial reversal of its livery to include elements of the Union flag along the body of its planes.

As part of the rationalization required to reduce costs in the early 1980s, BA cut down on many loss-making domestic routes in order to concentrate on strengthening its international activities. The licences for these routes were acquired by other airlines (some of which have since become BA franchises), even though some were owned by BA's competitors. These small airlines had reduced overheads and used aircraft which were more suited to short-haul, low-density routes. Accordingly, they were more able to compete with surface transport and offer feeder services to BA's international services, mainly in the UK but more recently in South Africa and Denmark. The franchise operations were managed through British Airways Express. Appendix 3 lists BA's franchise airlines as at 1997.

The precise relationship between BA and the franchise airlines varies. Brymon Airways, for example, is a fully owned subsidiary of BA and it was announced in 1999 that BA would acquire CityFlyer Express.

Following privatization, with few debts and the ability to raise large amounts of capital, BA was in a strong position to make major acquisitions to build a truly international airline. The obvious target was one of the major American airlines. Such an acquisition would give BA access to that airline's domestic route network and the opportunity to offer transatlantic passengers connections within both Europe and North America. In this way BA hoped it would overcome the ban on operating US domestic routes imposed by the US government discussed earlier.

BA and United Airlines announced a marketing partnership in 1987 and this was extended to a proposal for BA to participate in a buyout which would have left it with 15 per cent of United. The bid was withdrawn later when the other partners failed to raise sufficient finance.

In 1992 BA announced a conditional agreement to acquire up to a 44 per cent ownership of USAir. In return BA would inject much-needed capital into USAir. The proposal was withdrawn after the US government demanded concessions by the UK government which would have given US airlines traffic carrying rights within Europe.

In early 1993, a revised agreement was announced which stopped short of the fu
integration envisaged in the earlier proposals but did include BA directors joinir
USAir's board. A full programme of co-operation including codesharing and sharir
aircraft was announced at the same time. This 'strategic alliance' was approved by tl
US government and the alliance proceeded apace. However the alliance came und
strain in 1994 as USAir's losses mounted. In 1995, however, it became apparent that B
was seeking an alternative partner. BA disposed of its shareholding in USAir in ear
1997.

- In June 1996 BA announced plans for a 'broad alliance' with American Airlines, tl
second largest US airline. It was estimated that between them BA and AA wou
control over 20 per cent of transatlantic routes as well as having a significant sha
of total world traffic. The alliance required approval by both the UK and US gover
ments as well as the EU. Rival airlines lost no time in lobbying against the propos
which they perceived as a major threat. Prominent among these was Virgin Airway
Richard Branson placed large advertisements in British newspapers arguing th
approval of the alliance would lead to a reduction in competition and eventual
much higher fares across the Atlantic. Although both BA and AA proceeded wi
some elements of the alliance it became apparent that Brussels and the US governme
would require BA to give up a significant number of slots at Heathrow as a conditic
for approval. The proposals were quietly shelved in mid-1999.

Thus, BA's attempts to build an integrated partnership across the Atlantic have, at tl
time of writing, been fruitless. However, BA has had some success in other countries, albe
on a limited scale. Appendix 4 lists BA's subsidiaries and associated undertakings. Of the
the Qantas shareholding is the most significant as it represents a foothold in Australasi
Even this partnership was delayed until the Australian equivalent of the MMC approve
the investment. Ownership of the two French airlines gives BA access to domestic routes
France and up to 22 per cent of landing slots at Paris Orly airport.

In February 1999 BA announced the formation of the oneworld alliance – an allianc
between BA, American Airlines, Canadian Airlines, Cathay Pacific and Qantas (joined
August 1999 by Finnair and Iberia). The purpose of this alliance was to offer passenge
many of the benefits of a global airline even if the alliance members remain independer
Passengers travelling on a ticket issued by one of the members can share frequent fly
points, change tickets to another member at any member's ticket office, use each member
airline lounges and obtain assistance during transfer from staff of any member. The state
purpose of the alliance was to offer more convenient and seamless global travel to passe
gers and more airlines were expected to join the scheme.

It seems likely that until government restrictions on foreign ownership of nation
airlines are lifted that the oneworld 'global alliance' is the nearest that we are going
get to a truly global airline. There is already one competing alliance recently announced; tl
'Star Alliance' between Thai Airlines, Lufthansa, SAS, Ansett Australia, Air New Zealan
Varig, Air Canada and United Airlines. The test of their success will be whether or not the
can attract and keep passengers within the member airlines.

It is interesting to consider the comments made by Robert Ayling to a conference c
deregulation in 1993.

National interest is no longer the same as producer interest. The producer is less an arm of the state and more of a normal international business that happens to be based in the country. If the choice boils down to what is good for the consumer against what is good for the indigenous airlines, how is a nation to decide? And if a country wishes to maintain a multi-airline policy, but its market is too small to support one airline efficiently, should airline competitiveness or national policy be sacrificed? ... the nationality principle is weaker today than it ever has been.

Issues at the end of the decade

At the turn of the millennium, the airline industry as a whole was experiencing difficult times and BA was not immune. Two signs of these problems were the decline in profits in 1998 and 1999 shown in Appendix 6 coupled with the decline in the BA share price shown in Appendix 2. Since mid-1997 BA's share price underperformed the rest of the stock market. The initial trigger for this was the collapse of the Far Eastern economies in mid-1997 which severely reduced demand for air travel to and from that region. The effects of this were still being felt with no growth in that market for BA in 1998/99.

There were, however, a number of other reasons why profits declined:

growing competition stimulated by further deregulation throughout the world reducing entry barriers. Some routes, particularly those across the Atlantic, were suffering from overcapacity, leading to fare discounting;

general economic conditions throughout the world resulted in lower growth than expected. Furthermore passengers tended to downgrade and fly economy class rather than business class, thus reducing profit margins;

fuel costs began to rise sharply during 1999;

start-up losses of the new **go** subsidiary.

The company responded to these threats in a number of ways. These were outlined by Robert Ayling:

to focus on the premium end of the market (first and business class passengers) which attracted much higher margins than the low-fare economy market. In order to achieve this, older Boeing 747s and 757s were phased out and replaced by smaller Boeing 777s and Airbus A319s and A320s. The effect of this was to reduce capacity for economy passengers;

to raise the standards of service, particularly to Club Word passengers;

to continue the Business Efficiency Programme which was expected to achieve overall savings of £1 billion between March 1996 and March 2000;

to ensure that through staff recruitment and training, the company would have the correct mix of skills to deal with a wider range of passengers;

to continue to build the network of alliances to create a global airline.

During the 1990s BA sold off what it considered to be non-core activities, such as engine overhaul, aeronautical chart production, in-flight catering and its stake in the

Galileo International CRS. The refocusing strategy outlined above is consistent with this. However there is a curious anomaly in the creation of the **go** subsidiary. **go** is a low-cost no-frills airline competing in the 'rock bottom' end of the market which was fiercely opposed by competitors when it was launched in 1998. It is based at Stansted airport and uses leased aircraft to operate services to a limited number of popular European destinations.

Richard Branson of Virgin said of **go** in March 1998:

> I think the public should seriously consider boycotting **go** if there is an Easyjet plane or a Ryanair plane supporting an independent carrier. Unless BA say: 'We can afford the same fares at Heathrow and the same fares at Gatwick', I think that what they're doing is blatantly anti-competitive. If you look at the history of BA you will see the airlines that have been driven out of business – Laker, BCal, Dan-Air, Air Europe and others in the past – and see what happens when one of these airlines goes out of business – BA shoves its fares up almost immediately to high levels until another competitor comes along.

It was suggested that BA was opening a 'second front' in a different market where the key success factors were different to those in its core market.

Bibliography

Dienel, H.-L. and Lyth, P. (eds.) (1998) *Flying the Flag – European Commercial Air Transport Since 194* Macmillan, London.

Hanlon, P. (1996) *Global Airlines – Competition in a Transnational Industry*. Butterworth-Heinemann, Oxford

Marriott, L. (1997) *British Airways*, 2nd edn. Ian Allen Publishing, Shepperton, Surrey.

Rendall, I. (1988) *Reaching for the Skies*. BBC Books, London.

Appendices

Appendix 1. BEA/BOAC/BA fleet

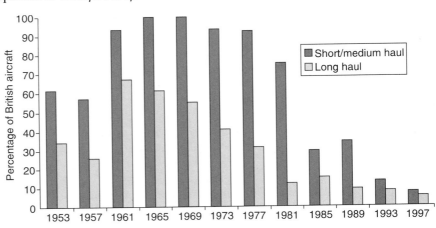

Source: annual reports

Appendix 2. British Airways share price relative to FTSE all-share index

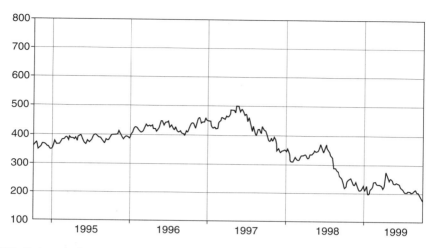

FTSE all-share index = 100.
Source: Datastream

Appendix 3. BA franchise airlines, March 1999

Airline	Destinations	Since
BASE	Holland	1998
British Mediterranean Airways	London, Beirut, Amman, Damascus, Tblisi, Alexandria	1994
British Regional Airlines (Manx Airlines (Europe) and Loganair)	Internal Scottish services	1995
Brymon Airways (100% owned by BA)	Plymouth, Bristol, Newcastle, Aberdeen, Southampton, Channel Islands, Eire, Paris	1994
CityFlyer Express	Gatwick, Newcastle, Leeds, Jersey, Guernsey, Antwerp, Dublin, Dusseldorf, Rotterdam	1993
Comair	Cape Town, Durban, Harare, Windhoek, Johannesburg	1997
GB Airways	Gatwick, Valencia, Nurcia, Jerez, Seville, Malta, Gibraltar, Madeira	1995
Maersk Air (UK)	Birmingham, Newcastle and other European destinations	1994
Sun-Air of Scandinavia	Denmark and Southern Scandinavia	1997

Source: British Airways annual report

Appendix 4. BA major subsidiaries, March 1999

Airline	Country	Equity (%)	Date
Qantas Airways	Australia	25	1992
Air Liberté	France	100	1996
Deutsche BA	Germany	100	1992
TAT	France	100	1997

Source: British Airways annual report

Appendix 5. BA return fares from London to New York in October 1999 (including taxes)

Class of Service	Fare
Concorde	£6342
First Class	£5590
Club World	£3396
World Traveller (Standard)	£880
World Traveller (Advanced Purchase)	£239

Source: British Airways

Appendix 6. British Airways group profit and loss accounts, 1995–99 (year ended March 31)

£ million	1999	1998	1997	1996	1995
Turnover	8915	8642	8359	7760	7177
Cost of sales	(8296)	(7978)	(7663)	(6903)	(6436)
Gross profit	619	664	696	857	741
Administrative expenses	(177)	(160)	(150)	(129)	(268)
Operating profit	442	504	546	728	473
Other income	214	243	262	206	167
Exceptional items	51	164	145	(1)	0
Profit before interest	707	911	953	933	640
Interest paid	(482)	(331)	(313)	(348)	(313)
Profit before tax	225	580	640	585	327
Taxation	(19)	(133)	(90)	(112)	(77)
Profit after tax	206	447	550	473	250
Extraordinary Items	0	13	3	0	0
Profit for Period	206	460	553	473	250
Dividends	(191)	(176)	(154)	(131)	(119)
Retained profit	15	284	399	342	131

Source: FAME and British Airways annual reports

Appendix 7. British Airways group balance sheets, 1995–99 (year end March 31)

£ million	1999	1998	1997	1996	1995
Fixed Assets					
Property	1331	1181	988	866	
Equipment	301	259	263	234	
Fleet	8207	7227	5726	5726	
Tangible assets	9839	8667	7588	6826	6163
Investments	402	388	684	531	471
	10 241	9055	8272	7357	6634
Current assets					
Stocks	84	75	78	104	70
Cash at bank and in hand	112	50	76	48	64
Debtors	1336	1432	1412	1374	844
Short-term loans and deposits	1051	688	598	1158	1451
	2583	2245	2164	2684	2429
Creditors: amounts falling due within one year					
Trade creditors	(1010)	(1000)	(983)	(1024)	(845)
Short term loans & overdrafts	(603)	(375)	(572)	(361)	(321)
Other current liabilities	(1468)	(1446)	(1605)	(1439)	(1154)
	(3081)	(2821)	(3160)	(2824)	(2320)
Net current assets (Liab.)	*(498)*	*(576)*	*(996)*	*(140)*	*109*
Total assets less current liabilities	*9743*	*8479*	*7276*	*7217*	*6743*
Creditors: amounts falling due after more than one year	(6356)	(5128)	(4208)	(4664)	(4653)
Provisions for liabilities and charges	*(32)*	*(30)*	*(58)*	*(59)*	
	(6388)	(5158)	(4266)	(4723)	(4653)
Total assets less liabilities	*3355*	*3321*	*3010*	*2494*	*2090*
Shareholders funds					
Issued capital	268	260	251	240	239
Reserves					
Share premium account	764	650	565	471	464
Revaluation reserves	290	294	297	302	304
Profit (loss) account	2033	2117	1871	1481	1083
	3087	3061	2733	2254	1851
	3355	*3321*	*2984*	*2494*	*2090*

Source: FAME and British Airways annual reports

Case Study 4

BAT INDUSTRIES PLC IN THE 1980s AND 1990s

David Campbell
University of Northumbria

The tobacco industry

Products and some key figures

As at the year 2000, the UK tobacco industry had sales of almost £14 billion. In terms of outputs, the industry produced four broad categories of tobacco product. By far the largest of these was cigarettes, accounting for over 90 per cent of tobacco sales by value. Loose tobacco was manufactured in two forms – for pipe smokers and for hand rolling smokers. The fourth category was cigars.

The problem with defining precisely which companies are a part of the UK industry arises because of the extent of transnational ownership. A wave of restructurings in the 1980s and 1990s significantly changed the industry structure such that there were fewer companies (reduction due to acquisitions and mergers) but they were typically larger and more internationalized.

A brief history of the industry

One of the most striking features of the tobacco industry has been the change in the view taken of it by society over time. As late as the 1940s, smoking was recommended by medical doctors to patients suffering from some conditions, and it was not until the 1950s that medical researchers started to suspect that smoking tobacco may have some negative effect on health. The strong cigarette, Capstan, was advertised in the 1930s and 1940s with the message that most doctors smoked and pointing out that many doctors recommended smoking to patients.

During the second world war, allied forces received a regular free ration of cigarettes each week. It was thought that smoking would reduce discontent among the ranks and many forces personnel who did not previously smoke began to do so during this period. By

1945 (at the conclusion of the second world war), 83 per cent of adult males in the UK smoked tobacco. It was only when deaths from a range of lung diseases increased that medical researchers began to suspect that there may be toxins in tobacco smoke.

The breakthrough came in the 1950s when one researcher, Richard Doll, discovered a link between smoking tobacco and certain lung diseases. The Doll Report was greeted with alarm by the industry and producers reacted to it in different ways. Imperial Tobacco (one of the largest producers) initially tried to discredit the findings by pointing to other research evidence. Duncan Oppenheim, who later became chairman of British American Tobacco, reported that many were taken completed by surprise by Doll's findings. 'We thought [before the Doll Report] that tobacco was a beneficial product' said Oppenheim.

In 1957, the UK government finally accepted at an official level that there was a link between 'heavy smoking' and lung cancers. Meanwhile, however, the industry producers were taking measures to offset their customers' concerns by introducing filters to many of their top brands (before this, cigarettes were not filtered). 'Independent' research commissioned by the tobacco industry attempted to persuade smokers that smoking was not as harmful as some would have them believe, even although evidence later emerged that by the mid-1950s, the producers knew the harmful effects of their products.

In 1962, President Kennedy, in trying to respond to health concerns over smoking, set up a committee to look into the subject under the chairmanship of the US Surgeon General. Although the tobacco companies knew about the addictiveness of tobacco by this time (in addition to its health implications) this information was withheld from the committee in their deposition of evidence. Accordingly, the Committee's spokesman, Luther Terry, concluded, notwithstanding Doll's evidence, that smoking 'contributes substantially' to health. It was thought that the powerful tobacco lobby in the USA had some influence in the Committee's deliberations. Meanwhile in the UK, the Royal College of Surgeons produced a report clearly linking tobacco smoking to lung cancer in 1964.

BAT – a brief history

The history of what became BAT Industries can be traced back to 1890 when one Mr Buck Dukes established the American Tobacco Company. Dukes took advantage of the (then recent) enlargement of the USA and the improvements in national infrastructure to develop his company into the first serious national tobacco producer in the USA. Within a few years, American Tobacco became a near monopolist in the US tobacco market, sourcing its raw materials from the tobacco growing states (the Carolinas, the Virginias and some others) and then shipping the processed leaf across the country. Consumption was in the form of tobacco that was rolled, smoked in a pipe or chewed. Ready-rolled cigarettes were relatively rare at this time because the technology for producing them on a mass scale was not yet available.

By the turn of the nineteenth century, just 10 years after its establishment, American Tobacco was exporting its products. In the UK, the many regional tobacco companies merged to act in collaboration to resist the threat of American imports into the UK. The result of this merger was the formation in 1901 of the Imperial Tobacco Group, which was based in Bristol.

For over a year, Imperial and American fought each other in a price war to win market share in the UK. The situation was resolved in 1902, however, when the two companies agreed to stay in their own countries but to market each other's brands in their domestic home countries based on a royalty payment system. It was one of the earliest uses of international licensing as a mechanism of international development and the arrangement served both companies' strategic ends. The loose partnership formed in the 'product swap' agreement was called British American Tobacco (BAT). Meanwhile in the USA, American Tobacco continued to build its share of the US market by acquiring many of the local tobacco companies which had previously only sold within their own state boundaries.

In 1911, BAT became a registered company in its own right on both sides of the Atlantic because it was forced to do so by an unforeseen legal dispute. American Tobacco was deemed by the US Supreme Court to be in breach of US anti-trust laws because of its dominant US market share. The company was ordered to demerge and Dukes divided the company up into five smaller units which would, under the provisions of the Sherman Anti-Trust Act (1890) be forced to compete with each other in future: American Tobacco Company; RJ Reynolds; Liggett & Myers Tobacco Company (Durham, NC, USA); Lorillard, and British American Tobacco Limited.

All of the demerged parts prospered in the buoyant market for tobacco products in the early years of the twentieth century. Whilst the other demerged businesses operated mainly in the USA, BAT split its efforts between the USA and the UK. In 1927, it strengthened its US market share with the acquisition of a major US rival, Brown & Williamson. As events unfolded in the 1980s and 1990s, BAT would be reunited with some of the demerged parts of the old American Tobacco company.

BAT benefited from the growth of tobacco smoking during the second world war. In the USA and the UK, servicemen were issued with generous tobacco rations ('C-rations' in the US army). The result of this state promotion of its products was that tobacco smoking reached its height in the late 1940s. Smokers were unaware of the health implications of tobacco consumption and smoking became an integral part of social and cultural life on both sides of the Atlantic. Most of the luminaries and role models of the period smoked openly and the practice was made to look glamorous and even sexy by the Hollywood stars of the day.

It was not until the mid 1950s and the publication of the Doll Report that the focus of BAT began to change.

BAT in the 1960s and 1970s

The controversy surrounding the painful realization in the 1950s that there was a link between tobacco consumption and some illnesses caused BAT to re-examine its product portfolio. The potential vulnerability of an over-emphasis on tobacco triggered a substantial amount of diversification in all parts of the industry, and BAT was to be no exception.

Throughout the 1960s and early 1970s, BAT made substantial investments by acquisition in several sectors other than tobacco. Its acquisitions in tobacco tended to concentrate upon developing its international portfolio. The modern form of the company was established in 1976 when BAT merged with Tobacco Securities Trust Company Limited – a UK-based investment company. The new company was called BAT Industries plc (which was still widely referred to as simply 'BAT').

By 1976, after the merger, BAT had developed its business to the point that although tobacco still formed the majority of product output by value, it had substantial interests in retailing, paper and pulp, cosmetics and some other minor sectors.

Tobacco division in the late 1970s

In tobacco, the company boasted over 300 brands of cigarettes, operating 90 factories in 37 countries together with a number of affiliated (part, rather than wholly, owned) companies in another 38 countries. This grew to interests in a total of 47 countries based around principal subsidiaries in the UK, Europe, Latin America, the Caribbean, Asia and Africa.

Its major tobacco subsidiaries were:

- Brown and Williamson (USA) – manufacturers of Kool, Raleigh and Viceroy brands;
- Interversa (Germany) – main brands included HB, Kim and Krone;
- Souza Cruz (Brazil) – main brands included Minister, Hollywood and Continental.

In addition, BAT's direct factories in the UK and USA produced and exported many of the top brands of the day – Benson & Hedges, John Player, Wills, State Express 555, Pall Mall and Lucky Strike. Its interests in other tobacco products was small in proportion to its cigarette business.

Retail division in the late 1970s

In retailing, BAT owned supermarket chains in the UK, the USA and Brazil. It also operated department stores and fashion shops in the USA and a developing retail interest in Germany.

Its major retail subsidiaries included:

- International Stores (UK) – a chain of 694 supermarkets and self-service stores in England and Wales;
- Gimbel Brothers (USA) – 38 department stores in the New York, Philadelphia, Pittsburgh and Milwaukee areas;
- Kohl Corporation (USA) – 92 supermarkets in Wisconsin and Illinois;
- Saks Fifth Avenue (USA) – 30 high fashion stores in major metropolitan locations throughout the USA;
- Supermercados Peg-Pag SA (Brazil) – 39 stores in or near the major cities of Sao Paolo and Rio de Janeiro.

In addition, BAT had other (less well-known) retail interests in the UK including Homefare, Kearley & Tonge and Ridgeways. BAT purchased Argos in 1979. The relatively new concept of catalogue shopping on the high street was thought to have significant growth potential and upon acquisition, Argos had 91 stores in England and Wales.

Paper division

The Group's paper interests included industrial and printing papers. Subsidiaries in the paper and pulping business (mainly mills and factories) were situated in the UK, Europe, Brazil, India and Africa.

In 1979, the company strengthened its interests in the paper sector with the acquisition of the remaining 50 per cent of Mardon Packaging International from Imperial Group (Mardon had packing and printing operations in Canada, USA, France, Germany, Eire and Zimbabwe).

Cosmetics division

The company's fourth major division, cosmetics, produced perfumes, cosmetics, toiletries and skin care products. Manufacturing of cosmetics took place in 41 countries and the products were sold in 143. The main brands in the cosmetics division included the Houses of Yardley, Lenthéric, Cyclax, Juvena and Morny.

It was during 1976 that Patrick Sheehy, then head of BAT's tobacco division, was appointed as Group deputy chairman. The company employed 148 000 people worldwide, 22 per cent of whom were in the UK, 29 per cent in the USA, 21 per cent in Latin America and 12 per cent in Asia.

Despite the reduction in the company's dependence upon its tobacco interests, BAT strengthened its presence in the US market by acquiring part of Lorillard for US$141 million. The BAT group chairman, Peter Macadam, said that, 'Our faith in the long term opportunities in tobacco has led us to acquire the overseas business of Lorillard'. Lorillard was one of the companies formed by the demerger of the original BAT in 1911.

BAT in the 1980s

Patrick Sheehy acceded to the Group chairmanship in 1982 by which time over 80 per cent of total assets by value were outside the UK. His experience during his career at BAT was primarily in its tobacco business but he had been deputy chairman to Peter Macadam since 1977. Whilst Macadam seemed relatively happy to guide the company as a well-diversified conglomerate, Sheehy felt the need to make some adjustment to the company's portfolio of businesses.

One of Sheehy's first major actions as chairman was to oversee the purchase of the US-based Marshall Field Company for US$368 million. In 1982 at the time of acquisition, Marshall Field operated 18 'full-line' department stores in Chicago and Texas, 24 Ivey's department stores in the Carolinas and Florida, and 15 Frederick & Nelson department stores in the Pacific north western US. The acquisition of Marshall Field also included a 50 per cent share in Chicago's 74 storey Water Tower Place, a retail, hotel and office complex.

In 1982, Patrick Sheehy described the company's approach to its international coverage:

> Geographically, we are well represented in the industrialized parts of the world and also in the more volatile regions where there are greater inherent risks, but where good growth prospects

can be discerned. Both types of area have a place in the Group's development and we will continue to strengthen our businesses and to extend them into new markets.

In his second statement as chairman (in 1983), Sheehy set out his perspective on the company's activities.

Although tobacco profits were significantly affected by difficulties in a number of markets [i.e. in different national markets], the balance was more than made good by the substantial profit increase achieved by our newer businesses.

These 'newer businesses' referred to in 1983 mainly comprised its major acquisition of the previous year. The acquisition of Eagle Star Holdings represented a significant departure from BAT's previous diversification strategy. At the time, the price paid by BAT of £968 million was the largest acquisition ever recorded on the London Stock Exchange. For BAT, the purchase of Eagle Star was the first foray into what Sheehy described as 'a business area which offered on an international scale the growth potential that we needed'. In order to help BAT to manage its new-shape portfolio, two Eagle Star directors joined BAT's main board. At the time of the acquisition, 70 per cent of Eagle Star's premiums came from customers located in the UK and it specialized in general and life insurance. Eagle Star employed 10 000 people, mainly in the UK

During the same year, BAT disposed of Kohl's food stores in the USA. Following the disposal of 12 stores in the Illinois the previous year, the increased competition in the retail sectors in the north eastern United States made Kohl's an unattractive prospect to keep as part of the group. Although proceeds from this partly offset the purchase price of Eagle Star, the major motivation behind the move was probably to begin the refocusing of the group's product and market portfolios.

In the early years of Patrick Sheehy's chairmanship, the company was organized into four main divisions: two manufacturing (tobacco and paper) and two service (retailing and financial services). Despite this, the majority of company sales and profits still came from its extensive interests in tobacco.

In January 1984, the company acquired Hambro Life Assurance for £664 million. The reasoning behind the acquisitions in financial services was made explicit my Mr Sheehy.

These moves [the purchases of Eagle Star and Hambro] secure a major foothold for the Group in a very exciting business area. . . . Together, these acquisitions have made this Group a major force in the fast-growing UK market for financial services, ranking second in terms of combined premium income, and with £9 billion of funds under management. The two companies are complementary. . . . They will operate under their own management and their own identity. Together, they form the new BAT Financial Services operating group.

During the same year, the company increased its shareholding in the German Horten chain of 58 department stores. Other retail investments included a near doubling of the number of Argos outlets from 91 when it was acquired in 1979 to 154 in 1984. The aim of 'national' coverage (in the UK) for Argos was almost completed.

It was decided to divest International Stores and it was sold in 1984 to the Dee Corporation for £180 million. This represented the beginning of a reconfiguration in the

Group's retail strategy. 'We believe that food retailing is a specialist business', remarke[d] Mr Sheehy, 'that does not fit into our long-term plans'. The board came to the sam[e] conclusions with regard to its cosmetics interests. British American Cosmetics was so[ld] to the Beecham Group (which merged to become part of SmithKline Beecham in the la[te] 1980s) for £125 million.

In the tobacco industry, BAT entered into a 'close and profitable' relationship with th[e] Spanish tobacco monopoly as well as developing the business in China (where the messag[e] of the health risks of smoking was less-developed). It became an expressed objective to se[ek] to develop new opportunities for tobacco in markets which had hitherto been the preser[ve] of state-owned national tobacco monopolies. Although Sheehy sought to reduce th[e] group's dependence on the tobacco sector, it remained the most profitable divisio[n]. 'Tobacco will continue for some years to be our major profit earner', Mr Sheehy said [in] 1985. He also noted the opportunities for tobacco sales in countries of the Far East and [in] Europe in countries that had previously been supplied only by a state-owned monopol[y].

Towards the middle of the 1980s, BAT's re-adjustment of its portfolio resulted in fo[ur] main divisions: tobacco, Wiggins Teape Group (an acquisition in 1985 into which the pap[er] division was subsumed), Financial Services and BAT Stores (comprising the non-foo[d] interests of the former retail division). The Financial Services division was significant[ly] strengthened in 1985 by the acquisition of Allied Dunbar and in 1988 by the acquisition [of] the US-based Farmers Insurance Group for £6 billion. The majority of acquisitions ov[er] this period were funded through internal resources (retained profits) and from borrowing[s]. The group expressed its satisfaction that it had not needed to raise new share capital for th[e] investments.

Wiggins Teape, BAT's paper products subsidiary, had principal subsidiaries in the U[K,] Belgium, France, Brazil and India but also operated office and distribution centres in [?] countries worldwide. Its products were marketed in 120 countries in all, making it th[e] largest paper exporter from the UK. In the USA, Wiggins Teape looked after Appleto[n] Papers Inc., which, like Wiggins Teape, produced high grade printing and writing paper [and] carbonless copying paper and its key brands, Conqueror, Orbit and Hi-Speed.

In terms of its geographical coverage, Sheehy said that it was a specific aim of th[e] company to acquire to increase coverage, reporting in 1986 that 80 per cent of turnov[er] and 82 per cent of profit were from activities in industrialized countries whilst the remai[n]-der arose from less developed economies, some of which were in the Third World. By 198[?,] however, this broad-brush approach was reversed and had been replaced with a focus o[n] Europe and North America.

'Our strategy is to concentrate our resources in the regions and activities offering th[e] best prospects', reported Mr Sheehy. 'We believe that our decisions to concentrate o[n] Europe and North America and to invest in financial services have proved to be wi[se] choices'.

Sheehy's strategy seemed to have paid off when the company announced record profi[ts] in 1989. 'Our impressive progress in just five years', Sheehy noted, 'first with Eagle Star an[d] Allied Dunbar and most recently with Farmers, makes it clear that we have acquired quali[ty] businesses with strong management teams. ... We are now the second largest Europea[n] based insurance group. ... The increase in private, rather than state, provision of pensio[ns] and other protection also provides exciting opportunities for expansion worldwide'. (In th[e]

UK, the deregulation of the financial services industry by the Thatcher government in the mid-1980s had created opportunities for pension companies to sell directly to individuals rather than just through corporate and public sector schemes.)

BAT in the 1990s

Despite the good results in 1989, the 1990s began with a major restructuring of BAT's entire business. The major decision was to reduce the Group's focus from four areas (tobacco, paper, retailing and financial services) down to just two (tobacco and financial services). The unwanted parts of the portfolio were disposed of by various means. Argos (the catalogue shop) and Wiggins Teape Appleton (the paper division) were demerged as independent public companies. Other parts were divested to other corporates: Marshall Field packaging, Saks Fifth Avenue, Breuners, Ivey's, Horten, Eurotec and VG Instruments were all sold off for good prices. Part of the capital from the demergers and divestments was used to buy back 55.4 million shares in order to increase the Board's control over strategy and to increase the ordinary shareholders' earnings per share (because the share volume on the stock exchanges was reduced by the buy-back).

At the same time, the company announced a significant increase in its tobacco developments in the Far East and in the (then) newly opened markets of Eastern Europe and the former USSR. Similarly, in financial services, Allied Dunbar announced expansion into Spain and Farmers increased its coverage in North America.

In 1990, Patrick Sheehy defended the company's decision to maintain its focus on the global tobacco markets. 'The dramatic increase in the proportion of the world's cigarette market now open to free enterprise [make these] the most exciting times I have seen in the tobacco industry in the last 40 years'. In the same year it was announced that, 'Following the Group's rapid and successful entry into East Germany', a joint venture had been set up with the leading Hungarian producer, Pecs. This led in 1991 to the acquisition of Pecs and to overtures to potential joint venture partners in Ukraine – the joint venture agreement was signed the following year..

The refocusing of the group onto tobacco as its only manufactured product helped to stimulate a sizeable export growth by volume in both 1991 and 1992 (24 per cent and 23 per cent respectively). Patrick Sheehy, in describing the causes of the increase said, 'With a full range of both US and UK style international brands [of tobacco products], no other company can cater so completely for the different tastes around the world'.

The newly opened markets in Central and Eastern Europe continued to prove attractive to Sheehy in seeking to increase the development of the tobacco side of the business. The Java factory in Moscow was the next acquisition in his sights – one of the largest tobacco producers in Russia. BAT's competitors, most notably Philip Morris Inc., were also developing partnerships and seeking out acquisitions in the former Communist countries of Central and Eastern Europe. During the early 1990s, the opportunities for expansion in the region were many and the two companies competed for joint venture partners and acquisition targets. It is likely that Philip Morris was more successful in this regard than BAT, acquiring as it did former tobacco monopolies in countries throughout the former Soviet bloc.

It was in 1994 that the company made its first reference to a growing new threat. '. . . investors may well feel disturbed by the wave of publicity over recent developments on the litigation front in the US. These are, however, early days and the tobacco industry will ultimately defend itself just as successfully as it always has in the past'. The litigation to which this statement referred was a 'class action' in some US states seeking compensation from the tobacco companies, including BAT, for patients' health problems associated with many years of smoking tobacco. The robust stand that BAT took against the litigants was reflected by its competitors, particularly by Philip Morris.

In the same year, the Los Angeles earthquake precipitated a gross loss for Farmers Insurance of US$1.7 billion, although this was not enough to offset a reasonable profits growth in the group's other sectors.

In 1995, Sir Patrick Sheehy retired and was replaced as Chairman by Earl Cairns. To begin with, the new chairman appeared to continue the strategy followed by Sheehy. Acquisitions of tobacco companies were made in Russia, Ukraine and Uzbekistan and new factories were opened in the Czech Republic and Poland to take advantage of the liberalization of the Eastern European markets. A third of the stock in the Polish Augustoiw factory was purchased in the same year and a joint venture was agreed in Cambodia.

By 1996, the threat of litigation had reached an advanced stage in the USA. Many media commentators were beginning to consider the possibility that the tobacco manufacturers might reach an out-of-court settlement with the claimants and some extraordinarily large figures were being mentioned in reparations. In an attempt to reassure investors, Cairns began his 1996 chairman's statement by saying optimistically that:

> We continue to believe that BAT Industries itself has no potential liability in any US tobacco litigation. This is principally because BAT Industries is a holding company, which supports its operating businesses without managing their affairs. Indeed, this has been confirmed by the three courts that, to date, have considered the issue of jurisdiction . . . There is considerable speculation about the prospects for some kind of settlement to the litigation. The US tobacco industry remains confident of its ability, ultimately, to win cases and has no intention of proposing a settlement. It would, however, be prepared to evaluate proposals from third parties to provide relief from all current and future suits, provided that they were in shareholders' interests.

During 1996, the company issued its proposals for yet another significant restructuring. Whilst it announced its intention to remain in its two strategic businesses (tobacco and financial services), the disparate companies in both divisions were integrated into two umbrella subsidiaries. The tobacco companies were subsumed into the new BAT subsidiary whilst the financial services companies (Allied Dunbar, Farmers, Canada Life, Threadneedle Asset Management and Eagle Star) were subsumed into British American Financial Services. The reason for this reorganization became clear the following year.

It was decided in 1997 to demerge British American Financial Services altogether from the BAT Industries Group. This represented a complete reversal of the strategy pursued under Sheehy and his predecessors in the 1960s and 1970s. BAT Financial Services was demerged and simultaneously merged with Zurich Insurance to form Allied Zurich. Shareholders in the former BAT Industries had their stock commuted into separate holdings in the two companies. Cairns noted that the remainder of the company was the 'only ree-standing investment in the international tobacco sector'. Cairns was alluding to the fact that whilst all of its major competitors were diversified (with interests in a disparate range f businesses), BAT was now a 'tobacco-only' company.

The City and the financial press were quick to suggest a link between the demerger of AT Financial Services and the looming threat of potentially damaging litigation against e major tobacco producers. 'At the time of writing', said Earl Cairns in 1997, 'it is npossible to predict the outcome of the deliberations on tobacco legislation between e Administration and the Congress in the United States. Four major suits have been ttled on terms which are consistent with the proposed legislation and which underline the S tobacco industry's commitment to a comprehensive solution'. The company's earlier ptimism with regard to the tobacco lawsuits appeared to have been misplaced. Many mmentators and the companies themselves began to countenance the possibility that a rge settlement might become necessary.

Following the reorganization, the chief executive Martin Broughton announced that, British American Tobacco's business strategy will be based on organic growth in its isting markets ...'. This approach seemed to draw a line under the Sheehy era which d placed such an importance upon growth through acquisition. Events, however, forced later rethink of this strategy.

The newly-elected Labour government in the UK announced that it planned to ban bacco sponsorship of sporting events and to end all tobacco advertising (i.e. that which as still permitted on billboards and in the press). This proved a difficult promise to fulfil, wever, as many sporting bodies that were reliant on tobacco sponsorship (especially otor racing and snooker) forcefully pleaded for more time to find replacement sponsors. espite this, however, it was clear that such constraints were probably inevitable and the bacco companies, including BAT, sought to prepare for the reduced exposure their oducts would have after the bans were finally implemented.

In November 1998, the cigarette makers in the US finally conceded that their attempt to ave off the litigation threat would not be successful and they collectively struck an out-of-urt deal requiring them to pay, between them, US$206 billion (£124 billion) in settlement tobacco health lawsuits (including BAT's US subsidiary Brown and Williamson) to be yable over several years. Agreement was reached between the major cigarette producers th representatives of the 38 states suing them for the cost of treating smoking-related nesses. In total, 46 states finally agreed to the deal, having been given a fixed time period which to sign up. Most approved the settlement as it included advertising restrictions d other anti-tobacco measures that would not be available through a jury award. The ttlement was a slimmed-down version of a tougher deal announced in June 1997. As part the deal, the tobacco companies agreed to pay US$1.45 billion for anti-smoking mpaigns and US$250 million to cut teenage smoking.

In July 1998, the four largest UK tobacco companies, including BAT, won permission launch a legal challenge to the government plan to place a complete ban on tobacco vertising (and a ban on smoking in public places) on the grounds that the government's ientific Committee on Tobacco and Health had failed to consult the industry before blishing its proposals.

The exasperation of BAT's Board at this and the actions in the USA showed in the 1999 rporate report.

Although the antics of the plaintiff's lawyers in the US seem set to continue, most people elsewhere in the world are prepared to take a common sense approach to smoking. Our own view is that an informed decision to enjoy the pleasures of smoking, while balancing those pleasures against the risks, is no more for criticism than many other lifestyle choices we all make.

On 11 January 1999, it was announced that Rothmans International was to merge wi BAT Industries (now comprising just the tobacco interests of the former group), creatin, combined operation valued at over £13 billion. The deal reinforced BAT's position as t second largest cigarette company in the world (after Philip Morris), giving it an estimat 16 per cent share of the global market. The newly-merged company's volume output w over 900 billion cigarettes a year.

The new chairman of BAT, Martin Broughton, explained the logic of the merger. 'T ... merger with Rothmans is entirely consistent with our strategy, especially as it brings leading positions in more [national] markets, strengthens our share in the premium se ment and provides further significant cost savings. The enlarged British American Tobac will be the clear market leader in the emerging markets, where most of the future growth expected.'

Appendices

Appendix 1. The cigarette and tobacco market by sector (£m and %) 1998

	Value (£m)	% Share
Cigarettes	12 122	94.1
Cigars	351	2.7
Hand-rolling tobacco	323	2.5
Pipe tobacco	90	0.7
Total	12 886	100.0

Source: Key note

Appendix 2. Index of total consumer expenditure and expenditure on cigarettes and tobacco at constant 1995 prices (1995 = 100) 1993–1998

	1993	1994	1995	1996	1997	199
Consumer expenditure	100	103	104	108	113	117
Cigarettes and tobacco	100	98	95	93	90	88

Source: Key note based on Office for National Statistics (ONS) data

Appendix 3. Prevalence of smoking among UK adults (%) 1986–1996

	1986	1988	1990	1992	1994	1996
Men	35	33	31	28	28	29
Women	31	30	29	28	26	28
All adults	33	32	30	28	27	28

Source: Office for National Statistics (ONS)

Appendix 4. The UK cigarette market by value and volume (£m and million pieces) 1993–1998

	1993	1994	1995	1996	1997	1998[a]
Value (£m)	9431	10 021	10 472	10 961	11 555	12 122
Index (1993 = 100)	100	106	111	116	123	129
Volume (million pieces)[b]	90 650	87 250	79 560	81 360	76 855	73 426
Index (1993 = 100)	100	96	88	90	85	81

[a] Key note estimates. [b] UK sales to trade, based on UK manufacturers' sales to the wholesale and retail trade, and estimates of imported goods.
Source: Office for National Statistics (ONS)/Tobacco Manufacturers' Association/Key note.

Appendix 5. Cigarette use by age and by socio-economic group (% of adults) and by rate of usage, 1998

	All users	Heavy users	Medium users	Light users
All adults	28.5	9.4	10.9	8.2
Men	28.0	10.2	9.2	8.5
Women	29.0	8.7	12.5	7.8
Age				
16–24	30.6	5.8	11.7	13.2
25–34	36.3	10.3	14.9	11.1
35–44	31.5	12.5	10.5	8.4
45–54	30.5	13.9	10.6	6.0
55–64	25.2	9.4	10.8	5.0
65+	16.9	4.9	7.0	4.9
Social grade				
AB	16.9	4.8	6.0	6.1
	25.5	7.4	10.2	7.9
	30.9	11.0	11.4	8.5
	36.4	13.2	14.2	9.0
	39.6	13.5	15.5	10.6

All users, smoke cigarettes; heavy users, smoke 20 or more a day; medium users, smoke 10–19 a day; light users, smoke fewer than 10 a day . Source: Target Group Index, © BMRB International 1998.

Appendix 6. BAT Industries plc, turnover and PBIT (1976–1998)

Year (19XX)	Turnover (£ billions)	Profit (before interest and tax, £ billion)
76	5.637	0.430
77	6.212	0.473
78	6.676	0.499
79	7.228	0.525
80	7.645	0.479
81	9.265	0.634
82	11.51	0.783
83	11.85	0.851
84	18.2	1.465
85	16.82	1.288
86	19.17	1.481
87	17.21	1.395
88	17.65	1.604
89	21.64	2.197
90	17.87	1.173
91	16.48	1.183
92	18.7	1.735
93	20.77	1.951
94	21.14	1.928
95	23.38	2.662
96	24.47	2.605
97	24.06	2.248
98	17.38	1.011

Source: BAT Industries annual accounts

Case Study 5

DE LA RUE FORTRONIC

John Ensor

Napier University

Ross McNichol

De La Rue Fortronic in association with the Chartered Institute of Marketing, UK.

Introduction

Fortronic was founded in the late 1970s in Dunfermline, Scotland. For a number of years it traded as an independent company, initially supplying transaction processing equipment to UK banks. It then identified and developed a niche market for electronic funds transfer and point of sale (EFTPOS) equipment and systems in the petrol industry. Further development of these systems subsequently led the company into the Dutch and Scandinavian markets where it became a major supplier.

In 1987, the company was acquired by the De La Rue group, which services the banking and financial industries throughout the world. The De La Rue group operates in over 100 countries, including China, supplying a wide range of products and services from banknotes and credit cards, to entire bank security systems and furnishings.

During the 1990s, De La Rue Fortronic, as it became, expanded in terms of both its markets and products. It opened regional offices abroad to help service the new markets. It also developed new products to support SMART cards and electronic purse systems, and was able to offer a full range of transaction processing services.

As at 1998, the De La Rue group consisted of approximately 50 separate businesses arranged into three divisions: security and print, cash systems and transaction systems. De La Rue Fortronic was part of the transaction systems division and employed over three hundred people organized into four regional offices. These were at Dunfermline and Manchester in the United Kingdom, Frankfurt in Germany and at Hartland, Wisconsin in the United States of America.

The De La Rue Fortronic organization

Dunfermline was the world headquarters and housed the senior management of the company. The sales and marketing staff for all countries were based there except those covered by Germany and the USA. In addition, the majority of the administrative staff and the manufacturing facility were located at Dunfermline. Manchester was the control centre for the UK support organization and co-ordinated all the activities necessary to install and maintain the company's products in the UK.

Both the German and US operations consisted of a sales and marketing function and service organization covering their respective territories. The German office served Germany and Eastern Europe with the US office serving the whole of North America.

At the same time as it increased its international presence, De La Rue Fortronic also expanded its product range. It no longer just supplied EFTPOS equipment to banking and retail environments, although these products and markets accounted for a substantial part of its turnover. The company also added a number of new products and services in the late 1990s, many of which employed new technologies. The new products included state of the art terminals and PIN-Pads incorporating SMART card support and a range of communication options. These new products allowed the company to enter growth markets such as electronic cash, customer loyalty and utilities pre-payment. The company also developed a number of services to complement its products. It offered data gathering and processing options which ranged from simple transaction collection to fully managed payment networks.

In January 1997, a dedicated product management department was set up, based in Dunfermline. This managed the onward development of existing products and co-ordinated all new product development activity across current markets. In addition, it researched potential new markets for the company's existing products and identified new areas of business for the company to exploit.

Almost all of the company's research and development was carried out at Dunfermline. However, some application software work was undertaken by the US and German offices and by certain distributors. Substantial investment in new development tools was made in 1998, mainly the installation of powerful workstations providing an integrated development environment.

The company had a custom-built manufacturing facility at Dunfermline from where it supplied all its current markets. This was converted in the late 1990s from a traditional assembly line to a modern cell manufacturing operation. The efficiency improvements which the changes brought about allowed volumes to increase while maintaining product quality.

The majority of the company's sales were made directly to end customers by its own sales force. However, the company also operated through independent distributors and agents when this was deemed appropriate (varying according to the part of world being serviced by the company).

While the company remained very strong in the UK, it continued to increase the number of overseas markets served. It exported its products and services to many international markets including North America, the Middle East and Europe. As at 1998, however, the UK still accounted for approximately half of all terminal shipments. The UK was also the most diverse market in terms of breadth of products and services supplied. These included terminals for EFT (Electronic Funds Transfer), customer loyalty, pre-payment and electronic purse applications as well as estate management and transaction processing services. The company had 35 per cent of the installed base making it one of the largest suppliers of terminals to this market. In addition, it was the largest supplier of terminals and transaction processing services to the utilities pre-payment sector.

Germany and the Netherlands were the company's largest overseas markets in the late 1990s, between them accounting for one third of total terminal shipments. The Frankfurt sales team sold terminals and PIN-Pads directly to customers in Germany. The majority of these were for EFT applications although there was also some interest in electronic purse systems. De La Rue Fortronic had 35 per cent market share, making it the largest of several suppliers. In the Netherlands, all shipments were to a local distributor that had exclusive sales rights for the country. This distributor took the basic De La Rue Fortronic products and developed software applications locally for its own customers. Like Germany, the majority of the products were for EFT applications although electronic purse and customer loyalty systems were becoming more popular at this time. The company had a dominant position in this market with a 65 per cent market share.

The Scandinavian countries of Norway, Denmark and Sweden accounted for the majority of the remaining terminal shipments. These markets were the responsibility of the UK-based sales team and took terminals and Pin-Pads for EFT applications. The company had been present in these markets for many years and had built up a substantial share of the market. Taking the three countries together, the company had 35 per cent of the installed base making it the single largest equipment supplier.

The North American market proved to be highly competitive and a difficult market to enter. However, 1996 was encouraging with volume shipments starting. Electronic purse terminals were shipped to Canada and both EFT and electronic purse terminals were shipped to the USA. Despite these shipments, the company's share of the vast North American market remained negligible at the date of writing. Of the remaining markets in which De La Rue Fortronic had a presence, its market share was very small.

The industry

The industry was served by a large number of suppliers. The majority of these were small companies that concentrated on their home region, although a number of large companies developed which supplied equipment on a global scale. Many of the smaller companies addressed niche markets, for example portable devices or specialist applications such as customer loyalty. Generally these manufacturers only supplied terminals. Several of the larger companies expanded from domestic market based into global international players and most offered a range of products and services rather than just terminals. De La Rue Fortronic saw their main competitors as follows.

Verifone

Verifone was the largest supplier in the industry with an installed base of nearly 5 million terminals, almost half of the world's total. In 1995 it shipped over 790 000 terminals, which was an increase of 13 per cent on the previous year. Two thirds of its revenue came from its domestic market, the USA. It had an installed base of approximately 206 000 terminals in the Asia/Pacific region. The company's main manufacturing facility was in Taiwan; however, it opened a new factory in China in the late 1990s where it claimed to have established a 30 per cent share of the market.

On the face of it, Verifone's strategy appeared to be one aimed to develop a presence in every national market. It was seen as having a production orientated philosophy whereby it developed new products which it then took to the market. It was sometimes perceived as having a 'take it or leave it' attitude especially towards smaller customers.

The company's sheer size meant that it could offer lower per unit prices and a wide range of supporting products and services. It was believed to be heavily involved in developing new products for electronic purse and internet commerce applications. It had joint ventures with, among others, Microsoft and Gemplus – a major SMART card manufacturer.

Hypercom

Hypercom was large and was also the fastest growing supplier of terminals. It had an installed base of 1.1 million terminals worldwide, one third of which were in Asia/Pacific. In 1995 the company increased its share of the US market by 4 per cent at the expense of market leader Verifone. During this period it shipped almost 300 000 terminals worldwide, half of which went to North America. The company operated manufacturing facilities in the USA, Australia, Brazil and Hong Kong. It was also active in China, with an office in Beijing, and claimed to have a 40 per cent of the Chinese market.

Hypercom's strategy appeared to be one of developing high specification, high quality products which addressed actual market requirements. The company offered a five-year warranty on its terminals compared to a 13-month warranty from Verifone. As well as terminals, the company offered PIN-Pads, network hardware and software and a terminal management system. Its product range was a significant strength in the past and had contributed to its rapid growth. A major weakness, however, was that the company had little SMART card or electronic purse experience. It was thought that this weakness might impede its efforts to enter the highly competitive European market and cause it problems in the Asia/Pacific market.

Ingenico

Ingenico was the largest European competitor and was based in France. It had an installed base of 400 000 units in Europe. It shipped over 110 000 terminals in 1995, 70 per cent of which went to Europe with most of the remainder going to the Asia/Pacific market. It had traditionally been strong in Australia and used this as a base to move into the economies of the Pacific rim where it had built up an installed base of some 68 000 terminals as at the case date. Although it opened an office in China, market share was tiny.

The company grew through acquisition and in the late 1990s, it bought Innovation Data Systems and EPOS of Germany. A particular strength was its experience with SMART card applications, having sold over 200 000 SMART card terminals. It was also strong in portable terminals and had considerable experience of radio communications. Ingenico was heavily reliant on Europe which was the most competitive market in the world and it lost some market share in Europe during 1995. With Hypercom having entered the European market, Ingenico became subject to even more competition in its home market.

Schlumberger/Diebold

Schlumberger, a European conglomerate involved in a number of industries, had an installed base of 350 000 terminals in Europe and was one of the biggest suppliers in France. In 1995 it shipped a total of 93 000 terminals, 70 per cent of which went to Europe. It was the largest supplier of terminals to the Middle East and Africa, shipping 15 000 units, a quarter of the regional total.

The company joined with Diebold, an American company, as part of its strategy for expansion. It hoped to use the partnership to enter the US market but early signs were not very promising, shipping only 10 000 terminals in 1995. It did not appear to have any plans to move into the Chinese or Asia/Pacific market.

The company had considerable SMART card experience since it was also a major supplier of SMART cards. This allowed it to offer a complete package to its customers, something most suppliers of terminals were unable to do. As at 1998, the company was heavily reliant on Europe but was attempting to enter the US market. In this regard, it was lagging behind both Europe and Asia/Pacific in the use of SMART cards.

Industry products

By 1998, there were a large number of developments under way in the industry. The most important of these were based on SMART cards and fell into three broad categories: SMART payment; electronic purse; and customer loyalty schemes. Regionally, Europe and Asia/Pacific led the way. The prime motivations in Europe were the banks' desire to combat fraud and reduce the cost of handling cash. In Asia/Pacific the developments were driven by direct government promotion of a SMART card infrastructure, coupled with the active exploitation by the banks of customer loyalty applications on credit/debit cards.

Magnetic stripe cards

Magnetic stripes are the common type of card used throughout the world. They most typically take the form of a black stripe on a credit or charge card. These cards are read by a Point of Sale (POS) machine. Information of all the transactions that have taken place during the day are polled (sent over the telephone line) back to a mainframe computer that updates the information into the customer's account. These cards cost about eight or nine pence each (sterling). This system only allows information to be read from the card.

SMART payment

SMART payment systems are seen as the successors to the magnetic stripe based credit and debit cards. The SMART card contains a microchip. This allows the cards to carry much more information. It not only means information can be read off the card, but additional information can be written down to the card during a transaction. The SMART card microchip can contain all the account details which the magnetic stripe cards have, along with additional security information which makes fraud more difficult. These cards are much more sophisticated than the magnetic stripe cards. They can also be encrypted, which means a password can be changed on the card after every transaction. They are considerably more expensive than magnetic stripe cards, and cost between one and five pounds (sterling) a card.

The advantage over the magnetic stripe is that information does not need to be polled back to a mainframe computer to update the customer's account. To give an example that illustrates the point: if a customer is using a SMART card for a customer loyalty scheme, points can be added directly to the card as purchases are made.

Europay, MasterCard and Visa co-operated in the development of an international standard for SMART card systems used for financial transactions. This standard, known as EMV, was implemented in cards and terminals which were deployed in a major trial in the UK in 1998.

A number of SMART payment scheme were already running in the Asia/Pacific region whilst the EMV trials were beginning. The Compass Visa card in Hong Kong claimed to be the world's first EMV-compatible credit card. The Loyalty Club card was a SMART credit card which was acceptable in Hong Kong, Singapore and Taiwan, while co-branded SMART Visa and MasterCards were issued by the Development Bank of Singapore. All of these schemes incorporated some form of customer loyalty application on the card as a value-added feature.

In China, the major development in the industry was the Gold Card project. This aimed to create a nationwide card authorization network by linking up various independent systems. SMART card technology is a fundamental part of this project.

SMART card technology led on to two further developments.

Electronic purse

An electronic purse system allows a cash value to be loaded onto a SMART card at a terminal. Subsequently, some of this value can be transferred from the card in payment for goods or services in a retail outlet. The card effectively becomes cash. If a customer has loaded £10 onto the card and then loses it, the customer has lost the £10 in the same way that he or she would if it were 'real' cash. The benefits, however, are that individuals do not have to carry pockets full of small coins. This could be especially beneficial if the system is installed on public transport systems or parking meters. Retail outlets do not have to take cash down to the bank every day, buses do not have to carry cash, and parking meters do not have to be emptied.

In the late 1990s, a number of independent electronic purse schemes began operating, the majority of them in Europe. However, these were generally incompatible with one another and a number of initiatives were begun that sought to produce globally-standardized schemes. The most prominent of the independent schemes were Mondex and VisaCash, both of which ran multiple large-scale pilots at the end of the 1990s.

Mondex was launched in the UK in 1995 and in Canada in 1996. VisaCash was launched in the USA at the Atlanta Olympics, where many sporting venues accepted only electronic cash for refreshments, souvenirs, etc. A UK pilot was launched in 1998. The schemes operated head-to-head in Hong Kong where 100 000 VisaCash and 40 000 Mondex cards were issued.

As at 1998, there were 17 electronic purse schemes operating in Europe, the majority of which were at the pilot stage. The participating banks claimed to have issued a total of 35 million cards by 1998. The longest running scheme, Danmont, was launched in Denmark in 1992. The largest was the GeldKarte scheme which was launched in 1998 in Germany. GeldKarte aimed to issue 20 million cards which could be used at 25 000 acceptance points.

European banks saw the electronic purse as a replacement for cash in small to medium sized retailers and at unattended points such as vending machines, public telephones and car parks. These markets were been identified by banks in the Asia/Pacific region. The Cash Card scheme was launched in Singapore in November 1996 with the cards being accepted in retail outlets, post offices and at vending machines. Approximately 250 000 transactions a month were paid for with these cards. The largest and most successful electronic purse application in the world was the Bus Card scheme in South Korea. This was launched by Seoul Bus in 1995 and 2.7 million cards had been issued by 1998. These were 1.9 million transactions made each day using Bus Card, one third of all bus journeys.

Customer loyalty schemes

Customer loyalty programmes were becoming increasingly popular as companies attempted to reward customers who gave them repeat business. As the cost of finding new customers is higher than gaining repeat business from an existing customer, this is often a sensible business decision. As at the case date, SMART cards were increasingly being used in this area and were proving to be very successful. In Europe, the Shell SMART scheme issued more than 4 million cards in the UK and then expanded into France. In Japan, 10 million cards were issued by the oil company Idemitsu Kosan for its Mydo scheme. Banks in the Asia/Pacific region saw customer loyalty as a powerful tool to increase their credit/debit card business, and the region became the biggest user of SMART cards for customer loyalty.

Appendices

Appendix 1. DLRF terminal shipments by country (1993–96)

Region	Percentage of total shipments
UK	47.3
Netherlands	24.1
Germany	14.4
Norway	6.2
Sweden	2.8
Denmark	1.6
Others	3.6

Source: DLRF terminal shipment analyses

Appendix 2. Terminal manufacturer data (by market share, 1998)

Territory	Verifone	Hypercom	DLRF	IVI	Ingenico	Telesinc	Others
China	30	40					30
Spain						45	55
France					40		60
Hong Kong	5	20					75
Japan	20	20					60
UK	10		35				55
Germany	20		35				45
Canada	20			60			20
Australia/New Zealand	10	25	10		10		45
India	40	20					40
Italy	10						90
Pacific Rim	40	30					30
Scandinavia	10		35		10	10	35
South Africa	25						75
Russia/Eastern Europe	30				10		60
Netherlands	20		65				15

Source: De La Rue Fortronic Research

Appendix 3. USA terminal market shares

Company	Market share (%)
Verifone	46
Hypercom	24
IVI	13
NBS	7
Datacard	7
Others	3

Source: Credit Card Management, April 1996

Appendix 4. Total terminal shipments by manufacturer, 1995

Manufacturer	Number of terminals
Verifone	790 562
Hypercom	293 550
Ingenico	110 400
Dassault	106 000
IVI	100 500
Schlumberger	93 000
Bull	80 000
De La Rue Fortronic	52 062
Dione	48 600
NBS Technologies	38 300
Others	350 580
Total	**2 063 554**

Source: The Nilson Report, October 1996

Appendix 5. Terminal shipments to North America by manufacturer, 1995

Manufacturer	Number of terminals
Verifone	523 528
Hypercom	153 750
IVI	96 000
Datacard	28 650
Checkmate	25 000
Atalla	14 500
Lipman	11 000
Schlumberger	10 000
Penware	9000
Others	52 600
Total	**924 028**

Source: The Nilson Report, October 1996

Appendix 6. Terminal shipments to Europe by manufacturer, 1995

Manufacturer	Number of terminals
Verifone	102 970
Dassault	75 000
Ingenico	74 800
Bull	70 000
Schlumberger	65 000
De La Rue Fortronic	51 000
Dione	40 000
G&D	27 000
Racal	23 250
Others	83 850
Total	**612 870**

Source: The Nilson Report, October 1996

Appendix 7. Terminal shipments to Latin America by manufacturer, 1995

Manufacturer	Number of terminals
Hypercom	82 500
Verifone	67 340
Dassault	10 000
Bull	5000
Ingenico	1600
Others	6600
Total	**173 040**

Source: The Nilson Report, October 1996

Appendix 8. Terminal shipments to Asia/Pacific by manufacturer, 1995

Manufacturer	Number of terminals
Verifone	85 724
Hypercom	55 300
Ingenico	30 000
Panasonic	16 800
Goldstar	15 500
Omron	15 100
NTT Data	9000
Intellect	7800
Dassault	6000
Others	47 270
Total	**288 494**

Source: The Nilson Report, October 1996

Appendix 9. Terminal shipments to Middle East/Africa by manufacturer, 1995

Manufacturer	Number of terminals
Schlumberger	15 000
Verifone	11 000
Dassault	10 000
Dione	8600
Racal	4200
Ingenico	4000
IVI	4000
Lipman	4000
Ascom	1500
De La Rue Fortronic	1062
Hypercom	1000
Others	760
Total	**65 122**

Source: The Nilson Report, October 1996

Appendix 10. Market sizes at at 1998 (thousands of terminals)

Territory	Market size
USA	6700
China	600
Spain	300
France	292
Hong Kong	270
Japan	230
UK	215
Germany	196
Canada	168
Australia/New Zealand	147
Pacific Rim	53
Scandinavia	48
Russia/Eastern Europe	32
Netherlands	28

Source: De La Rue Fortronic Research

Appendix 11. Growth in the world market for POS terminals (thousands of terminals). Includes projections

Year	Installed base at year end
1995	10 297
1996	11 193
1997	12 312
1998	13 543
1999	14 897
2000	16 387
2001	18 026

Source: De La Rue Fortronic Research

Appendix 12. Total world shipments of POS terminals (all suppliers: thousands of terminals). Includes projections

Year	Annual shipments
1995	2063
1996	2239
1997	2462
1998	2709
1999	2979
2000	3277
2001	3605

Source: De La Rue Fortronic Research

Appendix 13. A commentary on new and existing products from De La Rue Fortronic. (March 1998)

Overall 'lifetime cost' is recognized by De La Rue Fortronic as a critical customer issue. To address this, the company produces systems and tools which are flexible enough to suit any retailer environment as well as being adaptable enough to accommodate future requirements. The after-sales service and support packages including their unique Estate Management System (which provides configuration and software download, and handles unit replacement logistics) coupled with their Fault Identification Tool, complement a wide range of service and support options.

The product range

Eclipse TT41
The Eclipse TT41 is regarded by DLRF as a revolutionary product, which handles debit card, credit card and EMV (Europay, MasterCard and Visa), standard SMART cards as well as multiple SMART card applications including electronic purse, loyalty and pre-payment schemes.

It is described by the company as the most powerful and cost effective terminal of its kind, the Eclipse TT41 provides the flexibility to accommodate a range of printer options, multiple purses and applications. This, combined with De La Rue Fortronic's unique Estate Management System and Fault Identification Tool, ensures that users can minimize the total cost of ownership.

DLRF confidently expect the Eclipse TT41 to be the definitive transaction terminal for many years to come. Its built-in flexibility and practical modular design makes it a very cost effective product with the capability to accommodate a range of add-on devices without the need to replace the base unit. In fact, they have so much confidence in their technology that each terminal comes with a five year warranty.

Equinox EP41

The EP41 is a very recent product which has been designed by DLRF as a new generation PIN-Pad. Building on the Mondex and VisaCash developments, the new Equinox EP41 is regarded by the company as the definitive Purse Terminal. It can handle a range of electronic purse applications including Mondex, VisaCash, GeldKarte, ChipKnip and Proton. The Equinox EP41 removes the cash value from the customer's SMART card without requiring authorization or signature, making it quick and convenient for customers and staff. The terminal can be configured to handle the entire range of electronic purse applications.

Note: Clarification on the use of PIN-Pads.

There are two main ways a cardholder can verify a purchase.

1. By signature.
2. By use of a Personal Identification Number (PIN).

In the UK most credit and debit card transactions are verified by a customer signature. PINs are usually only required when a card holder requires cash from a bank cash machine.

In other markets, for instance Germany, the cardholder verification is done by means of a PIN. A PIN-Pad is a security device which is attached to a credit card terminal and allows the cardholder to enter their PIN without anyone else getting access to it. These units typically have encryption software, security keys, and physical, anti-tamper hardware to ensure the integrity of the system.

F95 Micropos EFTPOS Terminal

The Micropos is designed for retailers who have no previous experience of an electronic card payment terminal. It is a self install, fully programmable EFTPOS terminal with the built-in flexibility to connect to a wide range of peripheral equipment. Its ease-of-use provides immediate benefits for retailers across a wide range of sectors.

The terminal processes all major debit, credit, store charge and SMART cards. It excels at automating card transactions at the point of sales, reduces fraud and speeds up the payment process.

F105 Electronic Purse Terminal

The F105 Electronic Purse Terminal can be adapted to support various forms of cashless payment, including Mondex and Visa Cash.

It can operate as an off-line terminal, automatically transferring the required cash value from a customer SMART card to a retailer SMART card stored within the terminal. The transaction is completed without requiring authorization or signature, making it an ideal solution for staff and customers.

The terminal can also include a modem for onward transmission of the value of any transactions to the bank host. Either way, it offers sophisticated software for transaction management, management reporting and supervisory function, in a secure user-friendly manner.

Tripos – Internet Payment Solutions

Tripos is a set of Internet payment solutions from De La Rue which provides small merchants with a simple, hassle free route to the opportunities of electronic commerce.

The first part of the tripos solution is a Payment Server which is housed in a separate secure location, on a high performance UNIX workstation. This payment server can be utilized on thousands of web sites and once shoppers have selected their purchase, it will generate a payment options page. Card details entered by the shopper are then collected by the payment server.

The second stage is the Message server, which will establish a communication link with the terminal installed in the merchant's premises. Order details can then be sent automatically to the retailer's terminal or alternatively, the merchant can choose to poll his web site at pre-determined frequency, in order to download transactions to the in-store terminal. The final component is the Dispatch Trigger Mechanism. The purchasing cycle is completed when details of the transaction are communicated to the merchant's site. De La Rue has enhanced its new Eclipse TT41 transaction terminal to allow it to accept order details via the Internet, thus turning the merchant's everyday transaction terminal into an 'e-commerce' capable system. The Eclipse TT41 will print out the customer's name, address and details of the customer's order ready for dispatch.

Estate management

De La Rue Fortronic can provide an estate management service taking the problems of terminal ownership away from banks or retailers. The company can take care of Configuration Management, new Application Download, Unit Replacement Logistics and Fault Finding (using the Fault Identification Tool).

Pre-payment systems

One of the biggest growth areas for De La Rue Fortronic is fully managed payment services. Working with utilities such as Hyder, Scottish Power and Hydro-electric, DLRF can offer a complete turnkey service to utility companies in the UK. The company also operates a fully managed payment service taking responsibility for all aspects of the payment system from selection of payment points to full financial reporting.

The installation of over 2000 SMART card based pre-payment systems throughout the utility industries in the UK allows customers to purchase a value amount of electricity, water or gas which is loaded onto the customer's SMART card by the DLRF terminal. Details of the transaction are then stored for onward submission to the utility company. The customer then inserts his SMART card into the meter at home where the value of units purchased is transferred into the meter along with any other relevant information.

Customer loyalty schemes

De La Rue Fortronic has considerable experience in large, long-term multi-partner loyalty schemes, most notably Shell SMART. To date, the company has managed the installation of almost 3000 loyalty and payment terminals and designed and developed the core loyalty software and scheme security.

As part of the total service commitment, De La Rue Fortronic has also sourced the manufacture and personalization of over 4 million chip cards and managed the operational interface to other suppliers. The company continues to support existing and incoming manufacturers, host systems and data management suppliers.

The Shell SMART scheme is recognized as one of the largest electronic points collection schemes in the world. In addition, De La Rue Fortronic has recently reached agreement with Air Miles (British Airways loyalty scheme) to provide transaction terminals to support their Air Miles Dining Programme. Key involvement in such schemes firmly positions the company as a leading supplier in the customer loyalty market.

Appendix 14. Interview with Mike Keegan, chief executive of Mondex

Mike Keegan, CEO of Mondex, was interviewed on a programme called *Strategies for ftvision* introduced by Nigel Roberts. Key points he made:

- SMART card chips have the potential to carry retina images or fingerprint images as a security check;
- most SMART cards won't work with each other. Software doesn't work with each other, there is no common standard;
- consumers could load electronic cash onto their card either at a cash dispenser or via a phone at home. They would need an adapter on their phone with an LCD display. They could phone the bank, give them a PIN code and then access their account. Currently Chase Manhattan have a limit of $200 on their card. NatWest and Midland banks in the UK have a limit of £500;
- mondex are aiming to replace low value cash purchases, newspapers etc.;
- there is convergence between certain industry sectors: Telecoms, Banks, Post Office, and Retailing. Boundaries are blurring between them;
- one advantage of Mondex purchases are that merchants transfer that value to the terminal. The terminal can then send that to the bank for same day banking, improving cash flow and lowering costs;
- the credit card market is mature. MasterCard for instance has issued 400 million cards. The growth currently is in debit cards. Mondex will grow;
- Africa and Asia 'can perform a technology leapfrog', do not need to invest and develop payment systems such as the cheque clearing system etc. 'Retail Banking can be built on the telephone network rather than building bank outlets'.

N   RPORATED

George .

University ι   ιmbria

Company development

In 1998, with sales exceeding US$9 billion and a market share of 33 per cent, Nike was the brand leader in the global training shoe market. These figures represented an increase of 5 per cent compared to its market share figure of 28 per cent in 1995. This figure of 28 per cent was 10 percentage points ahead of Reebok's 18 per cent share and was more than double that of Adidas's 11 per cent share. Nike faced continued competition from Reebok, and also faced increased competition from a revived Adidas. Nevertheless, Nike remained the market leader and its 'swoosh' trademark was the most recognized in the industry ahead of the famous three stripes of Adidas.

Since its foundation by Phil Knight, Nike's record of growth has been strong. For the first 10 years of its history, its sales grew at an average rate of 82 per cent a year whilst its profits doubled every year. Accordingly, by 1980 it had overtaken Adidas as the largest seller of sports shoes in the USA. The 1980s and early 1990s saw the internationalization of Nike and by 1993, 20 per cent of sales were outside the USA, mainly in Europe where Nike held the largest market share at 20 per cent ahead of Reebok (17 per cent) and Adidas (16 per cent). Sales in the Far East also increased so that by 1996, Nike had a 12 per cent share of the Japanese market while Nike products also became widely available in the former Soviet Union. Nike was very much an American brand which became global.

Nike began life as Blue Ribbon Sports in 1957 selling cheap, but technically advanced, running shoes out of the back of a van. The company's founders, Phil Knight and Bill Bowerman, met at the University of Oregon where Knight was a student and moderate middle-distance athlete and Bowerman was his coach. Bowerman had developed the practice of modifying his athlete's shoes because he felt the original products were poorly designed. Knight capitalized on this idea and developed a business plan while at Stanford Business School, deciding that rather than manufacturing his own product, he would buy and market Japanese-made running shoes. This was a particularly bold idea as, at the time, Japanese products had a reputation for poor quality.

The Nike product concept

The brand name Nike was launched in 1972 at the US Olympic track and field trials where Knight and Bowerman sold running shoes targeted at serious athletes. The name Nike was taken from that of the Greek goddess of victory and the 'swoosh' trademark was introduced as a symbol of speed and the achievement of excellence. Initially, success came slowly but when in the mid-1970s Nike invented the impact-absorbing sole, there followed a sizeable increase in sales among both serious athletes and joggers. It was this development which allowed Nike to replace Adidas as the number one sports shoe company in the USA by 1980.

Since this time product design and development has remained at the heart of Nike's competitive strategy. Large sums are spent on developing materials which will wear for longer and absorb the damaging impacts of sporting activity on the body. The original concept of the impact-absorbing sole was further enhanced with the development of the Air principle based on a sole and heel which incorporated an air cushion. Although the benefits of this system may be questioned, it quickly became very popular with athletes and with fashion conscious youth.

Product design and development takes place at Nike's headquarters in Portland, Oregon, on the 75-acre *World Campus*. So well known is Nike's trademark that there is no name plate on the entrance to the Campus. A red swoosh is the only sign identifying the site's occupants. The swoosh also appears on the door handles and is even engraved into the after-dinner chocolates served in the executive restaurant! There are 2500 employees on site working primarily in R&D and marketing. Nike is reported to take good care of the workforce at its headquarters which features state of the art sports facilities, lakes, woods, restaurants, a hairdresser, a cobbler, a cash point and a nursery for employee's children. So strong is the loyalty to the company that some employees have a swoosh tattooed on their body.

Nike has always regarded itself as a business run by athletes for athletes. For this reason, product development has always been regarded as vital. Teams of designers work in informal and picturesque surroundings to develop new concepts to keep the company ahead of its rivals. There are laboratories and test tracks to test out new products. The product range expanded from running shoes into a range of high performance sports shoes covering most sporting activities. In addition to shoes, it began to produce a full range of sports apparel including shorts, T shirts, tracksuits etc. As the training shoe and sports apparel became fashion items, sales of all these products quickly expanded. More importantly, Nike accepted that the training shoe market has matured and embarked 'on a strategy to transform itself from a shoemaker into a global sports and fitness company' (*International Business Week*, 17 June 1996).

Nike is proud of its claim to be the technological leader in the industry. Continuous product development is considered necessary because Knight believes that there are seven-year brand cycles in the industry. Accordingly, Nike continuously innovates to stay ahead. Nike's success followed that of Converse and Adidas. It has not always been plain sailing, and Nike lost direction in the mid-1980s when Reebok took over from Nike as market leader in 1986. This was seen as the height of the crisis. It was this that galvanized Nike into action and led to the launch of the Air Jordan range of products linking 'shoes, colours, clothes, athlete, logo and television advertising' (Katz 1993). Such is Nike's commitment to research and development that some commentators have suggested that trainers could eventually measure the runner's pulse when running and cool the feet at the same time. *The Independent* newspaper (25 June 1996) reported that 'it is Nike's designs that are the most sought after by trainer connoisseurs'.

Vertical linkages and outsourcing

Although Nike briefly flirted with the idea of manufacturing its own products, it quickly realized that the main source of its competitive advantage lay in the design, development, marketing and distribution of sport apparel, rather than in manufacture. The products are manufactured more cheaply and to a higher quality standard in countries other than the USA. Once a new product has been designed and developed in Portland then its manufacture is outsourced to countries like Taiwan, China and Brazil (Appendix 1). Nike imposes stringent quality control standards on its manufacturers. Nevertheless Nike, Adidas and Reebok have come in for criticism of the allegedly low wages paid to workers in the factories producing their shoes, particularly when these are compared to the sums paid to the athletes promoting these products. This was highlighted by a report completed by Christian Aid which drew attention to 'the plight of many of the workers in these subcontracting factories. Its survey of conditions for workers in China, the Philippines and Thailand found that discrimination against trade unions, forced overtime, poor health and safety provision, and low wages were recurring problems' (*Ethical Consumer*, 1 February 1996). In response, Nike pointed to the fact that the wages in the factories were well above average earnings in other occupations in the same countries and that it insisted upon health care programmes for workers in its factories.

Nike also carefully vets the retailers that are allowed to sell its products. Not only are retailers checked for creditworthiness, but also for their expertise in sportswear. This is because Nike values its reputation as an authentic sportswear company and believe that retailers must be able to advise knowledgeably on Nike products. This expertise is felt necessary to strengthen the Nike brand image. Nike is valued by retailers not only because its products are popular among consumers but also because of the service that Nike provides to the retailers. Nike representatives have computers which provide information on the entire range of Nike products and the advertising campaigns that support them. Although Nike products command a premium price, a 'generous' proportion of this premium price goes to the retailer as well as to Nike itself. This is designed to encourage retailers to promote Nike products over other brands. Retailers also benefit from Nike's association with top athletes and the large-scale advertising campaigns to promote the products.

In recent years Nike has ventured into retailing itself. It opened a number of Nike Town Stores throughout the USA. There are a growing number of such superstores which sell Nike products exclusively. Those in Chicago and New York bear a strong resemblance to theme parks. They are heavily decorated with sports memorabilia and feature video walls showing famous sports events with pre-recorded crowd noises. These stores are devoted to Nike products and are based on the twin themes of Nike's history and that of its athletes. They include high technology and feature Nike's Ngage laser machine which not only measures the size of a customer's foot to the nearest millimetre but also indicates which

Nike products would be most suitable for the foot size. Nike Town Stores have expanded beyond the USA. London was the site of the first European branch. Nike Town Stores are regarded as the 'temples' of the business and are 'shrines' to its products. As Nike extended its product range and entered new market segments, influence over the retailing of its products was seen as vital to preservation of the reputation of the brand.

Promotions and endorsements

Marketing, promotion and brand name are as important to Nike's success as are product development and quality. Nike signed a number of top athletes to endorse and promote its products. In the USA, Michael Jordan is the supreme example of a Nike athlete but other top names like John McEnroe and Andre Agassi are also endorsees. In Europe, footballers Ian Rush and Eric Cantona were among those signed by Nike. Such athletes are paid substantial sums to wear and promote Nike products. This approach has shown some signs of success as, in the USA, 265 out of 320 NBA players wear Nike shoes. A sign of the loyalty of Nike's athletes, or perhaps of the sums of money paid to them, is illustrated by an incident at the Barcelona Olympics when Nike-endorsed athletes refused to wear Reebok shoes (the official shoes of the USA team) when they went to collect their medals. It is also interesting to note that Nike did not seek out the most 'clean cut' athletes but tended to opt for controversial characters like McEnroe and Cantona who, Nike believed, would generate more interest in its products, particularly among young people. There is evidence to support this view – Nike's UK advertisements were found to be the most popular among the key age range of seven- to sixteen-year-olds.

As well as endorsements from athletes, Nike used slogans and television advertising to enhance its brand identity. The best known of its advertising campaigns is the 'Just do it' slogan and more recently, 'Think global – dunk local'. The company spends substantial sums on television and other media advertising, and Nike's campaigns often generate controversy. The campaign timed to coincide with the Euro 96 football championships showed Eric Cantona leading a team of humans to victory over a team of demonic monsters. The evidence suggests that the controversy generated as much publicity for Nike as the campaign itself. A survey by BMRB suggested that many people believed that Nike was an official sponsor of Euro 96 when it was not. This is a convincing demonstration of the success of Nike's publicity machine.

In 1996 Nike launched a new campaign based around its top athletes using the Iggy Pop song *Search and destroy* while in 1998, it sponsored Ronaldo and Brazil in their World Cup campaign. Once again Nike was perceived as sponsors of the tournament in France when, in fact, it was not but arch rivals Adidas were. In the late 1990s, Nike sponsored such personalities as Tiger Woods, Michael Schumacher and Pete Sampras. In 1997, the company spent $5.6 billion on marketing and $4 billion on individual sponsorships. Michael Jordan alone was paid $70 million. *strength*

Markets and structure

Saturation of the US market was a major factor in stimulating Nike's expansion overseas. Nike's internationalization into Europe initially entailed the establishment of virtually autonomous subsidiaries. Each subsidiary had marketing, sales, distribution, IT and accounting functions. Each subsidiary also had a warehouse from which Nike products, obtained from factories mainly in Asia, were distributed to retailers throughout the country in question. Products offered to retailers varied from country to country and there was considerable variation in operational strategies between countries.

In the 1990s, however, the company brought in control procedures that allowed for much greater central control from the USA of both strategy and operations. At the same time, greater centralization of activities within Europe itself was introduced, reflecting the increasing similarity of the markets in which Nike operated. The company aimed to reduce the number of European distribution warehouses from 32 in 1994 to 5 by 1997, with European headquarters in the Netherlands and a main distribution warehouse in Belgium. Product ranges were also more standardized as were advertising and promotion. It is interesting to note, however, that there were still variations between the product ranges offered in Europe and the USA and to some extent between the advertising and promotional campaigns. These differences reflected differences in the popularity of different sports between Europe, where soccer is the number one sport, and America, where it is still a minority game. There were also differences in the athletes signed to endorse Nike's products reflecting the popularity of different athletes within Europe as compared to the USA.

Changes in the 1990s

It has not always been plain sailing and in 1997, Nike issued two poor profit warnings and made 1000 redundancies among US employees. This downturn had a number of causes. There was evidence of a shift in demand away from training shoes to 'brown shoe goods'. These hybrid walking/training shoes were manufactured by companies like Caterpillar, Timberland and Rockport. Rockport had a turnover of $500m in 1997 and, ironically, was owned by Reebok, which had lost the training shoe wars with Nike. There was also evidence that the sports apparel and training shoe markets had also become saturated.

Accordingly, Nike found itself with large quantities of unsold stock with the inevitable consequence that stock had to be sold at heavily discounted prices. To make matters worse, sales of Nike products on the 'grey market' increased. Tesco began to import Nike shoes into the UK to sell them at a reduced rate. Its advertisements added insult to injury for Nike by parodying Nike's 'Just do it' slogan with 'Just do it for less'.

Nike's troubles were exacerbated by economic problems in Asia where the majority of Nike's products were manufactured. There had been some bad publicity surrounding the conditions of employment of the workers employed by factories producing goods for Nike in the Asian region. There were claims that employees, including children, were forced to work for up to 14 hours a day for subsistence wages. Moreover, there were reports that workers suffered beatings at the hands of their employers. 'Anti-Nike' groups referred to 'The curse of the swooshstika'. These reports severely damaged Nike's image among young and middle-aged people who had become increasingly concerned about allegations of exploitation in the Third World.

The problems were not all of external origin. The size of the company had begun to cause communication problems and there was some evidence of low morale. Many employees felt that they had little say in the running of the business and felt that they had become remote from its management. There was also some evidence that Nike's American managers interfered rather too much in the running of the business in other parts of the world, particularly in Europe. For example, when Nike installed its new information systems in Europe, its American managers took over the project because they were unhappy with the progress being made by their European counterparts.

Nike at the end of the 1990s

Despite these problems, Nike had regained its market leadership by the turn of the millennium. Its swoosh logo ranked alongside the red can of Coca Cola and the twin arches of McDonald's as the three most globally recognized logos. In fact, so well recognized was the logo that Nike sometimes used its logo without the name itself. It became perceived as the most fashionable sportswear company in the world.

The threat from Adidas increased in the late 1990s particularly when Mel C of the Spice Girls regularly appeared wearing Adidas products. Nike was seemingly taken by surprise and reacted relatively slowly. Nevertheless, Nike reacted to this challenge and to the other threats to its business. The company lost a little of what some observers perceived as its arrogance and it made attempts to recultivate its workforce's goodwill. Nike also sought to improve the working conditions of workers in Asia and began to exert far greater control over its suppliers, forcing them to become model employers in their regions.

Nike once more became highly design-oriented and took advantage of the blurring between the markets for sportswear and fashion wear. It became successful in the growing fashion market which is no longer confined to those below 30 years of age. So strong is the Nike name that Americans often refer to their 'Nikes' rather than their training shoes. There are both advantages and dangers associated with Nike's entry into the fashion market. The market is characterized by the built-in obsolescence of its products. This has _Weakness_ the advantage that new products can regularly be designed and sold at higher prices, and that competition is more based upon design and brand than on price. The danger arises from the fact that fashion changes rapidly and a brand can become unfashionable very quickly at the same time as the development costs of new products are high.

Perhaps to counteract this problem, Nike sought to regain its association with its grass-roots athletes by introducing the Alpha range which represented the most scientifically designed and high tech of its products centred on the new Air Zoom Citizen trainer. Nike even changed its logo for these products. Alongside the swoosh were five circles to denote excellence of performance. This symbolized a return to the core values of the business which has always represented itself as the athlete's company. There was also a softening of the message conveyed in its advertising slogans from the harsher 'Just do it' to the more gentle slogan 'I can'.

Nike looked set to retain its position as a world market leader having fought off successive challenges from Reebok and Adidas. There were plans to expand the scope of Nike's business both geographically and in terms of the range of its activities. Phil Knight said that 'sport is the culture of the United States' and that, 'before long it will define the culture of the entire world'. This may prove to be an accurate extension of the concept of cultural convergence. Equally, it may be indicative of the kind of cultural arrogance which can precede the decline of such a business.

Appendix

Appendix 1. Nike's value system – the production and supply network

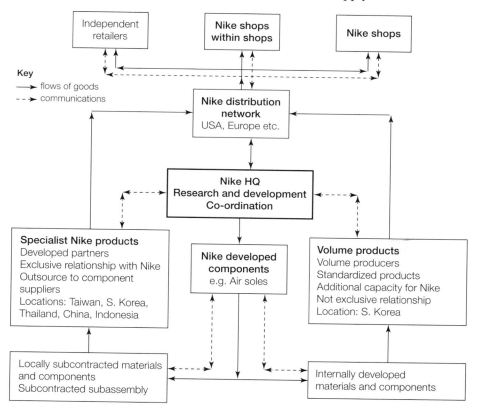

Source: adapted from Dicken (1998)

References and further reading

Dicken, P. (1998) *Global Shift – Transforming the World Economy*. Paul Chapman, London.

Jones, D. (1998) No more Mr Nike Guy, *The Sunday Times*, 23rd August.

Katz, D. (1993) Triumph of the Swoosh, *Sports Illustrated*, 16th August.

INDEX